# High-Stakes Testing:

## Coping with Collateral Damage

# Contents

# Preface

Early in the first decade of the 21st century, high-stakes achievement testing became the chief instrument that the U.S. federal government and state governments adopted for repairing what was deemed "the deplorable condition of schooling in America." However, as testing programs were implemented, it became clear that achievement testing as the prime solution for students' unacceptable academic performance was accompanied by a host of collateral damage in the form of vexing, unexpected, unwelcome problems.

The four-fold purpose of this book is to (1) describe the nature of high-stakes testing, (2) identify types of collateral damage that have attended the testing programs, (3) analyze methods different groups of people have chosen for coping with the damage, and (4) suggest lessons to be learned from the high-stakes-testing experience. The six groups of people whose coping strategies are inspected include (a) politicians and their staffs, (b) educational administrators and their staffs, (c) parents and the public, (d) test-makers and test-givers, (e) teachers, and (f) students.

# 1

# The Nature of Collateral Damage

The so-called "high-stakes" achievement-testing movement, which has gained so much momentum throughout the United States in recent years, has compiled a record of both successes and failures. In this book, the successes are periodically noted. However, the book's greatest concern is with the failures, because the causes of the failures are what need fixing if schools are to do justice to their students and to the society in general. Thus, the book's contents are chiefly about harm resulting from achievement testing and about how people who are involved with testing cope with the damage. The adjective *high-stakes* has been applied to the testing movement to suggest that the way the movement develops will yield serious consequences for students, school systems, and the society that schools are expected to serve.

The purpose of this opening chapter is to set the stage for subsequent chapters by introducing (a) some examples of the success of high-stakes programs, (b) some initial examples of collateral damage, and (c) two kinds of background information useful for understanding the rest of the book. Those two kinds are (a) significant characteristics of learners and (b) historical foundations of achievement testing.

At the start, it is important for readers to recognize the meanings assigned to the words in the title *High-Stakes Testing—Coping with Collateral Damage*.

*Testing* refers solely to the use of *achievement examinations* that are designed to discover how well students have learned what they have been taught. Other kinds of tests are of no concern here. Consequently, nothing will be said about intelligence tests or aptitude tests that are intended to estimate students' potential for coping with current or future tasks they might attempt. Likewise, no attention will be given to personality and attitude tests that are supposed to reveal aspects of people's psychological make-up.

1

The kinds of achievement tests on which the book focuses are the *standardized* variety, created by "experts," cast in printed or computerized versions, and administered to large numbers of students who are located in diverse communities that may be spread across an entire state, region, nation, or group of nations.  No attention will be paid to other sorts of achievement tests, such as ones created by teachers for use in their own classrooms.

The expression *high-stakes* means that the present-day testing movement can bear important consequences for students, their parents, and American society in general.  Among several desired outcomes, the reading-comprehension level of the nation's student population will likely increase, mathematics test scores will likely rise, and students' knowledge of science will likely improve.  At the same time, a variety of unwelcome effects may well result—more pupils failing to be promoted to the next higher grade, a greater incidence of school dropouts, <u>fewer students earning high-school diplomas,</u> a decrease in the variety of subject-matter taught in schools, and more.  The expression *collateral damage* refers to such unintended, unwanted harm done by the recent ways standardized achievement tests have been used.

The term *coping* means the methods people have attempted for solving—or at least for enduring—the difficulties that accompany high-stakes testing.

## Examples of Success

In the testing game, a school's success is measured by high test scores —or at least by improved scores—earned by students on state exams in selected subject fields.  The two fields examined nationwide since 2002 have been reading and mathematics.  In addition, some states have administered exams in such fields as written composition, science, and certain of the social studies, usually history and geography.

Reports of success have typically focused on increases in test scores from one year to the next, as illustrated in the following examples.

**Improved test scores.**  In Texas, under the newly adopted Texas Assessment of Knowledge and Skills test, third graders were required to pass the TAKS reading exam in order to move on to fourth grade.  Pretesting tryouts of the exam during the 2001-2002 school year suggested that 23% of the state's third-graders would fail.  But when the test actually counted in 2003, 96% passed the TAKS reading exam after three attempts.  Of those who had failed in their first attempt, 29% passed at the highest possible level on the third try (Galley, 2003).

In 2004, more of California's 8,000-plus public schools ranked higher in state achievement testing than ever before. On a 1,000-point scale, 21.5% of the schools scored in the desirable range of 800 or higher, reflecting high proficiency on state exams. A year earlier, only 15.5% of schools had scored as well (Azimov, 2004).

**Schools shed the "failing" label.** More than half of the 226 Arizona schools that the federal government said needed improvement on state exams did, indeed, increase student test scores in 2003. To help the 110 schools that had not improved, state officials sent principals and teachers from successful schools to demonstrate instructional strategies that had worked in high-ranking schools (Mendoza, 2003).

**More time is dedicated to reading and math.** On state reading and math exams in grades five, eight, and eleven, 21 Philadelphia schools that were restructured and given extra support by district officials outscored both charter schools and ones operated by private companies. The most prominent innovation in the 21 schools was that of doubling the amount of time spent on reading and math, so that in one school 120 minutes were spent on reading and literacy daily, and 90 minutes were dedicated to math. Teachers also assessed students' progress more frequently, analyzed the tests in greater detail, and discussed ways to improve instruction. Consultants helped teachers up-grade their methods and conduct after-school programs for low achievers (Snyder & Mezzacappa, 2003).

**Immediate improvements are mixed with long-term concerns.** In the state of Washington, educators welcomed the improvement in 2003 scores on the Washington Assessment of Student Learning (WASL) that was given to 230,000 students in grades four, seven, and ten. However, Superintendent of Public Instruction Terry Bergeson cautioned that the good news was accompanied by a sobering recognition that if future progress was not greater, many students might fail to pass all subjects on the WASL in 2008 when high-school graduation would depend on the test. If the 2003 trend did not change sufficiently, only 27% of the class of 2008 would earn diplomas, Bergeson warned. She said that if the schools did "business as usual," the outcome would not be "a happy one" (Shaw, 2003b).

**Students from disadvantaged minorities improve at a growing pace.** In the Salt Lake City public schools over the 1997-2003 period, non-Asian minority students' standardized test scores in reading and math rose at twice the rate of their white and Asian agemates'. The trend suggested that the district was improving the academic achievement of its most at-risk students without reducing the achievement of others. In the opinion of University of Utah Professor Patrick Galvin, it would still take years before the test performance of non-Asian minorities would equal that of their Asian and white peers, but the movement was definitely in the right direction (Lynn, 2003c).

North Carolina educators estimated that the state could eliminate the ethnic achievement gap in the next few years. Although the current gap between minority groups and whites was still quite large, during recent years the rise in the percentage of children performing at grade level had continued in nearly every school district. State reading and math test scores for African-American students in 2003 rose 10 percentage points to 67%. American-Indian and Hispanic students' passing rates rose above 70% for both groups. The minority students' success was not at the expense of white and Asian children, whose passing rates exceeded 90% in many school districts. In estimating the chances of the state achieving parity across ethnic groups in school progress, the state's superintendent of schools, Mike Ward, said the timetable was very demanding but "the trends suggest we can do this" (Simmons, 2003a).

**Summary.** It seems hardly surprising that progressively higher reading and math scores have been widely reported throughout the nation in recent years as schools' rewards for success and punishments for failure have become increasingly critical. Rewards have consisted of "effective schools" being lauded in the public press, commended by political and business leaders, and given monetary prizes. Punishments have included the condemnation of schools in the press, warnings of dire consequences for school personnel, permission for parents to move their children out of "failing" schools, and administrators losing control of their schools. Frightened by potential sanctions, administrators and teachers have redoubled their efforts to raise reading and math scores by means of increasing instructional time for those subjects, improving teachers' skills in the two fields, enlisting greater home support for students' reading and math progress, and hiring tutors to aid learners who fall short of the standards. In addition, more funds are being allocated to the high-priority subject fields. As one example, the National Science Foundation in 2003 granted $12.5-million to 46 school districts in the Philadelphia region to improve math and science education in grades 6 through 12 over the next five-year period, with the project annually affecting an estimated 117,000 students (Langland, 2003a).

Under such circumstances, scores in those aspects of reading and math measured by the tests are bound to improve nationwide. From that perspective, high-stakes testing has been, and will continue to be, a triumph. However, such a victory comes at a price. It requires trade-offs and is accompanied by collateral damage. The purpose of this book is to identify such damage and to analyze how people have tried to cope with it.

## Examples of Damage

The nature of collateral damage, its various causes, and ways of coping are described in detail throughout later chapters. However, to gain an initial hint of the diverse sorts of damage that can be involved, consider the following potpourri of incidents.

**Things that test-focused schools fail to teach and fail to assess.** In Boston's Mission Hill School that Deborah Meier founded several years ago, middle-school students have been required to present and defend their work twice a year in public exhibitions. In defense of such an assessment method, Ms. Meier said that, in the present-day achievement-testing climate, "the definition of being well-educated is your test score," whereas the qualities most resistant to measurement by tests—initiative, responsibility, creativity, critical thinking—are the exact skills schools should emphasize. Therefore, in addition to knowing facts, Mission Hill students have been required to identify thought patterns and connections, explain why material is relevant, and demonstrate that they understand diverse points of view (Paulson, 2002).

**Test standards altered.** In 2003, as Texas State Board of Education members reviewed the results of the field trial of a new statewide achievement test, there were guards outside the meeting room, and board members signed a secrecy pledge. The board members' worry was that thousands of Texas students would fail the state's new reading test and thereby be held back a grade. As a result, schools would suffer penalties under the federal government's *No-Child-Left-Behind Act*. To avoid such disaster, the board reduced the number of questions third-graders had to get right by lowering the standard from 24 out of 36 questions answered correctly to 20 out of 36 (Dillon, 2003a).

**Students tested on material they had not studied.** Because the aim of achievement testing is to discover how well learners have mastered material they have been taught, a test's items should all focus on what students have had a fair chance to learn. But in a telephone survey of 200 elementary-school teachers in Alberta, Canada, many charged that a significant portion of the province's tests measured for things that third-graders had never studied. Hence, teachers suggested that the standardized testing be discontinued (Achievement testing fails independent review, 1997).

Nevada high-school students have been required to pass tests in reading, writing, and math in order to earn diplomas. In 2003, there were 2,195 students—12% of the state's senior class—who had completed all of their course-work requirements but would not receive a diploma because they had failed the math portion of the state's graduation exam. In lieu of a diploma, each student would be given a *certificate of attendance,* a document usually not recognized by employers or four-year colleges as evidence of academic achievement. Part of the problem was that as many as 40% of students statewide had never taken algebra or geometry, which were included on the test. According to school officials, fast-growing and financially strapped school districts were often unable to find qualified math teachers (Fletcher, 2003).

**Frustrating inconsistency in test standards.** Teachers at a Boston suburban school district were astonished to learn that only 3% of their eighth graders' had earned an *advanced status* rating on the Massachusetts statewide math test. Yet only a short time earlier, 35% reached *advanced status* in mathematics on the nationally standardized Stanford Achievement Test. One student who had earned *advanced status* on the Stanford exam dropped to the *failure* category on the state exam. Two others with excellent records of daily class work fell from *advanced status* on the national test to *needs improvement* on the Massachusetts exam (Viadero, 2001).

**Increased school dropout rates.** A Rand Corporation analysis (*What Do Test Scores in Texas Tell Us?*, 2000) of what had been called the "Texas Miracle" revealed that the reason state test scores rose was not because of increased learning but, rather, because of increased dropout rates among students who were already struggling in school. Instead of receiving better instruction, lagging students were given high-stakes tests which they flunked. Discouraged, they left school. Critics of the "Texas Miracle" argued that low test scores often led to students giving up on school because they were dubbed failures. Critics noted that studies of retention policies showed that the chance a student would drop out of school increased by 50% for students held back once and reached 90% if held back twice (Bernstein, 2002).

A study of dropouts in New York City's schools suggested that growing numbers of students—most of them struggling academically—were being pushed out of the public schools and classified under bureaucratic categories designed to conceal their failure to graduate. Whereas official figures placed the city's dropout rate at around 20%, analysts claimed that number could rise to 25% or 30% if it included students who were forced out. The form of the official data made it impossible to determine just how many students were being forced out and what became of them. Administrators of high-school equivalency programs and experts who examined the school district's statistics said the number of "pushouts" seemed to be growing, with students shoved out at ever-younger ages (Lewin & Medina, 2003).

**High costs of implementing testing legislation.** Textbook companies have been among the businesses directly benefiting financially from the state testing programs. Selling instructional materials is a billion-dollar business that has enjoyed a consistent 7% annual growth, according to the American Association of Publishers. The 2001 federal legislation mandating testing guaranteed an even higher growth rate in the future. The National Association of State Boards of Education estimated that if properly funded, the nationwide testing mandate could cost states an additional $2.7-billion to $7-billion (Bernstein, 2002).

**Physical-education classes eliminated.** Studies of children's health status in 2003 reported that a quarter of U.S. American children were obese, a number that had doubled over the previous decade. Diseases associated with obesity and inactivity—diabetes, attention-deficit disorders, cardiovascular malfunction—were increasing rapidly. Poor eating habits and lack of exercise were cited as two principal causes of the obesity trend. Analysts estimated that three-fourths of high-school students currently had no physical education of any sort. As states placed more emphasis on passing standardized tests, time and money were being taken from physical education and used for teaching pupils test-taking skills (Deford, 2003).

**Political peril.** In early 2004, growing numbers of states reported that half or more of their schools were failing to reach the federal government's *No-Child-Left-Behind* standards. At the same time, funds to carry out the *No-Child* mandates were in short supply. Consequently, observers of the national political scene believed such news complicated President Bush's 2004 reelection effort. In other words, the *No-Child* program —acclaimed as a policy and political breakthrough by the Republicans in January 2002—was threatening to backfire on the president and his party in the 2004 elections. The president had hoped to enhance his image as a compassionate conservative by making the education program one of the highest priorities of his administration. But as news of problems with implementing the act continued to mount, that hope appeared to be fading (VandeHei, 2003).

An example of the effect of high-stakes testing on some individuals is the case of 19-year-old Eric Lira, a high-school senior who scored 286 on the Florida statewide reading test—one point below the passing standard.  Consequently, he would not receive a high-school diploma, even though he was earning A's in advanced-placement calculus and honors physics during the current semester, and he had a 3.3 (B+) grade-point average.  When Eric had immigrated to the United States from Nicaragua three years earlier, he had spoken no English.  Now, without a high-school diploma, he could not go to college.  He lamented that "My future is broke. . . everything. . . by one test" (Kronholz, 2003).  Across Florida in 2003—the first year that passing the state exam was required for graduation—more than 13,000 high-school seniors would not receive diplomas.  Observers suggested that such an outcome was becoming "a political nightmare" for Florida Governor Jeb Bush (Kronholz, 2003).

Jack O'Connell, California's state superintendent of public instruction, in late 2003 decided to postpone until 2006 the requirement that students pass a high-school graduation test in order to receive a diploma.  The exit-test requirement was originally scheduled for the 2004 graduating class, but a pilot study in 2003 showed that half of the English-language learners and 75% of special-education students who took a preliminary version of the test failed and, when the testing became official, would not be able to graduate.  The report also found that many students who failed had not taken the classes needed for passing it.  The superintendent's decision followed a State Assembly vote to remove the test as a condition of graduation (Wasserman, 2003).

A dispute over the *No-Child* requirements fractured Minnesota's conservative political body when Warren Grantham resigned from the Taxpayers League, where he had been in charge of its education advocacy group.  An avid supporter of the *No-Child Act*, Grantham spoke in the Senate against efforts by some members to have the state opt out of the federal program.  When he upset a pair of strong supporters of the opt-out movement by criticizing them publicly, party members forced him to relinquish his League post (Welsh, 2004b).

**Demonstrations and boycotts.**  In a highly publicized demonstration, thousands of protesters rallied against the Florida Comprehensive Assessment Test (FCAT) and condemned a new state policy that denied diplomas to students who did not pass the exam.  State Senator Frederica Wilson declared that the policy disproportionately harmed minorities.  The two-hour rally launched a boycott of such major Florida industries as tourism and citrus-growing.  The action was aimed at pressuring state officials to rescind the testing regulation.  Protesters also directed Governor Jeb Bush to grant amnesty to the Florida high-school seniors who would be denied diplomas and to 40,000 third-graders who would be held back because of poor state-test reading scores  (Pinzur, 2003a).

**Teachers feel like scapegoats.** A study of teachers' opinions by a nonpartisan research group—Public Agenda—reported that most of the 1,345 teachers surveyed said they were unfairly blamed for school short-comings, were being undermined by parents, and were distrustful of their bosses. A spokesperson for the National Education Association observed that teachers resented taking instructional time for practice tests and drills "that suck the life out of learning" (Feller, 2003).

**Testing consumes instructional time.** In California, high-school students were slated to take a High School Exit Exam, the Stanford 9 test battery, and the Golden State Exams. In addition, they had the option of taking Advanced Placement exams, the Scholastic Aptitude Test, and the American College Test. A California teacher, Vernonica Bennett, told the sponsors of the Public Broadcasting System's *Frontline* program that the spring-semester tests took away days of instructional time and turned teachers into proctors (Bennett, 2002).

**Students fear the exit exam.** Like many of his classmates, a high-school senior explained that he dreaded having to pass the high-school exit exam because he suffered monumental test anxiety. He said he became so frightened that he couldn't think straight. "When I get all nervous, it takes days to answer questions" (Tessler, 2003).

**Test success varies by students' socioeconomic status.** In 2003, state test scores varied dramatically among individual schools in Guinnett County, Georgia. At the high end were Riverside and Walnut, where only a few dozen students failed to meet the state standards. For instance, 98% of Riverside students either met or exceeded the standards for reading. In contrast, failing rates at Summerour and Lilburn middle schools exceeded 36%. Both of those schools had large numbers of students whose families were impoverished and a high percentage of parents who spoke a home language other than English (M. MacDonald, 2003a).

## The Book's Perspective

In order to place the above examples of collateral damage in proper perspective, I now need to explain the vantage point from which this book is written. It is important that readers understand that I am not an *anti-testing advocate*. I don't hate tests. I'm convinced that tests can be highly valuable instruments for promoting learners' progress. During 50 years of teaching, I created hundreds of classroom tests, wrote extensively about evaluating learners' progress (Thomas, 1960, 1965, 1986; Thomas & Brubaker, 1971, 1972), and developed standardized tests (Thomas & Titialii, 1973; Thomas, Titialii, Harris, & Harris, 1973a, 1973b).

Therefore, my concern throughout this book is not about testing itself but, rather, it's about badly constructed tests, the improper administration of tests, harmful uses of test results, unrealistic standards of performance, and a lack of attention to evaluation methods other than tests.

## The Book's Structure

Following this initial chapter, the book is organized in two major parts that portray the testing movement as an impromptu game or drama—a performance in which individuals play roles in ways that influence their own lives and others' destinies.

Part I, titled *Tasks of the Testing Game,* consists of four chapters focusing on stages of the educational-evaluation process. These are successive stages of the game.

> Chapter 2: What Should the Schools Teach?
> Chapter 3: What Should the Schools Evaluate, and How?
> Chapter 4: How Should Achievement Standards Be Set?
> Chapter 5: How Should Test Results Be Used?

Part II, titled *The Testing Game's Players and Their Coping Strategies,* identifies the game's principal performers and analyzes their roles, their influence on the testing process, and their attempts to deal with the damage that so often accompanies high-stakes testing

> Chapter 6:  Politicians and Their Staffs
> Chapter 7:  Educational Administrators and Their Staffs
> Chapter 8:  The Public and Parents
> Chapter 9:  Test-Makers and Test-Givers
> Chapter 10:  Teachers
> Chapter 11:  Students

The chapters of Part II are arranged in the order of the players' levels of authority or official power. Politicians (the U.S. President, members of Congress, state governors, state legislators, school-board members) are the actors who wield the greatest authority and thus are at the top of the hierarchy, while students—devoid of authority—are at the bottom.

The book's closing chapter, *Lessons to Learn,* suggests what guidance might be drawn for the future from the events portrayed in the preceding chapters.

With the foregoing introductory remarks in mind, we turn now to a pair of topics that provide useful information for understanding the book's contents: (a) significant characteristics of learners and (b) historical foundations of achievement testing.

# Learners' Characteristics

Such declarations as "All people are created equal" or "All students should be considered equals" are expressions of idealistic hope but certainly not descriptions of reality. In nearly all characteristics of importance for success in school, students are unequal—quite different from each other. In effect, the only way that all fourth-graders are alike is that they are all in fourth grade. In all other ways, fourth-graders vary—in height, skin color, acuity of eyesight, English-language fluency, social skills, self control, self confidence, fears, worries, contents of their consciences, brain-structure patterns, ambitions, motives, frustrations, study habits, their parents' child-rearing practices, and on and on. Thus, the daunting challenge teachers face is to equip such a variegated polyglot of individuals with the knowledge, skills, and attitudes specified in the schools' curricula. And not only are the learners at any grade level different from each other in so many ways, but the extent of variation among learners tends to increase with age.

Members of the public who are not experienced teachers typically fail to recognize the magnitude of individual differences among students. Early in my career as a teacher, I was told that the range of reading ability within any grade level in school would usually be the number of that grade. Hence, I could expect that in a typical third-grade class the children's reading abilities might range across three grades—from grade two (the child with the least reading skill) to grade four (the most skilled reader in the class). At the eighth-grade level, the range of reading abilities would spread over eight grades, with the least adept student reading at the average level of pupils in grade five and the most adept reading as well as the average twelfth grader. Since I was not convinced that such was actually the case, I collected the reading scores for third-grade and eighth-grade students who had taken standardized tests in a small city's school system. I was astonished to discover that the range of scores at each of those grade levels was not the number of the grade but, rather, twice that number. The least skilled third grader read no better than the average first grader, while the most skilled third-grader read as well as the average sixth grader. Among the city's eighth-graders, the poorest reader was no better than an average first grader, whereas the best reader was as good as an average college senior (Thomas & Thomas, 1965, pp. 304-309).

Studies of the variability among students—in virtually all other characteristics besides reading skill that affect success in school—reveal a similar extent of differences among learners who are of the same age or grade level. Consequently, ignoring this *rule of inequality* when teaching students and evaluating their progress can lead to many of the kinds of collateral damage identified throughout this book. In my experience, the most difficult task teachers face is that of accommodating the individual differences among the learners so that each student can progress in keeping with her or his own abilities, background of knowledge, and attitudes. Clearly, tutoring a single pupil is an infinitely simpler task than trying to teach a classroom of 30. Hence, educators are engaging in a futile exercise when they adopt an achievement-testing program that envisions all learners reaching the same high level of accomplishment—an exercise that invites the sorts of academic, personal-adjustment, and political problems described in the following chapters.

## A Short History of Achievement Testing

Achievement testing is not a recent invention. In China as early as the sixth century BCE,* applicants for posts in the government earned their positions by scoring high on civil-service examinations that required mastery of the Confucian classics. Between 200 BCE and 200 CE, additional subject fields covered by the exams consisted of the *Six Arts* of music, archery, horsemanship, arithmetic, writing, and knowledge of the rituals of both public and private life. The range of topics was later expanded to include the *Five Studies*—military strategies, civil law, revenue and taxation, agriculture, and geography. The fierceness of the competition candidates faced is suggested by the fact that during the Tang dynasty (618-907 CE), the passing rate among test-takers was around two percent. And from those ancient days until the early 1900s, such a civil-service-examination system remained in force in China.

In Europe, oral examinations that university students had to pass in order to earn academic degrees were required at Italy's University of Bologna by the early 1200s and at England's Oxford University in the 1600s. Written tests were introduced at Belgium's Louvain University in the mid-1400s, at Italy's St. Ignatius of Loyola in 1540, and at England's Cambridge and Oxford by the early 1800s.

Historically, the most significant achievement-test program in the United States has been the New York State Regents examination system. The Board of Regents was first established by the New York State Legislature in 1784 as a 16-member committee responsible for the general supervision of all of the state's educational activities. In 1864, as an effort to maintain high standards in secondary schools that sought public financial aid, the Regents voted to require public examinations of all stu-

---

* In keeping with modern usage, throughout this book the letters BCE (Before the Common Era) replace the earlier BC (Before Christ), and the letters CE (Common Era) replace the earlier AD (Anno Domini or Year of the Lord).

dents who applied for admission to academies and high schools. An 1877 statute authorized the Regents to give tests for high-school graduation and college admission. By 1925, Regents high-school exams were given in 68 different subjects. Students who passed the tests were awarded Regents diplomas. Over the decades, until the present day, the Regents curriculum guidebooks and the nature and number of examinations have been altered to conform with changing educational policies and practices (Folts, 1996).

As the years of the twentieth century advanced, increasing quantities of U.S. school systems adopted standardized tests that were available from commercial test publishers. The tests were designed to measure students' competence in such subject areas as reading, language usage, mathematics, science, history, and geography. Test results were used chiefly to compare schools in terms of national norms, showing how well the scores earned by students in a given school compared with the scores of students from a large sample of schools across the country. Standardized tests also helped colleges and universities decide which high-school applicants to admit for higher education. In elementary and secondary schools, test results were rarely used as the basis for the marks students received on their report cards, for promoting students to the next higher grade at the end of the school year, or for awarding high-school diplomas. Instead, decisions about report cards, grade promotion, and graduation were typically based on a combination of other measures—teacher-made tests, homework assignments, in-class assignments, and teachers' observations of students' class participation.

## International Comparisons

In the late decades of the twentieth century, a new educational movement—international achievement-test comparisons—served as a stimulus behind the current standardized testing movement in the United States and in other countries. The most extensive and influential of the cross-national testing activities were those carried out by the International Association for the Evaluation of Educational Achievement (IEA), which was originally a coalition of a dozen countries' research institutions, established in 1962 to conduct multinational research in education. In subsequent years, additional nations joined the association and participated in a series of assessments of student achievement in reading, mathematics, science, literature, civic education, French as a foreign language, English as a foreign language, and more. In each subject-matter area, tests were developed and administered to students in their nation's dominant language of school instruction (Postlethwaite, 1985).

The magnitude of the IEA studies can be illustrated with the reading-literacy investigation of 1990-1991 in which 210,059 students from 32 nations participated. Tests were administered to 9-year-olds and 14-year-olds—a total of 1,500 to 3,000 students in each nation, selected by means of representative sampling techniques. In addition, questionnaires were completed by teachers and parents in order to identify characteristics of schools and family life that might be correlated with different levels of students' success on the tests. The types of reading matter measured by the tests included word recognition, narrative comprehension, understanding expository writing, and the interpretation of documents. The tests were composed of multiple-choice items, a type deemed well suited to surveying a large quantity of skills in a short period of time. The test-makers decided that multiple-choice questions yielded results highly similar to those that would be obtained with open-ended (completion or fill-in) items.

In each of the IEA studies, test results were reported in terms of the average score of participants in every country, thereby permitting comparisons across nations. Consequently, some observers dubbed the IEA studies "the academic Olympics" because the results drew worldwide attention to differences in reading skill among the participating nations' students. The public press and political figures in countries that scored high in the testing announced the outcomes with pride, while the press and politicians in countries that scored low voiced distress at their students' poor showing. Consider, for example, the following rankings of nine-year-olds in reading skill. The top six countries in descending order were Finland, the United States, Sweden, France, Italy, and New Zealand. The bottom six in descending order were Cyprus, Portugal, Denmark, Trinidad/Tobago, Indonesia, and Venezuela (Elley, 1992, p. 14).

In addition to the reading investigations, the other IEA studies of greatest public interest focused on mathematics and science. Three such surveys were conducted, the first in the 1960s, the second in the 1980s, and the third in the 1990s. The 1990s Third International Mathematics and Science Study (TIMSS) was described as the largest, most comprehensive, and most rigorous international comparison of educational outcomes ever undertaken. The project involved 41 countries and more than a half-million participants. Students' mathematical and science knowledge was tested at grades four, eight, and twelve. Results were published in the form of each nation's averages for mathematics and science at all three grade levels. In the United States, politicians, educators, business leaders, and the general public were pleased with fourth-grade outcomes, which showed U.S. pupils scoring above the international average (mean) of 500 in both math (545) and science (565)—higher than 19 of the 26 nations participating in that portion of the study. However, the U.S. public was not so pleased with the eighth-grade results, which found American middle-school students only average in math (500) and not much higher in science (534). In math, American eighth-graders scored far below students in such nations as Singapore (643), South Korea (607), Japan (605), Hong Kong (588), Belgium (565), and the Czech Republic (554). In science, the U.S. eighth-graders lagged behind those in such places as Singapore (607), the Czech Republic (574), Japan (571), Bulgaria (565), the Netherlands (560), and Slovenia (560) (Stevenson, 1998).

Whereas U.S. political leaders and the general public were somewhat disappointed with the eighth-grade test outcomes, they were very disturbed by the twelfth-grade results, where the Americans fell well below the international average of 500—even lower in math (461) than in science (480). The countries surpassing the U.S. in math included the Netherlands (560), Sweden (552), Denmark (547). Switzerland (540), Iceland (534), Norway (528), France (523), New Zealand (522), Australia (522), and several more (Stevenson, 1998).

The 1990s TIMSS study confirmed conclusions drawn from the 1960s and 1980s IEA math and science surveys—that U.S. students' test scores in the upper grades were inferior to those of students in many other nations. As American pupils climbed the schooling ladder year by year, their performance—in comparison to that of students in other countries—appeared to grow worse. In addition to the IEA findings, other organizations that also conducted international testing programs drew similar conclusions. As a consequence, U.S. political leaders, members of the nation's business community, and commentators in the public press expressed their dismay that the education system of the most powerful country in the world was producing badly educated youths. The fate of the nation was deemed at risk, and critics charged that drastic measures would be needed to correct the schools' shameful performance. At both the state and federal levels of government, the primary device picked by officials in their attempt to remedy the problem would be high-stakes achievement testing that held schools accountable for producing well-educated children and youths. Thus, the educational reform movement was not generated from within the education system itself but, rather, was being forced on the schools by the business community and a worried public (Are we there yet?, 2002).

During the 1990s and into the early years of the twenty-first century, all states (except Iowa whose standards continued to be set by individual school districts) adopted statewide standards and testing programs. At an increasing pace, states were using the standardized test results for determining which students would be promoted from one grade to the next and which ones deserved high-school diplomas. Then in 2001, the movement to use high-stakes achievement testing as the primary stimulant for producing acceptable academic performance in the nation's schools reached its peak when the U.S. Congress authorized a far-reaching revision of the 1965 Elementary and Secondary Education Act (ESEA). On January 8, 2002, President George W. Bush signed the revised act into law as his administration's contribution toward repairing the country's education system. The aim of the program was reflected in the motto "No Child Left Behind."

## No Child Left Behind

When the U.S. Constitution was framed in 1787, the federal government was given no control over, or responsibility for, educating the nation's populace. Matters of schooling thus became the province of the states and local school districts. However, over the years since the nation was founded—and particularly during the latter half of the twentieth century—the federal government gradually passed legislation that affected education throughout the country. The legislation was usually in the form of providing funds to states and school districts that would furnish services for special purposes, such as assisting pupils who suffered physical or mental handicaps or ones considered socio-economically disadvantaged. The Elementary and Secondary Education Act of 1965 was the federal government's most ambitious and expensive venture of this sort until surpassed in magnitude, cost, and complexity by the 2001 *No-Child-Left-Behind Act*. The section of the ESEA law focusing on the needs of children from economically disadvantaged families was labeled *Title I*. Special funds and services were designed to help Title-I children succeed in school.

The centerpiece of the *No-Child-Left-Behind* legislation—and its most hotly debated feature—has been the nationwide achievement-testing provision. Understanding that provision's main characteristics is essential for comprehending the sorts of collateral damage described throughout this book. Thus, in the following paragraphs I identify a series of the most significant aspects of the testing scheme.

**In what subject fields do students take tests?** An earlier 1994 revision of the ESEA required schools to test pupils' reading and math skills at three grade spans (grades 3-5, 6-9, 10-12). That practice would continue until the 2005-2006 school year when every child's progress in reading and math should be tested each year in grades 3 through 8 and at least once during grades 10 through 12. In addition, beginning in 2002-2003, school districts would be obligated to test the English-language oral, reading, and writing skills of all students who were judged to have limited proficiency in English. By 2007-2008, states should test students' knowledge of science at least once during grades 3-5, grades 6-9, and grades 10-12.

The federal law also required that 95% of the students of each type in a school must take the tests and their scores reported. Therefore, no more than 5% of the students could be missing in the testing reports.

Although the *No-Child-Left-Behind Act* called for testing only in reading, math, and science, states could also elect to test in other subject areas, such as writing, history, geography, economics, foreign languages, civics, and the arts.

**Who creates the tests, and who sets the passing standards?** The national government does not prepare the tests, nor does it establish the standards students are expected to reach. Instead, each state is responsible for providing its own tests to fit that state's recommended curriculum. The task of building state tests is most often assigned to private companies that specialize in test construction. Each state also decides the test-score cutting points that separate four levels of student competence—*failure, basic, proficient,* and *advanced.*

In order to establish a state's standards for student achievement, state officials first set a *starting point* based on the performance of the state's lowest-achieving demographic group (such as an ethnic group) or the state's lowest-achieving schools. Officials then decide on the level of student achievement a school must reach after two years in order to show *adequate yearly progress.* At least once every three years, the basic, proficient, and advanced achievement levels must be raised until, by 2014, all students in the state are succeeding at the proficient level on state assessments in language arts (chiefly reading) and math. Underperforming schools may avoid such sanctions if they can demonstrate a 10% annual reduction in the number of students that are not meeting the proficiency goals.

As a result of states' freedom to set their own standards, they can differ from each other in how demanding their achievement criteria are. However, as an effort to maintain some degree of similarity among states' achievement aims, each state's test results are compared against an independent benchmark called the National Assessment of Educational Progress (NAEP), which consists of exams prepared by the federal government and given to a small sample of each state's fourth- and eighth-grade students in reading and math every other year. This provision, known as "NAEP comparability," is supposed to ensure that states are not setting standards that are unacceptably low. The *No-Child-Left-Behind Act* does not provide for penalties if students' scores on a state's own tests fall behind the state's NAEP results, but the act merely requires that the results of the two measuring instruments be made public.

**How are test results to be applied?** The results are used mainly for (a) judging individual schools' effectiveness, (b) tracking the progress of school-improvement efforts and reporting that information to federal and state officials, (c) informing communities of their schools' test outcomes, and (d) notifying parents of their children's academic success. The *No-Child-Left-Behind Act* does not recommend that achievement-test scores be used to decide whether children will be promoted from one grade to the next or will graduate from high school, but states may choose to use the scores for such purposes, and the U.S. Department of Education has encouraged such use.

*Judging schools' effectiveness.* Every school district is required to prepare an annual report card showing what percentage of students in each school scored at the defined failure, basic, proficient, and advanced levels on the state tests. The report must also offer information about the test success of students from eight subcategories—five ethnic groups (white, black, Hispanic, Native-American, Asian-American), students with limited English skills, ones in special-education programs, and ones living in poverty. In addition, the report must identify schools that need improvement, corrective action, or restructuring because their students' test scores have failed to advance sufficiently over the previous year (AYP—adequate yearly progress) for the school's population in general and for each of the subgroupings.

Every state must issue an annual report card summarizing student achievement throughout the state, with the data divided according to the same subgroups as those on the district report cards. State reports must include:

- State assessment results by performance level (basic, proficient, advanced), including (1) two-year trend data for each subject and grade tested; and (2) a comparison between annual objectives and actual performance for each student group.
- Percentage of each group of students not tested.
- Graduation rates for secondary school students and any other student achievement indicators that the state chooses.
- Performance of school districts on adequate yearly progress measures, including the number and names of schools identified as needing improvement.
- Professional qualifications of teachers in the state, including the percentage of teachers in the classroom with only emergency or provisional credentials and the percentage of classes in the state that are not taught by

highly qualified teachers, including a comparison between high- and low-income schools. (*Questions and Answers*, 2002)

The annual district and state reports must be published in forms available to members of the public via such media as newspapers, radio, television, and the Internet.

*Notifying parents of their children's performance.* School districts are required to make test results available to parents no later than the beginning of the upcoming school year. The law requires that the information be presented in an "understandable and uniform format, and to the extent practicable, in a language that the parents can understand." In addition, districts must notify parents if their child's school has been identified as needing improvement. If a school is so identified, districts must let parents know that they can send their child to a different public school whose students have made adequate progress on the reading and math tests. Districts must also notify parents annually about the professional qualifications of the teachers in their child's school (*Questions and Answers*, 2002).

**What happens to schools whose test scores fail to improve at the desired pace?**

- A school that has not made adequate yearly progress, as defined by the state, for two consecutive school years will be identified by the district before the beginning of the next school year as *needing improvement*. School officials will develop a two-year plan to turn around the school. The local education agency [such as a district school board] will ensure that the school receives needed technical assistance as it develops and implements its improvement plan. Students must be offered the option of transferring to another public school in the district—which may include a public charter school*—that has not been identified as needing school improvement.
- If the school does not make adequate yearly progress for three years, the school remains in school-improvement status, and the district must continue to offer public-school choice to all students. In addition, students from low-income families are eligible to receive supplemental educational services, such as tutoring or remedial classes, from a state-approved provider.
- If the school fails to make adequate progress for four years, the district must implement certain *corrective actions* to improve the school, such as replacing certain staff or fully implementing a new curriculum, while continuing to offer public school choice and supplemental educational services for low-income students.

---

* A charter school is a special type of tax-supported school that has been freed of many of the requirements that regular public schools are obliged to fulfill.

- If a school fails to make adequate yearly progress for a fifth year, the school district must initiate plans for *restructuring* the school. This may include reopening the school as a charter school, replacing all or most of the school staff, or turning over school operations either to the state or to a private company with a demonstrated record of effectiveness. (*Questions and Answers*, 2002).

**What rewards are provided for schools whose test scores improve at the desired rate?** States are required to furnish academic-achievement awards to schools that close achievement gaps between subgroups of students (such as between boys and girls or between Native Americans and whites) or that exceed test-score goals. States may use federal funds for cash bonuses to teachers in schools that have earned academic-achievement awards. States must publicize "distinguished schools" that made the greatest gains in closing the achievement gap between student subgroups or that significantly exceeded achievement goals (*Questions and Answers*, 2002).

**How are parents to be involved in the test-score improvement program?** The *No-Child-Left-Behind* law specifies steps school districts must take to ensure strong parent participation in planning, monitoring, and supporting children's progress. Such participation includes

- overall planning at the district and school levels; written policies on parent involvement at both levels; annual meetings; training; coordinating parent involvement strategies among federal education programs and evaluating those strategies and revising them if needed. (*Questions and Answers*, 2002)

*Summary.* Although the 2002 revision of the U.S. government's 1965 Elementary and Secondary Education Act includes far more provisions than those described above, the foregoing brief overview of key achievement-testing features should be sufficient for equipping readers to understand the legislation's influence on the types of collateral damage described in Chapters 2 through 11. Finally, it should be recognized that states are not obligated to abide by the *No-Child-Left-Behind Act's* requirements. But if they choose not to comply with the act, they forego the funds that the federal government would otherwise provide. For instance, in the state of Washington that would amount to about $600-million or 8% of the state's total expenditure on education (Shaw, 2003a).

# Conclusion

In early January 2002, President George W. Bush signed into law the first nationwide achievement-testing program ever required for American public-school students. That action, combined with states' current achievement-testing schemes, would subject schools and their students to the most ambitious, costly, time-consuming, and complex high-stakes testing they had ever faced. The purpose of this new testing movement was to correct what political leaders and a sizable portion of the American public regarded as the disgraceful ineffectiveness of the country's public schools. However, as the high-stakes testing plan went into action, it became clear that its implementation was plagued by a distressing mass of collateral damage. The dual purpose of this book is to identify multiple kinds of damage and to describe ways people have sought to cope with those kinds.

# Part I

## Tasks of the Testing Game

The purpose of achievement testing is to determine what students have learned in school and how well they have learned it. The process of deciding how effectively present-day high-stakes achievement tests perform this function can consist of answering four questions. The chapters that comprise Part I offer answers to those questions.

Chapter 2: What Should the Schools Teach?
Chapter 3: What Should the Schools Evaluate, and How?
Chapter 4: How Should Achievement Standards Be Set?
Chapter 5: How Should Test Results Be Used?

Each chapter first describes alternative ways that the chapter's focal question can be answered and then identifies types of collateral damage that can result from how that question has been answered in typical high-stakes programs. Each type of damage is not only described but is illustrated with one or more cases drawn mainly from newspaper accounts during the years following the 2002 introduction of the *No-Child-Left-Behind Act*.

# 2

# What Should the Schools Teach?

This book's analysis of achievement testing begins with the conviction that students should be tested only on those things that they have had a fair chance to learn. In order to determine what those fair-chance things will be, we first need to consider the purpose of schooling in terms of what we believe schools should teach. Thus, the first part of this chapter addresses the matter of what the schools *should teach*. The second part concerns the question of how the current high-stakes achievement-testing movement can affect what schools *actually do teach*.

## Deciding What the Schools *Should* Teach

One useful approach to the task of deciding what students should learn at school involves

- identifying the roles people can be expected to play in their lives,
- proposing which skills, knowledge, and attitudes people must learn in order to perform those roles efficiently,
- deciding which of those skills, knowledge, and attitudes the school should teach, and
- estimating the influence that high-stakes achievement testing likely exerts on how well learners acquire such skills, knowledge, and attitudes.

The following section is organized in terms of five typical life roles people fill in present-day America. The roles are those of *efficient worker, informed citizen, constructive group member, wise consumer,* and *enthusiastic user of discretionary time.* The discussion of each role involves progressing through the above four decision steps in order to arrive at a judgment of how high-stakes achievement testing can influence what students have a fair chance to learn in school.

Deciding on what the schools should teach involves not only analyzing roles people fill but also proposing what sorts of *support conditions* will affect how well people perform their roles. Those support conditions can be considered suitable things for schools to teach. For example, the role of *efficient worker* or *wage earner* not only requires that learners acquire particular skills, knowledge, and attitudes, but if workers are to function efficiently they need to enjoy good health. Therefore, good-health practices are support-learnings that are a worthy part of the curriculum because such practices contribute to the efficient performance of roles.

As a preface to our inspecting life roles, it is useful to recognize that roles are learned both outside the school (home, neighborhood, work place, church, recreational site, and more) and within the school. Over the decades, there has been a tendency for things that were traditionally learned outside of school to be assigned to the school. For instance, in the distant past many youths learned a trade by working alongside their parents (farming, carpentry, dressmaking, salesmanship, and the like). However, training for such occupations during the twentieth century was increasingly transferred to the schools. And as problems of illicit drug use, teen-age pregnancy, and sexually transmitted diseases increased, schools were also assigned to teach the young how to deal with such dangers. In short, during the past century, schools acquired a growing variety of things to teach. This shift of responsibility resulted from

- changes in the structure of American society that were caused by such events as (a) both parents entering full-time employment, (b) growing rates of divorce, (c) increasing immigration of people from diverse nations, (d) a shifting job market as a consequence of technological innovations, and (e) the spread of illicit-drug use.
- social problems that called for skills, knowledge, and attitudes that non-school agents (parents, pastors, children's peers, employers, television programs, club leaders) were not adequately providing for the nation's children and youth.

As proposed later in this chapter, high-stakes achievement testing may well be playing an important part in eliminating such added responsibilities from school programs or, at least, in greatly reducing the attention schools accord to those matters.

Consider, now, the five life roles for which schools help prepare students.

## Role 1: Efficient Worker

Most adults spend much of their time doing jobs that contribute to their own welfare and, usually, to the welfare of others. Workers produce goods (clothing, food, houses, cars), services (telephoning, laundering, banking, street sweeping), and beliefs (Christian, scientific, life-goals). Workers can be paid either in money or in goods (food, lodging) for doing their jobs. Or, as in the case of homemakers, workers can offer their services simply as a contribution to others' welfare. People who do not fit into this occupational-role category include young children, retirees, the infirm and disabled, the chronically unemployed, and the wealthy who live off investments without needing to work.

Vocational preparation, in the sense of the skills and knowledge people need to do their jobs well, can be divided into two levels or phases. One level is often referred to as *vocational education,* focusing on skills and knowledge useful in a variety of work settings. The other level is frequently called *vocational training,* focusing on skills and knowledge needed for doing particular kinds of jobs. Examples of vocational-education items are communication skills (speaking, understanding what others say, reading, writing), basic calculating (adding, multiplying, measuring), social competence (getting along well with fellow workers, subordinates, supervisors, clients), and work habits (doing one's best, accepting responsibility for one's performance, getting to work on time, endeavoring to improve). Examples of vocational-training skills are those of operating a metal lathe (for machinists), maintaining the shelf inventory (for supermarket employees), sight-reading (for members of a concert orchestra), and preparing a sermon (for the clergy).

Traditionally, schools have expected that their *vocational-education* task would be chiefly that of refining communication skills, social skills, and work habits that learners initially acquired at home. Three exceptions to this expectation have been those of children's learning to read, write, and calculate, so that acquiring these skills typically starts at school rather than at home. Furthermore, at an increasing rate, the schools' vocational-education task has become far broader as a consequence of societal change. According to U.S. census figures, by the opening on the twenty-first century, 20% of the nation's students were from homes in which English was not the language typically spoken. Over 47 million Americans age five and older used a language other than English in 2000 (Armas, 2003). Thus, the initial teaching of speaking and understanding English has become a further task assigned to schools. In addition, as more mothers entered the work force, children returning home after school were not as often supervised by a parent, so there were fewer opportunities for parents to teach acceptable social behavior and work habits.  Consequently, the schools have felt obliged to assume greater responsibility for promoting basic social behavior and work attitudes.

In the nineteenth century and well into the twentieth century, schools also accepted responsibility for *vocational training*, particularly in secondary schools.  Industrial-arts, business-practices, and home-economics departments taught skills needed in particular occupations—farmer, carpenter, auto mechanic, electrician, stenographer, secretary, accountant, chef, seamstress, and more.  However, as the nation's labor market has changed at an increasing pace, jobs available in the past have been replaced with new ones for which the schools do not offer specific training.  Thus, the role of public schools in vocational training has diminished, so that more employees now learn specific work skills either on-the-job or in special training programs.

A notable newcomer to the realm of vocational education has been the electronic computer.  Within no more than three decades, computers have become such ubiquitous features of American life—both at home and at work—that *computer literacy* has taken its place beside *reading literacy* and *numeracy* as a necessary part of vocational education.

In summary, whereas the schools' vocational-training assignment has diminished in recent times, their crucial role in vocational education has not only remained intact but has become increasingly important as society expects youths to stay in school longer and learn to be efficient workers in a highly technological twenty-first-century culture.

A question can now be asked about how well American schools have been fulfilling their responsibility for producing those efficient workers.  The answer, when viewed from the perspective of achievement-test scores in an international context, is "not very well at all."  The American business community, in particular, has been critical of the ostensibly low level of skill and knowledge of available workers, and the schools have been blamed for such shortcomings.  The schools are now expected to correct the problem, motivated and guided by high-stakes achievement testing.  In the present testing atmosphere, the main skills and knowledge for effecting the desired reform have been those of English language (particularly reading), mathematics, and science.

## Role 2: Informed Citizen

Citizens in the kind of democracy practiced in the United States enjoy a variety of rights and bear a variety of responsibilities.  If the American democracy is to operate as intended, its citizens must understand their rights and obligations and must fulfill them in daily living.  Although other institutions in American society contribute to such understanding (the family, mass-communication media, churches, clubs, teams), the public school has been the agency assigned the chief responsibility for citizenship education. To carry out that assignment, schools have traditionally adopted two main methods—formal courses and social-action activities.

The formal courses have been in the realm of the social studies and have often borne such titles as American history, civics, government, citizenship, and modern living. Here are three examples of lessons aimed at citizenship objectives.

- In a high-school course labeled American Problems, the instructor listed the following questions on the chalkboard as a guide to what students would be expected to write about after they viewed a videotaped episode from the television series *Law and Order*.
  —What crimes were committed in this episode?
  —What charges did the district attorney lodge against the three people who were arrested?
  —What proper police procedures did the defense attorneys accuse the arresting officers of violating? Do you agree with the defense attorneys? If so, why? If not, why not?
  —Do you agree with the jury's verdict? If so, why? If not, why not?

- Once each week, a middle-school social-studies teacher used episodes from a book entitled *Cases: A Resource Guide for Teaching about the Law* to explain various laws and to describe episodes in youths' lives that were related to those laws (Thomas & Murray, 1982). The class members were assigned to decide which of the depicted episodes were infractions of that particular day's law and which episodes were not. The laws concerned such crimes as theft, burglary, vandalism, illicit drug use, curfew violation, forgery, and disorderly conduct.

- A school's social studies for fifth-graders concerned the history and geography to the local community and region. During one three-week unit of study, class members focused on how, in the early days, their region had been transformed from a *territory* into a *state*. Questions class members were assigned to answer included: Why did citizens of the territory want to obtain statehood? Were any people against changing from a territory to a state; and if so, why? What procedure did the leaders have to go through to gain statehood? How were people's rights and responsibilities different between the territory and the state?

The phrase *social-action activities* identifies projects that furnish students an opportunity to apply their knowledge of democratic principles and practices. The following are typical activities.

- Students conduct a classroom or school-wide student-government election, including a campaign for candidates, debates over issues, and voting.

- Students participate in a simulated election that parallels an actual election in the adult society outside the school, such as an election to pass ballot initiatives (school bonds, environmental-protection laws, the death penalty for convicted felons) or to choose local, state, or federal office holders.

- Students carry-out community-development projects, such as planting trees, cleaning up cluttered neighborhoods, organizing safety patrols for protecting children on dangerous streets, taking meals to elderly shut-ins, and painting over graffiti on buildings.

Citizenship education that involves formal courses and social-action activities depends for its efficiency on the support of other school subjects, particularly on English-language communication skills—reading, writing, speaking, and understanding what other people say. Thus, language skills not only contribute to the efficient-worker role but also to the informed-citizen role.

## Role 3:  Constructive Group Member

The preparation for an informed citizen focuses chiefly on understanding society—particularly understanding the government—and on skills needed by citizens to exercise their rights and carry out their responsibilities.  Allied to the citizen role are skills and attitudes individuals need in order to get along well with others, that is, to perform as constructive group members.  The word *group* in this context is intended in a very broad sense to include collectivities that can range in size from two individuals (a pair of friends, a wedded couple, a tutor with a student) to many millions (all North-American Indians, all U.S. residents, all sixth-graders).  The most vital group in most people's lives is the family.  Hence, how to act constructively in the role of parent, grandparent, or sibling is particularly important.

Here are some typical comments that reflect people's assessment of how well individuals fulfill their constructive-group-member role.

- She's really a good sport.
- He tries to cheat his way through life.
- They both do more than their share of the work.
- You can usually expect her to pick a fight with someone.
- He's very even-tempered—never gets flustered.
- If she recognizes she's wrong, she'll apologize and try to make things right.

- If someone's in trouble, he'll offer to help.
- As a mother, she's really a good model of how to treat kids.

Schools use two main methods for promoting learners' personal-social relations—formal lessons and behavior-management techniques.

Formal lessons designed to foster positive social behavior come under such curriculum designations as character education, personal-social adjustment, moral development, and ethical training. The following examples illustrate the typical nature of such lessons.

- A kindergarten teacher read her pupils the story *Little Red Hen*, then asked the children questions about what they thought of the characters in the tale. "How would you feel if you were the little hen when the other animals wanted the food you had saved? What do you think the other animals should have done? Would you have shared your food with the others? If so, why—or why not?"

- After a junior-high-school class read Stephen Crane's novel *The Red Badge of Courage*, the teacher led a discussion of the propriety of the main character's actions and of what should be done about soldiers who acted as he had.

- Periodically, the teacher of a high-school class titled *Modern Living* posed moral-dilemma episodes for students to solve. Each episode consisted of an incident in which people were obliged to decide how to act in a moral-conflict situation. Class members were assigned to (a) decide whether the characters in an episode had acted properly and (b) defend that decision with a line of argument. As an example of a typical dilemma, here is an episode known as "the Heinz case."

  Mrs. Heinz was near death from a special type of cancer. The doctors thought one kind of drug might save her. The druggist who made the medicine she needed was selling it for ten times the amount it cost him to make it. The sick woman's husband, Heinz, did not have enough money for the medicine, so he went to borrow the money from everyone he knew, but he could collect only about half of what the druggist was charging. Heinz told the druggist his wife was dying and asked him to sell him the medicine cheaper or to let him pay later, but the druggist refused. The druggist said he had discovered the drug and he deserved to make money from it. So Heinz got desperate and later broke into the drugstore to steal the drug for his wife. The question then is: Should the husband have tried to steal the drug? Why or why not? (Adapted from Kohlberg, 1971, p. 156)

The expression *behavior management* refers to efforts of school personnel to get students to apply constructive-social-relations principles in daily life. Those principles include such precepts as:

- Give others a fair chance to express their opinions.
- Judge others on the basis of their behavior as individuals and not on the basis of their being from a particular age, gender, ethnic, religious, or social-class group.
- Keep your word.
- Don't bully other kids.
- During group activities, do your fair share of the work, and do it without complaining.
- Obey properly constituted laws and regulations.

The behavior-management efforts employed by teachers and administrators are sometimes referred to as discipline techniques, social-behavior guides, or classroom-management methods. Many opportunities to teach such principles arise spontaneously during daily school life in the form of episodes of either positive social behavior or undesirable behavior to which school personnel respond. Such opportunities appear in the form of pupils fighting on the playground, a girl befriending a new class member, a student stealing a classmate's cell phone, a boy sharing his lunch with a schoolmate who lost his lunch money, and more.

## Role 4: Wise Consumer

Although not all Americans are workers, virtually all Americans are consumers. Everyone beyond the age of infancy is obliged to make choices about what goods, services, and beliefs to accept or reject. The preparation for functioning as a consumer can derive from such varied sources as parents, siblings, peers, newspapers, magazines, movies, radio and television programs, the computer Internet, billboards, club meetings, the church, and the school.

The school's contribution to consumer education typically assumes the form of lessons or study-units in social-studies, science, health, home-economics, and industrial-arts classes. The following titles of lessons and study units illustrate the sorts of consumer knowledge that schools attempt to cultivate.

- How to Shop for a Bike
- Buying Wisely Over the Internet
- Junk Food and the Body You Want
- The Good and Bad of Credit Cards
- Reading the Back of the Package
- Smart Debt, Dumb Debt
- Ways to Plan a Budget
- Advertisers' Tactics

## Role 5: Enthusiastic User of Discretionary Time

A great part of most people's personal satisfaction with their lives comes during what is often called *free time, leisure time,* or *recreational time.* To me, such terms imply that during those "free" hours people are rather casual or lackadaisical about the activities they pursue. Thus, I prefer the expression *discretionary time,* which means that the individual is not duty-bound to invest those hours in a particular way, such as in a wage-earning job, in schooling, or in family obligations. Instead, the person has the option of deciding how to use the time. And the effort devoted to the chosen activity is often not at all casual but, instead, frequently involves intensive dedication and very hard work. Such can be the case with people who invest their discretionary hours in playing chess, building furniture, weight-lifting, learning a foreign language, practicing the cello, competing in figure-skating meets, writing a novel, cultivating orchids, painting landscape scenes, training animals, working in a political campaign, and far more.

One of the school's most vital contributions to enriching learners' personal lives is that of introducing students to knowledge and activities they can adopt as discretionary-time pursuits. Classes that offer such opportunities include ones in music, art, science (biology, geology, astronomy, physics, chemistry), literature, foreign languages, creative writing, dramatics, the dance, physical education, industrial arts, home economics, computer literacy, and social science (history, geography, psychology, sociology, anthropology, political science).

## Summary

In the foregoing discussion, I have proposed that the schools' stated objectives and curriculum content make a strong contribution to people's performing five roles (worker, citizen, group member, consumer, user of discretionary time) which, together, can constitute a satisfying and productive life. However, it is apparent that viewing the schools' task from the vantage point of role preparation is only one way of portraying the purpose of schooling. Another way is to see the school's job as that of fostering the growth of constructive personality traits—such virtues as honesty, courage, creativity, tolerance, diligence, and compassion. It's clear that role-preparation and trait-development are not in conflict. The two perspectives can be compatibly integrated, with virtues taught within a role-preparation framework.

Schools are forever negotiating what their contributions toward each role will be. As a result, new courses are added and old ones eliminated, the topics to be studied are revised, and different textbooks are adopted. Furthermore, the teaching methods and subject-matter content found in one school or in one classroom can differ from those in another school or classroom.

A variety of factors influence what the methods and curriculum content will be, including such factors as (a) state, school-district, and school curriculum requirements, (b) the opinions of influential community groups, (c) educational consultants from outside the school district, (d) books about education and articles in professional-education journals, (e) individual teachers' talents and subject-matter preferences, and (f) news in the public press and on television. A further influence on what is taught is the schools' ways of evaluating students' performance. As both teachers and administrators often observe, "The skills and knowledge that are evaluated are the ones most likely to be taught." Or, in a gloomier form, "If it's not to be evaluated, it won't be taught."

And that's the matter to which we next turn.

## Effect of Testing on What Schools *Do* Teach

Substantial evidence has accumulated to support the proposition that high-stakes achievement testing is causing schools to emphasize certain subjects, to de-emphasize some, and to eliminate others. And, as a further influence behind such curriculum change, the high-stakes movement has arrived at the same time that many schools face serious financial problems. Consequently, revisions of schools' curriculum patterns—that is, revisions of schools' contributions to the five life roles—have resulted from a combination of high-stakes testing and insufficient funds. In particular, the markedly increased time and money dedicated to teaching reading and math has diminished the time and money available for other fields of study.

Questions are continually being raised about whether those trade-offs have been wise. The key query is: How has high-stakes testing affected what schools *do teach* as compared to what schools *should teach*, and has any resultant collateral damage been worth the price? One sort of evidence bearing on this question is found in newspaper reports of schools' experiences. The following reports from across the nation identify traditional school subjects that have been reduced or eliminated, partly because of high-stakes testing. Each example begins with a title that suggests the nature of the ostensible damage. The description under the title then explains the type of damage and offers an illustrative case. The sorts of damage depicted in the examples include (a) teaching to the test, (b) the neglect of the study of history, (c) inadequate civic education, (d) social studies overlooked, (e) physical education eliminated, (f) the arts ignored, (g) the imposition of fees for students to participate in traditionally fee-free activities, (h) an increased burden of information to teach, (i) students' cultural heritage neglected, (j) testing postponed in certain subjects, and (k) recess and excursions reduced.

## Teaching to the Test

**Types of damage—Curtailed learning opportunities, more rote memorization.** Under high-stakes pressure, teachers can attempt to improve test scores by drilling students on the answers to specific test questions which are drawn from past state tests or from sample test items available on the Internet. Damage that can result from this practice includes

(a) limiting pupils' learning opportunities to the information required to answer particular test items rather than equipping students with a wide range of skills and knowledge and

(b) encouraging rote memorization of specific answers rather than promoting a comprehensive understanding of a field of knowledge and its underlying principles.

**Illustrative cases.** A study by the Rand Corporation of high-stakes testing in Texas reported that teachers said they were spending especially large amounts of class time on test-preparation activities. "Because the length of the school day is fixed, the more time that is spent on preparing students to do well on the TAAS [Texas Assessment of Academic Skills] often means there is less time to devote to other subjects" (Klein, Hamilton, McCaffrey, & Stecher, 2000).

An *Education Week* survey of the frequency of teaching-to-the-test in U.S. schools found that 20% of teachers were devoting either "a great deal" or "somewhat more" of class time to drilling on likely test questions. The survey team compared test-preparation teaching to junk food that gives a burst of energy (brief test-score gains) but no solid, long-lasting strength (permanent understanding). Test preparation is poor pedagogy when it bores students with continual testing, discourages teachers, offers bits of information out of context, turns classroom instruction into a series of multiple-choice questions, and drills on lower-level skills while neglecting writing and logical analysis (Marshall, 2003).

## Neglect of History

**Type of damage.** Critics have charged that the additional time and attention given to high-stakes-testing fields (primarily reading and math) has resulted in decreased emphasis on history in the curriculum. Consequently, students have fewer opportunities to learn the historical roots of their own community and nation, the rights and duties of citizens, and characteristics of cultures around the world. Thus, youths are inadequately prepared for their role as citizens in a democracy, and particularly for understanding causes and effects of such social problems as ethnic and religious conflicts, crime, war, economic change, family dysfunction, sexual exploitation, and the like.

**Illustrative cases.** At a gathering of about 7,000 middle-school and high-school students at Montgomery College to celebrate Maryland History Day, teachers expressed their concern that history was "on the public school chopping block" since Congress neglected the social studies when they passed the *No-Child-Left-Behind Act*. According to Peggy Burke, executive director of the Maryland Humanities Council, social studies were so drastically reduced that some school had completely eliminated them. Mark Stout, coordinator of secondary-school social studies in Maryland's Howard County, said, "If it ain't tested, it ain't taught" (Bowler, 2003a). John F. Jennings of the Center on Education Policy predicted that schools in high-poverty neighborhoods would be the ones most likely to neglect the social studies as teachers dedicated most of the school day to teaching reading and math. Jennings called reading and math instruction "the galactic black hole that's going to suck up all the resources" (Bowler, 2003a).

The Denver-based *Rocky Mountain News* reported in late 2003 that with so much attention in schools on reading and math under the *No-Child Act*, other subjects were in danger of neglect. The *News* cited a Thomas B. Fordham Institute's study of state targets for U.S. history which found standards dismally inadequate, with Colorado's history provision deserving a mark of "D" (Colorado's awful history standards, 2003).

## Civic Education Inadequate

**Type of damage.** The nature of citizenship in a democracy has traditionally been the focus of a secondary-school class titled *Civics* or *Citizenship Education* or *American Government*. Or, matters of citizenship have at least been included in units of study in social-science classes at various grade levels. Topics addressed in such classes have usually included the structure of American government, the duties assigned to different government levels (federal, state, county, city), current issues of law and governance, and citizen's rights and obligations. However, research surveys have suggested that schools have been negligent in teaching about such matters in recent times. Whereas some states test students' knowledge of civics, many do not; and it is clear that citizenship education has been left out of the federal government's *No-Child-Left-Behind* testing program. Consequently, the amount of emphasis placed on citizenship instruction has declined.

**Illustrative case.** A survey of 632 youths' knowledge of political matters revealed that more Americans between ages 15 and 26 could name the make-believe city where the Simpson cartoon family lived than could identify the political affiliation of their states' governors or could name the political party that controlled the U.S. Congress. The survey report from the National Conference of State Legislatures concluded that American youth failed to understand the meaning of citizenship, were not interested in the political process, did not know how to participate in American democracy, and didn't seem to care (Bushweller, 2003).

## Social Studies "Put on the Back Burner"

**Type of damage.** Not only have history and civics been neglected, but other aspects of the social studies have been set aside as well. Therefore, pupils are entering high school with less adequate backgrounds in geography and world cultures than they had in the past.

**Illustrative case.** All public schools in North Carolina are required to teach the state's curriculum, which includes subjects such as social studies and science. But from the viewpoint of evaluating students' achievement, elementary and middle schools are accountable only for how well they teach reading and math. As a result of this neglect of assessing pupil's command of social-studies skills and knowledge, students enter high school poorly prepared for social-studies classes. According to Carol Vogler, a high-school teacher and past president of the North Carolina Council for the Social Studies, much social-studies foundational learning that elementary schools traditionally provided has recently dwindled. Even though the material continues to be in the printed course of study, teachers spend so much time on the tested subjects of reading and math that there is little or no time left for the non-tested field of social studies (Silberman, 2003b).

## Physical Education Eliminated

**Type of damage.** The traditional curriculum field that has most often disappeared from students' school day has been physical education, a field that typically has included health and safety education.

**Illustrative cases.** Studies of curriculum change across the nation show physical education classes have increasingly been squeezed out of the school day, a trend that parallels a national increase in childhood obesity. Whereas 40% of high-school students enrolled in gym classes in 1991, by 2001 hardly 30% took gym. Observers believed the decline in required physical education was related to the fact that in 1980 only 5% of school-age children were severely overweight, while 20% were obese in 2001. With the increased pressure to teach for passing reading and math tests under the *No Child Left Behind* plan, more schools found physical education a luxury they could no longer afford (Kemper, 2003).

By 2004, Illinois was the only state in the nation to require physical education from kindergarten through high school. However, Illinois schools routinely obtained waivers to drop P.E., so that in 2004 at least 91% of elementary schools, 45% of middle schools, and 31% of high schools did not offer P.E. five days a week. A study revealed that 99% of waivers requested by school districts had been granted. A spokesman for the Chicago school system explained that school officials would like to have students engaged in more physical education but the top priority was to improve pupils' reading skills (Ritter, 2004).

## Education in the Arts Jeopardized

**Type of damage.**  The content of the *No-Child-Left-Behind Act*, like much recent state legislation, was strongly influenced by corporate leaders in the business community who wanted the schools to produce efficient workers who were well versed in communication skills (reading, writing), mathematics, and, to a lesser extent, science. Hence, in the *No-Child* plan, as well as in many state plans, testing has focused on language and math, often with the intent to include science later. Thus, the focus of current high-stakes programs is chiefly—and in some cases exclusively—concerned with only the first of the five life roles described earlier in this chapter, that of *efficient worker*. As a consequence, schooling that traditionally included attention to such other roles as that of *enthusiastic user of discretionary time* is—in the opinion of many concerned educators and members of the public—in danger of becoming a thing of the past.

**Illustrative cases.**    A study by the National Association of State Boards of Education concluded that the arts and foreign languages were at risk of disappearing from the curriculum offerings across the nation (Manzo, 2003b).

Elementary schools in North Carolina have been reducing the time spent on second-language learning so as to have more time for basic reading and math in English. Fewer than 20% of the state's public elementary-school pupils received once-a-week language lessons in 2004, compared to 50% a decade earlier (Silberman, 2004a).

A survey of 1,000 school principals in Indiana, New Mexico, New York, and Maryland showed that as schools paid more attention to reading and math, the curriculum was narrowing. A fourth of the principals reported decreased instruction time for the visual and performing arts, while only 8% reported increased time (Bowler, 2004a).

In Salt Lake City, 250 protestors in front of the state capital building urged the repeal of the Utah state legislature's bill SB154 that required major changes in public education, including additional instruction in math, language, reading, and science. But parents and teachers at the rally feared the elimination of music, drama, art, technical education, and sports. A similar demonstration was held at Valley High School in the southern Utah town of Orderville, an area represented by Senator Tom Hatch, sponsor of SB154. The bill was the result of recommendations from the Employers' Education Coalition, which consisted of business executives that Governor Mike Leavitt had appointed to propose ways of improving schooling in Utah. The chairman of the coalition, Fraser Bullock, said the contents of the legislation were precisely what employers wanted. However, the protesters disagreed. They passed out petitions calling for repeal of the law, claiming that they already had more than a thousand signatures (Rolly, 2003).

Raymond Park Middle School in Warren Township, Indiana, lost its two arts teachers, and home economics classes were eliminated, along with most foreign-language and physical-education classes. In place of funding an art department, the school board hired a business consultant from Texas who introduced a model called "total quality management." The model called for reorganizing the curriculum into three-week segments, each segment ending with a test (Dobbs, 2004).

In Missouri, recess was scaled back in the Olathe school district, the Renaissance Festival was eliminated in Blue Valley, and the fifth-grade band program was dropped in DeSoto. Faced with the demands of the *No-Child* program, administrators were restructuring the school day in an effort to accommodate the federal requirements and still maintain a well-rounded curriculum (Blobaum & Kowalczyk, 2004).

## Participation Fees Introduced

**Type of damage.** Tight budgets cause a rapid increase in schools charging fees for students to participate in extracurricular activities that traditionally had been free and were considered important contributors to a well-rounded education. The large amounts of money required to conduct high-stakes testing and its provisions (data analysis, tutoring, reports to parents) are among the reasons for the fee assessments.

**Illustrative cases.** A survey of fees charged by a sample of Massachusetts schools revealed that Tahanto Regional Middle/High School in Boylston assessed students $50 each year for such after-school activities as the math team or jazz band. The school charged student-athletes $225 for their first sport and $125 to play a second sport, but no more than $525 per family. At Holliston High School, parents paid $875 to have two children in sports. Weston public schools introduced a student activity fee for the entire school year, charging $100 for children in grades 3 through 5; $175 for grades 6 through 8; and $230 for grades 9 through 12. All Weston students paid at the same rate, whether to play basketball, solve equations on the math team, or join the high school's social awareness club. The fee was expected to bring $250,000 into the school coffers (Sweeney, 2003).

## Information Overload

**The type of damage.**  In their attempt to predict every bit of knowledge that might appear on high-stakes tests, state and county curriculum departments often prepare voluminous collections of information that teachers are expected to "cover" with their classes prior to testing time. In terms of students' learning, the result may well be a very hasty grasp of a few "facts" about many topics, but with no in-depth understanding of anything.

**Illustrative case.**  A Maryland ninth-grade teacher reported that the state's schools were straining to prepare students for the new tests by mastering the contents of two three-inch-thick curriculum guidebooks. However, there was so much material to be covered that even with her best students there was no way she could teach even a major portion of the lessons in a meaningful way.  All of the information was "important" because any of it might be on the state test.  When she tried to cover everything, she could do no more than refer to each item once and move ahead.  She said that was "not how children (or adults) learn" (Roush, 2003).

## Students' Cultural Heritage Neglected

**Type of damage.**   Recent decades have brought greater public awareness of the ethnic diversity of the U.S. population and of a desire for people of all cultural backgrounds to respect and maintain important features of their ethnic heritage.  One claim for attention has been particularly poignant—that of American Indians, whose land was wrested from them by European invaders and whose culture was denigrated and largely replaced with European forms.  The recent awakening of the public conscience to the desirability of people to learn about—and be proud of—their cultural origins has served to popularize multicultural education, with its increased focus on minority groups' backgrounds. However, the effort to give more time in the school day to the heritage of ethnic groups has come into conflict with the need for teachers to spend more time on English language and mathematics so students are well prepared for state tests.  Because the consequences of low test scores are so serious, the conflict is typically resolved by neglecting cultural studies in favor of more time on English and mathematics.

**Illustrative case.** North Carolina's Robeson County schools enroll more than half of the state's 20,000 Native American school children, and 60% of the teachers in the county are Indian. But there is little concern in school for Indian culture, because the teachers are obliged to focus on preparing children for state tests. Only occasionally and informally is attention paid to native traditions. For instance, Lynn Blanks, a second-grade teacher at Magnolia Elementary school prepared a table display of local Indian artifacts—arrowheads, a grinding stone, the painted jawbone of an animal, and the like—in celebration of Native American Heritage Month. She regarded the display as particularly important for her pupils, since two-thirds of them were Indian. But she was astonished when one of her second graders asked when they were going to see some real Indians. She answered, "Honey, *you* are a real Indian" (Simmons, 2003b).

## Testing Postponed in Selected Subjects

**Type of damage.** As already noted, instruction is bound to be more intense in those subject areas that are included in high-stakes testing. Therefore, if states' financial problems require the postponement or elimination of tests in certain subjects, teachers will not feel compelled to emphasize those subjects in their instruction, because there will be no public reports of students' level of knowledge in such fields.

**Illustrative cases.** Faced with tight budgets and new tests that must be developed, some states reduce the number of grade levels or subject fields for testing, with most cutbacks in subjects other than reading and math. During 2002, Oregon saved $4.5-million by eliminating writing tests for 3rd, 5th, and 8th graders, postponing science tests for 5th and 8th graders, and removing extended-response parts of math exams for 5th and 8th grade students. In the same year, Missouri saved $7.1-million by not giving science and social-studies tests, and Massachusetts cut costs by withholding history and social-studies tests (Hoff, 2002).

## Recess and Field Trips Reduced

**Type of damage.** Curtailing the time for children to relax between intensive periods of study may reduce learning efficiency and contribute to pupils' dislike for school. In addition, the elimination of visits to instructive sites outside the school restricts students' understanding of how school subjects apply to daily life.

**Illustrative cases.**  A survey of school districts around Washington, DC, showed that many had cut back on recess and field trips in order to spend more time on reading and math, resulting in complaints that the *No-Child* law made school "too much of a chore" (Mathews, 2004).

Many principals reported that children do not learn as well without breaks.  Rima Vesilind, a principal in Fairfax County, Virginia, said she protected recess because pupils worked hard during most of the day and she felt they need some free time in which to enjoy their friends (Mathews, 2004).  At Deale Elementary School in Virginia, recess periods were shortened, and less time was allowed for assemblies, chorus, band, and orchestra.  In 1998, when Virginia Standards of Learning tests were first required in Spotsylvania County, the number of field trips was cut.  In 2004, excursions were reduced from six to two at Maryland's Bradley Hills Elementary and the school's traditional book club discussions of literature were dropped (Mathews, 2004).

## Conclusion

The results of nationwide testing in reading and mathematics have made it abundantly clear that a program of high-stakes exams can stimulate increased test scores in reading and math.  But such testing is costly, both in terms of money and time.  The task of preparing, administering, and scoring standardized tests is a very expensive business, running into many millions of dollars for each state each year.  Therefore, funds used for high-stakes testing are not available for other educational purposes—programs in other subject fields, teachers' salaries, library books, band instruments, excursions, athletic facilities, and more.  In addition, many hours of classroom-instruction time are required for preparing students for high-stakes testing and for administering the tests.  Because of the serious punishment schools must bear when students do poorly on the obligatory exams, teachers are willing to reduce attention to other parts of the curriculum in order to improve students' chances of succeeding in the tested fields.  As a consequence, subject fields that are not examined can suffer instructional neglect—collateral damage from high-stakes testing.  Critics have wondered whether the loss of subject-matter that students might otherwise have studied is worth the gains in reading and math scores.

It is apparent that not all students suffer the same loss of subject-matter as a consequence of high-stakes testing.  Comparisons of schools have shown that the extent to which subjects other than reading and math are neglected vary markedly from one place to another.  The loss is minimal in schools that are liberally funded and that draw pupils from homes where parents have advanced education, speak English fluently, and promote their children's academic success. In such schools, a high proportion of students are motivated to succeed with their studies, are well fed, and are generally "well behaved," so they do well in reading and math without an undue amount of instruction. Thus, their teachers have sufficient time and facilities available for giving instruction in science, social studies, the humanities, and the arts. Far less favored are schools in run-down and often dangerous urban neighborhoods that draw their clientele from families in poverty—largely ethnic-minority families whose home language is other than the standard English used in schools. Children who attend those schools frequently are ill-fed, are often boisterous, and fail to attend class regularly. If teachers are to prepare such learners to do well on reading and math tests, then a great deal of class time—and perhaps after-school tutoring—must be dedicated to the task. Consequently, little time will be left for social studies, science, and the arts. In sum, high-stakes testing in reading and math results in students in socio-economically privileged schools receiving a much broader education than do those in socially disadvantaged schools.

An oft-debated issue is the matter of which fields of learning should be the focus of high-stakes testing. Apparently few observers, if any, question the emphasis on reading, since reading skill is vital for success in all five of the life roles proposed earlier in this chapter and for all of the school's academic pursuits. But giving mathematics the same level of attention as reading is questionable, particularly when tests include mathematics beyond the simplest functions of algebra—mathematics that most adults seldom if ever encounter in daily life. So a question can be posed about why science should not be regarded as important for people's lives as math—or even more important than any math beyond the most basic arithmetic? And as another alternative to math testing, what about urging students to become well-informed, active citizens of the American democracy by testing their knowledge of government and of people's rights and responsibilities? In view of the low level of participation among young adults in public elections in the United States, might not greater stress on the study of civics be warranted so as to encourage young citizens to become actively involved in determining who runs the government and how?

In summary, the high-stakes testing required by the *No-Child-Left-Behind Act* raises crucial questions about the relationship between what the schools *should teach* and what the schools *actually do teach*. Those questions include:

- Are politicians in Washington and in state capitals well qualified to decide which subjects should be given priority for study in all of the nation's public schools, regardless of the nature of individual communities and their populations?

- Does high-stakes testing in two or three subject-matter areas do more overall harm than good in terms of providing students with a well-balanced education—an education that prepares them to perform well in all five life roles?

# 3

# What Should Schools Evaluate, and How?

Answering the question *"What* should schools evaluate?" is quite simple. Schools should evaluate students' progress toward all learning goals. Otherwise, how would anyone know how well instruction was succeeding? In contrast, answering *"How* should evaluation be performed?" can be complex and controversial. In order to explain where high-stakes testing fits into the *how* of assessing student progress, this chapter describes

- Alternative ways to evaluate students' achievement,
- Strengths and weaknesses of different types of test items as evaluation instruments, and
- Kinds of collateral damage that can result from limiting a school's assessment methods to high-stakes achievement testing.

## A Host of Evaluation Methods

School personnel have available a variety of methods for judging students' achievement. The following are examples of such methods as listed under three categories—direct observation, the inspection of student work products, and written tests.

- Teachers depend on *direct observation* of students' performances when students
  —Orally answer teachers' questions
  —Give speeches
  —Participate in class discussion
  —Work on small-group projects
  —Engage in physical activities

—Carry out laboratory experiments

—Work problems at the chalkboard

—Operate equipment (computer, lathe, sewing machine)

—Perform in dramatic, musical, or dance events

—Demonstrate a process (how to use a voting machine, how to prepare fried chicken, how to search the computer Internet, how to create a clay vase on a potter's wheel)

—Participate in a project (clean up the classroom and school yard, conduct an election, plan a party, publish a newspaper)

- Teachers analyze such student *work products* as

—Written essays, term papers, stories, poems, journals

—Answers in workbooks

—Exhibits and collections related to science, mathematics, social studies, literature, or the arts

—Graphic displays (drawings, maps, charts, photographs)

—Created objects (a wood carving of a fox, an electric motor, a party dress, a miniature model of a pioneer village)

—An Internet web page

- Teachers depend on *achievement tests* for judging students' skill in answering questions and solving problems that are cast as true-false, multiple-choice, matching, completion (fill-in), short-answer, or essay items.

It is thus apparent that achievement tests serve as only one method for assessing students' progress. Other important methods are teachers' observations of students' performances and teachers' analyses of students' work products.

Not only do school personnel have a variety of methods for judging students' progress but also a variety of ways to summarize students' achievement. Those summaries can assume such forms as test scores, written notes, judgments entered into a computer file, comments dictated into a tape recorder, check lists, rating scales, report cards, and photographs or videotapes of students' performances and work products.

Whenever judgments of achievement are limited to a report of test scores in a few subject-matter areas, other significant realms of students' education are left unrecognized. The result is a distorted picture of what students have learned and how well they have learned it.

## Test-Item Types—Strengths and Weaknesses

The ability of a test to measure how well students have achieved learning objectives depends partly on the types of items that comprise the test, because all item types are not equally effective for measuring different objectives. In other words, no single kind of test item is well suited to assessing all kinds of learning. This point can be demonstrated by brief analysis of five popular item types—true-false, multiple-choice, completion, short answer, and essay.

## True-False Items

Here is a typical true-false item.

**T   F**   1. The Bill of Rights was not part of the original United States Constitution but was a separate document.

True-false items of this sort can be dismissed outright as accurate evaluation tools, because they suffer from too many weaknesses. Students who know nothing about the Bill of Rights can get the item right 50% of the time by pure guess, since the chance of getting a two-option question correct simply by guessing is 1/2. Furthermore, such a phrase as "a separate document" is imprecise. Does it mean "a later amendment" or "an entirely different document, not associated with the Constitution"? Problems caused by such imprecision can mislead students into getting the question wrong when they actually know the information.

## Multiple-Choice Items

Here is a typical multiple-choice item, prefaced with the directions explaining to test-takers the nature of their task.

*Directions:* Read each question and the four possible answers under the question. Then write an **X** on the line in front of the best answer.

1. A farmer grows only enough crops and has only enough cows and pigs to feed his own family. He has no food left over to sell. What kind of farming would this be called?
   ____ subsistence farming
   ____ sharecropping
   ____ cash-crop farming
   ____ primitive farming

A multiple-choice item consists of a question accompanied by several possible answers. Test-takers are asked to select which of those answers is the best. The number of options from which students can choose may vary from two to five or six, with four choices perhaps the most frequent type. Two-or-three-choice forms are used with younger pupils, and four-to-six-choice types with older ones.

For the purpose of evaluating students' progress, multiple-choice items offer a variety of attractive advantages, thereby making them the most popular type on high-stakes tests. Multiple-choice questions are effective for assessing how well students can choose—from among several alternatives—the (a) solution to a problem, (b) date of an event, (c) names of people, places, and events, (c) definition of something, as well as its purpose, cause, or effect, (e) similarities and differences among things, (f) wrong answer, (g) mistaken belief, (g) and more. In addition, multiple-choice items can cover a broad range of information in a short period of time, are easy for students to mark, and are easy for testers to score by hand or by machine.

But while multiple-choice questions test students' ability to *recognize* or *identify* which of the displayed answers is the best one, they do not measure students' ability to *recall freely* from memory the answers to questions. That is, the four or five alternatives from which the best answer is to be chosen are already provided on the test. Hence, students are not required to create a proper answer but merely to recognize the most suitable answer from among the proffered alternatives. Therefore, multiple-choice items are not appropriate for measuring a pupil's ability to recall and present facts, plan a way to solve a problem, or organize ideas and present them.

Multiple-choice items are somewhat susceptible to guessing. The chance of a student guessing the right answer without actually knowing the desired information is 25% for a four-choice item (1/4) and 20% for a five-choice item (1/5).

## Completion or Fill-in Items

Some test questions require pupils either to complete or fill-in a statement that is unfinished.

The United States Congress consists of two legislative bodies that are called (a) The House of Representatives and (b) _____.

Who was the author of the novel *Moby Dick*? _____

A principal advantage of completion questions is their ability to test students' *unaided recall* of facts, rather than only the skill of recognizing which of several displayed options is best. It is virtually impossible by "pure guess" to give a correct answer to a completion question. Another advantage of fill-in items is that they can sample an extensive array of facts in a short period of time. But compared to multiple-choice questions, completion and short-answer items are more difficult to score, since they require a test-corrector to decide how well each student's written word or phrase matches the test-maker's notion of a right answer.

## Essays

The following are essay questions from four subject-matter fields.

- **Science.** Imagine that a friend asks you what the "water cycle" is and how it works. Explain exactly how you would answer your friend's question.
- **History.** Why is Abraham Lincoln known as one of the greatest American presidents?
- **Literature.** In Mark Twain's novel *Huckleberry Finn,* was Huck prejudiced against Negroes? Support your answer with examples of events in the story.
- **Auto mechanics.** A woman tells you that when she turns on the ignition to start her car, the car sometimes starts and other times doesn't start. Explain how you would go about (a) discovering the cause of the problem and (b) deciding how to fix it.

Whereas multiple-choice and completion items are well adapted to measuring pupils' command of facts and definitions, essays are better for testing students' ability to organize facts into a well-reasoned argument or a plan of action. Essays are also more appropriate for testing pupils' skill in analyzing the advantages and disadvantages of proposed actions, such as the city's program for unsnarling traffic or the high-school principal's plan for controlling students' use of drugs and alcohol.

One reason essay questions are rarely found in high-stakes testing is that most students require considerable time in which to compose an answer, so that a very small sample of what has been taught can be assessed during a normal testing period. Furthermore, composing a fluent essay requires considerable writing skill. Consequently, unless the aim of the test is to evaluate students' writing skill (rather than command subject-matter content and manner of reasoning), students who know the subject but do not write fluently are unable to display what they have learned. In addition, scoring essays is very time-consuming and is highly influenced by the personal opinions and tastes in writing style of the people who correct the essays.

Some high-stakes testing schemes do include one or two essay items. When the purpose of those items is to evaluate students' command of the mechanics of writing (spelling, subject-verb agreement, consistency of tenses, and the like) and when students write their essays on a computer, then computer programs can readily score the essays. However, computers are not capable of judging such things as the logic of the writer's line of reasoning, wise choice of vocabulary, emotional tone, point of view, consistency of argument, objectivity in presenting evidence, and other important aspects of written composition.

Hence, while essay items can be excellent devices for assessing many higher-level skills that the school aims to promote, essay questions are seldom found on high-stakes tests.

Finally, it's important to recognize that test-makers have available far more item types than those described above. In effect, our overview has failed to cover the complete arsenal of item types that test-builders can draw from. Yet, brief as it is, the overview should provide a sufficient background for understanding kinds of harm that have accompanied present-day high-stakes testing programs. But before inspecting such damage, we can profit from considering the topic of test validity.

## Achievement-Test Validity

The expression *test validity* refers to how well a test does what it is supposed to do. Questions about validity deserve attention because a significant amount of the damage from high-stakes testing has been caused by validity problems.

There are various kinds of test validity. *Predictive validity* is reflected in the question: "How accurately does the test foretell how well a person will perform a given task at some future time?" For instance, the more precisely a student's grades in college are foretold by a test the student took on entering college, the higher that test's predictive validity. In contrast, *diagnostic validity* concerns the question: "How accurately does the test identify the strengths and weaknesses of a person's performance in some aspect of life?" Examples of aspects are reading, math, general science, basketball, driver safety, house construction, knowledge of the law, and the like.

But the type of validity of primary interest in high-stakes testing is different. It has usually been called *content validity*, with its intent reflected in the question: "How well have students learned what they have been taught?" Or "How well have students mastered what they have had a fair chance to learn?" At first glance, determining a test's content validity might seem fairly straightforward; a list of what students are expected to learn is simply compared to the test's items. So, the greater the percentage items that focus on things students are expected to learn, the greater the test's validity.

But, however simple the validity-checking task might seem, in practice it can be very tricky, indeed. For example, it is necessary to pay attention to the distribution and quality of the test items to make sure that items sample each section of the content in a balanced matter, that the test directions are easily understood, and that questions are clearly worded. It is also important to recognize that test-makers typically create questions focusing on what those test-makers believe students should know (knowledge) or should be able to do (skills). But the resulting test content may not match the content of the printed course of study of a particular school system. Therefore, students can end up being tested over material that the school system never intended them to learn; and the result is low test scores. To avoid this problem, states have increasingly insisted that test-makers base test items solely on the state's own curriculum content. Yet, even that requirement may not ensure that a test measures what the students had a fair chance to learn, because teachers often do not strictly follow the printed curriculum manual. They may spend more time on some topics than on others, leave out material they consider less vital, add extra material they believe is important, and fail to clearly explain certain concepts or skills. Time constraints may also require that some topics be slighted. Under those conditions, the test does not accurately measure what the students were taught or had a fair chance to learn.

The content-validity problem is further complicated by individual differences among learners, as dramatically demonstrated in cases of children with physical and psychological disabilities and those with a limited command of English. Such pupils have trouble taking tests that require English-language reading and writing skills.

In sum, problems of content validity can contribute significantly to the collateral damage that accompanies high-stakes testing.

# Collateral Damage from High-Stakes Tests

When the evaluation of students' progress is limited to the sorts of tests used in the current high-stakes movement, resulting damage may include (a) momentous decisions about a student as based on a test score, (b) the fate of a school determined by the test scores of one group of students, (c) unstable test scores, (d) the questionable quality of tests, (e) harm resulting from testing errors, (g) learners confronted with a strange, confusing situation, and (h) conflicts within a school's staff.

## Momentous Decisions That Affect Individual Students Are Based on a Single Test Score

**Type of damage.** Using standardized achievement tests as the only means of assessing the skills, knowledge, and attitudes students have acquired will produce a distorted picture of what students have learned. This damage is particularly grave when a student's score on a single test determines whether that individual will be promoted to a higher grade or will graduate from high school. As the National Center for Fair and

Open Testing warns, crucial decisions affecting a student's fate can be based on a single test score because any particular test can evaluate only a small part of a subject area or only a few human abilities. Even a reading test may cover no more than a few reading skills and not the entire range of ability to understand and apply what is read. Whereas a multiple-choice math exam can reveal students' computational skills and ability to solve routine problems, it does not show how well students can apply their knowledge to problems met in daily life (*Fair test*, 2003).

**Illustrative cases.** All public high-school students in New York State have been required to pass Regents exams in English, mathematics, world history, American history, and one science subject. In late 2003, after State Assemblyman Steven Sanders (chairman of the education committee in the New York State Legislature's lower house) completed three days of legislative hearings, he announced that both educators and members of the public overwhelmingly agreed that Regents tests played too large a role in determining students' futures. Sanders charged that everybody wants high academic standards but it is unreasonable to expect any student's entire range of abilities to be measured accurately by a single exam given on a particular day (Hoff, 2003e). Sanders suggested that Regents-exam scores should be only one of a variety of factors local school officials use in deciding whether a student should graduate.

In Massachusetts, state-education officials implemented legislation requiring high-school seniors to pass a graduation exam in order to receive a high-school diploma. After the exams were scored, Boston officials reported that, according to past policies, high-school students deserved a high-school diploma if they met the city's requirements in English, math, and other subjects, as well as in attendance. Among the 636 Boston seniors who did not pass the graduation exam and were thus denied diplomas, 455 (72%) had fulfilled all of those conditions. In responding to this news, John Mudd, a representative of the Massachusetts Advocates for Children, charged that Boston was "serving up 455 kids on the state altar of the high-stakes exam" (Rothstein, 2003a).

## The Fate of a School Determined by the Test Scores of One Group of Students

**Type of damage.** As described in Chapter 1, during the opening years of the twenty-first century, American public schools were threatened by punishment that was far more severe and widespread than any imposed before. Those sanctions—stipulated in laws passed by the U.S. Congress and state legislatures—applied to all public schools whose students did not improve their reading and mathematics test scores at a rate dictated by federal and state formulas. For instance, recall the *No-Child-Left-Behind* requirement that:

> If a school fails to make adequate progress [in test-score improvement] for four years, the district must implement certain *corrective actions* to improve the school, such as replacing certain staff or fully implementing a new curriculum, while continuing to offer public school choice and supplemental educational services for low-income students.
>
> If a school fails to make adequate yearly progress for a fifth year, the school district must initiate plans for *restructuring* the school. This may include reopening the school as a charter school, replacing all or most of the school staff or turning over school operations either to the state or to a private company with a demonstrated record of effectiveness. (*Questions and Answers*, 2002).

To incur such sanctions, it was not necessary for a school's student population in general to fall short of federal targets. Instead, the punishment could be imposed if the scores if any of the *No-Child-Left-Behind* subgroups (whites, African-Americans Hispanics, Native-Americans, Asian–Americans, limited-English, special-education, poverty) failed to advance at the required pace. Therefore, a school that served students in an economically-distressed, crime-ridden urban ghetto could suffer those sanctions even if its staff was doing an admirable a job of teaching under extremely difficult societal conditions.

**Illustrative cases.** In Maryland, 131 schools were relegated to the failing-schools list in 2003. Schools could be placed on the needs-improvement roster if they failed to meet only one of 18 standards, such as those applying to the eight *No-Child-Left-Behind* subgroups. Like many schools across the country, Maryland's Magnolia Elementary reached most of the goals set under the *No-Child Act,* but the school's special-education pupils' standardized-test scores fell below the cutting mark. At Broad Acres and Burnt Mills schools in Montgomery, pupils passed in all 18 required categories but were kept on the failing list since they had not yet met the performance standard for two years in a row (Bowie, 2003).

In the state of Washington, shortfalls in test scores among special-education students at Alki Middle School and Columbia River High in the Vancouver district prevented both schools from achieving the federal government's standard of adequate yearly progress. In Camas district, students in all pupil subgroups except that of special education far exceeded state targets. But because only 47.5% of fourth-grade special-education pupils met the reading target rather than the 56.2% required by the state, Camas was listed among the state's 125 districts that were cited for failing to make acceptable progress (Gilbert, 2003).

When the *No-Child-Left-Behind* standards were applied in Missouri during 2003, nearly half of the state' 2,055 schools failed to meet federal criteria in language arts and math. Several schools that fell short of the target had been among the top 10 performers on Missouri tests in 2002, along with many more schools cited as outstanding for their performance on state tests. This paradox resulted from the federal law holding schools accountable for (a) how well ethnic, special-education, and limited-English subgroups performed on tests and (b) ensuring that at least 95% of students in each group were tested  (Bower, 2003a).

## Unstable Test-Score Gains

**Type of damage.** If a school's test-score gains or losses for a given year are not good predictors of what will likely happen the following year or two, then test scores are not stable indicators of a school's quality. Therefore, it is appropriate to withhold rewards or punishments for schools until a trustworthy trend over a series of years is apparent.

**Illustrative case.** Walt Haney, a Boston College professor, analyzed the trends in state test results for individual Massachusetts schools over the 1998-2001 period and reported that the principals of four elementary schools in 1999 had received $10,000 each for their pupils' notable gains on the state's high-stakes tests. In 2000, test scores declined in three of those schools. Haney noted that among all elementary schools that rose at least 10 points in 2000 over their 1999 scores, most showed declines in 2001, with the declines frequently as much as the previous year's gains. The tendency was for schools that did better the first year to do worse the second year, and vice versa. He concluded that the 1999 scores were not suitable evidence of improved quality of schooling because, especially in small schools, score averages could vary widely from one year to the next because a different population of students is tested each year and the contents of tests and their manner of administration change somewhat year by year (Haney, 2002).

## Questionable Quality of Tests

**Type of damage.** Dramatic increases in students' test scores may be suspect when, in the past, such increases have been due, at least partly, to defects in the way the tests were constructed and standardized.  Consequently, the public may come to doubt the worth of high-stakes tests as measures of students' learning and of school quality.

**Illustrative case.** The remarkable 2003 gains in fourth-graders' math scores across New York State became the target of testing-experts' questions about the quality of the tests. Alfred S. Posamentier, dean of the

School of Education at City College, questioned the reliability of the test when there were dramatic changes from one year to the next. He said the test should be analyzed to make sure it was the same level of difficulty as its predecessor. He mentioned his experience as a member of a committee that reported serious flaws in the way the state's Math-A Regent's exam had been prepared, so that the test had to be rescored (Gootman, 2003c).

## Harm Resulting from Testing Errors

**Type of damage.** Mistakes in the creation, administration, and scoring of tests can result in various kinds of harm, including (a) a waste of financial resources and (b) emotional distress and a waste of time for students and school personnel.

**Illustrative cases.** The state of Minnesota employed the company NCS Pearson as the prime contractor for managing the state's Comprehensive Assessments and Basic Standards Test. However, the arrangement went awry when Pearson used the wrong answer key on 47,000 tests. Consequently, about 8,000 high-school students were listed as failing when they actually had passed, with several dozen not permitted to attend graduation ceremonies because of the error. A resulting class-action lawsuit was settled by the company agreeing to pay the school $7-million in reparations (Anti-FCAT group, 2003).

Just before students in Georgia were scheduled to take state tests in grades 1 through 8, education officials suspended the test sessions when they learned that 270 of the intended test questions were available to students, teachers, and parents on an Internet site—a state "item bank" that districts used for practice. The president of the Southern Regional Education Board in Atlanta said that states needed to adopt quality-control measures to reduce costly errors in the future (Olson, 2003c).

Difficulties in New York City with the 2004 reading test included (a) some teachers having pupils practice on the 2003 test, thereby giving children a preview of questions that would be repeated on the 2004 exam, (b) some questions appearing on television, so makeup exams had to be postponed, and (c) items on the answer sheets for the makeup test, which was taken by 2,400 pupils, failed to match items in the test booklet. Jane Hirschmann, a critic from a group called Time Out From Testing, warned that schools should not use a single score on a test to determine a pupil's future, particularly when a test used for high-stakes purposes was "unreliable, invalid, and [the testers] just can't get it straight" (Herszenhorn, 2004c).

### Learners Confronted with a Strange, Confusing Situation

**Type of damage.** The expression *test anxiety* refers to the distress students often experience when confronted by a test, and particularly when faced with a testing situation that deviates from usual classroom activities and promises serious consequences for test-takers. Such is the situation in most high-stakes achievement testing.

**Illustrative case.** In Texas, a comparison between typical classroom activities and the administration of state achievement tests led a teacher-education expert to conclude that requiring pupils to spend several very anxious hours choosing among answers to reading and math questions, with only occasional restroom breaks, was quite at odds with children's daily classroom experience that permitted them to get help from teachers and classmates (Casas, 2003).

### Conflicts Among School Personnel

**Type of damage.** Controversies within a school can arise whenever staff members disagree about what constitutes improper aid to students who are taking tests.

**Illustrative case.** In a lawsuit, Jean McKay, a former administrator at the West Oak Lane Charter School in Philadelphia, charged that she was fired from her job three days after she had informed district authorities that members of the school staff had given students answers to questions on state achievement tests. According to the complaint, on the testing day another administrator visited a classroom and ordered pupils to take time out to check their answers. When the same administrator visited a different classroom, she helped some pupils with test questions and suggested ways that others should change their answers. She also took advantage of a rest break in the testing session to teach a brief lesson on telling time, thereby helping pupils answer test questions about time. McKay reported that three days after her phone call to district officials, she went to the school and discovered that all of her files, documentation, and personal notes about the testing activities were missing (Woodall, 2003).

## Conclusion

The line of logic offered in this chapter has been built on the following sequence of convictions.

- The ultimate purpose of schooling is to improve the way students' act, that is, to enhance learners' ability to act wisely in present and future decision-making situations. To accomplish this purpose, the typical school curriculum confronts students with a wide variety of learning objectives to master.

- School personnel—and particularly teachers—have three main ways of judging how well students achieve the objectives: (a) direct observation of students' behavior, (b) the analysis of students' work products, and (c) oral and written tests. Each evaluation method is accompanied by particular strengths and limitations.

- The sorts of test items found on achievement exams—and especially the sorts used in high-stakes testing—are suitable devices for assessing progress toward only a limited number of the typical school's learning objectives. Multiple-choice questions, as the most popular item type, measure only students' ability to *recognize* which answer, among a few choices, is the most suitable. They do not measure students' *free-recall* of answers to questions, as do completion and short-answer items, which are rather rare in high-stakes testing. Neither multiple-choice nor completion items measure students' ability to plan, compose, create, evaluate, make complex comparisons, analyze in detail, or formulate answers about complicated issues. Nor do such items permit students to qualify their answers to questions by citing conditions under which one answer would be more suitable than another. Therefore, many of the objectives that schools have traditionally sought to promote are not assessed by high-stakes tests, particularly when the tests focus on so few subject-matter fields as reading and mathematics.

- The limitations of high-stakes achievement testing—as the foundation on which to base serious negative sanctions against students and schools—call into question the wisdom of both the *No-Child-Left-Behind* program and state testing programs in their current forms. It seems obvious that far more adequate evaluation methods are needed for judging how well individual students and their schools are fulfilling the expectations society holds for them.

# 4

# How Should Achievement
# Standards Be Set?

After subject-matter fields have been chosen as the bases for judging students' achievement, and after tests have been selected as the instruments of measurement, education authorities face the task of deciding how many of each test's questions a student must answer correctly in order to pass. In the case of tests used to fulfill the requirements of the *No-Child-Left-Behind Act*, standards must be set for distinguishing among four levels of performance: *failure, basic, proficient*, and *advanced*.

The purpose of this chapter is to identify

- Alternative ways to set standards and
- Collateral damage that can accompany the setting of levels in high-stakes achievement-testing programs.

## Alternative Ways to Set Standards

Every evaluation of student progress involves comparing the student's performance against a criterion. Among the available types of criteria, five of the more popular are (a) the ideal student, (b) the attainable level, (c) other students, (d) each student's own record, and (e) some combination of a-through-d. The following brief overview of those alternatives describes their key features and their relationship to high-stakes testing.

### The Ideal Student

It is possible to conceive of the level of knowledge and skill that would be displayed by a person who is ideally fitted to participate constructively in society and to attain an optimal degree of self-fulfillment. This standard is particularly appealing to business executives as they search for new employees who they hope will display all worker-virtues at a high level of efficiency. However, to apply such a standard, education officials are obligated to specify how many test items—and at what level of difficulty—a student must pass in order to achieve the ideal-student standard.

In judging the desirability of this criterion, some critics claim that the ideal level of attainment is too high if only a very small proportion of learners earn acceptable marks, as so often occurs in schools that enroll a high percentage of students from disadvantaged social backgrounds or ones who suffer physical and mental handicaps. Other critics complain that the ideal level is too low if an excessively large proportion of students receive extremely high ratings. According to a news-magazine report, the dean of admissions at a prestigious law school said his office paid no attention to an honorific *magna cum laude* or *cum laude* title from Harvard University because so many students (83.6% in 1993) had such titles attached to their degrees (Leo, 1993).

## The Attainable Level

A less stringent criterion than the ideal-student standard is one based on an estimate of the amount of knowledge or skill that most—or perhaps all—students can reasonably attain. Such a criterion is established in terms of the number of test items that someone—such as a teacher, test-maker, or administrator—believes most students can answer correctly if they have studied diligently.

The attainable-level standard assumes that an educational program should enable all—or nearly all—participants to master all of the learning objectives. Having a high proportion of learners fail to achieve the objectives signifies that the instruction has been very poor, or that the methods of evaluating student progress have been faulty, or that the achievement standards have been unreasonably strict.

Whenever all (or most) students reach or exceed the attainable level, all (or most) students are able to progress up the educational ladder at a regular pace and feel successful. However, if all, or nearly all, students are to pass, then the standard must be set at a level which the least adept can reach and which the great majority can exceed. But setting such a low expectation may result in the average and above-average students not being challenged to exert their best effort, for they lack the incentive to learn far beyond the limits of such an expectation. In the public press, a critic of the "inflation of standards" complained that:

> For whatever reasons (and the feel-good self-esteem movement is surely one), marks have broken free of performance and become more and more unreal. They are designed to please, not to measure or to guide students about strengths and weaknesses. Give A's and B's for average effort and the whole system becomes a game of "Let's Pretend". . . . What happens when

[students] join the real world where A and B rewards are rarely given for C and D work? (Leo, 1993, p. 22)

On the other hand, if the attainable level is set so high that few learners reach it, the mass of students who fall below the pass line can view themselves as failures. Such an experience may motivate some to greater effort in order to score higher in the future. However, for those who already have been working diligently and still fail, the experience can lead to discouragement—to giving up and dropping out.

## Other Students

Another popular way to assess achievement is to compare students' performances to the performance of their classmates, grademates, or agemates. Thus, the assessment process consists of ranking students by the test score each earned. Students in the top ranks are awarded the best marks. Those in the bottom ranks are assigned the worst marks. By comparing students with each other, schools avoid the risk of setting an attainment level that is unreasonably high or unreasonably low.

Adopting the student-comparison criterion requires that some individual (teacher, administrators, test-creator) or group decides the cutting score between the students who pass and those who fail. This is a subjective decision, based on opinion, not fact. For example, a committee may decide that 80% of the students should pass and only 20% fail. Or, as a more lenient standard, the cutting point could be the score that separates the lowest 10% of students' scores from the upper 90%. And that decision can be influenced by such factors as the decision-makers' beliefs about

- how many test items students should answer correctly at a given grade level to warrant students being considered *minimally adequate* in the field of knowledge that the test samples;
- what percentage of students can be dubbed *failures* without generating undue political consequences, such as parents' objections, public demonstrations, and demands that the officials who have set the standards be ousted from their positions; and
- the present stage of the testing program—with less demanding standards being acceptable early in the testing program (such as during the first year of the *No-Child-Left-Behind* plan) than later in the program (such as in the fifth year of the plan).

Typically, standard-setters not only determine the cutting score that distinguishes between *pass* and *fail* but also identify cutting scores that separate different levels of *pass* from each other, such levels as *basic, proficient*, and *advanced*.

## Each Student's Own Record.

This criterion is founded on the belief that judgments of each student's progress should focus on the amount of skill and knowledge which that particular learner gains over a given period of time. For every individual, that amount should be adjusted to that person's apparent learning potential. Students with higher potential should be expected to acquire more during the same time period in which students with lower potential gain less. Therefore, the adequacy of a student's present performance is judged by how much the individual has progressed beyond his or her own past performance in light of that person's estimated learning ability.

This individual-progress approach has been extolled as the mode of standard-setting best suited to promoting the goal of "Let each become all that she or he is capable of being." However, the approach has been criticized on several counts. Critics have suggested that comparing a student's progress only against that person's own past record can give the less apt learners a false sense of their actual ability. Consequently, after receiving high grades for their modest achievement in school, they suffer a rude shock in the world beyond school when they fail to compete successfully with their more competent agemates. Furthermore, parents and employers typically wish to know, not just how a youth measures against his or her own potential, but also how that youth compares to others the same age. An individual-progress report fails to yield that sort of information.

There is also a school-wide version of the individual-progress method. Achievement standards within a school may be adjusted to the apparent capabilities of the particular student population. Thus, the percentage of students awarded passing marks in a socially depressed inner-city school may be quite similar to the percentage in a private school attended by a highly select group of socially privileged students. However, the labels *failure, basic, proficient,* and *advanced* in the two schools can have quite different meanings in terms of academic accomplishment.

Such high-stakes testing programs as that of the *No-Child-Left-Behind* plan do not accept individual progress as a proper criterion on which to base judgments of achievement.

## The Hybrid *No-Child-Left-Behind* Approach

The method of standard-setting mandated by the *No-Child-Left-Behind Act* is a hybrid scheme that combines features of the ideally-educated-person, attainable-level, and student-comparisons perspectives.

The *ideally-educated-person* element is most obviously represented by the act's aim to have virtually all public-school pupils proficient level in reading and math by 2014—and probably in science as well.

The *attainable-level* element is found in the stage of progress that the *No-Child-Left-Behind Act* proposes for each year between 2002 and 2014. The act recognized that students' 2002 scores in many schools would fall well short of *proficient.* But with more effective instructional methods being increasingly adopted, students could be expected to improve their scores annually at a regular pace. Thus, a higher attainable level would be set for each year after 2002 until the ideal would be reached in 2014.

The *student-comparisons* element of the *No-Child* program is found in the proportion of each group of a school's learners (Black, Native-American, handicapped, etc.) that should pass the tests during any given year in order for the school to avoid the failure label.

Because the *No-Child Act* is a federal law, applicable throughout the United States, the standards set by the act would, at first glance, appear to produce uniformity across the nation. However, such is not the case, because each state has the right and responsibility to (a) devise its own reading and math tests and (b) set the test-score levels that distinguish among *failure, basic, proficient,* and *advanced.*

As explained in Chapter 1, the *No-Child Act* authorizes state officials to establish a 2002 *starting point* based on the performance of the state's lowest-achieving demographic group (such as an ethnic group) or the state's lowest-achieving schools. Officials then decide on the level of student achievement a school must annually reach above that starting point in order to show *adequate yearly progress.* At least once every three years, the basic, proficient, and advanced achievement levels must be raised until, by 2014, all students in the state are succeeding at the proficient level on state assessments in language arts (chiefly reading) and math. Under-performing schools may avoid such sanctions if they can demonstrate a 10% reduction in the number of students that are not meeting the annual proficiency goals.

Two examples of the way states may set their goals are the Kentucky and Louisiana plans. The Kentucky aim is to have all schools reach a Kentucky-Core-Content-Test score of 100 (on a scale of zero to 140) by 2014. A score of 100 would indicate that, on average, a school's student population was proficient under a system of four performance classifications—novice, apprentice, proficient, and distinguished. At the rate of gains reported in 2003, the state's elementary schools would have an accountability index of 102.1 by the target date, thereby slightly exceeding the standard. However, at their 2003 pace, middle schools would be only at 92.1 and high schools at 88.2 by 2014. In 2003, 14 of Kentucky's nearly 1,200 public schools had already reached or exceeded 100 (Wolfe, 2003).

By 2003, the Louisiana plan had become quite complex, with schools' assessment scores awarded on a 250-point scale based overwhelmingly on standardized test scores. The LEAP (Louisiana Educational Assessment Program) or Graduate-Exit-Exam scores counted for 60% percent, Iowa Tests (a traditional, nationally standardized battery) for 30%, and combined attendance and dropout rates for 10% of the final tally. The state adopted a long-term goal of pushing every school above 120 points by 2014. The previous goal had been 100 points by 2009. A five-star rating system—with 5 as the highest—replaced labels such as *academically below average* and *school of academic excellence*. A new category titled *academic warning* applied to scores between 45 and 60. Finally, 2003 was the last year that all schools with scores over 100 would be regarded as acceptable, because the passing score would be raised to 120 in 2004 (M. Brown, 2003a).

In practice, the *No-Child Act's* procedure for establishing a state's standards has proven to involve a substantial amount of personal opinion on the part of state officials and has resulted in dramatically different standards from one state to another. As a consequence, at the outset of the *No-Child* program, such a state as Mississippi had few if any schools dubbed failures, whereas Michigan and California had many. Thus, whether a school would be deemed a failure could depend not simply on its students' test performance but on the school's location. This could occur if the tests in one state were much easier than those in another state and if officials in one state set higher standards than those in another. In effect, a school could suffer because its students were not competing on a "level playing field" from state to state.

Discrepancies among states' standards were demonstrated by researchers at the Northwest Evaluation Association in Portland, Oregon, when they compared the difficulty levels of reading and math tests in 14 states. The investigators expected to find variation among states, but they were amazed by how differently states defined "proficient performance." Among the states that were studied, Colorado and Texas had the lowest reading and math standards. Colorado's passing score for reading proficiency was set so low that 82% of fifth-graders throughout the country could exceed it. In contrast, the reading-proficiency standard in South Carolina was set so high that only 27% of the nation's fifth-graders could achieve the goal. It was also the case that students on the Washington state side of the Columbia River who failed to meet reading and math standards could have been judged proficient if they had lived on the Oregon side of the Columbia (Hammond, 2003c).

Discrepancies across states—due, at least partially, to differences in test-difficulty and achievement standards—are shown in Table 4-1 by the percentages of a state's schools accused of failing to make adequate

yearly progress (AYP) when judged by each state's own application of
*No-Child-Left-Behind* criteria.

---

Table 4-1

**Schools Failing to Make Adequate Yearly Progress in 2003**

| State | Number of Schools | Percent of schools |
|---|---|---|
| Alaska | 283 | 58% |
| California | 3,219 | 45 |
| Connecticut | 157 | 16 |
| Delaware | 98 | 57 |
| Florida | 2,525 | 87 |
| Georgia | 846 | 42 |
| Kansas | 183 | 13 |
| Minnesota | 143 | 8 |
| Montana | 179 | 21 |
| Ohio | 829 | 21 |
| Oregon | 365 | 32 |
| Pennsylvania | 1,428 | 51 |
| West Virginia | 326 | 45 |
| Wyoming | 55 | 15 |

Source: As first appeared in *Education Week,* September 3, 2003.

---

Factors other than test difficulty and standard-setting that contribute
to the differences in the incidence of failing schools include the ethnic
mix of a state's school population, the proportion of students from low
income families, and a state's percentage of students with limited-
English skills.

In summary, the *No-Child-Left-Behind Act* mandated a method for designing achievement standards that (a) combined features of several approaches to standard-setting and (b) depended on each state's political
and educational authorities to apply the method as they saw fit. This
process has resulted in marked differences across states in the content
and difficulty level of tests and in the rigor of achievement standards. A
host of collateral damage has accompanied the application of the *No-
Child-Left-Behind Act's* approach to standard-setting. The nature of such
damage is the matter we next address.

# Standard Setting and Collateral Damage

The kinds of damage identified in the following cases include (a) a high incidence of failing schools, (b) excellent schools dubbed failures, (c) the one-size-fits-all error, (d) increased non-promotion rates, (e) high-school graduation rates markedly reduced, (f) problems of specifying graduation rates, (g) rules changed in the middle of the game, (h) federal/state discrepancies, and (i) inconsistency across states.

## High Incidence of Failing Schools

**Type of damage.** Reports that large numbers of schools have failed are followed by decreased public confidence in the schools' personnel. A survey in 2003 estimated that 26,000 (28%) of the nation's 93,000 public schools fell short of the adequate-yearly-progress standard, hence "fueling predictions that the law could eventually label nearly all schools as failing" (Dillon, 2004d). The failing label discourages competent, hard-working teachers and administrators who have been doing their best under difficult conditions—such conditions as inadequate family support for children's schooling, large numbers of students from non-English-speaking homes, a shortage of funds for teaching supplies, oversize classes, and insufficient time for teachers to prepare lessons and correct students' homework.

**Illustrative cases.** The adequate-yearly-progress formula has varied from state to state. Some states in 2003 had just 8% of their schools fail to show sufficient progress, while others had 90% (Kossan & Konig, 2003). During 2003, states identified more than 23,812 schools as not making adequate progress, and at least 5,200 were in need of improvement (meaning they had missed the minimum-passing mark for two or more consecutive years). The 23,812 figure was up from 3,826 schools identified as low-performing under state accountability systems in 2002 (Olson, 2003e).

In September 2004, as the *No-Child* program was completing its third year, the school term began with 12 million students attending schools that had not met the program's yearly-progress goal for two years in a row. Federal officials reported that 24,000 public schools—one quarter of the nation's total—had fallen short of the progress they would need to reach *proficiency* by 2014 (Archibald, 2004c).

Here is a sample of "failed-schools" reports from three states (Missouri, Illinois, Arizona) and the District of Columbia.

Under the *No-Child-Left-Behind* standards, over half of Missouri's public schools were accused of not making sufficient progress. In many instances, the math and reading test scores for the students overall had improved from the previous year but the school was still labeled "failing" because not every subgroup defined by the federal law had met the standard. Officials noted that there were as many as 40 different ways a school could fall short (Robertson, 2003).

In Illinois, 43.8% of the state's public schools were cited for not meeting yearly-progress targets, either because (a) fewer than 37% of each subgroup passed the math and reading tests or (b) fewer than 95% percent of students in each subgroup took the tests. In addition, elementary schools were required to maintain an attendance rate of at least 88% and high schools were obligated to have a graduation rate of at least 65% (Rossi & Grossman, 2003b).

Over 25% of Arizona public schools failed to raise test scores enough to meet the federal requirement for yearly progress in 2003 (Kossan & Konig, 2003).

For a second consecutive year, 68 (46%) of the 149 public schools in the nation's capital fell short of the acceptable-progress goal in 2004. The federal government's plan to transfer students from failing schools to successful ones could not be implemented, especially at the secondary-school level where 18 of the district's 20 middle schools and 12 of the 15 high schools were declared substandard. Consequently, there were far too few openings in the successful schools to accommodate the hundreds of potential transfer candidates (Archibald, 2004c).

## Excellent Schools Dubbed Failures

**Type of damage.** School personnel and members of the public are confused and distressed whenever schools that were judged exemplary by one set of standards are called failures by another set.

**Illustrative cases.** In Illinois, several schools that had the highest overall scores on state tests were listed as failing, alongside some of the state's lowest-performing schools. Schools in Evanston, Oak Park, and River Forest ranked high in test results for their students as a whole, but fewer than 40% of their black, special-education, and poverty-family students passed one or more of the state tests. Under the state's rating system, the three subgroups were not given credit for having made significant progress in math scores over the previous three years (Grossman, 2003a).

In Georgia, some of the highest-rated high schools in the Atlanta region were listed among the state's failures. But education officials cautioned that the list should not be taken at face value, because the schools ran afoul the 95%-testing requirement in one or two subgroups. For example, even though 98% of the students at Northgate High School in Coweta who took the math test passed it, the school was placed on the failure list because four students had not taken the exam (Tofig, 2003a).

Of the 846 schools in Georgia that were cited for not making adequate progress, 536 failed because fewer than 95% of students in one or more subgroups took the tests (Robelen, 2003).

In Michigan, even before the official announcement of which schools had passed, the news media learned that some of Metro Detroit's top-performing schools would be on the list of failures. Critics claimed that the appearance of traditionally highly rated schools on such lists would confuse parents and distract officials' attention from the schools that needed the most help. As examples of highly regarded schools that were cited as failures, Vandenberg and Stevenson elementaries had more than 90% of fourth-graders proficient in math and reading, as compared to statewide averages of 65% math and 75% in reading. But Vandenberg was charged by the state with not having enough special-subgroup students tested. In response, Vandenberg officials pointed out that almost half of their students were learning English as a second language. When President George W. Bush had visited the school in May 2002, he had called it a school that exemplified "the philosophy of our 'No Child Left Behind'" (C. MacDonald, 2003).

## The One-Size-Fits-All Error

**Type of damage.** The *No-Child-Left-Behind Act,* like many of the states' own high-stakes plans, was devised to hold every child and every school to the same standard, without regard for differences between individuals in their potential for succeeding. As noted earlier, all children were expected to be proficient in reading and math by 2014; and all were supposed to advance toward that goal at the same regular pace from 2002 to 2014. However, an overwhelming amount of evidence from research on child development, social psychology, and student learning indicates that such a one-size-fits-all expectation is ridiculously naïve and bound to fail.

**Illustrative cases.** An Educational Testing Service review of social research identified 14 societal factors that distinguish students who do well in school from ones who do poorly. Three of the factors appeared in early childhood—(1) birth weight, (2) lead poisoning, (3) hunger and nutrition. Six involved schooling conditions—(4) rigor of the curriculum, (5) teacher preparation, (6) teacher experience and attendance, (7) class size, (8) availability of appropriate classroom technology, and (9) school safety. Five concerned home conditions—(10) reading to young children, (11) amount and kind of television watching, (12) parent availability and support, (13) student mobility, and (14) parent participation. On each indicator, black and Hispanic students were at a distinct disadvantage. Paul Barton, author of the report, said the results very clearly showed that in all 14 conditions, their were significant gaps between the minority and majority student populations. Most obvious were discrepancies between students from lower-income families and higher-income families in 11 factors that reflected inequalities in "those aspects of school, early life, and home circumstances that research has linked to achievement" (Barton, 2003).

The outcome of high-stakes testing in Pennsylvania and New Jersey in 2003 were typical of the testing results throughout the country. Over 200 schools in Pennsylvania and more than twice that number in New Jersey were flagged as needing improvement, mostly because special-education students scored much lower than their age peers. In Pennsylvania, 14.6% of students with disabilities reached math proficiency compared with 52.3% of all students, and 16.9% reached proficiency in reading compared with 60.3% of all students. In the *No-Child-Left-Behind Act*, only 1% of the students could be exempted from the standard because of profound retardation. Yet, according to other federal legislation, children become entitled to extra services in public schools for such impairments as autism, Down syndrome, mental retardation, blindness, and hearing loss—a spectrum that extends to learning disabilities related to reading, such as dyslexia. In addition, as explained by Jack Jennings of the Center on Education Policy in Washington, a portion of the students were "cognitively disabled," but the federal law did not set different standards for them. "So when the teachers say it doesn't make sense, they are right—it doesn't" (Langland, 2003b).

In North Carolina, less than half of the state's 2,200 public schools met federal standards, primarily because special-education students failed to reach the *No-Child* benchmark. Such outcomes inspired some educators to recommend replacing the one-size expectation with an individual-growth model for judging pupil achievement. As an example, Melanie Gillie, a special-education teacher at Millbrook Elementary School in Raleigh, noted that her pupils had made significant progress in test scores in math and reading over the previous year. But she was disappointed that the children were still failures by the *No-Child-Left-Behind* standard. She suggested that the law needed to recognize the growth rate of special-education students and assess their performance at the level at which they were currently functioning, because most of her pupils were not just one grade level below their agemates, they were two or three below (Silberman, 2003a).

Typical high-stakes-testing plans fail to take into account the socioeconomic and cultural backgrounds of a school's clientele, thereby holding the same expectations for schools in crime-ridden inner cities as schools in wealthy suburbs. Consequently, instances of conflicting assessments of a school's quality can occur. John Marshall Elementary School, located in a high-crime district of Boston, was identified by Schools Superintendent Thomas W. Payzant as a model of "effective practices" two years in a row. At the same time the school was placed on the *No-Child* list of schools failing to make adequate yearly progress on math tests. Payzant complained that educators are frustrated when their schools appear on two different lists—one good and the other bad—that send mixed signals about "what they're doing right and what they're doing wrong" (Tench, 2003).

Analysts of educational conditions in Cleveland, Ohio, observed that the poorer and more ethnically diverse a school district was, the more difficult it was to achieve the many goals that, according to federal law, must be reached by a certain percentage of a school's students. In Cleveland that meant 82 standards had to be met. Less-diverse and wealthier suburban districts had far fewer standards to meet because they had fewer subgroups. (Okoben, 2003)

A report published at the end of 2003 identified reasons that 3,000 of California's 7,669 public schools were cited as "needing improvement" under the *No-Child-Left-Behind* law. The results showed that many of the 3,000 schools were so identified because a single subgroup—such as disabled learners or those of Asian ancestry—had fallen short of a target. Consequently, the likelihood a school would fall into the "failing" category increased with the number of different subgroups the school served (Dillon, 2003b). For example, two Oakland elementary schools—Manzanita and Golden State—were equal in overall test scores. But pupils at Manzanita came from diverse socio-cultural groups (black, Latino, Asian, low-income, limited-English), thereby obligating the school to reach 18 federal-law assessment targets. In contrast, Golden State served primarily black pupils (some from low-income homes), thereby resulting in only six subgroup targets. In test performance, Manzanita pupils met 17 of their 18 targets, but since the school's black students narrowly missed the proficiency target in math, the entire school was charged as needing improvement. Golden State, on the other hand, met its six targets and was judged successful. Bruce Fuller, an education professor at the University of California in Berkeley, noted that the law penalized schools that had a more diverse population. "It's not that those schools are less effective for average students, it's just that they have all these targets to hit" (Dillon, 2003b).

## Increased Non-Promotion Rates

**Type of damage.** The number of students who are obliged to repeat their present grade increases when school systems require students to pass tests in reading and math at the end of the school year in order to be promoted to the next grade, whether or not their daily work during the regular school year had been satisfactory.

**Illustrative cases.** In 2002, the Philadelphia public school system established a two-part policy that applied to students who did not pass language-arts and math tests at the end of grades 3, 8, and 12. The policy required failing students to (a) attend summer school as a means of improving their test performance and (b) repeat the same grade for another year if they did not earn a satisfactory mark on tests at the end of summer school. At the close of summer school in 2003, nearly 13% (2,312) of the 17,675 students who had attended failed the tests again and were thus required to repeat their former grade (M. M. Dean, 2003).

By 2004 the Chicago school system had been retaining between 7,000 and 10,000 students each year. However, researchers at the University of Chicago concluded that the policy of making failing students repeat a grade did not help pupils do better the next year, so that "retention should absolutely be a last resort." In particular, retention increased the likelihood that eighth-graders would drop out of school. One study of retention showed that 78% of students who repeated two grades dropped out before age 19 (Rossi, 2004).

## High-School Graduation Rates Markedly Reduced

**Type of damage.** Failing to earn a high-school diploma places a student in jeopardy for getting a good job or pursuing further education. Employers with well-paying jobs available usually avoid the risk of hiring youths who did not even graduate from high school. Likewise, colleges generally reject applicants who lack high-school diplomas.

**Illustrative cases.** With the arrival of the June 2003 high-school graduation day, Florida education officials announced that 13,000 seniors statewide would not graduate because they had failed the state test (Rabin, 2003). Of the 636 Boston seniors who did not pass the Massachusetts exam, 455 or 72% had met all the city's traditional graduation requirements but would not receive diplomas because they had failed the newly required exit test (Rothstein, 2003a). In Nevada, 2,195 students or 12% of the state's senior class had completed all of their course-work requirements but would be denied high-school diplomas because they had scored too low on the math portion of state high-school graduation test (though only 2% failed the reading test). Instead of diplomas, the failing students would be granted *certificates of attendance*, which are frequently considered meaningless by employers and four-year colleges (Fletcher, 2003).

## Problems in Specifying Graduation Rates

**Types of damage.**  High schools' graduation rates, which depend increasingly on students' test scores, are difficult for states to calculate accurately enough to satisfy *No-Child-Left-Behind* standards for dropout reductions.  The federal law defines the graduation rate as the percentage of ninth-graders who finish high school and earn "a regular diploma."  However, that percentage fails to account for students who neither graduated nor dropped out, such as ones who transferred to another school during their high-school career.  Therefore, if many students transfer, the school that they left is blamed for large numbers of students failing to be on the graduation list.  And by schools not appearing to raise graduation rates at the pace required in the *No-Child Act,* they could suffer such sanctions as the dismissal of faculty members and administrators, or be closed or taken over by the state.

Mike Kirst, a Stanford University professor of education and co-director of a research group callled Policy Analysis for California Education, warned that it was unwise to base high-stakes decisions on standards that are confused and that involve so much disagreement among states, localities, and the federal government.  David Rogosa, a Stanford statistician, added that graduation figures are largely "capricious and arbitrary in their arithmetic and should not be high-stakes components" (Azimov, 2003b).

A further sort of damage that can result from the strict graduation-rate requirement is the reporting of false graduation figures. For instance, U.S. Education Secretary Roderick Paige, who helped design the *No-Child* program, had created a similar approach in Houston, Texas, when he was the city's superintendent of schools until 2000.  Under the Houston plan, school principals who reduced dropout rates won money, and those who did not lost their jobs.  However, under such pressure, many principals falsified data, thereby hiding more than 3,000 unreported dropouts that were discovered in a later audit (Azimov, 2003b).

**Illustrative cases.**  The fact that education officials have been unable to accurately measure graduation success creates problems for schools whose graduation rates appear low.  For instance, at McClymonds High in Oakland—and at more than 650 other California high schools that received federal funds for poor students—educators feared that the state might take over their school if they fell short of "adequate yearly progress."  Before the graduation-rate requirement was introduced, progress had been measured by test scores and the percentage of a school's students tested.  But the task of making adequate progress now became more demanding, so that missing the graduation-rate mark for two consecutive years could mean the school would be closed down or taken over by state administrators (Azimov, 2003b).

Inconsistent attendance-reporting methods from one school to another made it impossible for Utah officials to track attendance and graduation rates in 2002-2003. One high school counted every class period a student missed, whereas another counted only how many days the student was absent, no matter how many classes were skipped. As a result, officials could not determine which schools had fulfilled federal requirements and which had not (Lynn, 2003e).

In the state of Washington, problems of calculating graduation rates resulted in conflicts between state and school-district officials over what the rates really were. The original report issued by the Office of the Superintendent of Public Instruction stated that 79% of ninth-graders ultimately graduated from high school. But a revised estimate, based on a different method of calculation, reduced the figure to 66% and generated disagreements between the state office and school districts. The revised figures lowered graduation rates in some school districts by as much as 17%. For instance, the new OSPI estimates reduced the rate in Seattle from 70% to 53% and in Bellevue from 79.1% to 76% (Solomon, 2003).

## Rules Changed in the Middle of the Game

**Type of damage.** Pupils, their parents, and their teachers can be upset when the standards are raised during the testing process and children fail to be promoted.

**Illustrative case.** After Texas third-graders finished taking the state reading test in 2004, officials announced that getting 22 out of the test's 36 items correct would no longer suffice. Twenty-three correct items would be the new passing score. As a result, 3,339 of the state's children who had earned scores of 22 were in danger of being retained in third grade for another year (Benton, 2004).

## Conflicts Between Federal and State Standards

**Type of damage.** Confusion and frustration for students, educators, and the public result when federal standards for schools conflict with state or school-district standards. And the confusion mounts whenever a state has more than one evaluation system of its own.

**Illustrative cases.** In the federal government's National Assessment of Educational Progress (NAEP) "nation's-report-card" program, only 31% of the cross-section of Maryland eighth-graders who were tested rated *proficient* in reading. However, nearly 60% of those same students were deemed *proficient readers* when measured by the Maryland-School-

Assessment-Test standards (Bowler, 2003b). State tests vary considerably in type and quality, according to Michael Cohen of Achieve Inc., a nonprofit group concerned with academic standards. He noted that Maryland's test was difficult, but the passing score was so low that the state could easily show adequate yearly progress. Cohen explained that Texas started low and then moved the bar up, whereas Maryland began at aq rather high level (Bowler, 2003b).

People can also be perplexed by discrepancies between federal and local school districts' standards of success. For instance, according to the *No-Child-Left-Behind* program, 83% of Chicago's public schools were failing by the end of 2003. However, when judged by the district's own rating system, only 53% (292 schools) were on or near academic probation, with 19% of the ostensibly unsatisfactory schools actually receiving bonuses of $5,000 to $10,000 from the district because the schools' test scores had improved (Grossman, 2003d).

Conflicting federal, state, and district standards have been only one source of confusion in Colorado, where state officials adopted two competing systems for judging the quality of schooling. The first system was created in 1998, requiring school districts to report their status on a long list of measures that included not only academic-achievement scores but also data on school safety, the use of technology, and financial controls. Then another accountability scheme added in 1999 required schools to publish performance and safety data on school-appraisal report cards. Although the two systems used much of the same data, they handled it in such different ways that a school could look good by one system and bad by the other (Colorado must revisit school standards, 2003).

## Inconsistency Across States

**Type of damage.** Because officials in each state determine the nature of the tests students take and how many test questions students must answer correctly in order to be judged proficient, there are significant differences from one state to another in the percentage of students making adequate yearly progress. When some states' standards are more demanding than others, the citizens of states in which a large proportion of students receive failing marks are shocked by how poorly their public education system seems to operate in comparison to states in which a small proportion of students are identified as failing. However, reports of failure rates are a function not only of students' mastery of reading and math, but also of the tests' difficulty and of the strictness of standards. Therefore, such reports do not necessarily reflect the comparative quality of different states' schooling practices.

**Illustrative cases.** As noted earlier, during 2003 the percentage of schools charged with failing to make adequate yearly progress was 87% in Florida, 45% in California, 21% in Montana, 13% in Kansas, and 8% in Minnesota. Much of the difference between such extremes can be accounted for by different states holding different standards. As an example, South Charlotte Middle School is one of North Carolina's wealthiest communities. In 2002, more than 95% of South Charlotte students passed both the state reading and mathematics tests. A few miles away, in another wealthy community, more than half of the students at Fort Mill Middle School failed the state mathematics test, and three-quarters failed the reading test. One important cause of the difference between the two schools' test success is that Fort Mill Middle School is located across the state line in South Carolina (Fessenden, 2003).

## Conclusion

It seems hardly necessary to argue that achievement standards in testing programs should be realistic—that is, reasonably attainable—so that collateral damage will be held to a minimum. Whenever high-stakes testing programs are judged by this *realistic* criterion, it's apparent that much of the damage suffered in recent high-stakes testing programs has come because standard-setters failed to recognize the achievement limitations imposed on learners by the nature of human development and societal conditions. In effect, evidence from both human-development research and astute people's observations suggests that certain standards in high-stakes programs have been absurd. One such goal in the *No-Child-Left-Behind Act* has been the expectation that all public-school pupils would be at a *proficient* level in reading, math, and science by 2014. Equally ridiculous has been the requirement that a school's students advance to that goal by equal-sized annual steps from where they stood in 2002. Educational progress rarely involves equal steps along a straight path. Instead, progress is typically by stages—by spurts and plateaus, surges and hesitations (Elmore, 2003).

Other problems with high-stakes standards have not been the result of standard-setters' ignorance about human development but, rather, have been the result of people's philosophical convictions that cause them to disagree about the proper purpose of schooling. For instance,

- Should the aim of public schools be to enable each learner to reach his or her potential—potential that is the combined product of the individual's genetic inheritance, family influences, personal ambitions, surrounding culture, and societal events? Should each learner's progress be judged in relation to that person's potential rather than against the achievement of agemates or of an ideal student? And should grade promotion and graduation depend on how hard each learner tries to make the most of his or her aptitude rather than on how closely he or she has approached a single standard that is held for all other students?

- Or, should the purpose of public schools be to offer each learner the same chance to study the same set of skills and knowledge, and then should each student's progress be judged in terms of how much of those skills and knowledge the student has mastered? Finally, should grade promotion and graduation be based on the proportion of the skills and knowledge regarded as necessary for advancement?

It is also the case that people's beliefs about such matters as "sufficient competence" and "fair treatment" can lead to their disagreeing about which test-score levels should determine the designations *failure, basic, proficient,* and *advanced.* Should the cutting points between such levels be quite strict, so that many learners fail and only a few earn ratings of proficient or advanced standing? Or should lenient standards be set so that few students fail, many score at the basic level, most are judged proficient, and a goodly number are deemed advanced?

The opinions people hold about such philosophical issues are obviously affected by conditions in their own lives—conditions that influence their own welfare and the fate of individuals and institutions they value. Consequently, parents of an autistic ten-year-old can view math standards differently than does the owner of a machine shop which employs 50 workers and the owner wants them all to be "math smart." An immigrant teenager from Mexico can subscribe to different English-language standards than does a university professor of English. A marine biologist can favor different science-education standards than does a parish priest. Because people so often hold contrasting opinions about such matters, disagreements about what constitutes proper standards of achievement in schools are bound to continue. In short, it is unrealistic ever to expect complete accord regarding standards.

# 5

# How Should Test Results Be Used?

Achievement tests can be used for making many kinds of decisions about education, as suggested by the following list of 16 applications of test results.

*Six traditional functions:*
Diagnosing individual learners' strengths and weaknesses
Designing learning methods suited to individuals' aptitudes
Diagnosing a group's strengths and weaknesses
Designing instruction that corrects a group's shortcomings
Assigning students marks or grades
Predicting students' future performance

*Five specified No-Child-Left-Behind functions:*
Distinguishing between good schools and bad schools
Rewarding successful schools and punishing failing ones
Transferring students from failing schools to successful ones
Informing people of students' achievement-test performance
Providing tutors for students whose test-scores have been unsatisfactory

*An increasingly popular state-mandated function:*
Determining students' promotion and graduation

*Four frequently affiliated functions:*
Controlling the curriculum
Evaluating school personnel
Motivating school personnel and students
Improving instruction

The three aims of Chapter 5 are to describe each of the above functions, to inspect the role each plays in typical high-stakes-testing programs, and to illustrate types of collateral damage that may be associated with such functions.

# Six Traditional Functions of Test Results

From the viewpoint of enabling all learners to achieve their potential, the most constructive use of test results is for diagnosing a student's learning strengths and weaknesses so that methods of instruction can be designed to eliminate—or at least to reduce—the weaknesses. These same functions of diagnosing weaknesses and designing remedial methods can also be applied to groups, such as a single class, a subgroup within a class, or all classes at a grade level. Two further traditional uses of tests have been those of assigning students marks, as on report cards, and of predicting how well learners will likely succeed in their future education.

## Diagnosing Individuals' Strengths and Weaknesses

An achievement test that is organized in sections, with each section focusing on a limited set of learning objectives, can be a valuable tool for determining the extent to which a student has achieved the skills and knowledge of a particular lesson or unit of study. By scanning the pattern of an individual learner's correct and incorrect test answers, a diagnostician—usually a teacher—can distinguish between things the student has already mastered and things that call for additional study. How well this diagnostic function can be performed depends on (a) the structure of the test and the form in which test results are reported, (b) the diagnostician's skill and diligence and (c) classroom teaching conditions.

**Test structure and the report of test results.** The task of diagnosing a learner's strengths and weaknesses consists of identifying the student's pattern of right and wrong test answers and asking, "Why did this person get these particular items wrong but get those other items right?" Such a task is most easily accomplished if the test has more than one item focusing on each learning objective—that is, several focusing on each type of skill or knowledge. For example, if a third-grader gives the wrong answer to the test's only subtraction problem that requires carrying, the teacher may not be able to tell what misconception led to that error. Or perhaps the mistake might not be a misconception but the result of carelessness or a misreading of the problem. However, if several items concern the same process—such as carrying—then the pattern of the student's answers can offer the diagnostician a more helpful clue to the cause of wrong answers.

For a standardized test that is corrected by a testing company, the teacher's task is eased if the report of a student's performance that is received from the testing company is broken down into subsections, with each subsection focusing on a particular type of learning objective. With such a report in hand, a teacher can scan the scores a student earned on each subsection and gain a quick impression of how well the student had mastered different objectives. Then the test items within low-score subsections can be analyzed in detail to reveal the particular learner's misconceptions and careless errors.

Collateral damage—in the form of a teacher not being able to discover a student's learning strengths and weaknesses—occurs whenever (a) only a total test score for each student is reported to the teacher and (b) the teacher does not have available a copy of the test that was given. And whenever a student's test results are returned to the diagnostician without test scores reported for each of the test's subsections, then another sort of damage occurs: the diagnostic task consumes excessive amounts of time and bother.

Many testing programs do not allow for this diagnostic use of tests, because teachers receive only pupils' overall final scores and no copies of the tests. Nor are parents allowed to inspect their children's tests in order to discover the specific sorts of knowledge in which their offspring must improve in order to pass high-stakes exams.

Consider, for example, an episode from Florida's testing program. After a high-school senior had been denied a diploma because he had failed the graduation test, his father asked to see the test in order to understand which kinds of items his son had missed. Although a Leon County judge ruled that the father had a right to inspect the test, that decision was reversed by an appeals-court judge who argued that making the test questions public would cost Florida millions of dollars for creating a new test each year. As an alternative, the state made sample questions available and sent parents a report telling the areas of math and reading in which their child did well or poorly (Hegarty, 2003)

Such states as Massachusetts, Maine, New Hampshire, and Virginia publicly publish test questions and answers. In Massachusetts, questions and answers are posted on the Internet weeks after students take the test. However, parents do not have access to their own children's tests (Hegerty, 2003).

**Diagnostician's skill and diligence.** Analyzing a student's pattern of right and wrong test answers requires skill in estimating what sort of thinking on the part of the test-taker might have led to such answers. Teachers can differ markedly from each other in the skill and diligence they bring to that task.

**Classroom teaching conditions.** The extent to which test diagnosis will be performed, and how well, also depends on such conditions as (a) class size (the fewer the students, the more reasonable it is to expect test diagnosis) and (b) whether classroom aides are available to help with the analysis.

## Designing Individualized Learning Activities

From the standpoint of improving students' learning, the obvious value of test diagnosis is to guide teachers in estimating the causes of poor test scores and to aid them in designing such remedies as simplified explanations of concepts, additional practice of skills, tutoring, work sheets, specialized reading materials, medication, and the like. If the school's only response to students' low total test scores is to assign them bad marks or require that they stay in the same grade another year, the likelihood that learners will reach their potential is not very great.

## Diagnosing a Group's Strengths and Weaknesses

In such schemes as the *No-Child-Left-Behind* program, the concern is not so much for the individual learner as for groups of learners. Schools are publicized as failing when a substantial portion of their students do poorly on reading and math tests. And if teachers are to raise test scores at the pace required in the *No-Child Act*, they are best prepared to do so if they recognize the specific skills and knowledge in which the bulk of their students are weak. Teachers can thus profit from (a) receiving reports of testing results in the form of the percentage of students who, for each test item or test subsection, gave incorrect answers, (b) recognizing the nature of those incorrect answers (as shown by students being required to display their computation procedure on a math test or by their improper choices on a multiple-choice reading test), and (c) having a copy of the test in hand so as to estimate the sort of thinking that led to the errors. When those three conditions are not provided in a high-stakes-testing program, teachers are left uninformed about which skills and knowledge their students have failed to master.

## Designing Instruction to Correct a Group's Shortcomings

Whenever the poor command of a particular skill or of an item of knowledge is widespread in a group, as revealed in a report of test results, a teacher can devise corrective measures that apply to the entire group. In terms of teacher time and effort, such group remediation is obviously more feasible than trying to help each learner individually.

## Assigning Students Marks or Grades

Evaluations of students' learning have traditionally led to assigning them a symbol of their level of achievement. That symbol is often a letter (A, B, C, D, F), a percent representing the proportion of the learning task the student performed correctly (80%, 63%, etc.), or a comment written at the top of an assignment on in a margin ("Nice work," "Better than last time," "Far below your ability level," "You need to study harder"). Such marks can be given for individual assignments or can represent an overall assessment of a combination of assignments, such as the sum of weekly test results for a semester.

In terms of accurately reflecting learner's achievement, collateral damage can result if the mark or grade is based entirely on a high-stakes test, because, as noted in Chapter 3, standardized tests are insufficient for evaluating students' command of much of what schools are expected to teach.

## Predicting Students' Future Performance

A report on how well students have learned in the past is often useful for predicting how well they will succeed in the future. A standardized-test score is one indicator of that past learning. Among the tests used for this predictive purpose, perhaps the best known in the United States are the Scholastic Aptitude Tests (SAT) used by colleges for deciding which applicants they will accept as students. The SAT tests are of two varieties, SAT I and SAT II.

SAT I is a single standardized test designed to measure "verbal and mathematical reasoning skills students have developed over time and skills they need to be successful academically." SAT II consists of 22 tests, each focusing on a separate subject, such as writing (with an essay), literature, United States history, world history, math, biology, chemistry, physics, English-language proficiency, and several foreign languages. College applicants can take one or more of the SAT II exams (About SAT, 2004).

Whereas such tests are helpful as predictors of success in college, they are far from perfect. Students who score high on the tests usually get higher grades in college than those who score lower, but not invariably. Thus, to improve the prediction of student performance, college-admission officials typically collect other information in addition to test scores, such as applicants' study habits, motivation, and dedication (consistently working hard, not giving up in the face of obstacles).

State tests given at various grade levels (such as 3, 6, 8, and 10) in present-day high-stakes programs are also often used for predicting pupils' future academic success, particularly when decisions are made about (a) classes to which students will be assigned (gifted, regular, remedial) and (b) tracks into which students will be directed in high school (college prep, general, vocational). However, using standardized-test scores as the exclusive evidence on which to base such decisions can lead to collateral damage by limiting the future opportunities of students who did not score well on the tests but who are strongly motivated and have performed well in school when measured by such non-test evidence as class participation, daily assignments, and individual and group projects.

## Five *No-Child-Left-Behind* Functions

As explained in Chapter 1, the *No-Child-Left-Behind Act* uses testing as the centerpiece from which other functions of the school-reform act derive, including the functions of

(a)  distinguishing between good schools and bad schools,
(b)  rewarding successful schools and punishing failing ones,
(c)  transferring students from failing schools to successful ones,
(d  informing people of students' achievement-test performance, and
(e)  providing tutors for students whose test-scores have been unsatisfactory.

Types of collateral damage relating to such functions are identified in the following paragraphs. In addition, two further kinds of consequences of implementing the *No-Child* provisions have been (f) high costs and (g) an avalanche of paper work. Typical damage related to those two features are discussed near the end of this section.

### Distinguishing Between Good and Bad Schools

Although federal and state officials usually dislike such expressions as *good schools* versus *bad schools* or *successful schools* versus *failing schools,* those expressions are used by the general public, the press, and school personnel when referring to what high-stakes-test results imply. But federal and state officials, who are sensitive to the likely feelings of disadvantaged segments of society, will tend to cast the good-school/bad-school distinction in less pejorative language. For example, Secretary of Education Roderick Paige said it was quite likely that a school, which has been judged successful on the basis of the average performance of the overall student population, can have one or two subgroups of students who have not done well on tests. Paige suggested that it was insulting to say a school was failing, because "We think it's still a great school, but it needs improvement because it's not educating all the kids" (Olson, 2003e).

No matter how the distinction between satisfactory and unsatisfactory schools is worded, the schools that are accused of inadequate yearly progress can be expected to adopt strategies that enable them to appear adequate. As shown in the following examples, some strategies are accompanied by collateral damage.

**Type of damage—Good schools get bad-school rating.** The high proportion of schools deemed unsatisfactory under the *No-Child-Left-Behind* standards is, to a great extent, a result of the law's requiring all subgroups of students (ethnic, socioeconomic, ability) to do well on state tests in order for a school to be judged adequate. Consequently, many schools in which most students have earned satisfactory test scores still are publicized as doing a poor job, thereby sullying the school's reputation in the eyes of the public.

**Illustrative case.** In Johnson County North Carolina, Micro-Pine-Level School, by most measures, did a fine job. Pupils had been cited for making exceptional gains on state tests, thus earning each teacher a $1,500 state bonus. The two most recent recipients of the county's teacher-of-the-year awards were on the Micro-Pine-Level staff. And under the *No-Child-Act* standard, the school had made adequate progress overall, with 86% of the students proficient in reading and math. The school was also satisfactory in 15 subgroup categories but was rated as unsatisfactory for falling short of the standard in special education. Micro Pine Level's 45 special-education students had not made adequate progress under the federal formula for North Carolina. The students' handicaps ranged from speech impediments to mental retardation. In order for the school to be credited with adequate progress, 74.6% or 34 of the students would have had to score at the proficient level on the math test (Winerip, 2003).

**Type of damage—Improved schools continue to bear *failing* label.** According to the *No-Child Act*, a school must improve for two years in succession in order to shed the "insufficient yearly progress" designation. Such a policy is considered unfair by staff members and parents in schools which, after one year on the failing list, exceed the passing mark the following year and are still dubbed "failing."

**Illustrative cases.** In 2002, Penniman School in Cahokia, Illinois, was judged unsatisfactory by *No-Child-Left-Behind* standards. However, after an intensive effort by teachers, supported by a new curriculum and new principal, Penniman exceeded the standards in 2003, yet continued to bear the brand of a school that failed. Jeff Burkett, Penniman's principal, questioned how the "chart" could show "we are a failing school with all the great things that are going on here" (Aguilar, 2003).

Thirty schools in Maryland improved enough to meet all the state targets for reading and math in 2003, but they were not eligible to be removed from the failing-school list until they showed two consecutive years of improvement (Bowie, 2003).

**Type of damage—Confusion over different rating systems.** Some states have their own method of rating schools, a method different from that of the *No-Child* program. As a result, schools judged satisfactory by state criteria may not be satisfactory by federal standards, and vice versa. As a result, people can be perplexed about which report of school quality they should accept.

**Illustrative case.** In Oregon, 330 schools fell short of the federal performance targets based on their 2003 language and math test scores, but only 39 schools were rated less than satisfactory by the state's own standards. The state's method judged schools not only by how many students passed reading and math tests but also by student attendance, dropout rates, the percentage of students tested, and a school's improvement over time. Whereas the state graded schools on overall performance, the federal system broke down test scores by subgroups (minority, low-income, special-education, second-language), resulting in many more schools ending up on the federal failing list than on the state list. In effect, Oregon's grading scale was more lenient than the *No-Child* scale. By federal standards, at the beginning of 2004 a larger number of Oregon schools than ever before were declared unsatisfactory. Out of 29 high schools that got low ratings, 10 had satisfactory test scores but had not tested at least 95% of their students. For example, Ashland High, which was among the highest scoring schools in the state, was placed on the failing list because only 93.8% of its students had been tested (Hammond, 2004a).

# Rewarding Successful Schools, Punishing Failing Schools

The responses of federal and state governments to schools' test scores —and especially to test-score trends from one year to the next—comprise a mixture of rewards and punishments. Rewards are typically in the form of (a) favorable publicity for high test scores and (b) cash payments that may be used for school purposes or may be distributed among teachers and administrators for their personal use. Punishments include (a) a school's being burdened with the "failing-school" label, (b) parents being allowed to transfer their children to another school, (c) obligatory tutoring of low-scoring students, (d) visiting consultants requiring changes in the schools' curriculum, staff, or administrative procedures, (e) the dismissal of staff members, (f) the take-over of the school by managers from outside, and (g) temporarily or permanently closing the school. The following kinds of collateral damage can result from the positive and negative sanctions adopted in high-stakes testing programs.

**Type of damage—Disappointment at a reduction in rewards.** When a school and its teachers have received cash bonuses for their students' high test scores, they tend to expect payments of equal size in the future if their students again perform well. But administrators and teachers can be less than delighted if future payments are cut back.

**Illustrative case.** In 2004, a larger number of Florida's schools scored higher on state tests than in 2003, so that more schools achieved "A" status and deserved cash rewards. However, because the state fund from which bonuses were paid was reduced (from $137.5-million in 2003 to $117.2-million in 2004) and more schools were obliged to share the total, the amount any school system received in 2004 was less than in 2003. For example, Hillsborough district had been given $9.3-million for 110 high-scoring schools in 2003 but only $8.5-million for 106 schools in 2004. The award to Pinellas schools in 2004 was $1.5-million short of the 2003 total. Such changes led to administrators and teachers voicing disappointment in having their expectations dashed (Brown, 2004).

**Type of damage—The impossibility of a school's ever escaping punishment.** The nature of a school's student population is a critical factor in determining whether it is realistic to expect the school ever to rise from the ranks of failing schools because school personnel are unable to correct some of the most powerful conditions affecting students' success on state achievement tests—such conditions as physical/mental disabilities and home environments in which English is rarely spoken.

**Illustrative case.** Terry Bergeson, superintendent of public instruction for the state of Washington, complained that the *No-Child-Act's* one-size-fits-all standard did not take into account the diversity of children in public schools, with pupils coming from families in which a total of 201 different languages were spoken. Bergeson predicted that schools with large limited-English-speaking populations would never get off the "needs-improvement" list (Gilbert, 2003).

**Type of damage—The law's faulty limited-English provision.** Schools with a high proportion of students whose native language is not English are confronted with an unsolvable dilemma. Students classified as having limited-English skills are expected to score as high on state tests as students whose English is considered adequate. But when a limited-English pupil gains sufficient mastery of English to qualify as fluent, he or she is transferred out of the limited-English group and placed in the English-speaking category. Under such a system, the school can never get the limited-English group to earn satisfactory scores on the state's language test because students who become proficient in the language are moved out of the group. Hence, the school will forever be deemed "failing."

**Illustrative case.** In Fort Lupton, Colorado, ten-year-old Claudia Hernandez, the daughter of Mexican immigrants, learned her English at Butler Elementary school. When her teacher gave her a dictionary as a gift, Claudia studied at home by playing school with her younger brother. She served as the teacher, and together the two youngsters looked up words. She reported that "I'd write out the definitions and memorize them, and my English just kept getting better" (Dillon, 2003b). Through such effort, she earned the right to transfer out of the limited-English category and into the mainstream. However, the catch-22 feature of the *No-Child* legislation meant that Butler Elementary would not be credited for their limited-English students successfully mastering the school's dominant language of instruction.

## Transferring Students Out of Failing Schools

In the *No-Child-Left-Behind* law, the student-transfer provision is intended to offer learners an alternative to remaining in a school whose test results have been judged substandard. As noted in Chapter 1, if a school has not made adequate progress in test scores for two years in a row, students must be offered the opportunity to move to another school in the district. However, a variety of problems have arisen during the efforts to effect transfers.

**Type of damage—Many candidates, few openings.** The main problem facing the transfer plan has been that of finding enough openings in non-failing schools to accommodate all of the pupils from failing schools who have a right to transfer under the federal law.

**Illustrative cases.** Because of the high incidence of failing schools in Chicago during 2003, education officials were obliged to set up a lottery system to determine which of the 48,000 high-school students eligible for transfer would be permitted to take the district's only 123 vacant seats. When the lottery was first run, some low-scoring schools had accidentally been left out. Thus, the lottery was rerun, with the result that 222 students, rather than 123, qualified for transfers. School officials announced that all 222 students could move, because it was the school's effor. Disney Magnet High School had the district's greatest demand, with 3,300 youths applying for the school's 44 available places (Rossi & Grossman, 2003a).

**Type of damage—Families reject transfer opportunity.** Many students who qualified to leave a low-performing school turned down the opportunity for various reasons—they liked the teachers in their neighborhood school, traveling to a distant school would be difficult, parents felt the neighborhood school was safer, and children wished to remain with their friends.

**Illustrative cases.** The Center on Education Policy reported that for the 2003-2004 school year only 2% of eligible students nationwide transferred out of a low-performing school, primarily because "most parents are not really interested in having their kids move," according to Jack Jennings, the Center's director (Few students fleeing, 2004). But the low percentage was also affected by many school districts still struggling to make transfer choices available. Often the available successful schools had no room for transfers. And in remote rural areas—as well as in such states as Alaska and Hawaii—there were no available schools close by, so students would have to take a daily plane ride to make the transfer scheme work.

Six school districts around San Francisco Bay informed tens of thousands of parents that their children had a legal right to transfer immediately from their low-achieving school to a better one, but few accepted the offer. Of 51,716 letters sent to parents in six Bay Area districts where there were state-designated "schools in need of improvement," just 1,018 students—fewer than 2%—asked to exercise their legal right to attend a higher-achieving school (Azimov, 2003a).

In Ohio, out of 16,830 students in Cleveland who were eligible to transfer, only 35 chose to do so. Of 750 eligible in Euclid, five transferred. In Lorain, 33 out of 1,133 moved; in Akron 76 out of 4,088; in Maple Heights, 51 out of 1,500. Warrensville Heights had only one transfer request (Okoben, Ott, Reed, & Matzelle, 2003).

When the Chicago school district distributed transfer opportunities by means of the lottery, barely half of the lottery winners showed up at their new schools. At the elementary and high-school levels, 270,757 students were eligible to apply for transfers, but only 19,246 students sent in applications for the available 1,097 seats. At the opening of the 2003-2004 school year, only about half (529) of the students who had won lottery seats appeared at their newly assigned schools. For example, 18 of 44 arrived at Disney Magnet High, 22 of 44 went to McCosh High, and 13 of 42 showed up at Stockton Elementary (Lawrence, 2003; Rossi & Grossman, 2003a).

In Virginia during the 2003-2004 school year, 19,030 students enrolled at 43 schools statewide were eligible to demand transfers to a different school, but only 432 students (2.2%) chose to shift (Wermers, 2003a).

**Type of damage—Overcrowded schools.** Large numbers of transfers can result in overcrowding the recipient schools.

**Illustrative case.** In New York, during the first week of the 2003-2004 school year, some of the better performing middle schools were already struggling with overcrowding as a result of receiving 8,000 transfers from the past year's failing schools. Then a newly published report identified 43 additional schools as falling short of achievement standards, thus qualifying thousands of additional students to move (Gootman, 2003b).

**Type of damage—Increased disparities in class size.** When students have a chance to move from a school that has unsatisfactory test scores to one that has acceptable scores, the average class size in the former school can shrink and in the latter school can expand. As a result, a teacher's burden of giving individual attention to students in the "failing" school is lightened and in the "successful" school is increased.

**Illustrative case.** Significant differences among Portland, Oregon, high schools in the number of students per class resulted from the opportunity under the *No-Child* law for students to transfer out of low-performing schools. In high schools that lost enrollment, teachers routinely saw 90 to 130 students a day and had classes averaging 22 students or fewer. In contrast, at schools that accepted transfer students, teachers regularly met 160 to 200 students a day in classes averaging 30 students or more. A science teacher in a school that received transfers complained that grading students' work was "driving teachers crazy. [School officials] ought to have this all planned out before school ever starts" (Chestnut, 2003a).

**Type of damage—Recipient schools' test-score levels are jeopardized.** Accepting a large number of students from low-performing schools could reduce subsequent test scores in the schools to which those students transferred.

**Illustrative case.** In Belleville, Illinois, the superintendent of schools rejected the transfer requests of students from low-performing East St. Louis schools because he said that such transfers could place his own schools in danger of landing on the failing list the following year. He believed it would be "virtually impossible" to prepare students to earn passing scores in a single year's time (Aguilar, 2003).

**Type of damage—Unrealistic choices.** A lack of viable options prevents students from taking advantage of the *No-Child Act's* provision that allows them to transfer out of a failing school. For instance, there are usually few high-achieving schools willing to take such students, and many parents are not interested in uprooting their children from a familiar and nearby school for the marginal instructional improvement they might reasonably expect.

**Illustrative case.** Fewer than one-third of Chicago's lowest-performing schools gave parents a chance to move their children to another school in 2003. The problem of parents finding a suitable school was exacerbated by the fact that the city had 365 failing schools while just over

15% of the better-performing schools (38 out of 240) were required to accept transfers. However, the task of finding places for students to move was simplified by the fact that only 10% of the eligible students asked to transfer, and only half of those requests were approved (Russo, 2003).

**Type of damage—Taxpayers burdened with supporting out-of-district students.** If pupils from a "failing" school transfer to a non-failing school that is located in a different school district, the taxpayers of that recipient district must assume the burden of financing the education of the transferees.

**Illustrative case.** Brent Clark, superintendent of the Belleville, Illinois, school district refused to allow East St. Louis high-schoolers to attend Belleville schools, on the grounds that it would not be fair to expect Belleville taxpayers to foot the bill for out-of-district students, since the federal law provided districts no financial incentives for accepting transfers (Aguilar, 2003).

## Informing People of Students' Test Performance

A provision of the *No-Child Act* whose intention has been widely acclaimed is that of furnishing parents and the public more complete and up-to-date information about how well students—as individuals and as groups—are reaching the schools' goals. Therefore, the test-results reporting system mandated by the act has been designed to:

A. Inform people of individual students' mastery of learning objectives—such people as:
   (a) the parents
   (b) the students' teachers
   (c) counselors
   (d) tutors
   (e) the students themselves
   (f) the students' school principals

B. Inform people of how well a group of students (such as ones who attend a particular school) have mastered learning objectives. Such people include:
   (a) the students in that group
   (b) those students' parents
   (c) other students who are in the process of choosing a school to attend
   (d) the parents of those other students
   (e) administrators (principal, superintendent, board of education) of the schools that the evaluated students attend
   (f) federal and state legislators
   (g) government agencies that fund, supervise, or monitor schools

(h) college admissions officers
(i) employers
(j) the general public

Although the aim of the reporting system has been lauded, its implementation has come under attack. One problem has been the *No-Child Act's* focusing solely on reading and math, so that reporting state test scores in only these subjects—or perhaps in science and social-studies as well—fails to furnish a well-balanced view of learners' school progress. Furthermore, limiting reports to test scores fails to include information about students that derives from other evaluation methods, such as daily class work and teachers' observations. In addition to these shortcomings, the reporting system has been accused of confusing parents, members of the public, and school personnel.

**Type of damage—Distressed parents.** Critics of the *No-Child* Act have complained that the law unintentionally exposes parents to a host of bad news, such as the schools their children attend are doing a poor job, there are no openings at other schools to which their children might transfer, and moving children from a school with low test scores may damage the recipient school's record of test success (Russo, 2003).

**Illustrative case.** In January, 2004, on the second anniversary of the inauguration of the *No-Child-Left-Behind Act*, President Bush visited West View Elementary School in Knoxville, Tennessee, to praise the pupils who had dramatically raised reading and math test scores. This was at the time that 47% of the state's 1,650 public schools were reported to have failed to make adequate yearly progress. Observers suggested that the president apparently did not recognize that (a) the *No-Child* act was under attack by many school administrators, who considered it a rigid intrusion they could not afford, and (b) the state's first round of school evaluations in 2003 had shaken the confidence of some parents instead of reassuring them. Mary Ann Blankenship, assistant executive director of the Tennessee Education Association, reported that when she led 100 workshops focusing on implementing the act, she had not "found any place where people are happy with No Child Left Behind" (Allen, 2004).

## Providing Tutors for Low-Scoring Students

Most educators—perhaps all—would agree that tutoring is an excellent device for accommodating the marked differences among learners in abilities and background experiences. Tutoring, when done properly, involves a continuous series of exchanges between a tutor and a student. The tutor begins with a specific learning objective—a skill or piece of knowledge—and assesses the student's mastery of that objective by posing a question to answer or a task to perform. Then, by observing the student's performance, the tutor can (a) judge the extent to which the objective has been mastered, (b) estimate the causes of any shortcomings in the student's response, and (c) propose ways of correcting such causes. Hence, tutoring consists of guiding a learner through a graduated sequence of tasks that are adjusted to that particular person's ability to perform the tasks.

Because tutoring is so well suited to caring for the individual differences among learners, the idea of including a tutoring provision in the *No-Child-Left-Behind Act* has been widely applauded. Some 8,000 schools across the nation that have concentrations of children from low-income families have qualified for federal tutoring funds (Connors, 2004). However, attempts to put the provision into practice have been accompanied by several sorts of collateral damage.

**Type of damage—Low proportion of students apply for tutoring.** Far fewer families apply for tutoring services than are entitled to such help. Various reasons have been identified for this apparent lack of interest. In some cases, parents or their children wish to avoid the bother involved with after-school or weekend sessions that may require special transportation arrangements. Other parents believe the tutoring may do little good. And some critics have charged that school systems have often been lax in telling parents (a) that children who fared badly on high-stakes tests are entitled to free individual help, (b) the nature of that help, and (b) how to apply for tutoring services.

**Illustrative cases.** Only 12.5% of the 243,249 pupils in New York City who were eligible for free tutoring in 2002 actually received help. According to observers, poor communication with parents was a significant cause for the low numbers. Information about the tutoring program that had been sent to parents and to groups offering tutoring services was meager, confusing, and often discouraged enrollment. As a result, the city spent less than half of the $27.5-million that the law provided (Gross, 2003a).

In contrast, during 2003, one-third more children in low-scoring New York schools were tutored, due largely to improved outreach to eligible families, earlier notification, clearer correspondence, and help from new parent coordinators. A total of 40,369 students—19% of those eligible—signed up for the help to which they were entitled because they attended schools that had failed to meet federal standards for at least two years (Gross, 2003b).

In Chicago only 11% of eligible families (14,931 of 133,000 low-income parents) responded to the school district's letter offering children extra help from any of 10 private tutoring agencies, including such well known companies as Sylvan and Kumon, or from their own public schools. The disctrict planned to spend $20-million on 10,000 students in the form of after-school programs, Saturday school, reduced class size, teacher mentoring, extra materials, or full-day kindergarten. A spokesperson for the board said the system had waged an "aggressive campaign" to publicize the services, but some critics disagreed. They claimed that many parents had failed to receive the letters or did not understand the letters, while others rejected the offer because transportation to the tutoring sites was not included (Rossi, 2003a).

Of the 7,500 students in the New Orleans public schools who were eligible for tutoring during the 2003-2004 school year, just 489 signed up. Most of them students were scheduled to attend after-school sessions at least twice a week—sessions conducted by seven state-approved private companies and nonprofit groups (Rasheed, 2003).

A report issued in 2004 by the nonpartisan Center on Education Policy said that, across the nation, 25% of eligible children were currently receiving tutoring, a decrease from 46% during the 2002-2003 school year. (Senators take agency to task, 2004).

**Type of damage—Difficulty in selecting a suitable tutoring source.** In a given school district, a variety of organizations may offer to furnish tutoring. School officials and parents can find it difficult to choose which of those sources to patronize, because the costs and services can vary significantly from one provider to another.

**Illustrative case.** In Minnesota, 45 organizations applied to the state Department of Education to become providers. Among the applicants were (a) such familiar names in the for-profit-tutoring business as Kumon North America, Sylvan Education Solutions, and Kaplan, (b) faith-based bodies, such as the Salvation Army, (c) non-profit organizations, like the Twin Cities Boys and Girls Clubs, and (d) school districts themselves. Some providers offered one-on-one tutoring, whereas others worked with children in small groups. Prices differed significantly, ranging from $9.17 per after-school session for one provider to $40 or more an hour for several others. The school district's program in St. Paul had six students per instructor in two-hour sessions four times a week. Those students received a snack, and ones who lived farther than one mile from the school were taken home by bus. The Sylvan Education Solutions program had six students per instructor in one-hour sessions two or three times a week—about one-fourth of the instruction time offered by the St. Paul School District—and no transportation (Welsh, 2003).

**Type of damage—Commercial tutoring companies charge high fees.** The individual help for children with low test scores can be furnished by private tutoring companies, nonprofit groups, or the public schools themselves. Under federal regulations, the cost of tutoring per child for a school district can vary substantially from one school system to another, ranging from about $800 to $2,000 per student annually, depending on how much a district receives in federal Title-I money for children from low-income families. Critics have complained that the fees private companies often charge are exorbitant, thereby reducing the number of needy students who can receive help.

**Illustrative case.** During the 2003-2004 academic year, 100,000 students in the Philadelphia schools qualified for tutoring. The federal law entitled providers of tutoring services to charge as much as $1,815 per student. However, Paul Valla, the school district's chief executive, objected to giving that much money to profit-making companies which had sprung up expressly to do such work. Valla said he was not averse to outside providers, but to spending $1,800 per student. He said his aim was to "serve the most children possible with the highest-quality program." He estimated that only 12,500 students would get tutoring if each went to an outside provider. In contrast, more than 40,000 could be helped through the district's program at a cost of $300 per student while providing 120 hours of instruction compared with as little as 30 hours from some private providers (Mezzacappa, 2003).

**Type of damage—Unspent funds used for other purposes.** Under the *No-Child Act,* a school district can keep whatever Title-I money it does not spend on tutoring, then use those extra funds for whatever district officials choose. Thus, the funding system potentially provides districts with a financial disincentive to aggressively promote tutoring. For instance, officials may neglect to inform parents adequately of the availability of tutoring.

**Illustrative cases.** The amount of unspent funds could range from as much as $37-million for a large city like New York to several thousand dollars for smaller cities (Connors, 2004).

## High Costs

The massive demands for data collection, data reporting, and furnishing extra services (tutoring, teacher upgrading, modernizing learning materials) that high-stakes testing has placed on school systems has come at a time that states have suffered serious income short-falls.

**Type of damage—Trying to do more with less money.** In the face of the *No-Child-Left-Behind* requirements and the depressed economy, state education departments have been hard pressed to fulfill their responsibilities. Many states have been forced to dismiss employees after their legislatures cut administrative spending. Although officials have tried not to eliminate jobs, they often have had to reduce spending on collecting data and on assisting struggling schools, which have been two essential components of the *No-Child-Left-Behind* program (Hoff, 2003b).

**Type of damage—Inadequate federal funding.** School districts face high costs for administering obligatory state and federal testing programs without receiving adequate funds from the state or federal government to cover the costs. Many state officials, as well as some members of Congress, have complained that the *No-Child Act* was woefully underfunded by the federal government. In the first two years of the act, Washington increased K-12 spending by $7.8 billion, but that was only a 1% increase in all of the money—local, state and federal—spent on primary education. The increase was supposed to enable the states to help all school children improve, not just the economically disadvantaged ones for whom Title-I money had been furnished in the past (States voice doubts, 2003).

**Illustrative cases.** Near the end of 2003, the budget passed by the Alabama legislature resulted in (a) the elimination of all consultants who had been hired to help struggling schools, (b) the department of education being unable to fill its 51 vacancies, (c) funds for textbooks being cut, and (d) aid for teachers' professional development being reduced. In Kentucky, a $4-million budget cut eliminated regional education-assistance centers that helped schools carry out federal program mandates. Similar difficulties were experienced in South Carolina when the state education department's workforce was downsized by 15%. In California, the dissemination of faulty data about the annual progress of local schools was blamed on the loss of researchers in a 13% reduction of the state education department's staff (Hoff, 2003b).

## An Avalanche of Paper Work

Implementing high-stakes-testing programs—and particularly the *No-Child-Left-Behind Act*—has required enormous amounts of additional paper work for teachers, administrators, and clerical staff in order to record and report test results for individual students and sub-groups of the school population.

**Type of damage—Teachers' time and energy diverted.** The *No-Child* plan obligates teachers to take time away from planning lessons and from helping students in order to complete the required paper work.

**Illustrative cases.** At an increasing pace, teachers have posted their complaints on the Internet. A teacher in Houston wrote that at her school the main focus was on doing paperwork, so on a typical day "I have a list of 10 things that I absolutely HAVE to get done, and teaching isn't even on the list" (Schmitten, 2003).

Another reported that teachers in her school district were over stressed and confused by so much paper work that "they don't have time to breathe, much less have . . . lessons that deal with social behavior in the classroom" (Re: Here is what NCLB has to do with it, 2003).

After 24-years of aiding Title-I children, a distressed Alabama teacher challenged advocates of high-stakes testing to

> Test me—test my students—but do it fairly. Don't threaten me with closing my school down. Not until I see you (federal and state department) walk into my classroom, teach my students the same skills with the same materials or lack thereof, and have them score higher on this or that particular test. Not until I see you spend $4,000 out of your own pocket on that classroom every year. Not until I see you sit up until midnight because the paper chase is becoming unending. (AAE Teachers weigh in, 2003)

## Grade Promotion and High-School Graduation

The terms *social promotion* and *tested promotion* identify two different policies for determining which students should be advanced from one grade level to the next for the upcoming school year. *Social promotion* is the practice of moving children up a grade level each year, so they can stay with their age peers, regardless of how well they have met the learning goals of the grade they were in during the past year. *Tested promotion* or *earned promotion* is the practice of requiring learners to achieve above a set minimum standard in order to move to the next higher grade. Failing to reach that standard results in students repeating the same grade for another year. Although these two policies may appear to be diametrically opposed, they are often combined in practice. Whether a student under an *earned-promotion* policy moves up to the next grade can depend not only on the student's test scores but also on a teacher's judgment about such things as (a) the number of subject-matter fields (language arts, math, science, social studies) in which the pupil failed to reach the minimum standard, (b) whether the student tried hard to succeed, and (c) the effect that flunking might have on the student's self-confidence. At an increasing rate, school districts have abandoned social promotion in favor of promotion determined by tests, particularly tests in reading and math, but sometimes in other subjects as well.

Most high schools have traditionally awarded graduation diplomas to students whose class work has been judged satisfactory, with the judgment based on the adequacy of homework assignments, class participation, periodic tests, term papers, group projects, and the like. However, in recent years a growing number of states and school districts have based high-school graduation chiefly—or often exclusively—on high-stakes-test scores.

The dual purpose of adopting a tested-promotion policy has been to (a) motivate students and their teachers to work hard and (b) ensure that students arrive in the next higher grade with a proper background of achievement from the previous grade. The dual purpose of the graduation-test policy has been to (a) stimulate students and their teachers to work hard and (b) ensure employers and the public that high-school graduates are competent in the fields in which they were tested, especially in language and math.

## More Learners Fail to Advance

Typically, a school's success is judged partly on how many of its students advance regularly through the grades, rather than being held back to spend a second or third year at the same grade level. Two types of damage accompanying the adoption of high-stakes testing have been (a) increased numbers of students repeat a grade and (b) all evidence of student progress other than state test scores have been eliminated in determining whether pupils will be promoted.

**Types of damage—More grade repeaters, fewer graduates.** A major consequence of school systems changing from social promotion to tested promotion has been a dramatic increase in (a) students flunking and thus being obliged to spend another year in a grade and (b) students failing to graduate from high school.

**Illustrative case.** In 2003, over 59,200 Louisiana fourth-graders took the LEAP-21 tests (Louisiana Educational Assessment Program for the Twenty-first Century) that measured command of English language arts, math, science, and social studies. Among the pupils tested, 6,500 or 11% failed. More than 12,000 eighth-graders also failed the LEAP, and at least 17,500 failed the state's high-school exit exam (Rasheed, 2003).

**Type of damage—Daily work fails to compensate for test failure.** Traditionally, decisions about students' eligibility for promotion and graduation have been founded on various sources of evidence, particularly on daily class assignments and periodic tests. However, when such decisions are based solely on students' state test scores, those whose daily work has been judged satisfactory but whose state test scores are low cannot be promoted or graduate.

**Illustrative case.** In Louisiana, only 125 out of the 220 senior-class members at Fortier High School graduated in May 2003. At least 30 of those who did not graduate had earned passing marks on daily class work but were denied diplomas because they failed the graduation test. Throughout the school system, 28% of the seniors did not graduate in 2002, most of them because they did not pass the state exam (Rasheed, 2003).

# Grade Overcrowding

**Type of damage—Too many students in a grade.** When large numbers of students fail tests required for promotion to the next higher grade, the grades at which the tests were administered suffer overcrowding.

**Illustrative case.** For the 2004-2005 school year, New York City imposed strict promotion requirements for third graders that education officials estimated could result in 15,000 children (one in five) being forced to repeat the grade, four times as many as were left back in 2003. Promotion would depend on children's standardized reading and math test scores, with pupils who scored in the lowest of four rankings automatically held back. However, some educators questioned the merits of the plan, warning that similar efforts, including one in New York in the 1980's, were expensive and failed. They cited research that showed students forced to repeat one grade are much more likely to drop out of school, and those forced to repeat twice are almost certain not to graduate. The cost of implementing the program was estimated at $25-million. Critics noted that holding back a large number of third graders would mean far higher test scores on the fourth-grade high-stake exams in 2005, when Republican Mayor Michael R. Bloomberg—a strong proponent of the grade-retention plan—would be up for re-election. Eva S. Moskowitz, a Manhattan Democrat suggested that it was "awfully politically convenient" to avoid having the lowest-performing pupils retained in third grade so that the fourth grade scores would "look a lot better" (Herzenhorn, 2004b).

# Held-Back Pupils Could Have Succeeded

**Type of damage—Low-scoring pupils not promoted.** A substantial amount of research evidence compiled over the past few decades has suggested that pupils who are held back to repeat a grade will seldom improve the second year and would have been better off if they had been promoted and given extra help in overcoming their deficiencies.

**Illustrative case.** When New York City officials ordered strict compliance with the 2003 non-promotion policy for third graders who earned low test scores, Dr. Leonard Golubchick called the policy a "big mistake." Golubchick was the principal of Public School 20 on the Lower East Side, one of the city's poorest schools, attended by the children of immigrants. Every year several PS-20 pupils failed the citywide third-grade reading test with a score of 1. However, Dr. Golubchick managed to raise extra money to pay for additional aides and facilities so that most low-scoring third-graders improved enough to advance to fourth grade with passing scores. To produce such success, pupils were placed in reading groups suited to their individual skills and needs; and those who lagged behind their classmates were given extra time at the computer each day, using the Sound Reading Solutions program for phonetics and the Read Naturally program for fluency. Thus, every child could progress at his or her own rate (Winerip, 2004a).

## Increased Disparities in Class Size

**Type of damage—Marked differences in class sizes in adjacent grades.** Unless adjustments in the number of classes provided at a grade level are made in response to large numbers of learners being retained in their former grade, marked differences can appear in the size of classes. This is most dramatically displayed in schools that use state tests for promotion decisions at only certain grade levels, such as grades 3 and 9. In those instances, third-grade and ninth-grade classes become overcrowded, while the size of fourth- and tenth-grade classes markedly declines.

**Illustrative cases.** Holding back 40,000 third graders in Florida for the 2003-2004 school year would inevitably swell the size of third-grade classes and diminish the size of fourth-grade classes (Pinzur, 2003a). The same result could be expected in Massachusetts between ninth- and tenth-grade classes when retention rates for ninth-graders jumped from 6.3% in 1995 to 8.4% in 2001. Twelve Massachusetts districts held back more than 20% of their ninth-graders, with three districts retaining between 27% and 38% (Edley & Wald, 2002).

## Increased Dropout Rates

A school's ability to hold onto students—not have them drop out of the education system—is one criterion usually included in judgments of a school's success. In numerous districts, high-stakes testing has been accompanied by higher dropout rates as state test scores have become the most important—or exclusive—measure of student success.

**Type of damage—Low-performing students eliminated.** When a school is threatened with punitive sanctions for its students having scored low on language and math tests, teachers and administrators are tempted to get rid of the least successful scholars in order to raise the test-score average. Methods of removing low-performers can be either direct (flunk them, suspend them, expel them) or indirect (neglect them, harass them, make no effort of save them).

**Illustrative cases.** In Chicago, during the 2001-02 school year, 17,400 students—17.6%—dropped out of the public schools, an increase from 13.5% in 1992. At a public hearing of the Illinois senate's education committee, the state's superintendent of education, Robert Schiller, joined other speakers in blaming the *No-Child* law as an important cause behind the dropout increase. The speakers claimed that the *No-Child* program exerted pressure on school officials to "push out truant, low-performing students" whose poor test performance lowered a school's test scores, thereby reducing the school's chances of achieving adequate yearly progress. William Leavy, director of a Chicago alternative school, agreed that the district's dropout problem was "largely a push-out problem" for the "neediest kids [who had] the least support" (Grossman, 2004).

In 2003, the *New York Times* reported that 500 students per year had been pushed out of Brooklyn's Franklin K. Lane High School by means of shifting students into one bureaucratic category or another so as to avoided increasing the school's dropout rate. This was apparently not an isolated case, as New York City's Public Advocate, Betsy Gotbaum, contended that 160,000 students, or at least 20%, had been pushed out of the city's public schools during three previous school years. In Birmingham, Alabama, 522 students were expelled in 2000 for "lack of interest" prior to test administration; school officials admitted eliminating students in order to remove low-achieving ones from the test pool. In Miami, Florida, an elementary-school principal wanted to "weed out problematic students who live outside the school's attendance area—and who may be dragging down standardized test scores." Houston, Texas, officials were charged with failing to report thousands of dropouts because school personnel wanted to collect bonuses for high accountability ratings. Critics blamed the push-out problem on administrators, counselors, and teachers who had no confidence in the ability of struggling students to graduate (Standardizing unfairness, 2003). The New Hampshire Center for Public Policy Studies reported that the state's high-school dropout rate over the 2001-2002 period continued at 23% to 25% (Ramer, 2004).

# Four Frequently Affiliated Functions

Four additional test functions that typically accompany high-stakes programs are those of controlling the curriculum, evaluating school personnel, motivating personnel and students, and improving instruction.

## Controlling the Curriculum

As proposed in Chapter 2, whenever school administrators and teachers suffer serious consequences if their students do poorly on tests, teachers usually dedicate more time and attention to the skills and types of knowledge measured by the tests. Instructors, in effect, teach to the tests. Ergo, the material treated on the test becomes the curriculum. Other material in a school's published course of study is set aside.

Therefore, even though using standardized tests to determine what is taught does help ensure that teachers concentrate on the kinds of skill and knowledge the test-makers consider important, that advantage is paid for by the neglect of other important learnings.

**Type of damage—Restricted learning opportunities.** Teaching to the test restricts teachers' freedom to fashion instruction to the needs of individual students and to extend learners' educational experiences beyond the test contents. Hence, students get a "bare-bones" education, particularly when testing is limited to two or three subject-matter fields, such as reading, math, and science.

**Illustrative case.** While shrinking the curriculum by permitting tests to determine what is taught is unfair to all students, perhaps gifted students suffer the greatest loss. When a researcher, Tonya Moon, surveyed 2,500 teachers and visited 50 classrooms, she discovered that teachers in high-stakes-testing programs were spending large amounts of time on test preparation, including using worksheets mimicking state test questions. As a result, little or no time was left for activities that were particularly engaging for gifted students, such as art, music, physical education, field trips, and more complex science and social-studies topics. Moon concluded that material not on the test no longer deserved to be taught, particularly when administrators so strongly pressure teachers to get high test scores that educational standards "become more like a checklist" (Pappano, 2003).

## Evaluating School Personnel

In the high-stakes-testing era, teachers' destinies can be affected by two types of tests—state achievement tests taken by their students and teacher-knowledge tests taken by teachers themselves. Test scores from both of these types are often used as measures of teachers' competence.

**Types of damage—Students' low test scores as inadequate evidence of the quality of teaching.** Teachers are rewarded—often with praise and sometimes with cash—for high scores their students earn on state tests. At an increasing rate, teachers are also being blamed and punished for their students getting low test scores. Certainly the quality of teaching has some effect on students' test performance, since students can't do well on tests if they haven't had a fair chance to learn what the tests measure. But it's silly to imagine that the only variable affecting students' success on tests is their teacher's ability and diligence. Success depends also on a test-taker's motives, interests, energy level, inherited neural structure, schooling background, family support, emotional control, peer influences, immediate testing context, and more. These additional, highly potent influences are typically beyond a teacher's control.

And since the teacher cannot fix them, the teacher should not be blamed for the effect of such conditions on students' exam scores.

It is also the case that a person who is an effective teacher for one type of learner may not be an effective teacher for another type. Hence, in a third-grade class, a Spanish-speaking child, recently arrived from Mexico, may thrive more adequately under a particular teacher's tutelage than does an intellectually gifted but boisterous child of over-indulgent parents who are long-term residents of the community. Classroom observations of the two pupils may suggest that the Spanish-speaking newcomer is making admirable progress, whereas the gifted classmate is often disrupting the class and wasting time. And the teacher is at wit's end, not knowing how best to deal with the hyperactive pupil. But on state tests the gifted pupil scores much higher than the newcomer. So what do those test scores tell us about the teacher's success with the two pupils?

In summary, while students' standardized-test scores are partially a reflection of how well teachers have prepared students for those tests, the scores certainly do not accurately reflect how effectively a teacher promotes each student's overall welfare. Using students' test scores as *the measure* of teacher quality is a serious mistake.

**Types of damage—Tests as inadequate measures of teaching skill.** In an effort to improve the quality of teaching in America's schools, the *No-Child-Left-Behind Act* has included the goal of having all of the nation's classrooms staffed by highly qualified teachers. The evidence of a teacher's qualification has usually been a state or national certificate. Typically an individual earns certification by taking an acceptable series of college courses and, in many cases, passing one or more tests. Those tests are usually of three types designed to measure (a) general knowledge, (b) command of subject-matter skills and knowledge, and (b) knowledge of the education profession and teaching practices.

For example, candidates for certification in Florida need to pass the following:

A 120-item, multiple-choice Professional Education Test focusing on general knowledge of pedagogy and professional practices.

A General Knowledge basic-skills battery consisting of three multiple-choice tests (math, reading, English-language skills) and an essay.

One or more Subject Area Exams designed to measure content-area knowledge, usually in multiple-choice format. However, some subject tests also require an essay (such as English for grades 5-9 and Spanish for K-12).

Spanish K-12 and French K-12 are administered in a language lab, and German K-12 has an interview. Speech 6-12 has a videotaped portion.

Candidates applying for a Professional Certificate and those adding a subject area to a Professional Certificate must pass a subject area exam in the field(s) in which they seek certification. (Description of the FTCE Tests, 2004)

Nobody questions the importance of teachers' general knowledge, of their command of the subject matter they are expected to teach, or of their knowledge of teaching practices. Thus, gaining evidence about teachers' mastery of such fields is important. But it is a grave error to assume that scores on a selection of multiple-choice and essay questions accurately reflect a teacher's effectiveness. Paper-pencil tests obviously fail to assess such vital teacher characteristics as

- skill in explaining concepts and procedures,
- a knack for generating students' interest in what is taught,
- diligence in preparing lessons and in evaluating students' work,
- an understanding of factors that influence children's behavior,
- the ability to maintain classroom control,
- an absence of ethnic, religious, or social-class prejudice, and
- skill in adjusting teaching methods to the individual differences among learners.

In sum, certification on the basis of test scores is useful but does not ensure that a teacher is competent, nor does a lack of such certification mean that a teacher is not proficient. A proper assessment of a teacher's effectiveness requires multiple evaluation techniques—observations of the teacher's interactions with students, interviews with students, information about the tasks assigned to students, and the quality of students' performance on assignments and tests (written multiple-choice and essay items, oral responses, discussion contributions).

## Motivating Students and School Personnel

In view of the serious punitive sanctions that schools and students suffer when students get low test scores, it is apparent that high-stakes testing strongly motivates most students, teachers, and school administrators to take whatever measures they think necessary to raise test scores. Many students respond with greater effort to the threat that they will be denied promotion or graduation if they fail state tests. Most teachers appear to try harder to improve students' test performance and thereby avoid blame for their school being labeled a failure. For instance, in Buffalo, New York, the school district's math and science supervisor, Franco DiPasqua, attributed the 2004 remarkable rise in the district's math-test scores to hard-working teachers and students, along with new textbooks and a revised curriculum. DiPasqua said students were taking the math exam seriously, as they saw more of their peers failing to graduate because they had not passed it. He said, "There are so many people working hard to make sure these kids are successful" that schools should give themselves proper credit (Pasciak, 2004).

**Type of damage—Neglect of important learnings.** However useful tests may be in focusing teachers' and students' efforts on reading, math, and other tested subjects, the extra attention paid to those subjects can result in the neglect of nontested fields, as was shown in Chapter 2.

**Illustrative case.** In a poll of school principals in Maryland, more than 50% of the respondents reported decreases in social studies instruction, while 40% predicted further cuts in teaching time for the arts (Bowler, 2004a).

## Improving Instruction

The high-stakes movement has directed a great deal of attention to improving the quality of teaching, particularly the teaching of reading and math in schools whose students fared badly on state tests.

As a step toward raising the quality of instruction, the *No-Child-Left-Behind Act* has required that school districts plan to have all teachers fully licensed by the end of the 2005-2006 school year. In addition, districts have been obligated to promote the professional development of teachers, of staff members responsible for services to pupils, and of school administrators in order to increase their content knowledge, teaching skills, and dedication.

A typical example of an effort to foster improved instruction is the state of Virginia's awarding the Consortium for Interactive Instruction $638,000 a year for five years to support training activities that increase teachers' use of educational technology. The plan offers a variety of professional-development opportunities, including on-line instruction via the Internet, live two-way audio and video communication, and face-to-face training through a series of workshops and seminars ranging from one day to a full week, with all such services available at no charge (Callahan, 2004).

The high-stakes movement's emphasis on the inservice upgrading of teachers—with millions of dollars available for that purpose—has spawned a host of consultants and companies offering teacher-training services touted as effective for raising students' performance on state tests. These recent entrants into the teacher-training business, along with the textbook and teaching-materials companies already in the field, have confronted school districts with the problem of deciding on which of the multitude of entrepreneurs' programs will most likely lead to improved test results.

In summary, lawmakers at both federal and state levels have viewed teachers as critical functionaries in improving the quality of schooling, as that quality is reflected in standardized test scores. Thus, students' test outcomes—which legislators, the business community, and a vocal segment of the general public regard as very unsatisfactory—have directed renewed attention and more funds toward improving teachers' skills and knowledge. In such a manner, unacceptable test results may lead to improved instruction.

But the effect of high-stakes testing on teachers and on instructional methods has not been entirely positive as shown by the following negative effects of high-stakes testing on teaching methods and on veteran teachers who lack full certification.

**Type of damage—Inferior teaching methods adopted.** Studies of teaching in a high-stakes environment have revealed an increase in the use of instructional methods that foster rote memorization and segmented learning rather than analytical thought, broad understanding of issues, and creativity.

**Illustrative case.** A survey of more than 4,500 teachers nationwide showed that their concern for testing had influenced the time they spent using different instructional methods, such as whole-group teaching, individual seat work, cooperative learning, and studying problems similar to those on the test. The survey distinguished between *high-stakes states* (in which tests bore quite serious consequences, such as affecting high-school graduation and school accreditation) and *low-stakes states* (in which test consequences were not so crucial). In high-stakes states, 40% of teachers reported that their schools' test outcomes affected their daily teaching, whereas in low-stakes states only 10% of teachers reported such influence. Over 60% of respondents agreed that the testing program led to some teachers using methods that were contrary to their own beliefs about effective schooling (Olson, 2003b).

**Type of damage—Teachers abandoning the profession.** The effort to ensure that all classrooms are staffed by "fully accredited" teachers has been accompanied by some unwelcome results. For instance, there are veteran teachers who lack complete state credentials but whose performance in the classroom has been laudatory. Yet, under the strict application of the *No-Child-Act's* rules, those teachers must acquire full accreditation or be dismissed. However, not all of them are willing to go through the retraining procedure required by credentialing agencies. Some—if forced to retrain—would prefer to quit teaching, thus ending what has been valuable service to students. Keeping experienced teachers on the job is especially important in view of studies suggesting that nearly 30% of teachers nationwide leave the profession within three years and 50% are gone within five (Lynn, 2004b). The problem of capable teachers resigning is particularly acute in rural communities and in stressful inner-city schools.

## Conclusion

This chapter's discussion suggests that the greatest impact of high-stakes testing on individuals and schools has resulted from the use of standardized achievement tests for:

- Distinguishing between good schools and bad schools in terms of reading and math test scores
- Rewarding successful schools and punishing failing ones
- Controlling the curriculum
- Informing people of students' achievement-test performance in reading and math
- Determining students' promotion and graduation
- Providing tutors for students whose test-scores in reading and math have been unsatisfactory
- Motivating school personnel and students to work hard in the areas of reading and math

High-stakes testing appears to have had relatively little influence on:

- Diagnosing individual learners' strengths and weaknesses
- Designing learning methods suited to individuals' aptitudes
- Accurately evaluating school personnel
- Accurately assigning students marks or grades
- Diagnosing a group's strengths and weaknesses in all subject-matter areas
- Designing instruction that corrects a group's shortcomings in all subject-matter areas
- Transferring students from failing schools to successful ones
- Predicting students' future performance in all subject fields
- Improving instruction (other than in reading and math)

The collateral damage accompanying high-stakes testing has consisted chiefly of unwelcome consequences for students, parents, and school personnel. Prominent among those consequences have been:

Great numbers of the nation's schools dubbed "in need of improvement" (an expression widely interpreted as a euphemism for "failing")

Large numbers of students denied grade-promotion or a graduation diploma

Increased dropout rates

Teachers and school administrators blamed for students' low test scores, whereas other socio-cultural factors have played a strong role in affecting students' test performance

Too few students receiving tutoring

Increased disparities in class size

Students overloading some schools and under-occupying other schools

Certain components of the traditional curriculum (science, social studies, the arts, physical education, health education, and more) neglected so as to provide more time for teaching reading and math

A dramatically increased financial burden imposed on schools by high-stakes testing programs

A growing flood of paper work imposed on school personnel for implementing testing programs and submitting reports to government officials and parents

Some school personnel using devious methods in an attempt to fulfill requirements of high-stakes programs—such methods as encouraging low-scoring students to leave school

In summary, the uses of test results in high-stakes programs has led to such desired outcomes as improved student scores on standardized reading and math tests, but the uses have also been accompanied diverse forms of troublesome collateral damage.

# Part II

## The Testing Game's Players and Their Coping Strategies

The chapters of Part II focus on six types of players who engage in high-stakes-testing activities.

As explained in Chapter 1, the Part-II chapters are arranged in the order of the players' levels of authority or official power. Politicians (members of Congress, state governors, state legislators, school-board members) wield the greatest authority and thus are at the top of the hierarchy, while students—having no authority—are at the bottom.

Each chapter in Part II lists types of collateral damage often faced by the people who are the subject of that chapter. The account of each type of damage includes (a) a description of the type, (b) strategies that people may adopt to cope with the damage, (c) one or more cases illustrating the coping method in practice, and (d) problems that may remain after the coping technique has been applied.

# 6

# Politicians and Their Staffs

The words *politics* and *political*, as intended throughout this book, refer to the exercise of authority, control, and power for determining who gets tested, why, and how. The word *politicians* is used to mean individuals who have been elected to office and, in their official roles, influence the achievement-testing process. The expression *their staffs* refers to people who are officially responsible for helping politicians carry out their functions. The six types of politicians of interest are (a) the U.S. President, (b) members of Congress, (c) state governors, (d) state legislators, (e) the heads of state education departments, and (f) members of school-district boards of education. Such office-holders have been chosen by the voters of the constituencies they serve.

The six types of politicians form a hierarchy of authority that descends from the U.S. president at the top to members of local school boards at the bottom. The word *authority* means the official power invested in a particular office. In general, the higher an individual is located on this administrative structure, (a) the greater the official power available to that individual and (b) the larger the number of people affected by the office-holder's decisions. Thus, members of Congress have greater authority than state legislators, and state legislators have greater power than school-district board members.

The following discussion is divided into four parts. Parts 1 through 3 describe incidents that illustrate politicians' strategies for coping with collateral damage at three levels of government (Part 1 = national, Part 2 = state, Part 3 = school-district). Part 4—the conclusion—summarizes key features of the chapter's contents and identifies two attributes of politicians that often affect their decisions about educational matters.

The incidents in Parts 1 through 3 have been selected to illustrate typical political attempts to deal with collateral damage that results from high-stakes testing. The description of each incident begins with (a) a title reflecting the kind of coping strategy the incident illustrates, (b) the kind of collateral damage the event entails, (c) one or more coping strategies adopted by political figures who were involved in such an event, (d) the description of one or more cases illustrating the type of damage and the attempted coping strategy, and (e) problems that may remain after the strategy has been applied.

## National-Level Politicians

The significant political figures at the federal level are (a) the U.S. President and his staff (especially personnel of the U.S. Department of Education) and (b) members of Congress and their staffs. These functionaries play four main roles in the high-stakes-testing game. They set regulations that public schools throughout the nation are expected to obey, they provide funds to help schools implement the regulations, they monitor schools' progress toward achievement-testing goals, and they publicize which schools succeed and which fail in pursuit of those goals.

The collateral damage suffered by politicians in Washington consists of unwelcome criticism they receive from the public press and from such constituents as state officials, school-district administrators, teachers, parents, and students. As ways of coping with damage, national-level politicians may (a) reassure the public that the testing program has been well conceived, (b) recommend patience, (c) publicize supporters' endorsements, (d) cite survey results, (e) reject critics' charges, (f) prematurely declare victory, (g) hold fast to high-stakes principles, (h) express confidence in high standards, (i) redefine terminology, (j) increase funding, (k) alter testing conditions or revise standards, and (l) accept responsibility for flaws in the program. In the following pages, the strategies are presented in an order that moves from the most unyielding and defensive reactions (rejecting all criticisms) to the most conciliatory (admitting weaknesses in the *No-Child* program and weighing solutions).

### Reassure the Public

**Type of damage—Loss of public's confidence.** Whenever the populace learns of serious problems arising in a government-sponsored program, political leaders and their staffs are in danger of losing public confidence, thereby placing their reputations and jobs in jeopardy. Over the period 2002-2004, as news of troubles with high-stakes testing spread at an accelerating pace, the sponsors of the *No-Child-Left-Behind Act* recognized that the program was developing a tarnished image.

**Federal politicians' coping strategy.** One popular strategy for repairing a blemished persona involves hiring public-relations experts to mount a campaign reassuring the public that the program is in good health and bound to succeed. Such efforts are sometimes referred to as "cheer leading." They typically involve the use of mass-communication media for publicizing successful cases of school reform while rationalizing away—or simply ignoring—problems, mistakes, and damage.

**Illustrative case.** In early 2003, as news of collateral damage from the high-stakes testing plan spread at a growing pace, the U. S. Department of Education appointed eight members of a special outreach team assigned to "clear up" public misconceptions about the *No-Child-Left-Behind Act*. The team's work supplemented the efforts of existing political appointees and career staff members. Some observers believed the team was an attempt, as the 2004 presidential-election approached, to promote President Bush's public image as the rescuer of American education. The eight team members' salaries totaled more than $507,000. According to the team leader, "Now we have the ability to combat misinformation and correct the record, and ultimately to better inform the public about the significance of this law" (Davis, 2003).

The sort of enthusiastic optimism expressed by sponsors of high-stakes testing and its allied features is reflected in such comments as the following, which Secretary of Education Roderick Paige offered at a conference of the National Association of State Boards of Education.

> Never before has this nation made such a commitment to educate every child, regardless of race, family income, or zip code. In the year since *No Child Left Behind* first became the law of the land, we have seen great progress. States have moved forward on all fronts. . . . This is what true reform looks like. Things are getting done. The American people think we're on the right track. A recent poll shows:
> - 91% want high standards and accountability,
> - 91% want annual report cards to parents on school performance,
> - 91% want a highly qualified teacher in the classroom,
> - And across the board demographically, the majority of Americans—66% —believe that high standards and accountability are more important to improving our schools than increased funding.
>
> President Bush's 2004 education budget will ensure that we stay on track. Despite all the priorities competing for our tax dollars—strengthening our economy, defending our nation, and expanding opportunities for all Americans—the President's budget boosts education funding to $53.1 billion—historic levels for our nation's children. (Paige, 2003)

**Remaining problems.** One difficulty for politicians is the accusation that the program's sponsors have used funds that are needed for more important purposes. As a spokesman for one U.S. senator complained,

"We're a little disappointed they're not spending this money on a way to provide more support for the No Child Left Behind Act, instead of engaging in some artful public relations campaign" (Davis, 2003).

Opponents also charge that public-relations efforts are a waste of time and energy. A lobbyist for the American Association of School Administrators said of the Department of Education's outreach team, "It always strikes me as kind of silly and fruitless because the truth is . . . that people locally don't pay a lot of attention to that [public-relations] stuff. I guess [the *No-Child-Left-Behind* supporters] feel if they don't push their issue, it will somehow get left behind" (Davis, 2003).

## Recommend Patience

**Type of damage—Loss of voters' confidence.** Much-publicized attacks on provisions of the *No-Child-Left-Behind Act* by state and city officials have threatened to weaken the public's confidence in Washington politicians.

**Politicians' coping strategy.** A technique for quelling disapproval of a program that's still in its early stages is to advise critics to be patient.

**Illustrative case.** In October, 2003, after the *No-Child* law had been in operation for 22 months, Chicago's Mayor Daley declared that the law should be changed because it was creating a logistical nightmare and was unfairly stigmatizing schools as failing when they were actually progressing. In reacting to the mayor's criticism, Secretary of Education Roderick Paige replied, "It is much too premature to start talking about changing the law. I think the law is fine as it is" (Rossi, 2003b).

**Remaining problems.** School personnel and the public cannot be expected to wait forever before they request—or demand—that high-stakes-testing programs be revised. Therefore, when cautioned to be patient, people are prone to ask, "How long must we wait for the legislation to operate as it should? How soon can we ask that the law be repaired?"

## Publicize Supporters' Endorsements

**Type of damage—Value of testing programs doubted.** Opponents of high-stakes testing frequently quote the opinions of experienced teachers, school administrators, educational researchers, and psychologists who believe it is a serious mistake to depend on high-stakes testing for determining the fate of individual students and of entire schools. Because such critics are intimately involved with the daily conduct of schooling, their opinions are often trusted by parents whose confidence in testing programs is thereby diminished.

**Federal politicians' coping strategy.** To counteract negative publicity that dissatisfied educators initiate, proponents of high-stakes programs can gather a coterie of satisfied educators to openly support the legislation.

**Illustrative case.** At the end of 2003, as disapproval of the *No-Child-Left-Behind Act* mounted, the Washington-based Education Trust (a strong proponent of high-stakes testing) collected more than 100 African-American and Hispanic school superintendents and other educators who voiced support of the law's strict accountability provisions. Diana Lam, New York City's deputy chancellor for teaching and learning, praised the *No-Child Act* for providing "A culture of accountability, and this includes the accountability provisions of No Child Left Behind, is the best way to ensure that our schools improve teaching and learning for every child" (Olson, 2003e). Although the superintendents did not endorse every feature of the act, they strongly supported the need to account for the test performance of such subgroups as blacks, Hispanics, and Native-Americans.

**Remaining problems.** How effectively defenders of high-stakes testing use their own group of educators to nullify the accusations of educators who criticize testing depends on such factors as (a) the amount of publicity given to the opinions of each group, (b) the number of educators on the two sides in the controversy, (c) the prestige of the members of the contending groups in the eyes of the public, and (d) the kind of evidence and logic each group offers to buttress its position.

## Cite Survey Results

**Type of damage—Diminished faith in testing programs.** In the public press, critics of achievement testing often claim that the entire testing process does more harm than good by (a) failing to provide a well-balanced evaluation of students' learning, (b) causing students anxiety, and (c) focusing teachers' efforts on preparing students for tests. Such publicity can weaken the public's faith in high-stakes plans.

**Federal politicians' coping strategy.** In order to counter critics' charges, proponents of high-stakes programs can cite the results of surveys in which most students, school personnel, or parents report their satisfaction with testing.

**Illustrative case.** In 2002, the Public Agenda organization issued the results of its fifth annual *Reality Check* survey of secondary-school students' opinions of achievement testing. The survey report began with a headline declaring that "few students are unsettled by testing" and finished with the conclusion that "public school students nationwide appear to be adjusting comfortably to the new status quo" (Schaps, 2002). In support of the survey's conclusions, the chief executive officer of International Business Machines, Louis V. Gerstner, published an editorial in *The New York Times* asserting that "the great majority of middle and high-school students are comfortable with the increased testing in public schools" (Schaps, 2002).

**Remaining problems.** The effectiveness of using survey results to convince the public of the value of testing can be impaired whenever opponents to testing publicize weaknesses either in the survey methodology or in the way the survey's sponsors interpreted the results. For example, following the publication of the Public Agenda report, an article in *Education Week* gave examples of biased questions in the survey—questions that guided students toward seeming to favor testing and seeming to feel little or no anxiety in test situations. The author of the *Education Week* critique concluded that a large amount of information in the form of test scores was available for appraising the intended outcomes of testing—such as students' reading and math skills—but there was hardly any systematic information about how high-stakes testing influenced teachers' morale and willingness to stay in the profession, a school's social atmosphere, the comparative time spent on different subjects, the quality of instruction, and other important features of schooling (Schaps, 2002).

## Reject Critics' Charges

**Type of damage—Flaws exposed in lawmakers' evidence.** The public's faith in politicians drops whenever critics publicize errors in the evidence on which politicians apparently based educational legislation.

**Federal politicians' coping strategies.** One way political figures and their staffs can respond to such charges is to dismiss critics' accusations as false, unfair, mean-spirited, and politically motivated.

**Illustrative case.** In late 2002, Austin High School in Houston was rated "exemplary" by Texas education officials, and the entire Houston school district was lauded by a private foundation as the best in the nation. The Austin High award was based heavily on the school's reporting that, during the 1990s, the proportion of students who left school without graduating had declined from 14% to 0.3%. But in late 2003, Austin High's rating was dropped to "low-performing"—the bottom rung on the school-quality ladder. At the same time, the entire Houston district was accused of having rigged the school-performance data that would subsequently lead President Bush to use Houston as a model for his *No-Child-Left-Behind* program. The accusations resulted from investigators from outside the district reanalyzing Houston's statistics and charging that officials at Austin High and a dozen other high schools had either manipulated or falsified the data on which they had based reports of impressive progress, including the claim that Houston had significantly reduced the achievement gap between white and ethnic-minority students. The charges drew nationwide attention because Roderick R. Paige had been Houston's school superintendent before President Bush appointed him as the U. S. secretary of education (Dobbs, 2003).

In responding to his critics, Paige called the accusations "inflammatory" and "very unfair," adding that people who leveled such attacks were ones who believe it is "fundamentally wrong" to assess student achievement and who have a "vested interest" in preserving a dysfunctional status quo (Dobbs, 2003).

In a speech to Houston business leaders in December 2003, Paige said his detractors tried to find fault with the *No-Child* law for their own political gain and not because they were interested in quality education. He argued that some people dislike change and they "have a good thing going with the old system. Rather than working to make reform a reality, they want to derail it" (Paige: Houston schools criticized, 2003).

On a later occasion, Paige contended that much of the criticism of the *No-Child Act* was "ingenuous. There are some (people) who mean to distort. They have a different ideology. There's nothing unreasonable about this [*No-Child*] bill" (Liberman, 2004).

**Remaining problems.** Defending problematic educational practices by accusing critics of ignoble intentions, political motives, or ignorance—but failing to support the charges with objective evidence—is unlikely to convince perceptive members of the public that the accusations are unfounded.

## Prematurely Declare Victory

**Type of damage—Citizens distrust office holders' promises.** Officials often commit themselves publicly to the dates on which goals of their programs will be reached. But frequently, when those dates arrive, progress toward the goals is still short of the commitment, thereby inviting observers to reproach officeholders for failing to fulfill their promises. Politicians may thus be accused of ignorance, exaggeration, lack of foresight, a cavalier disregard for reality, cronyism, and other unattractive traits that cause voters to doubt the office holders' ability and integrity.

**Federal politicians' coping strategy.** One technique for warding off potential criticism is to announce that the goal has indeed been reached on time, even when that claim is not quite true. Premature declarations of victory are like post-dated checks or promissory notes that the public is expected to accept as the real thing—as cash on the line.

**Illustrative case.** In June, 2003, President George W. Bush chose the White House rose garden as the site for proclaiming that every state now had a federally approved plan for ensuring that all of the nation's students will be proficient in reading and math by 2014. However, reporters who searched for details of the plans discovered that the president had used the word *approved* in a rather loose fashion, thereby giving the misleading impression that the task of designing acceptable proposals had been completed. At the time of the president's announcement, only five states' plans had been fully approved, and another six would be approved as soon as changes had been completed (Olson, 2003c).

In December, 2003, Secretary of Education Roderick Paige announced that "Every single school in our nation now has an accountability plan that covers every student. This is revolutionary. This alone is a powerful change of culture" (Olson, 2003d). However, a survey of the 50 states and the District of Columbia by *Education Week* found that many states were straining to get their current methods of assessing schools into line with federal regulations. Michael Cohen, president of a group concerned with schooling standards, said there was "massive confusion, owing to the stapling together of state and federal accountability systems, and pretending that we have one, unified system" (Olson, 2003d).

**Remaining problems.** When a commander during wartime proclaims victory before the battle is actually over and the public then discovers that the proclamation was unwarranted, trust in the commander declines. Thus, premature declarations are usually successful only in the short term. Such claims hold off critics for the moment, but each additional time a politician's ploy is exposed, the public's confidence in the politician erodes even further. It's rather like the fable of the boy who cried wolf.

## Hold Fast to the Principles of High-Stakes Programs

**Type of damage—Public loses faith in officials.** If, in the early stages of a new program, sponsors of the program admit that their plan was seriously flawed from the beginning, the public's faith in their ability to do their job properly can deteriorate.

**Federal politicians' coping strategy.** A program's creators steadfastly defend the basic principles—if not the details—on which the program was founded, despite any complaints opponents may issue.

**Illustrative case.** At a ceremony celebrating the launch of the *No-Child-Left-Behind Act* in 2002, President Bush had said, "I admit, I haven't read it yet. . . . But I know the principles behind the bill." Two years later, on the second anniversary of the act's implementation, he declared his continuing confidence in the law, regardless of educators' criticisms (Allen, 2004). Then, nearly half way through the third year of the *No-Child Act*, he insisted that "I don't care how much pressure [states and school districts] try to put on the process, I'm not changing my mind about high standards and the need for accountability, because I know the promise that holds out" (Sanger & Rutenberg, 2004).

**Remaining problems.** Discerning members of the public are not likely to place much faith in the arguments offered by a program's defenders unless those arguments are backed with convincing evidence that critics' complaints are ill-founded. Merely saying "Believe me," without furnishing persuasive supporting data, may not be accepted as adequate.

## Express Confidence in High Standards

**Type of damage—Officials accused of setting unrealistic standards.** When serious problems of implementing testing legislation are increasingly exposed, office holders responsible for the legislation can be accused of stupidity for setting unrealistic achievement standards.

**Federal politician's coping strategy.** A popular response to such accusations consists of officials asserting that the standards are proper and realistically achievable if only school administrators and teachers do their jobs properly.

**Illustrative case.** In September 2003, *Washington Post* writer Jay Mathews declared that never in the nation's history had there been a greater gap between "the authors of a major piece of federal legislation and its executors—in this case, the 90,000 public schools across the country" (Mathews, 2003). In particular, school personnel disagreed with the *No-Child Act's* requiring steady test progress by the kinds of children who faced the greatest difficulty preparing for tests—special education students, recent immigrants with meager English skills, and children living in poverty. But lawmakers in Washington still said they were confident they had done the right thing. They typically defended the *No-Child Act* by both (a) claiming that perfection is within reach and (b) not knowing what other options were available for achieving higher learning performance on the part of the nation's students. For instance, creators of the *No-Child* legislation said they did not see any way to fix education in American other than to attempt the remedies contained in the act (Mathews, 2003).

**Remaining problems.** Educators who oppose the *No-Child-Left-Behind Act* may offer alternatives to the act's provisions and cite both anecdotal evidence and research to support their proposals. Consequently, as news of collateral damage from testing mounts, legislators have an increasingly difficult time defending the act in its original form.

## Redefine Terminology

**Type of damage—Too many schools bear failure label.** Whenever large numbers of schools are called failures because their pupils fared badly on a test, many troubled parents can vent their distress by blaming government officials for failing to make sure mass failures don't occur.

**Politicians' staff members' coping strategy.** Members of the Department of Education in Washington who are responsible for implementing federal education legislation may seek to placate exasperated parents by rephrasing official regulations in a manner that seems not to denigrate either schools or pupils.

**Illustrative case.** When the Arizona state education department released the names of 220 Arizona schools that federal officials charged with failing to meet performance standards, Jo Ann Webb, a U.S. Department of Education spokeswoman, said the report did not necessarily mean a school had "failed" its students. Rather, "It means the school can do better and it needs to improve. It means there are certain areas the school needs to pay attention to" (Kossan, 2003b).

**Remaining problems.** As newspaper editors can attest, attempting to repair or retract a news story after it was first published can be a chancy venture. Newspaper readers often fail to see the retraction, so they continue to believe the original story. Or the revised account may serve to heighten readers' curiosity about the motives behind the retraction. Hence, politicians' efforts to rephrase bad news about test results in order to render the results less offensive to students, school personnel, and parents may have the opposite effect—cause constituents to question the politicians' integrity.

## Increase Funding

**Type of damage—Officials accused of failing to finance testing adequately.** Testing programs of the magnitude envisioned in the *No-Child-Left-Behind Act* are extremely expensive. Not only is the creation, administration, and analysis of tests very costly, but additional large amounts are needed to finance the tutoring of under-performing pupils, the upgrading of teachers' skills, and the purchase of instructional materials. One of the most frequent criticisms of the *No-Child* plan has been that the program has been drastically underfunded by the federal government.

**Federal politicians' coping strategy.** The response most likely to quiet critics is to increase the funding of testing programs.

**Illustrative case.** In January 2004, at the outset of the *No-Child* program's third year, President Bush submitted to Congress a budget that would furnish significantly more federal money for the nation's schools than had been provided in previous years, including a $1-billion increase for Title I programs, a $1-billion increase for children with disabilities, and four times the amount spent on reading programs. President Bush said, "The No Child Left Behind Act is a great piece of legislation, which is making a difference around our country. Public education, we've got to get it right. It's the gateway to hope" (Curl, 2004).

**Remaining problems.** While welcoming more money, critics may continue to complain that the increased funds still fall far short of the amounts needed to do the job right. The ostensible money gap between what would be required to implement the *No-Child Act* and what had been provided by the federal government became the focus of the criticism aimed at the Republican administration by Democrats, including ones who had helped vote the act into law. For example, Democratic Congressman John M. Spratt, Jr. claimed that in 2003 President Bush had tried to cut funds to 46 education programs covered by the law (Curl, 2004).

## Alter Testing Conditions, Revise Standards

**Type of damage—Too many schools declared failures.** Among the most egregious flaws in the *No-Child-Left-Behind Act* has been the requirement that disabled students meet the same achievement standards as those held for their non-handicapped agemates. Many of the nation's schools were burdened with the "failing" label only because, under the act, the test scores of handicapped students were below the level considered acceptable for all groups of students. Not only did schools' reputations suffer, but the handicapped could be humiliated for being the cause of their school's shame.

**Federal politicians' coping strategy.** In an effort to repair the damage, political leaders directed the U.S. Department of Education—as the agency responsible for implementing the *No-Child Act*—to correct the act's objectionable standards for pupils with mental disabilities.

**Illustrative cases.** The federal government's first steps toward fixing flagrant faults in the *No-Child Act* appeared in December 2003 with the U.S. Department of Education announcing new rules governing test standards for the mentally handicapped. In the original version of the act, no more than 1% of students who were rated *proficient* could be pupils having a "significant cognitive disability" and thus allowed to be assessed by means other than a standard grade-level test. But the new rules permitted each state to decide what levels of disability would be sufficiently severe to permit the use of alternative evaluation methods (Mollison & Tofig-Cox, 2003). In addition, under the revised regulations, school districts could apply to their states to exceed the 1% maximum if they could show they had "larger populations of students with the most significant cognitive disabilities and had effectively designed and implemented assessment practices for students with disabilities" (Goldstein, 2003).

The next effort to repair the *No-Child* plan appeared in February 2004 when the Department of Education announced that states could grant a one-year transition period for English-language learners in their first year in U.S. public schools, which meant that recent immigrants would be temporarily excluded from their schools' test results. About 5.5 million students, or 12% of all those in grades 1 through 12, would be covered by the new regulations, resulting in an estimated 20% decrease in the number of schools falling short of their academic targets because of such students' poor test results (Dobbs, 2004a).

A third step toward relaxing the *No-Child* regulations allowed non-certified teachers more time to earn certification. And a fourth measure, announced in March 2004, allowed schools to reach the target of 95%-of-students-tested by averaging percentages over a period of three years rather than having to meet the 95% goal each year. For instance, a school that tested only 93% of students one year could reach the 95% average by testing 97% of students the next year. Schools also would not have to count students who missed testing because of a medical emergency (Bush administration, 2004).

**Remaining problems.** Whereas the revised rules helped accommodate learners with severely limited cognitive capacity, the rules failed to care for the needs of many other special-education children who suffered disorders that diminished their ability to learn as effectively as most of their agemates. Those maladies included autism, attention deficit disorder, dyslexia, dyscalculia, blindness, deafness, and more. Peggy Cochran, executive director of the Missouri National Education Association, said that even with the adjustment, "there is still not enough flexibility." She feared that all students could not reach the proficient level, particularly because in Missouri "proficient" had been defined as "above-grade-level work" (Bower, 2003b).

Another difficulty not solved by the revised rules was that of ensuring uniformity of standards for the disabled throughout the nation, since each state set the level of disability that qualified a student as "severely disabled" and each state determined how that level would be measured.

## Accept Responsibility for Flaws

**Type of damage—Increased criticism of officials.** As public awareness of weaknesses in a program continues to mount, politicians who
either sponsored or supported the program face a growing stream of
criticism.

**Federal politician's coping strategy.** One way to deal with critics is to
admit that the program does, indeed, contain defects that need correcting. This is the *mea culpa*—my fault—tactic. When accepting blame for
program flaws, politicians gain credit for integrity and humility, even
though they also expose themselves to censure for having displayed a
lack of wisdom when originally voting the program into law.

**Illustrative cases.** Some members of Congress publicly have voiced
doubt about how judicious they were in supporting the nationwide
achievement-testing plan. Alaska Republican Senator Lisa Murkowski
said she believed the intent was fine, "but did we think through all of the
provisions?" (Bacon, 2003, p. 42).

In mid-2003, four U.S. senators—including Democratic Senator Mark
Dayton of Minnesota—sponsored a bill that would allow states and
school districts to get waivers from the achievement-test requirements.
In order to receive waivers under the proposed Student Flexibility Act,
states would need to demonstrate academic progress on their own.
Dayton claimed that the change represented "sanity in the midst of testing frenzy" and argued that testing had become "the cheap version" of
education reform (Hotakainen, 2003).

Near the end of 2003, Senator John Edwards of North Carolina, who
had voted for the *No-Child Act* in Congress, pledged to "fix" the act,
partly by changing its testing requirements. At the same time, Democrats on the Senate Committee on Health, Education, Labor, and Pensions
sent a letter to committee Chairman Judd Gregg, calling for hearings on
the law's implementation. The letter proposed that the committee hold
hearings focusing on the concerns in so many communities about the *No-
Child* legislation (Olson, 2003e).

**Remaining problems.** Merely admitting faults in legislation does little
good unless politicians follow up their confession of guilt with remedies
that repair the flaws without generating new kinds of damage.

# State-Level Politicians

State politicians include governors, state legislators, elected heads of
state departments of education, and members of the staffs of such officials. State politicians serve both as intermediaries and initiators. As
intermediaries, they receive orders from the federal government and

pass those orders on to school districts. As initiators, officials create laws that affect public schools throughout the state—laws that can bear on such diverse matters as curricula, student evaluation, pupil attendance, length of the school year, funding, textbooks, personnel certification, transporting students, the quality of buildings, school lunches, and more.

In the realm of high-stakes testing, the interaction of state politicians with the federal government and with school districts has been a mixture of abrasive and amicable relations. State officials' coping strategies have included (a) redirecting the blame for testing problems, (b) demanding that the *No-Child-Left-Behind* law be changed, (c) threatening to abandon the federal program, (d) threatening to sue the federal government, (e) emphasizing teacher training, (f) coopting members of protesting groups, (g) expanding the public-information system, (h) accentuating positive features of high-stakes testing while de-emphasizing negative aspects, (i) lowering achievement standards, (j) raising achievement standards, (k) providing extra funds for students from poor families, (l) offering multiple chances to pass tests, (m) providing alternatives to tests, (n) furnishing different school-leaving certificates, (o) providing special incentives, (p) remaining firm but offering alternatives, and (q) rationalizing failure figures.

## Redirect the Blame

**Type of damage—State officials risk public censure.** When a state's or school district's schools show up badly as measured against the federal government's criteria for judging the quality of schooling, state officials may fear that they themselves will be blamed by the voters for the schools' unsatisfactory test scores.

**State politicians' coping strategy.** To avoid responsibility for a regrettable situation, a politician can place the blame elsewhere. In the case of high-stakes testing, this ploy involves state politicians arguing that the fault for the schools' poor performance lies in irrational standards imposed by the federal government.

**Illustrative cases.** Reactions of politicians in New York and Arizona to the federal government's list of "failing schools" are typical of the reactions in numerous other states as well.

After federal officials cited more than 40% of New York City schools (497 out of 1,200) as falling short of the *No-Child Act's* targets, the chairman of the state assembly's education committee called the federal regulations arbitrary, unreasonable, and "screwy." He noted that one small subgroup in a school might have low test scores, while all other subgroups were succeeding and 90% of the overall school population passing the exams; but the school would still be on the failing list. A deputy commissioner of the New York State Education Department said that many of the schools on the under-performing list were faring far better than the schools on the state's own traditional list of schools (Gootman, 2003a).

When Arizona's state department of education released a report on 220 schools that federal officials said had failed to meet performance standards for two to four years, the state's superintendent of public instruction, Tom Horne, called the federal standards unfair. He suggested that parents should put more faith in state rankings which located schools in four categories—underperforming, performing, highly performing, or excelling. Horne pointed out that many of the schools that failed under federal standards were also labeled "underperforming" by the state method. But Arizona's formula for ranking schools was so different that some of the 220 schools ranked as poor performers by federal standards would qualify as "performing" and even "highly performing" under the Arizona criteria (Kossan, 2003c).

**Remaining problems.** In order to accept state officials' claim that federal standards are faulty, members of the public must agree with the arguments state officials present to support their charge. But if people don't agree, then the state officials' stratagem of blaming the federal government is of no avail.

## Demand Changes in the *No-Child-Left-Behind Act*

**Type of damage—School personnel impugned.** School principals and teachers who have been doing a good job can feel demoralized and outraged when they are expected to work miracles with students who come with very different ability levels and social backgrounds. In many instances, teachers with a long history of success are labeled "not qualified" according to federal standards.

**State politicians' coping strategy.** In an effort to mollify educators who feel aggrieved by what they consider irrational requirements of legislation, state officials can (a) publicly agree that the law is unreasonable and (b) identify which of its features should be changed in order to render it both fair and feasible.

**Illustrative cases.** In Oregon, State Superintendent of Public Education Susan Castillo urged federal officials to make major changes in the *No-Child-Left-Behind* law. She objected to the law's requiring the immediate upgrading of teacher qualifications, more testing of special education students, rural schools being held to the same standards as urban schools, and basing judgments of a school's quality on the test results of a single group of students, such as low-income students or ones who speak English as a second language (Hammond, 2003b).

In late February 2004, many of the nation's governors called for revising the federal *No-Child* regulations. The tenor of the criticisms was reflected in the opinion voiced by Governor Gary Locke of Washington, who called the *No-Child-Left-Behind Act* a "very needed, well-intended law," but "we need much more flexibility, and we need to fully fund it" (Richard & Robelen, 2004).

Instead of merely asking that faults in the *No-Child Act* be corrected, Republicans and Democrats in the Oklahoma legislature joined forces to demand that Congress repeal the act entirely (Dillon, 2004c).

**Remaining problems.** Efforts to correct weaknesses in federal legislation will not succeed if (a) federal officials believe the law is correct in its present state or if they are unwilling to admit they erred in originally voting for the law, or (b) the changes that states propose are considered unfeasible by the federal government—particularly if those measures would require substantial federal funding.

## Opt Out of the Federal Program

**Type of damage—States lose control of the education system.** Because under the U.S. Constitution the authority to regulate education is vested in the states rather than in the national government, states are not legally obligated to abide by most types of federal legislation that concerns schools. However, with few exceptions, states do participate in federal programs in order to (a) receive funds provided for those programs by the federal government and (b) avoid the bad publicity that can follow a refusal to participate in programs that most other states accept.

**State politicians' coping strategy.** State authorities can either reject a federal program outright or, before accepting the program, demand changes in it that ameliorate its objectionable features.

**Illustrative cases.** In 2003, the Hawaii legislature passed a resolution discouraging the state schools superintendent from complying with the federal law. Lawmakers in New Hampshire, Vermont, and Maine contemplated bills to prohibit spending state money on costs associated with implementing *No-Child-Left-Behind*. In early 2004, the State of Virginia's Republican-controlled House of Delegates, by a vote of 98 to 1, passed a resolution calling on Congress to exempt states like Virginia from the *No-Child-Left-Behind* program's requirements. The resolution stated that the *No-Child* law was the "most sweeping intrusion" into state and local control of education in the nation's history and would cost "literally millions of dollars that Virginia does not have." No Republicans voted against the resolution, a fact that House Education Committee Chairman James H. Dillard II (R-Fairfax) said is proof that "the damn law is ludicrous" (Becker & Hilderman, 2004). Republican lawmakers joined Democratic counterparts in Arizona, Indiana, Minnesota, New Mexico, Wisconsin, Wyoming, and several other states in opposing provisions of the *No-Child Act*.

As Utah officials struggled to meet the requirements of the act, a state legislator, Margaret Dayton, drafted legislation that would ignore the law and the $103-million of federal money the state would receive for participating in the federal program. Dayton asked, "Does Utah want this much intrusiveness or do we want our schools to be more accountable to parents and their communities?" (Lynn, 2003d).

**Remaining problems.** In Utah, a potentially insurmountable barrier confronting Representative Dayton's proposed legislation was the loss of the $103 the state would receive if it joined in the *No-Child* program. Although Utah officials were very dissatisfied with many of the federal law's mandates, at the same time they felt they could not do without the federal funds. For example, a spokesman for Granite School District pointed out that his district used its annual $13-million in federal money to hire reading specialists, reduce class sizes, and finance drug-and alcohol-prevention programs. He said that losing those benefits "would be devastating" (Lynn, 2003d).

## Prepare to Sue the Federal Government

**Type of damage—States unable to implement *No-Child Act*.** The most persistent complaint about the *No-Child Act* is that the funds provided by the federal government to meet the law's requirements have been woefully inadequate. Without sufficient money, the act is bound to fall short of its goals.

**State politicians' coping strategy.** Persuade the courts to demand that the federal government fully finance the *No-Child Act* or else rescind it.

**Illustrative case.** A first step toward filing a lawsuit against the federal government was taken in mid-2004 by Wisconsin's attorney general, Peg Lautenschlager, when she issued an opinion that the wording of the law made clear that the federal government "can't make states or school districts pay the law's mandated costs for improved education" (Richmond, 2004).

In mid-2003 the National Education Association (NEA)—the country's largest teachers union with over 2.3 million members—called for states to join the union in suing the federal government over the *No-Child Act*.

Although the union did receive the verbal support of the Democratic Governors Association, the governors favored "rigorous discussions" with the administration instead of a lawsuit (Union left behind, 2004).

**Remaining problems.** Lawsuits can be extremely expensive, which means that funds for educational purposes must be diverted to pay lawyers' fees and court costs. Furthermore, the court system often advances at a very slow place, so schools are obliged to continue operating under present conditions (underfunded, in the *No-Child* case) until a final judgment is issued.

Suing the federal government can also be politically dangerous, because federal officials could retaliate against the plaintiffs. By mid-2004 at least 30 state legislatures, including some headed by Republicans, had complained about the *No-Child* law, but none had agreed to join the NEA's proposed court action. Patty Sullivan, deputy director of the Council of Chief State School Officers, explained that it would be both awkward and unwise for states to sue the federal government which monitors and funds so many of the states' important education programs (Union left behind, 2004).

## Emphasize Inservice Teacher Training

**Type of damage—Office holders shamed.** Politicians can suffer humiliation when large numbers of their state's schools are judged unsatisfactory under the *No-Child-Act's* standards.

**State politicians' coping strategy.** On the assumption that ineffective teaching is an important cause of students' low test scores, officials can call for more and better inservice teacher education.

**Illustrative case.** Out of the 1,098 hours of classroom instruction required annually in Michigan schools, 51 hours could be used for teacher training or professional development. In 2004, the state's governor, Jennifer Granholm, proposed that all 51 hours be devoted to upgrading teachers' skills in the areas of reading and math (Hornbeck, 2004).

**Remaining problems.** Limiting professional development to improving instructional techniques in reading and math neglects the need for better training in other subject fields and in the skills of counseling students, working with parents, using computers, and the like.

## Recruit Members of Protesting Groups

**Type of damage—Officials accused of ethnic discrimination.** The problems that accompany high-stakes achievement testing are typically more serious for students from one segment of society than those from other segments. For example, a higher than average rate of test failure occurs among children with disabilities and those from (a) particular ethnic groups (blacks, Hispanics, Native Americans), (b) homes where a language other than English is spoken, and (c) families at the poverty level. Consequently, political activists representing those segments of the population often attack public officials for prejudice against their groups and for not properly adjusting schooling opportunities to the needs of the disadvantaged.

**Politician's coping strategy.** In an effort to stave off charges of prejudicial treatment of a particular group, a politician may coopt members of that group, publicly enlisting them in the politician's cause.

**Illustrative case.** In Florida, after education officials announced in 2003 that large numbers of high-school seniors had failed the state's graduation test, leaders from the black community threatened to boycott the state's citrus and tourist industries unless the state's Republican governor arranged for the seniors to receive high-school diplomas. Some of the state's prominent Democrats joined in criticizing Governor Jeb Bush, who reacted by labeling the threat "politically motivated." As the governor was publicly defending the Florida testing program, he was flanked by State Senator Larcenia Bullard, a black Democrat and vice chairwoman of the Senate education committee. During his speech, Bush turned to Senator Bullard and said, "To suggest that we have a lower standard, a lower expectation for one group of kids, Larcenia, just doesn't make sense. I know you understand that" (Pinzur, 2003a).

**Remaining problems.** Members of the dissident groups may not accept the coopted individuals as suitable spokespersons for their groups and may brand such recruits *traitors, turncoats, renegades,* or *Uncle Tom*s.

## Expand the Public-Information System

**Type of damage—Officials accused of withholding information.** Parents and the general public can be confused and frustrated about the status of academic performance in their school when information regarding the condition of other schools is unavailable. Hence, they blame state officials for failing to report comparative data in the public press.

**Politicians' coping strategy.** Officials seek to dispel criticism by devising better methods of disseminating information about test scores through the news media, particularly via the Internet.

**Illustrative case.** Virginia's Governor Mark R. Warner announced a $1-million to $2-million data base on the Internet that would allow the public to compare schools' performance statewide and within districts. The information would also be on file in libraries. The database would include (a) attendance, dropout, and graduation rates, (b) enrollment trends, (c) student-teacher ratios, (d) descriptions of the age, ethnic, and socioeconomic conditions of the student population, and (e) some national figures for comparing Virginia with the rest of the country (Melton, 2003).

**Remaining problems.** When school funds are in short supply, officials may be reluctant to take money away from essential teaching and administrative activities to finance an expanded information scheme.

## Accentuate the Positive, Deemphasize the Negative

**Type of damage—True status of schools distorted.** As a high-stakes testing program advances from one year to the next, news of continuing low student scores can diminish the public's faith in the proposals by legislators and education-department officials for improving the education system.

**Politicians' coping strategy.** Public reports of test results can begin with a glowing account of whatever evidence of progress can be gleaned from the test outcomes. Then, any results that readers might find disappointing can be mentioned only later in an article and without fanfare.

**Illustrative case.** In late 2003, the opening paragraphs of a typical newspaper account of California's test-based Academic Performance Index informed readers that 90% of the state's high schools had scored higher on the index than in 2002. Nearly 80% had met the target they had set for themselves, so that overall percentages of improvement were significantly higher than in 2002 (Oberthur, 2003).

However, eight paragraphs later, following a detailed description of the state testing program, a less cheerful and somewhat contradictory picture of results appeared. The article noted that the 2003 scores showed that only 21% of the 6,448 schools that were measured had achieved the state target score of 800. About one-quarter of the elementary schools met the statewide standard (a 3% gain over 2002), but the proportion of middle schools that hit the target had dropped two points (16% in 2002 to 14% in 2003) and only 7% of high schools reached the goal (an increase of 1% over 2002) (Obserthur, 2003).

**Remaining problems.** People who have studied the entire article rather than only the opening paragraphs are apt to recognize that state officials have apparently sought to convince the public that the legislators' policies resulted in miraculous educational improvements when, in truth, such improvements—if any—had been quite limited. As a consequence, confidence in politicians' policies and public-relations strategies can decline.

## Lower Achievement Standards

**Type of damage—Officials blamed for high student-failure rate.** As large numbers of students fall below the passing scores set by state officials, politicians can incur the ire of school personnel, parents, and students who consider the standards too strict.

**Politicians' coping strategy.** One obvious way to increase the number of students passing tests is to lower the existing passing mark, or at least to postpone implementing a planned raising of standards.

**Illustrative cases.** News accounts from Texas and New York demonstrate how and why politicians lower test targets.

A standard-reduction strategy was recommended by members of the Texas Board of Education in late 2003. Aware of the bad public impression that would result from high failure rates on the state's standardized test, board members voted to keep in place a lower passing score rather than moving the standard up as previously intended. For instance, on the seventh-grade math test, 73% of students had passed in 2002; but if the standard were raised in 2003 to the intended level, only 62% would have passed (Elliott, 2003).

New York's Regents, who govern the conduct of the state's public education system, traditionally issued diplomas representing different levels of academic accomplishment. The top students who took the most demanding Regents tests were awarded the prestigious Regents diploma. In 1996, passing Regents exams became a requirement for high-school graduation, with the new requirement phased in gradually, starting with one exam and a passing score of 55 (for school districts that thought 65 would be too tough, and that was most districts) and aiming at five exams (English, math, American history, world history, and a science) with a passing score of 65. But in October 2003, the Regents retreated in their requirements. First, for at least two more years, students could pass the exams with scores of 55 rather than 65. Second, the provisions for students with disabilities would be extended by five years. Third, the standard for the physics-science requirement would be reduced to a single introductory course. Fourth, the math curriculum would be simplified, cast in greater detail, and the test made easier (Arenson, 2003a)

**Remaining problems.** Reducing standards, or failing to carry through with a standard-raising plan, invites censure from critics who contend that (a) low expectations lead to low performance and (b) being "too soft" encourages students to fall short of their true potential. Reducing standards can also diminish the public's confidence in state officials by implying that the officials didn't know what they were doing when they first set the standards.

## Raise Achievement Standards

**Type of damage—Officials accused of causing students to hold low educational goals.** Members of the public—and particularly members of the business community who hold high academic expectations for the schools—can blame students' low test performance on educators' setting achievement expectations too low. According to such critics, two interlinked sorts of harm result from holding low standards. First, unless students are challenged to reach their highest potential, they are not going to be motivated to do their best in school. Second, if students leave school with inadequate skills and knowledge, they will not be able to do the jobs required in a technologically advanced society; consequently, America could suffer in the modern world's stiff economic competition.

**Politicians' coping strategy.** Officials can increase the test-score levels that define such categories as *failing, minimally passing, proficient,* and *advanced.*

**Ilustrative case.** In Missouri during 2003, the state standard required at least 19.4% of all students in any subgroup to perform proficiently in communication arts, and at least 9.3% to do the same in math in order to achieve adequate progress. By 2005, the state planned to raise the targets to 38.8% in communication arts and 31.1% in math, with this increasing pace intended to carry schools to 100% proficiency by 2014 (Robertson, 2003).

**Remaining problems.** Because the difficulty level of test items affects the ability of students to correctly answer the questions, an exam containing many hard problems can prevent a large number of students from earning satisfactory scores, thereby causing their schools to miss the achievement targets. As the pressure for schools to hit increasingly higher targets mounts, personnel in schools that enroll large numbers of low-income, limited-English, and disabled students can be tempted to adopt illicit testing and reporting methods in order to avoid negative sanctions. Test administrators cheat by giving students improper help at testing time, altering test scores, and falsifying reports of test outcomes.

## Provide Extra Funds for Students from Poor Families

**Type of damage—Disadvantaged students given too little support.** Students from socially and economically disadvantaged backgrounds have more difficulty succeeding on tests than do students from non-disadvantaged families. Such group differences are revealed in the test reports required by the *No-Child-Left-Behind Act.*

**Politicians' coping strategy.** Extra funds can be provided for services (tutoring, counseling, healthful meals) that enhance disadvantaged learners' chances of earning satisfactory test scores.

**Illustrative case.** Education Trust—an advocacy group for the disadvantaged—reported in late 2003 that states differed significantly in the amount of funds provided to help minority and poor students succeed in school. Nationwide, school districts whose students were mainly white and middle-class received an average of $1,000 more per-pupil in state and local funds than did districts with large numbers of socially disadvantaged students. According to the Trust, districts serving low-income students needed at least 20% more funds per-pupil in order to furnish the same quality of education as that provided for non-disadvantage students. Oregon was one of the 17 states furnishing that much extra money (Hammond, 2003a).

**Remaining problems.** Offering extra funds to districts that serve many minority and poor children reduces the amount of money available to other districts.

## Provide Multiple Opportunities to Pass Tests

**Type of damage—High proportions of students fail state tests on their first try.** If pupils are allowed only one chance to take high-stakes tests, many will likely fail, resulting in very low rates of promotion and graduation. As a result, parents may blame legislators for setting unreasonable standards and may accuse school administrators and teachers of failing to do their jobs properly.

**State politicians' coping strategy.** Legislators pass laws permitting students numerous chances to take state tests.

**Illustrative case.** In March 2004, Washington state lawmakers approved a bill to allow high-school freshmen to retake part or all of the Washington Assessment of Student Learning (WASL) up to four times. If students still did not pass, there would be alternative ways for them to show they had learned what was required. Without the legislation, teenagers would have had only a single chance to pass the exam in their sophomore year. In 2003, hardly more than one-third of students passed on their first attempt (Shaw, 2004).

**Remaining problems.** Providing multiple testing opportunities raises the cost of testing programs by using more staff time for administering tests and by requiring alternate versions of a test so that students will not remember specific items from one testing session to the next.

## Offer Alternatives to Test Performance

**Type of damage—Inaccurate judgments of students' competence.**
Students who perform well in class work but do poorly on high-stakes
tests are not being evaluated fairly if grade promotion and high-school
graduation depend solely on test scores.

**Politicians' coping strategy.**  A wider variety of evidence than just test
scores is adopted for determining whether students deserve to be promoted or to graduate—such evidence as oral responses in class, homework assignments, in-class written work, and contributions to small-
group projects.

**Illustrative cases.**  In New York State, a member of the Board of Regents implored legislators to create an appeals system that allowed students who failed the Regents exams to graduate from high school if they
could show solid performance in their classes and could meet other criteria.  The Regent urged legislators to explore other methods than test
scores—such as portfolios of students' work—for deciding whether students deserved a high-school diploma.  In support of the proposal, a
former school principal in East Harlem, Deborah Meier, blamed the state
testing system for failing to measure most of the qualities she believed
were important in an educated person, including the ability to speak effectively, write a well-reasoned document, do independent research, and
logically assess conflicting evidence (Arenson, 2003b).

Massachusetts adopted an appeals system in 2003 for students who
had missed the state's passing score of 220 by only a few points, but who
had compiled a good attendance record and whose classroom work was
comparable in quality to that of students who had passed the test.
Among the 60,000 students who were tested, 3,000 had failed.  More than
79% (2,373) of the failing students then submitted appeals. After the appeals were screened by a committee and ruled on by the state education
commissioner, 1,191 (50%) were approved.  In defense of the appeals
plan, a spokeswoman for the Massachusetts Department of Education
said the scheme did not represent a lowering of standards but simply
was intended to be fair to students who were "doing 220-level work in
the classroom every day but simply can't do it on a test. They sit down
and take a test and freeze" (Arenson, 2003b).

**Remaining problems.**  Officials may oppose the creation of an appeal
system if they believe it might be abused by allowing incompetent students to graduate, thereby defeating the intent of raising achievement
levels by means of a rigorous testing program.

In the New York case, the notion of an appeal system was rejected by a
Regents Board member who thought it could damage the whole Regents

assessment system by opening a large loophole: "The question is how to create an appeal system" strict enough to keep it from becoming "a wide-open barn door." The existing Regents' scheme was defended by Richard P. Mills, the state education commissioner, who contended that, with the tests, children in New York State were "learning more now than a decade ago." Mills was strongly supported by Joel I. Klein, the New York City schools chancellor, who said that the standards needed to be highly demanding: "Whatever the elements of arbitrariness, whatever the imperfections, we are on the right course" (Arenson, 2003b).

## Offer Alternative School-Leaving Certificates

**Type of damage—Poor employment opportunities.** As well-paying jobs in an increasingly high-tech society require advanced levels of education, students who fail to graduate from high school face a bleak employment future. Thus, youths who lack a high-school diploma typically qualify for only low-skill, insecure jobs that promise little chance for promotion to more satisfying, lucrative positions. The danger of failing to receive a diploma has increased substantially as more states require students to pass high-stakes tests in order to earn a regular diploma.

**Politicians' coping strategy.** Some states have turned to awarding more than one form of school-completion credentials. In addition to regular diplomas, a *certificate of attainment, certificate of attendance,* or *second-tier diploma* may be given to learners who fail the state exit test but have fulfilled course and attendance requirements. High-school dropouts can also later earn a high-school graduation-equivalency GED (General Educational Development) certificate and thereby demonstrate that they have fulfilled high-school requirements.

**Illustrative case.** In December 2003 the Maryland State Board of Education authorized a system of diplomas that would take effect in 2009, thereby enabling current seventh-graders six years to prepare for their high-school graduation. According to the plan, different diplomas would be awarded to students depending on how many of the four state tests they passed: (a) algebra I, (b) English, (c) national, state, and local government, and (d) biology. Students passing all four tests would earn a state diploma. Those passing three tests would earn a local county diploma. Others could be eligible to receive one of two diplomas for special-education students (Sedam, 2003). However, by February 2004 the Board—responding to parents' concerns that some diplomas would be considered inferior—substituted a different solution to the graduation-test problem. The maximum score on each test would be 800. If students failed one of the four tests, they would still be able to graduate if the combined total of all four scores was at least 1,613 (Mui, 2004).

**Remaining problems.**  In alternative-diplomas schemes, such school-leaving documents as certificates of attainment may be regarded by students and the public alike as inferior credentials—unwelcome consolation gifts or booby prizes.  Even GED (General Education Development) papers are often viewed by employers as second-rate documents.

Under Maryland's fail-one-test plan, critics could claim that flunking one test very badly should not be acceptable, so that at least some minimum score should be reached on each test to qualify students for a diploma.  .

## Provide Special Incentives

**Type of damage—Schools fall short of the required number of test-takers.**  Students who object to the state-test requirement for high-school graduation may intentionally avoid taking tests, or they may not bother to prepare themselves adequately for the exams.  Consequently, schools can suffer sanctions under the *No-Child-Left-Behind Act* if fewer than 95% of the members of each subgroup take the state tests or if many of the students who are tested earn low scores.

**Politicians' coping strategy.**  As an additional means of motivating students to do their very best on state tests, officials offer students special recognition in the form of symbols of high merit at the time of high-school graduation.

**Illustrative cases.**  Minnesota Governor Tim Pawlenty proposed the creation of a *Seal of Honor* that would appear on the high-school diplomas of students who earned high scores on the Minnesota Comprehensive Assessments and who met other criteria.  The proposal called for two different seals.

- Governor's Honors, given to students who met state and local requirements, passed state tests, and had at least a 2.5 grade-point average.
- Governor's Advanced Honors, given to students who met state and local requirements, scored in the top two levels of the state tests, had a 3.5 or better grade-point average, and finished two years of foreign-language study (Welsh, 2004a).

Oregon has provided a Certificate of Initial Mastery for high-school students who (a) pass state tests in English, writing, and math and (b) complete eight classroom work-samples in writing, math, and speech. Students who earn a certificate are authorized to wear a special purple tassel on their hat during graduation ceremonies (Anderson, 2004).

**Remaining problems.** For many students who avoid state tests or are reluctant to study diligently in preparing for exams, certificates of merit can be inadequate incentives for changing their behavior.

## Remain Firm but Offer Alternatives

**Type of damage—Tarnished public image.** Mass demonstrations against a public official—with petitioners demanding that the official correct a bad decision—can draw widespread attention to the office holder's alleged incompetence, dishonesty, or unwarranted stubbornness. Hence, such publicity does not bode well for the official's political future.

**Politicians' coping strategy.** Office holders, like most people, are loathe to admit that their past judgments about important matters have been faulty. Therefore, one way they can appear stalwart in defending their past decisions, while still meeting petitioners' demands, is to hold fast to past judgments but at the same time to offer alternative methods of fulfilling the critics' desires.

**Illustrative case.** As noted earlier, when large numbers of Florida high-school seniors failed the state achievement tests and thus would not receive regular diplomas, the students' supporters conducted mass demonstrations, petitioned Governor Jeb Bush to grant amnesty to the seniors, and threatened to boycott key Florida industries. In responding to the demonstrators, the governor's staff reported that the governor was away at the time but an aide would give him the petitions. Bush's press secretary said that, instead of altering the graduation policy, the governor had prepared a new program that could enable students who had failed the state tests to earn a general-equivalency diploma in the future (Pinzur, 2003a).

**Remaining problems.** Dissatisfied parents can argue that a general-equivalency diploma is rarely accorded as much respect as a regular high-school diploma.

## Rationalize the Failure Figures

**Type of damage—Politicians suffer criticism.** Officials can come under attack when large numbers of schools are labeled failures because students have not reached the test-score levels the officials had set.

**Politicians' coping strategy.** To ease the sting of a school's "failure" label, politicians and their staffs can rationalize disappointing test outcomes by interpreting the results to imply that such scores "are really not all that bad." Officials may also claim that problems of test construction are universal and not unique to their own situation. In addition, they may attempt to divert attention away from problems of test construction and test standards by placing the blame for students' poor performance on teachers' inefficient instructional methods.

**Illustrative case.** The New York State deputy commissioner of elementary, middle, and secondary education—James A. Kadamus—used rationalization when responding to questions about why so many schools were dubbed failures and why so many students flunked state math exams. In explaining why 497 schools were cited as substandard, Kadamus proposed that some of the schools might be close to the cutting score that divided *pass* from *fail*, so even though the schools had problems, "I wouldn't use the term 'failing,' because you could be five percentage points from" the cutting score and be on the failure list (Gootman, 2003a)

On another occasion, Kadamus was asked why thousands of the state's high-school seniors had failed the math test, but would still be allowed to graduate. He responded that the math test may not have been quite fair and thus needed some readjustment. Citing New York's long history of preparing Regents' exams, Kadamus implied that test-construction problems were not at all unusual—and, besides, the fault might not be with the test but with teachers' ineffective instruction. He suggested that the test aimed at a level of performance that was new for all students and until now the schools had not found the proper methods to raise students to that level (Hoff, 2003a).

**Remaining problems.** Members of the public may not be satisfied with a politician simply offering excuses for a high incidence of school failures instead of acting to fix the testing system. Furthermore, skilled and dedicated teachers can resent being blamed by political figures for low scores in testing programs that set unreasonably high standards for students who are of varied levels of ability and are from diverse sociocultural backgrounds.

## School-District Politicians

School-district politicians are mostly school-board members elected to office by the district's voters. However, sometimes the governance of a school district will be under the control of political figures other than an elected school board, such figures as a mayor, a city manager, or a state-appointed administrator (C. MacDonald, 2003). Five strategies attempted by school boards to cope with collateral damage are those of (a) forewarning the public of impending trouble, (b) cautioning state officials to move carefully, (c) dismissing opponents, (d) transferring the administration of public schools to private groups, and (e) raising achievement standards.

## Forewarn the Public of Impending Trouble

**Type of damage—Public shocked by sudden bad news.** Local boards of education often foresee the criticism they are likely to incur from their constituents as a result of students in their district failing to meet the test standards set by state and federal officials.

**School board's coping strategy.** To prepare the community for the bad news that will result from instituting high-stakes testing, board members can warn the public of the imminent trouble, can mention that they are trying to work out solutions, and can place the blame—at least by implication—on state and federal officials.

**Illustrative case.** The board of education in Granite, Utah, announced that over the coming weeks, educators, business leaders, legislators, parents, and higher-education leaders would be refining the state board of education's Performance Plus plan. The plan would require elementary school pupils to read proficiently by the end of third grade and to pass tests in reading, writing, math, and science at all grade levels. In middle school and high school, students would pass each course only if they earned a grade of C or better in class work and performed satisfactorily on year-end standardized tests. The plan also required middle-school students to pass classes in pre-algebra, eighth-grade English, and science before they could enter high school. High-school students would need to complete 18 units of credit in core classes, rather than only 15 units, and display core skills in order to graduate. Students who fell short of those standards would take remedial classes or tutoring until they could pass the tests, provided the legislature furnished the $202-million that state education officials estimated the program would cost (Lynn, 2003b).

**Remaining problems.** In speculating about difficulties that could result from the Performance Plus program, Utah board members suggested that students would drop out of school for being labeled failures, even when they received remedial help. To estimate the effect of the plan on individual students, the Performance Plus criteria were applied to four recent Granite graduates' records. This exercise showed that a pair of straight-A students "would likely have had to give up music or advanced placement classes, and two C students might not have graduated on time because of D's or F's in ninth-grade courses" (Lynn, 2003a). Such examples that appeared in the newspapers warned the public that troubles were apparently in the offing.

## Caution State Officials to Move Carefully

**Type of damage—Board members in danger of censure.** Whenever schools are branded as failures, school-board members become the targets of criticism, blamed by parents and assailed in the public press for irresponsibility, stupidity, or malfeasance.

**School board's coping strategy.** In an effort to forestall potential disaster, school-board members warn state officials of dire consequences that could accompany the adoption of a proposed high-stakes testing program.

**Illustrative case.** In the same Utah district that forewarned the public of imminent bad news, the school board advised state leaders not to "jump on the competency-based-education bandwagon" before considering the potential for skyrocketing student dropout rates and a rapid growth in class sizes, along with "a slew of other unintended consequences." Board members predicted that without intensive tutoring and other services, thousands of struggling students would fail to advance through the grades, much less graduate under a proposed statewide plan to increase graduation standards (Lynn, 2003a).

**Remaining problems.** Political pressure from a variety of sources can defeat board members' attempts to effect changes in a proposed state plan. One source of pressure can be the federal government through its legislation and the accompanying funds, as in the case of the *No-Child-Left-Behind Act.* Another source can be influential business leaders who view education from the perspective of a business-management model, which sees schools—like manufacturing plants—as consisting of inputs (raw materials), through-puts (the fashioning of raw materials into products by employees and equipment), and outputs (finished products whose quality is judged by testing). A further source are state legislators and their "expert consultants" who have formulated the proposed innovation and are reluctant to accept advice from local school boards.

## Fire Foes

**Type of damage—Politician's goals blocked.** Political leaders who are in control of a school board can find their education policies opposed by other board members, thereby holding up the implementation of those policies.

**Board chairperson's coping strategy.** Dismiss opponents from the board.

**Illustrative case.** After a new state law gave New York City Mayor Michael Bloomberg control over the city's public schools, the mayor replaced the former school board with a 13-member Panel for Educational Policy. The mayor appointed eight of the panel members, with the remaining five selected by the city's five borough presidents. In March 2004, the mayor introduced a plan to base third-grade children's promotion to fourth grade solely on reading and math test scores, a plan that could mean 20% of the pupils (15,000 of the city's 74,000 third-graders) would be held back. As the mayor's proposal was about to be voted on by panel members, Bloomberg ousted from the panel three members who, he realized, would vote against his plan. He then appointed three new members who he knew would vote in favor of the proposal, and so his plan was promptly approved. In response to critics who condemned the mayor's arbitrary dismissal of panel members, Bloomberg said that the state legislature had given him control over the city's schools and that panel members "are my representatives, and they are going to vote for things I believe in" (Herzenhorn, 2004b).

**Remaining problems.** Politicians who summarily discharge individuals for holding views contrary to their own can incur the wrath of influential individuals and groups who may then retaliate. In the New York case, parents, elected officials, and union leaders were reported to be incensed at the mayor's arbitrary actions (Herzenhorn, 2004b).

## Privatize School Administration

**Types of damage—A multitude of students fail tests.** A high incidence of high-school dropouts and a low percentage of students passing state tests can plague a school district that is strapped for funds.

**School board's coping strategy.** The control of a city's public schools can be transferred to a private corporation which applies a model from the business world to refashion a traditional type of school system.

**Illustrative case.** In St. Louis, Missouri, half of all public high-school freshmen quit school before graduation, and fewer than 7% of juniors scored at the *proficient* level on a state reading and writing test. At the same time, the school district was short of funds to operate the schools in their present form. In an effort to improve students' performance, the school board awarded a New York corporation a $4.8-million contract to overhaul the school system. The corporation brought to the task a 20-year history of reorganizing companies but had never before used its business model for massively restructuring public education. After taking control of the district, the 17-member management team closed 16 schools, dismissed more than 2,000 employees, changed bus routes, and contracted out food services and textbook distribution to private companies. In addition, the team members cut more than $60-million from the budget without laying off any classroom teachers. They also hired 94 reading coaches and ensured that each kindergarten, first-grade, and second-grade teacher had no more than 23 pupils (down from 25 the previous year) (Simon, 2003, p. A8).

**Remaining problems.** The changes wrought by the consultants were met with strong hostility by vocal members of the community. So many parents of black pupils were distressed that several civic leaders urged families to boycott the opening day of school. The head of the teachers union said she believed the quality of education might suffer since she felt the new administration had "poisoned the atmosphere." While she agreed that it might make good economic sense to close 16 schools whose enrollment was declining, she estimated that those schools, in the opinion of parents, were "the only safe, stable haven in their neighborhood" (Simon, 2003, p. A8).

## Raise Achievement Standards

**Type of damage–Unreasonably low performance goals for students.** Just as state politicians can be criticized for tolerating low achievement standards, the same charge can be leveled at district boards and administrators.

**School board's coping strategy.** Board members can respond to critics by demanding higher performance from students, either in the form of more challenging subject-matter requirements for graduation or more stringent test-score levels.

**Illustrative cases.** School-district officials in Portland, Oregon, in late 2003 declared that all freshmen entering high schools in 2004 would be required to pass a course in algebra in order to graduate at the end of their senior year. In keeping with this plan, the city's high schools eliminated general math classes and offered freshmen only algebra or higher-level math courses as a means of preparing them for tenth-grade state achievement tests and for college entrance (Chestnut, 2003b).

Education officials in Howard County, Maryland, set higher achievement goals in 2003. While presenting a state-of-the-school-system report that described the targets, Deputy Superintendent Kimberly Statham said, "The consequences of contentment are much, much too great. We have to keep getting better" (Bishop, 2003). In the Howard plan, every school and student group would meet adequate-yearly-progress standards in 2004, at least 70% of students would perform proficiently in math and reading in 2005, and 70% of each student group (ethnic, economic, English-fluency, learning-ability) would be proficient by 2007.

**Remaining problems.** Unless officials recognize the dominant causes of—and feasible remedies for—unsatisfactory test scores, raising the bar that students are expected to hurdle produces higher, rather than lower, rates of student failure. Elevating standards is particularly futile when the causes of poor test performance are chiefly in the nature of a school's pupil population, such as large numbers of students who suffer from poverty, poor health conditions, inadequate family support for schooling, destructive peer influences, dangerous neighborhoods, limited English skills, physical handicaps, and psychological disabilities. Raising the bar also produces more failure whenever low test scores are caused to a significant degree by poor quality teaching that results from teachers' inadequate instructional skills, low dedication to the job, and difficult working conditions—such conditions as large classes, unruly students, an overload of responsibilities, and insufficient instructional materials. Fortunately, these in-school factors are things district officials can do something about, in contrast to many of the negative factors behind poor test performance that reside in children's' out-of-school lives. Consequently, whenever in-school factors appear to be a significant cause of low test scores, raising standards is reasonable if measures are adopted to improve those factors.

# Conclusion

The coping strategies described throughout this chapter reflect perspectives from which politicians at national, state, and district levels view schooling. It seems clear that elected public-office holders differ from each other in numerous ways—in family backgrounds, ethnic origins, personal wealth, social values, religious affiliation, forms of recreation, length of time in office, and more. Yet, despite such diversity, many politicians appear to share in common certain attributes that can affect their opinions about educational matters. The purpose of this conclusion is to propose two such attributes and to suggest how they may influence politicians' decisions about high-stakes testing.

## Winning Election and Remaining in Office

*Proposition 1: Most politicians' fervent hope is to get into office and securely remain there.*

People who seek political office apparently do so out of various motives, including desires to:

- Improve the quality of life in their nation, state, or community by sponsoring legislation that fosters the general welfare.
- Gain personal prestige from the notoriety associated with holding public office.
- Enjoy a sense of power from having the authority to make decisions affecting other people's lives.
- Pass legislation that benefits a particular group (ethnic, occupational, religious, gender, social-class) or that promotes a particular

belief system (capitalism, socialism, atheism, Darwinism, high-stakes testing).

- Enhance their personal financial condition, not only by the salary and side benefits of the office they seek (expense account, retirement provisions, support services), but also by the opportunities for social contacts that could lead to present and future profits.
- Do the job of policymaking more satisfactorily than have past office holders or than other candidates for the position might do.

Whatever the combination of motives that inspires a particular candidate, that combination cannot be satisfied without the person's besting other contenders in elections. It is therefore necessary for the candidate to convince the majority of voters that he or she is better fitted for office than are competing aspirants. Hence, the purpose of a political campaign is to influence voters' judgments by

(a) publicizing a candidate's name, policies, and such personal virtues as honesty, sincerity, friendliness, fortitude, wisdom, sensitivity to constituents' needs, and experience relevant to the requirements of the political office at stake, and

(b) demeaning—either directly or by implication—the qualifications of competing candidates.

Accomplishing this image-management task costs money. At the school-district level, campaign expenditures can range from hundreds of dollars (in small districts, when incumbents face little opposition) to many thousands (in large districts, when competition is stiff). At the state and national levels, legislators' campaign costs can stretch from the hundreds-of-thousands of dollars into the many millions. Most of these funds do not come from the candidates' own coffers but, rather, from the contributions of people (a) who agree with the office-holder's qualities (as often reflected in an incumbent's voting record) and/or (b) who expect the office-holder to support legislation that advances the contributors' beliefs or welfare. Thus, when politicians accept funds to promote their election, they incur obligations. Their financial supporters expect that, once in office, politicians will (a) initiate and endorse legislation that their supporters favor and (b) furnish supporters special access to the office-holder and government agencies.

How, then, does such a view of politics relate to high-stakes testing? The answer is that it helps account for (a) why high-stakes-testing programs have been introduced at an accelerating rate over the past decade and (b) why those programs have assumed their particular form. One force behind the testing movement has been the widespread publicity given to international studies showing U.S. students scoring below those of various other nations on academic achievement tests. Parallel to the testing studies, a series of reports, such as *A Nation at Risk* (National Commission of Excellence in Education, 1983), portrayed schooling in the United States as fatally flawed.

> If an unfriendly power had attempted to impose on America the mediocre educational performance that exists today, we might well have viewed it as an act of war. As it stands, we have allowed this to happen to ourselves. We have even squandered the gains in achievement made in the wake of the Sputnik challenge. Moreover, we have dismantled essential support systems which helped make those gains possible. We have, in effect, been committing an act of unthinking, unilateral educational disarmament. (National Commission of Excellence in Education, 1983, p. 5)

The American public—appalled to learn that the youth of the most powerful nation in the world were academically inferior to the youth of far less influential nations—was ready for proposals about how to fix America's schools.

At the same time that disappointing news about America's schooling appeared, the nation's job structure was in transition. At a rapidly growing pace, American industries were moving overseas to take advantage of markedly lower labor costs in Latin America and Asia. And industries that remained in the United States increasingly adopted robotics to replace hand labor. Thus, if the country was to remain an industrial leader, its workers would need the advanced skills and creativity that new high-tech processes required. The nation's schools would be expected to produce such workers—adept communicators (reading, writing, speaking) and inventive analysts (science, math). To fill the need for a highly educated work force, industrialists and business leaders launched a vigorous campaign to remedy what they believed were defects in American education. The campaign included (a) sponsoring school-choice programs, charter schools, and school vouchers that furnished parents alternatives to traditional public schools, (b) requiring high academic standards for all students, and (c) urging states and the federal government to make schools openly accountable for the quality of their students by imposing high-stakes testing. At the national level, this campaign resulted in the adoption by Congress in 2001 of the Bush administration's *No–Child-Left-Behind Act* that took effect in January 2002.

Given the public's distress about American students' disappointing test scores and the business community's demand for a well-educated labor force, it seems hardly surprising that legislators at both the state and national levels felt compelled to support high-stakes testing if they were to remain in office. The majority of voters—and, particularly, the lawmakers' financial backers—expected the politicians to do something dramatic to repair the schools. High-stakes testing seemed to be that something.  Both the motto and goals of the *No-Child-Left-Behind* plan had a public appeal that politicians could hardly ignore.  Everyone agreed it would be great to have students of all ethnic origins and of all ability levels achieve at a high academic level.  Everyone agreed that it would be marvelous to have all classrooms staffed by teachers of impressive skill and dedication.  And everyone agreed that such outcomes should be produced at relatively modest cost.  Consequently, even though the *No-Child* plan was a Republican initiative, a high proportion of Democrats in Congress joined the Republicans in voting the proposal into law.  Voting for the act looked like a good way to stay in office.

Only when weaknesses of the *No-Child* plan began to appear over the period 2002-2004 did a significant number of politicians begin assailing high-stakes programs.  A typical critique was one by former Vermont Governor Howard Dean as he sought the Democratic nomination for president in 2004.  Dean acknowledged that the ideals expressed in the *No-Child* legislation were admirable, but he considered the methods of pursuing those ideals to be very unrealistic.  The features of the *No-Child* plan that Dean attacked included (a) its great expense, (b) the expectation that the states would pay most of the costs, (c) the rigidity of the program's standards, and (d) the one-size-fits-all expectation for schools' yearly progress, so that "26,000 of America's 93,000 schools 'failed' to make adequate yearly progress in 2003, and many are not receiving the additional support they need to improve" (Dean, 2004).

## Suffering from Inadequate Knowledge

*Proposition 2:  Politicians have little understanding of the multiple factors that affect students' academic success and of how those factors can interact.*

The provisions of the *No-Child Act*, as well as the components of states' high-stakes-testing legislation, suggest that the politicians who voted such measures into law were poorly informed about (a) child and adolescent development and (b) the teaching process.  Perhaps the fact that, when they themselves were pupils, they had spent more than a dozen years in classrooms, and thus they now believed they understood what schooling is all about.  However, seeing teaching from behind a pupil's desk produces quite a different sort of knowledge than does seeing it from a teacher's perspective.  Whereas a pupil need only adjust his or her ability and interests to the instruction the teacher offers, a truly successful teacher must accommodate instruction to the varied ability levels and attitudes of 30 or so different learners.  This is a feat requiring skill in analyzing individual pupils' talents, learning styles, misconceptions, interests, motives, family circumstances, and peer influences.  The teacher's task also requires a command of diverse instructional methods, an understanding of conditions under which each method will work, and the flexibility in classroom practice that allows the use of varied methods.

Most politicians—predominantly trained as lawyers and business executives—lack the experience that would equip them to understand what it takes to be a successful teacher. As a consequence, they often seem prone to pass laws that set unrealistic standards of achievement and that restrict the flexibility school personnel need to promote each child's progress. Among the components of the *No-Child-Left-Behind Act* that are ridiculous—in view of the realities of human development, societal forces, and classroom conditions—are the requirements that (a) all students be *proficient* in reading and math by 2014 and (b) progress toward that goal be made in regular increments (straight-line improvement) between 2002 and 2014.

# 7

# Educational Administrators and Their Staffs

The term *administrators* refers to educational personnel who are appointed to direct the conduct of schooling at national, state, school-district, and school levels. Administrators serve in policy-making and supervisory roles. They do not teach students, nor do they usually carry out such services as counseling, testing, tutoring, nursing, transporting, or serving lunch.

At the national level, the most important administrators are the secretary of education and the secretary's support staff in the U.S. Department of Education. At the state level, the key administrators are the state superintendent of public instruction and the superintendent's staff in the state department of education. Administrators within a school district are responsible for organizing and directing the school system's operation under such titles as superintendent, associate superintendent, curriculum director, budget director, and supervisor of instruction. In individual schools, the chief administrator is usually the principal, often aided by assistant principals, a dean of students, a director of business operations, a facilities manager, and the like.

Chapter 7 is divided into five parts. Part 1 concerns administrators' coping strategies that are of nationwide scope. Part 2 analyzes strategies at the statewide level, Part 3 at the district level, and Part 4 at the individual-school level. Part 5, titled "Conclusion," suggests ways that typical characteristics of administrators may help explain their coping behavior.

# Nationwide Coping Strategies

At the national level, the connection between the politicians from the political party in power and the administrators in the U.S. Department of Education is so close that it is virtually impossible to tell them apart. That intimate relationship was demonstrated in Chapter 6 where the nation's president and the secretary of education expressed identical opinions and adopted similar coping strategies in responding to ostensible damage from the *No-Child-Left-Behind Act*.

**Main types of damage—Diminished public faith in the *No-Child* plan and resentment at federal intrusion into states' rights.** As newspapers reported a growing spate of problems with implementing the federal testing program, the sponsors of the plan were in danger of the public's doubting Washington politicians' ability to govern. Critics charged federal officials with destructive meddling in the conduct of schooling and with underfunding mandatory programs.

**Coping attempts.** In addition to the national government's strategies described in Chapter 6, federal administrators and their staffs have (a) sent representatives around the nation to mollify distressed school personnel, parents, and state legislators, (b) yielded slightly on a few standards, and (c) assigned demeaning labels to critics.

## Send Staff Members on Appeasement Missions

**Federal administrators' coping strategy.** In an effort to stop—or at least to reduce—politically harmful criticism, representatives from the U.S. Department of Education traveled across the nation, defending the *No-Child Act* at gatherings of perturbed state legislators, school personnel, and parents.

**Illustrative case.** One evening in late February, 2004, Ken Meyer

was smiling gamely from a gloomy high school stage at an audience of disgruntled teachers and parents to whom he had been introduced as "a bigwig from Washington," come to Utah to explain President Bush's centerpiece education law. . . . Mr. Meyer's job is to barnstorm the country, part goodwill diplomat, part flak-catcher, calming emotions and clarifying misunderstandings. He is one of many Bush administration officials traveling to explain the 700-page law. Since Feb. 8 [2004], at least 10 other department and White House officials have spoken in nine states.

"I've been in some, I don't want to say hostile, but very contentious environments" in recent months, Mr. Meyer said. "Places where I wondered whether I'd get out of there with my skin intact. This law is largely misunderstood by the public because of its enormity, so people get emotional about it, and you've got pent-up frustrations." (Dillon, 2004b) (Copyright © 2004 by The New York Times Co. Reprinted by permission)

**Remaining problems.** Federal-government representatives who attempt to soothe local critics with explanations and promises are not likely to succeed with their task if they fail to effect the changes the critics demand. Such has been the case with states' and local districts' complaints that the federal government has (a) underfunded obligatory programs, (b) set unreasonable test-performance standards for disabled and limited-English pupils, and (c) imposed unreasonable annual test-score targets, particularly for schools that enroll large numbers of children from economically disadvantaged homes.

## Yield Slightly on a Few Standards

**Federal administrators' coping strategy.** To deal with the most persistent complaints from school systems, officials in the U.S. Department of Education reluctantly altered the *No-Child* requirements in small ways so as to diminish criticism without weakening the law's intent.

**Illustrative cases.** Between December 2003 and April 2004, the Department of Education announced minor adjustments in implementing the *No-Child Act*: Students who had recently immigrated from non-English-speaking cultures would be allowed more time to gain English proficiency. Teachers who lacked full certification would be allowed more time to earn certificates. The reading and math skills of acutely disabled students could be evaluated by means of special testing procedures. Students who failed to show up on testing days because of serious medical emergencies would not be counted against the requirement that the school test at least 95% of the students in any of the law's required subgroups. Schools could average test-participation rates over three years to reach the 95% level rather than having to meet that standard each year (Robelen, 2004a; Schemo, 2004).

By mid-2004, more than 40 states had requested permission to revise some *No-Child* regulations. For example, Connecticut officials asked that tutoring or transferring children to other schools apply only to subgroups of students who failed to make annual targets, not to the entire school population. Many states requested more time and flexibility for testing special-education students. However, Raymond J. Simon, the U.S. Department of Education's assistant secretary for elementary and secondary education, rejected a variety of proposed changes on the grounds that "Our goal is to wring every ounce of flexibility out of the law, but not to change the law" (Olson, 2004c).

**Remaining problems.** Opponents of the *No-Child Act* charged that meager adjustments in implementing the act failed to correct such fundamental problems as (a) limiting evaluation to multiple-choice tests, (b) treating all schools as if their student populations were alike, (c) judging teachers' competence on the basis of a standardized test, and (d) usurping states' and school districts' authority to fashion curricula and evaluation methods to suit the nature of their communities.

## Call Critics Bad Names

**Federal administrators' coping strategy.** Frustrated by faultfinders' attacks on the *No-Child* testing program, federal officials on occasion have publicly affixed unsavory labels to the program's critics.

**Illustrative case.** In late February 2004, Education Secretary Roderick Paige called the National Education Association a "terrorist organization" after the 2.3-million-member teachers union criticized the *No-Child* plan's implementation. Paige made the comment while speaking to the nation's governors at a private White House meeting. Later he said his remark had been "a bad joke; it was an inappropriate choice of words" (Tanner, 2004).

**Remaining problems.** During a presidential-election year, the secretary's comments were seen as potentially damaging for the Republican Party, in that the *No-Child-Left-Behind Act* had been touted as the showpiece legislation of the Bush administration's domestic program. Not only could the remarks incur the ire of the nation's largest teachers union but, according to the chairman of the Democratic National Committee, the comments might also be seen by the public as "comparing those who teach America's children to terrorists" (Feller, 2004).

Jeffry R. Ryan, the Massachusetts teacher of the year refused to attend a conference in Washington honoring the nation's top educators in March 2004 because Ryan resented Paige's comment. Ryan, responding to Paige's dismissing the remark as a bad joke, said, "Terrorism isn't funny. I just couldn't show up and shake that man's hand after he made those remarks" (Teacher of year, 2004).

# State Coping Strategies

Administrators at the state level have attempted a variety of coping strategies, including those of (a) furnishing extra help to low-scoring schools, (b) providing fix-up teams for failing schools, (c) identifying improvement factors, (d) advocating a growth model, (e) preferring states' own evaluation systems, (f) reanalyzing school-performance data, (g) adopting alternative tests for special students, (h) urging Congress to abolish the testing law, (i) delaying the increase in standards, (j) fudging cutting scores, (k) not reporting failing schools, (l) granting waivers, and (m) altering teacher-qualification rules.

## Offer Special Help to Low-Scoring Schools

**Type of damage—Causes of low scores are not remedied.** In schools whose students perform poorly on tests, likely causes of low scores may go uncorrected so that unsatisfactory test results continue year after year.

**State administrators' coping strategy.** Extra help in altering certain causes of students' poor test performance (teachers' inadequate training, shortage of suitable learning materials, ineffective administrative leadership) can be offered to school districts.

**Illustrative case.** In 1999, before the *No-Child Act* was introduced, the North Carolina Department of Education distributed $19.6-million to seven school districts who students were the lowest performers on state tests. The special funds were used to reduce class size to a maximum of 15 pupils in kindergarten through third grade. The state also offered to pay the salary and an annual bonus of about $17,000 for three years for "teacher on-site specialists" to work in troubled schools. Each impaired district could have up to five such teachers. In addition, the state would pay the salaries and a 25% bonus for replacement principals in low-performing schools (Johnston, 1999a).

**Remaining problems.** The superintendent of one of the seven low-scoring districts said he was not enthusiastic about the on-site specialists. "We're talking about coming to a remote, academically disadvantaged area. If they wanted to be teaching in an area like this, they'd be here already" (Johnston, 1999a).

## Organize Fix-up Teams for Failing Schools

**Type of damage—Lack of progress with existing personnel.** Some observers of low-performing schools have questioned the ability of those schools' current personnel to mount the corrective measures that would raise students' test scores. Thus, continued low performance could be expected in the future.

**State administrators' strategy.** One solution involves recruiting especially skilled teachers and school administrators to help fix the problems at "failing" schools.

**Illustrative cases.** The Arizona Department of Education in late 2003 introduced a plan to recruit highly competent teachers and administrators to help 136 under-performing schools. Rather than import national consultants, state officials sought well-trained local experts, including master teachers, successful principals, and school-district business officers. The dual intent was (a) to develop a group of specialists readily at hand to help schools year after year and (b) to have the specialists teach their newly acquired skills to colleagues back in their own schools (Kossan, 2003d).

**Remaining problems.** Some Arizona educators were concerned about the quality of team members. One principal said she would welcome some veterans to help train a host of new teachers at her school by showing new teachers how to manage a classroom and by offering experienced teachers new instructional techniques that were supported by recent research. But she was worried about the quality of the fix-up-team members and about how much power they would have to effect change (Kossan, 2003d).

## Identify Improvement Factors

**Type of damage—Large numbers of students fail tests.** As a result, students become discouraged, more drop out of school, and schools suffer punitive sanctions.

**State administrators' coping strategy.** Different schools' pupil populations can be analyzed to reveal factors that apparently influence why pupils in one school produce better test results than those in another.

**Illustrative case.** Researchers in Illinois identified 27 schools that produced high test scores despite serving poor children. Although more than half of the students were from low-income families, at least 60% of them met state standards in reading and math during 2003. All groups —special education, ethnic, bilingual—reached the *No-Child-Act* standard for adequate yearly progress. The research team, upon comparing those schools with others that enrolled poor children but had low test scores, discovered four characteristics that distinguished the higher-ranking schools from the others—strong leaders, an emphasis on early literacy, high-quality professional development, and more learning time. For instance, Violet Tantillo, principal of Jefferson School in Berwyn, said that reading was the most important subject at her school where 79% of the pupils qualified for free or reduced-fee lunches and where 75% of the children were Hispanic (Grossman, 2003b).

**Remaining problems.** Whereas spending so much time on reading helps ensure that children command a skill vital to success in most school subjects, it also reduces—and may eliminate—time for social studies, math, science, the arts, and languages.

## Adopt an Alternative Growth Model

**Type of damage—Successful schools appear to be failures.** Some observers charge that the *No-Child* model of school progress is too rigid, so that it fails to recognize schools whose students are improving but do not fit the pattern dictated by the *No-Child Act*.

**State administrators' coping strategy.** Models of school improvement, other than the *No-Child* variety, can be devised to more adequately accommodate the differences among schools, their student populations, their staffs, and the surrounding communities.

**Illustrative case.** In 2004, a group of 14 chief state school officers proposed a school-improvement "growth model" as an alternative to the *No-Child* approach. The state chiefs argued that, under the federal mandate, states lacked the freedom to adopt more suitable models for judging schools' progress (Archibald, 2004b).

**Remaining problems.** The 14 sponsors of the "growth model" hoped that their organization, the Council of Chief State School Officers, would endorse the proposal, but that hope was shattered when more than 80 black and Hispanic school superintendents across the nation strongly objected to such a change, asserting that altering the *No-Child's* design which revealed achievement gaps between whites and minorities would "send the wrong message" about how schooling in America has traditionally favored whites over other ethnic groups (Archibald, 2004b).

## Give Priority to States' Evaluation Systems

**Type of damage—Downgraded accountability.** Before the federal government passed the *No-Child-Left-Behind Act*, most states already had their own assessment programs in operation. In many cases, state leaders feared that replacing the existing programs with the federal plan would downgrade school accountability.

**State administrators' coping strategy.** A state's evaluation system can be given priority over the federal testing plan, or the two can be merged.

**Illustrative case.** In Kentucky, a group of 24 school superintendents in December 2003 told the State Board of Education that they wanted to retain CATS (Commonwealth Accountability Testing System) as the state's school-accountability instrument because CATS covered seven subject areas with both multiple-choice and written-response questions as well as a portfolio of a student's writing over time. In contrast, the *No-Child* program focused solely on reading and math. In their appeal to the Board, the group said that "a vast majority" of Kentucky's 176 su-

perintendents endorsed the plan to incorporate the new federal requirements into the state system without lowering high academic-
achievement standards. The group added that, in addition to reducing
school accountability, "scrapping CATS would limit students' development of real-world skills and reduce the amount of assistance offered to
low-performing schools" (Superintendents: Replacing CATS will harm
schools, 2003).

**Remaining problems.** Some states' evaluation systems are incompati-
ble with federal requirements, particularly in regard what constitutes
"proficient" test performance. Consequently, merging the two becomes
difficult or impossible. In addition, if the results of federal and state
testing standards are reported separately, parents can be confused about
which report is the more valid whenever there is a discrepancy between
the two. This puzzlement is particularly disturbing when schools are
judged unsatisfactory under the federal plan but not under a state program.

## Reanalyze School-Performance Data

**Type of damage—Schools burdened with undeserved failing label.**
The complex requirements of high-stakes programs can result in schools
being unjustly deemed inadequate.

**State administrators' coping strategy.** School districts can appeal a
state department's appraisal and thereby prompt a reassessment of test
outcomes.

**Illustrative cases.** As a result of school districts complaining that they
did not deserve a failing label, some state departments of education have
become more diligent about cleaning up erroneous data and recording
information accurately. In Texas, the number of schools meeting annual
improvement targets rose from 74% to 81% following such appeals. The
proportion of Mississippi schools that were credited with adequate
yearly progress rose from about 50% to 75% after the state changed one
criterion for rating schools. In Georgia, 840 of the state's 2,000 schools
were reported in late 2003 to have fallen below the *No-Child-Act's* passing level. After 430 of the "failing schools" appealed to have their situations reviewed, state officials reevaluated the cases and determined that
117 schools should be removed from the "unsatisfactory-performance"
list (Olson, 2004a; Tofig, 2003b)

**Remaining problems.** The more frequently people read of errors in
calculating test results, the less confidence they have in the testing system. The situation is particularly frustrating for schools that were first
labeled failures but were subsequently removed from the failure list after

the test scores were reappraised; a later revision of the earlier report may not be sufficient to repair the damage that the original report did to the school's reputation.

## Adopt Alternative Tests for Students with Special Needs

**Type of damage—Students with disabilities fare badly on regular tests.** Special-education students' physical and psychological disorders can impair their ability to take tests that are built for their non-disabled agemates.

**State administrators' coping strategy.** Special tests or special provisions for taking regular tests can give exceptional students a fair opportunity to display what they have learned.

**Illustrative case.** In 2004, special-needs students in Arizona could take the state standardized test (Arizona Instrument to Measure Standards—AIMS) that matched their skill level rather than their grade level. Hence, children with "significant cognitive disabilities" were allowed to take AIMS below their grade level or to take AIMS-A, an alternate exam for school-age children who functioned at a pre-kindergarten level. The selected pupils included ones with mild, moderate, or severe mental retardation; multiple disabilities with retardation; or multiple disabilities with sensory impairment and retardation. It also included students whose academic performance was within the same range as students with mental retardation. In 2003, 25,000 special-needs students took AIMS below their grade level, but in 2004 that number was cut in half, with the remaining 12,500 taking grade-level AIMS with accommodations, "such as extra time for the test, permission to use a calculator, or consent to have the test read out loud" (Galehouse, 2004).

**Remaining problems.** Employers and college-admission officials—and oftentimes parents—are typically interested in knowing how well students perform when judged by the same standards as their agemates. Hence, such officials are not satisfied with receiving test results for students who (a) have not taken the same tests as everyone else or (b) did not take tests under the same conditions. Therefore, such people may be unwilling to consider candidates for employment or college admission who took tests designed for the physically or psychologically handicapped.

## Press Congress to Abolish High-Stakes-Testing Law

**Types of damage—Disheartened administrators.** Dissatisfied educators complain that the *No-Child-Left-Behind Act* is too punitive and is underfunded. Requiring students to perform at a level beyond their ability is demoralizing for both the students and their teachers. Especially objectionable are the law's (a) punishing schools that serve disadvantaged students, (b) requiring too much data collecting, (c) failing to assess how much progress schools make with individual students, and (d) being designed to give public schools a bad reputation (Hammond, 2003d).

**State administrators' coping strategy.** Critics of high-stakes testing laws can assemble educators from different levels of the schooling hierarchy to meet with members of Congress, urging the lawmakers to scuttle the act entirely rather than to try repairing it.

**Illustrative case** A collection of Portland-area educators and parents asked Senator Ron Wyden to have Congress stop trying to fix the *No-Child-Left-Behind Act* and, instead, to eliminate it altogether. The group complained that the law was basically too defective to be fixed. The penel members included a variety of individuals—four school superintendents, two school-board members, top administrators from four cities, teachers from Portland, and parent-teacher-association leaders from three communities (Hammond, 2003d).

**Remaining problems.** Politicians who had originally voted in favor of the *No-Child Act* would less likely support a proposal to eliminate the law than ones who had not voted for it. Furthermore, members of Congress who wished to maintain amicable relations with the George W. Bush administration might be expected to resist efforts to abolish the *No-Child* plan.

## Delay the Raising of Standards

**Type of damage—Likely high incidence of failures.** Administrators often begin a high-stakes-testing program with a lower passing score than they believe is desirable. They adopt a low initial standard because they fear too many students might otherwise earn failing marks, thereby setting off a public outcry that the evaluation system was unfair. On the belief that the pressure exerted on students and teachers by high-stakes testing will result in significantly improved student test scores as the years advance, administrators can consider it feasible to raise the passing standard periodically without eliciting critics' claim that the standard is unreasonably high. However, the schools' recent test results may suggest that a planned higher standard would produce an unacceptably greater number of failures and would foment widespread attacks on state decision-makers.

**State administrators' coping strategy.**   Authorities can delay the implementation of a planned higher standard in order to promote the impression that they are still dedicated to high standards but, at the same time, are reasonable, compassionate individuals.

**Illustrative case.**   In late 2003, New York State officials postponed for three years an intended increase in the passing score on high-school exit exams because the present rate of failures suggested that thousands of students would likely be denied diplomas if the standard were raised. The state commissioner of education, Richard P. Mills, said that the next three years would witness a "renewed, rigorous, and relentless statewide effort" to raise student achievement from the present passing score of 55 (on a 100-point scale) to a new passing score of 65 on tests in English, math, world history, American history, and one science subject (Hoff, 2003c).

**Remaining problems.**   Proponents of high standards may accuse officials of cowardice or double-dealing for officially setting high standards, yet failing to put them into practice.   In addition, school-district personnel may be confused about which standard to apply and when to apply it.

## Fudge the Cutting Scores

**Type of damage—Schools fail to make hoped-for progress.**   In pursuing the goal of having all students at or above the proficiency level by 2014 on reading and math tests, state officials hope to have test scores rise substantially from one year to the next.   Whenever scores do not improve at the desired rate, officials fear they will be blamed.

**State administrators' coping strategy.**   One way to convey the appearance of substantial annual growth in test scores is to lower the cutting points between score categories from one year to the next.   Adopting such a ploy means that this year a lower test score is accepted as signifying proficiency than was accepted last year.

**Illustrative case.**   The Minnesota Department of Education reported that 2003 language-arts and math test scores improved markedly over 2002 scores.   However, the joy occasioned by such apparent progress diminished when analysts revealed that state officials had lowered the cutting scores in 2003.   As a result, fifth-graders' average reading score was reported as improving from 75 to 81, whereas it actually had not risen at all.   The percent of third-graders passing the reading test, reported as up 10 points from 67% to 77%, actually rose only four points—67% to 71%.   By the officials' lowering the standard in 2003, only

143 schools throughout the state were accused of not making adequate yearly progress. An additional 50 would have joined those ranks if the original passing standard had been applied (Walsh, 2004).

**Remaining problems.** Whenever misleading reporting practices are exposed, the public is apt to doubt other claims of progress that state officials report, thereby diminishing faith in the school system.

## Avoid Reporting Failing Schools

**Type of damage—The disgrace of being labeled a failing school.** Under the *No-Child Act,* schools without a majority of fourth- and eighth-graders testing at a *proficient* level for reading and math suffer the disgrace of being dubbed *needing improvement* and may also face sanctions that could lead to a takeover or closure by the state after a fifth year of unsatisfactory progress.

**State administrators' coping strategy.** In an effort to avoid sanctions that low test scores provoke, personnel at the state or district level can neglect to report all of the schools that have fallen below the set standard.

**Illustrative case.** By early 2004, the total of 5,200 schools listed as low-performing—from among the nation's 91,380 public elementary and secondary schools—was 40% lower than the U.S. Department of Education's list of 8,652 schools needing improvement the previous year. Observers noted that, as the years advanced, the number of low-performing schools should be increasing as standards were annually stiffened. Thus, it appeared that many low-performing schools were not being reported for the 2003-2004 school year. Secretary of Education Roderick Paige suggested that some districts and states were "playing games" to avoid being held accountable for poor teaching. "There will be those that will push the envelope and try to game the system" (Archibald, 2004a).

**Remaining problems.** Suspicion that a state or district intentionally avoided reporting all failing schools may cause federal officials to withhold support funds. Newspaper reports of proven incidents of such mendacity can damage the school system's reputation in the eyes of the public.

## Grant Waivers

**Type of damage—High rates of non-promotion and non-graduation.** Students' lives can be damaged by their failing to be promoted from one grade to the next or by their being denied a high-school diploma. Furthermore, parents of such students can threaten the tranquility of administrators' lives by complaining that their offspring have been treated unjustly.

**State administrators' coping strategy.** A system can be established for granting exceptions to the strict application of promotion and graduation standards.

**Illustrative cases.** In Massachusetts, students who missed passing the state graduation test by less than five points and who had a good record of school attendance could appeal for a waiver. In 2003, 50% of such appeals were granted. That percentage rose to 93% in 2004 as a result of (a) district superintendents becoming more adept at filing waiver applications and (b) state officials considering additional conditions in students' lives (Rothstein, 2004b).

Early in 2004, the California State Board of Education granted the Santa Cruz School District a waiver exempting students from the law requiring one year of algebra in order to earn a high-school diploma. Within the next few months more than 200 other districts applied for the same waiver (Schools get Waivers, 2004).

**Remaining problems.** When one waiver is permitted, other districts will apply for exemptions as well. If all such appeals are honored, then the intent of the law is defeated. But if only a few applications are granted, officials are open to charges of favoritism and corruption.

## Alter Teacher-Qualification Requirements

**Type of damage—Many teachers labeled "unqualified."** When school districts introduce a policy of requiring teachers to pass written tests over the content of the subjects they teach, veteran middle-school and high-school teachers may fail the tests and thereby not meet the federal standard of "fully qualified."

**State administrators' coping strategy.** Teachers who fail content-area tests can earn qualified status by demonstrating their competence in other ways.

**Illustrative case.** The Pennsylvania Board of Education in mid-2004 eliminated the requirement that all teachers must pass content tests in order to be considered properly qualified. The new rule applied to seventh- and eighth-grade teachers who had elementary or general certification and who taught math, science, English, or social studies. The revised regulation also applied to the fields of special education and English-as-a-second-language. In 2003, nearly one-quarter of such teachers had failed the content tests. But the new rules provided teachers a three-year extension called "bridge certification" founded on such evidence of competence as satisfactory teaching experience, attending inservice-education sessions, completing or teaching college classes in their subject field, writing professional articles, tutoring, and winning teaching awards (Mezzacappa, 2004).

**Remaining problems.** Critics of Pennsylvania's alternative-certification policy complained that it permitted teachers who were under-qualified to stay in the classroom. Baruch Kintisch of the Education Law Center assailed the policy as being too vague to tell what a teacher must do to become highly qualified. He feared that standards of subject-matter knowledge were being lowered for teachers who worked with the most vulnerable students (Mezzacappa, 2004).

# School-District Coping Strategies

District superintendents and their immediate assistants ply their trade amidst social pressure from a variety of sources, both within and outside the school system. Strategies they adopt in response to the pressure include those of (a) blaming the legislators who passed the high-stakes-testing laws, (b) filing lawsuits, (c) demanding changes in high-stakes legislation, (d) adopting a different auditing method, (e) holding students back, (f) awarding themselves high marks, (g) delaying decisions, (h) searching for achievement-gap causes, (i) adopting multiple corrective measures, (j) offering students multiple chances to pass tests, (k) intensifying English instruction for immigrants, (l) substituting alternative evaluation methods, (m) developing a different evaluation system, (n) trying new curriculum designs, (o) furnishing cash rewards for test-score improvement, (p) hiring more and better teachers, (q) offering incentive pay, (r) offering teachers bonuses, (s) providing special teacher training, (t) improving the system for reaching parents, (u) requiring summer-school attendance, (v) tutoring, (w) improving classroom visits, (x) rescuing dropouts, and (y) feeding test-takers. In the following pages, the 25 strategies are presented in a sequence extending from ways of resisting, evading, or altering the demands of high-stakes plans to ways of accommodating those demands.

## Blame the Lawmakers

**Type of damage—Public disgrace.** The announcement that hordes of schools have been called failures on the basis of students' test scores typically sets off public attacks on a school district's administrators. Critics may charge administrators with incompetence and demand that officials be investigated, reprimanded, demoted, or dismissed.

**District administrators' coping strategy.** To explain and defend their schools' performance, administrators can fault federal and state legislators for what local school personnel view as unreasonable requirements in state education laws and in the federal *No-Child-Left-Behind Act.* The strategy of publicly blaming lawmakers can serve two aims of local school personnel: (a) deflect the blame for "failed schools" and "failing students" from district personnel to agencies farther up the political-authority hierarchy and (b) embarrass legislators into correcting flaws in education laws by subjecting them and their staffs to publicized censure.

**Illustrative cases.** Matters addressed in the following examples include (a) contradictory laws, (b) unrealistic standards, and (c) inappropriate criteria.

*Contradictory laws.* As a result of the conflict between two federal laws, 30 Maryland elementary schools failed to meet the *No-Child* standards because teachers had given test aid to thousands of third-graders who had disabilities or limited English skills. An earlier law had provided for teachers to read test questions to students with limited English skills and to special-education students whose individual education plans required such accommodation. However, under the *No-Child-Act's* rules, test scores must be thrown out if children receive such help. In 2003, the private company responsible for scoring the Maryland exams discarded the entire test of any child who had received help (Mathews & Mui, 2003).

*Unrealistic standards.* Nearly two-thirds of New Jersey high schools fell short of the *No-Child Act's* standards in 2003. According to Edwina M. Lee, executive director of the state's School Boards Association, it would be possible for an entire school to be accused of insufficient progress "if only six students . . . did not pass the state test." The Association, representing more than 600 New Jersey school districts, planned to lobby Congress to change the way academic progress was reported under the federal law (Callas, 2003).

*Inappropriate criteria.* Commenting on the high incidence of Arizona schools receiving unsatisfactory ratings under the *No-Child* law, Paul Koehler said that the federal government's formula for determining adequate yearly progress was too new to be reliable, had no record of success, and was not the best way to judge a school's quality. Koehler, director of WestEd research service, noted that the federal formula was not even applied in the same fashion from state to state (Kossan, 2003b)

**Remaining problems.** The public may not believe the claim that schools' low test scores have been the result of defects in state or federal testing requirements. Instead, the public may interpret the claim as an attempt by school personnel to divert attention from their own incompetence.

## File Lawsuits

**Type of damage—Inadequate yearly progress.** Many school districts contend that they lack enough money to achieve the level of adequate yearly progress required in the federal *No-Child* law.

**District administrators' coping strategy.** Officials use lawsuits as a means of forcing state legislators to raise the state's financial contribution to public schools.

**Illustrative cases.** In 2003, four Nebraska school districts filed a lawsuit contending that the state's current funding levels left the districts without enough money to offer full-day kindergarten, smaller classes, summer school, and other services needed to provide an adequate education. The Omaha attorney representing the four districts said that whenever large numbers of children were not becoming proficient, they were "almost by definition" failing to receive the sort of education they deserved under the state's constitution and education laws (Hoff, 2003b).

School officials in Reading, Pennsylvania, filed a suit contending that the state, in enforcing the federal *No-Child* law, had (a) misinterpreted the district's methods of teaching thousands of Spanish-speaking immigrants and (b) required the impoverished city to offer tutoring and other services for which there was no money. A school-board member explained that they were not trying to make a political statement but were simply pointing out that the *No-Child* law could "overwhelm a school system's ability to meet its requirements, especially when a district is as financially stressed as we are." In particular, money from the state was not sufficient for translating tests into Spanish for Reading's large number of Hispanic students (Dillon, 2004a).

**Remaining problems.** Using the courts in an effort to correct ostensible defects in testing programs can be a very expensive venture, particularly in view of the high fees that lawyers charge. Furthermore, litigation can drag on for months or years as a result of crowded court calendars and of legal tactics employed to slow the decision-making process.

## Cooperate in Demanding Changes in the *No-Child Act*

**Type of damage—Many schools fail to meet standards.** When large numbers of schools fall short of the *No-Child Act*'s achievement goals, many school staff members can be frustrated by being blamed for the unacceptable test scores.

**District administrators' coping strategy.** School superintendents organize a coalition which, by dint of its large number of participants, is able to exert more political pressure on federal officials than would be possible if the superintendents operated individually.

**Illustrative case.** An alliance of 138 superintendents, representing more than one quarter of Pennsylvania school districts, in a March 2004 rally drafted a position paper citing "critical flaws" in the *No-Child-Left-Behind* law—flaws related to (a) rules requiring testing of special-education students and students with limited English and (b) the perennial complaint that Congress failed to fully finance the law's mandates (Langland, 2004).

**Remaining problems.** The larger the number of people within an alliance, the greater the likelihood that there will be differences of opinion among participants about what needs fixing in high-stakes testing and how best to present the alliance's case. Such differences can cause conflicts among alliance members, delay the group's actions, and weaken the case the group ultimately presents.

## Adopt an Auditing Method That Minimizes Dropouts

**Type of damage—High incidence of dropouts.** A widely recognized indicator of a school system's efficiency is the number of students who drop out before graduating from high school. Low dropout rates are seen as signs that the school system is in very good shape, indeed. High dropout rates are interpreted to mean the schools are not doing their job properly.

**District administrators' coping strategy.** There are various reasons students abandon the education system before they complete high school, and different methods of calculating dropout rates involve different ways of categorizing those reasons. Thus, school systems that use an auditing method which minimizes the number of school leavers labeled *dropouts* gains a reputation for being highly efficient in serving the needs of the diverse population of children and youths.

**Illustrative cases.** In 2003, the public press reported that a Houston, Texas, high school had changed its dropout figures and that 14 other Houston schools had filed incorrect dropout reports. The news attracted nationwide attention, particularly because Roderick Paige had been the superintendent of Houston's schools before his appointment as U.S. secretary of education. The Houston schools had been cited as a model district at the time the *No-Child-Left-Behind* act was being designed to hold schools more accountable than in the past for student attendance

and performance. However, an *Education Week* analysis of dropout figures in Texas showed that in 108 high schools, at least 70% of the students were at risk of academic failure. About half of those schools
reported that their dropout rates were 1% or less, even though enroll-
ments had declined 30% or more between grades 9 and 12. Other states'
accounting methods often resulted in similar discrepancies. In Maine,
the dropout rate was publicized as 3% when the high-school graduation
rate was 87% (Archer, 2003).

**Remaining problem.** Whenever investigators expose questionable
dropout-auditing practices, the public may suspect that school officials
have been less than honest in reporting other aspects of schooling as
well, such as financial expenditures, employees' working hours, individuals' use of school equipment and supplies, travel expenses, and the
like. This is the problem expressed in the adage, "The thirteenth stroke
of the clock casts doubt not only on itself but on the other twelve strokes
as well."

## Hold Students Back at Critical Testing Junctures

**Type of damage—Massive low test scores.** It has been the custom in
most states to use high-stakes tests only at selected grade levels, such as
grades 3, 8, 10, and 12. Schools suffer negative sanctions if many students fail to pass at those junctures.

**Administrators' coping strategy.** One way to help ensure that a high
proportion of students meet the test standards is to retain weak learners
for another year in the grade prior to the grade in which state tests are
administered.

**Illustrative case.** In Texas, a statewide test has been traditionally administered to high-school sophomores. Investigators discovered that in
many Houston high schools, students were routinely held back in ninth
grade as provided by a district policy that permitted administrators to
exclude weaker students from the tenth-grade test results. For example,
at Austin High School in 2001, there were 1,160 students in ninth grade
and 281 in tenth grade. Perla Arredondo, the daughter of Mexican immigrants, was typical of the held-back students. She spent three years in
ninth grade before being advanced to eleventh grade and "then she was
so discouraged she dropped out" (Dobbs, 2003).

**Remaining problems.** As shown by the Austin data, retaining students in order to imply that a high percentage are succeeding in school
can result in (a) marked imbalances in the number of students at different grade levels, (b) more students dropping out of school on the verge

of the critical testing points, and (c) the public's receiving an erroneous impression of a school's effectiveness.

## Award Themselves High Marks

**Type of damage—Bad publicity.** Parents and the general public become alarmed whenever schools are judged by an outside agency to be unsatisfactory. In the case of high-stakes testing, the outside agency is usually the state education department, often operating under federal rules.

**District administrators' coping strategy.** School district personnel can attempt to counter bad publicity by issuing self-evaluations that cast their schools in a favorable light.

**Illustrative case.** Michigan in 2002 introduced a system of assessing school effectiveness from two perspectives—(a) students' scores on the Michigan Educational Assessment Program tests and (b) each school staff's self-appraisal in which a letter grade (ranging from A for "excellent" to F for "failure") is assigned for each of 11 school-quality indicators:

Family involvement
Student attendance and dropout rates
Teacher quality and professional development
Curriculum alignment
Extended learning opportunities
Arts and humanities programs
Advanced coursework
School facilities
Performance management systems to determine if children have gained
  critical skills
Continuous improvement programs
Four-year education and employment plan for students after graduation
(MacDonald & Feighan, 2004)

An overall report of school quality was based two-thirds on test results and one-third on a school's self-appraisal. In early 2004, state officials reported that 76% of schools statewide that had failed to meet federal test-score standards over the past four years had awarded themselves A's in the self appraisals, thereby saving those schools from getting a failing grade that would have resulted in sanctions. In Detroit, staff members of 82 schools that had fallen short of national standards for at least four years gave themselves a grade of A, so none of the city's 250 schools were listed as failing (MacDonald & Feighan, 2004).

**Remaining problems.** Whenever there is a marked discrepancy between a school's test results and the staff's self-appraisal, the public is apt to think the staff's appraisal is unduly self-serving. David Plank, co-director of Michigan State University's Education Policy Center, said there was an obvious problem with the policy of self-reporting, since it involved asking educators to describe how they rated on the set of assessment criteria without the state having any way of appraising the accuracy of the reports (MacDonald & Feighan, 2004).

## Delay Decisions

**Type of damage—Unreasonable standards for disabled students.** Many educators and members of the public believe it's wrong to hold students who suffer learning impairments to the same performance standards as their non-impaired age peers. However, testing schemes like that of the original *No-Child Act* have held all students to the same standard.

**District administrators' coping strategy.** A board of education may decide to deviate from state or federal regulations by setting what the board considers fairer achievement standards for handicapped students. But in order to avoid trouble with state and federal officials—and thereby risk the loss of funds—a school superintendent may delay the implementation of the board's decision in the hope that more lenient standards for the disabled will be set at state and federal levels. This same delaying tactic may also be adopted in cases of other imposed conditions that local schools regard as unfair or unworkable, such as (a) achievement standards for immigrants with limited English skills and (b) a provision for tutoring that is underfunded.

**Illustrative case.** In western New York State, the superintendent of the Holland School District delayed for more than a month the implementation of a district board-of-education ruling that the passing grade on social-studies, global-studies, and English-language-arts tests for students earning a Regents graduation diploma in 2004 should be lowered from 65 to 55. The superintendent had held off imposing the new rule in the hope that the state would issue a decision on passing grades for special-education students and thereby render the local board's decree unnecessary (Werbitsky, 2004).

**Remaining problems.** Delaying the application of a local rule becomes futile if the higher authority in the educational power structure fails to change its policies. In the Holland case, faculty members had originally sought a 55 passing grade (on a 100-point scale) for the district's increasing population of special-education students. However, state education officials worried that a 55 standard for special-education students and 65 for others would represent a double standard, so the officials did not accede to the Holland request (Werbitsky, 2004).

## Search for Achievement-Gap Causes

**Type of damage—Conspicuous subgroup achievement differences.** When the *No-Child-Left-Behind Act* required that schools report test scores for different subgroups (ethnic, limited-English, impaired) rather than simply reporting for the school population as a whole, marked test-performance discrepancies between groups showed up. Educators were urged to eliminate—or at least reduce—the between-group achievement gaps.

**District administrators' coping strategy.** School districts adopt a two-step process—(a) attempt to identify causal factors behind the groups' test-score differences and (b) try to correct causes that are within the power of school personnel.

**Illustrative case.** An example of the way the *No-Child* accountability system could expose subgroup differences was revealed in test scores at George Washington Middle School in Alexandria, Virginia. For the school population as a whole, 60% of the students were proficient in reading/language arts and 77% proficient in math. But when test results were analyzed by subgroups, 96% of white students were found to be proficient in both subjects. However, only 53% of blacks and 39% of Hispanics were proficient in reading/language arts; and 64% of blacks and 57% of Hispanics were proficient in math. Thus, it became the administrators' task to analyze students' home situations, peer relationships, and the classroom teaching methods and materials so as to estimate significant causes for the group differences and propose ways of improving those causal factors that could feasibly be affected by school personnel (Archibald, 2003).

**Remaining problems.** Because the causes of poor test performance can be different from one student to another, the task of cause-analysis is a difficult and time-consuming venture that is often beyond the skills and available time of a school's personnel. Furthermore, many of the most potent causes are not amenable to the efforts of teachers, principals, psychologists, social workers, and the like. Such causes include family attitudes and child-rearing practices, poverty, dangerous neighborhoods, malnutrition, drug and alcohol use, peer influences, and destructive TV programs.

## Adopt Multiple Corrective Measures

**Type of damage—Schools risk punishment.** Low student test scores not only endanger schools' reputations but make schools vulnerable to such punitive sanctions as the replacement of teachers and administrators, take-over by a private company, or closure.

**District administrators' strategy.** Rather than trying a single solution for students' unsatisfactory test performance, a school system can attempt multiple kinds of improvement.

**Illustrative case.** In Indiana, education officials attributed the markedly improved state-test scores in the Southern Hancock School District to a combination of six innovations:

- An updated fifth-grade math curriculum credited with raising the proportion of sixth-graders passing the state test from 77% to 88%.
- More time spent on writing activities, so that 86% of sixth-graders met the language-arts standard compared with 77% the previous year.
- A revised high-school math curriculum that identified students' strengths and weaknesses through the analysis of their math tests, thereby raising the number of sophomores passing the state test to 86%—representing improved annual progress for five consecutive years.
- English-language laboratories for freshmen who needed extra help in addition to their regular English classes. Thus, sophomores passing the language-arts exam rose from 79% to 88% in a single year.
- A summer-school record enrollment of 325 students—14% of the district's K-8 population.
- State remediation funds distributed to classroom teachers willing to hold tutoring sessions with students before and after school hours (McCleery, 2003).

**Remaining problems.** The number and types of corrective measures a school can provide are limited by a variety of restrictions—funds, time, staff members' skills, school facilities and supplies, students' abilities and motivation, and parents' cooperation.

## Offer Students Multiple Chances to Pass Tests

**Type of damage—High rate of student failures.** Many students fail state achievement tests on the first try, thereby endangering their chance for grade promotion and graduation.

**District administrators' coping strategy.** A frequently adopted policy is that of furnishing students multiple opportunities to retake the tests.

**Illustrative cases.** In 2003, Massachusetts began requiring students to pass the Massachusetts Comprehensive Assessment System (MCAS) examination at some point in their high-school career in order to earn a high-school diploma. Between grades 10 and 12, members of the graduating class of 2003 had six chances to take the test. As a result, 95% of the state's 2003 senior class passed. The figure included 1,228 successful appeals for special consideration, with the 1,228 representing about 2% of the total 60,000 seniors. When members of the 2003 class were tenth-graders, just 68% had passed the MCAS. At that time only 29% of Hispanic students had passed, but by the time they were seniors 83% succeeded. Even more dramatic was the improvement of students with limited English skills. Whereas barely 7% passed on their first try, by their senior year 82% had earned satisfactory scores (Rothstein, 2003c).

A special graduation ceremony in December 2003 honored 80 Boston high-school students who had failed the MCAS test the previous spring and thus could not graduate in June. But after attending summer school, the 80 had earned passing scores. At the December commencement exercise, School Superintendent Thomas W. Payzant told the students, "The diploma you walk away with tonight is worth more than previous diplomas from Boston public high schools and other public high schools in Massachusetts" (McElhenny, 2003).

In June 2004, Baltimore school officials sought to increase graduation rates by allowing seniors who had failed a class to retake their final exams and earn a diploma. In response to teachers who complained that the new policy let students off too easily, the recently appointed director of Baltimore high schools, Frank DeStefano, said, "If you've been working hard all semester and you screw up on one test on one day, we will help you. The standard stays fixed, but time can be altered" (White, 2004).

**Remaining problems.** Simply offering failing students a chance to retake a test is rarely sufficient for equipping them to succeed on the next try. It is also necessary to diagnose individuals' weaknesses and furnish them ways to overcome their shortcomings. For example, in Boston a special night school was established in a poverty section of the city for students who had consistently failed the state exam (Rothstein, 2003c).

## Intensify English Instruction for Immigrants

**Type of damage—Immigrants' graduation delayed.** Students who have recently arrived in the United States from countries in which English is not the native language usually face a difficult time with high-stakes tests. Even when youths come with an exemplary record of achievement in such subjects as math and science, their progress in American schools is impeded by their substandard English skills. The problem is particularly severe in school systems that have no regular bilingual program.

**District administrators' coping strategy.** Special intensive-English classes or tutoring sessions are furnished to hasten limited-English students' progress toward graduation.

**Illustrative case.** After voters in Massachusetts approved the state's English-immersion program that eliminated regular bilingual classes, the Lawrence school district launched the New Comers Program that moved immigrant students through the high-school curriculum and prepared them for the Massachusetts Comprehensive Assessment test by providing an additional load of three English classes each day. The Lawrence public-school population was nearly 84% Latino. About 27% of the students were classified as having limited English proficiency compared with 5% of students statewide (Conti, 2004).

**Remaining problems.** By spending so much time in English classes each day, students are restricted in the number of other subjects they can study. Thus, the emphasis on English curtails the breadth of the education that limited-English students are able to pursue.

## Substitute Alternative Evaluation Methods

**Type of damage—Many pupils held back.** When a school system institutes a policy of not promoting pupils who fail to earn high-enough test scores, large numbers of pupils can be retained in their present grade for one or more additional years.

**District administrators' coping strategy.** Pupils who fail state tests can still be promoted if their achievement is deemed satisfactory when judged by other methods of evaluation, such as daily class work or alternative standardized tests.

**Illustrative case.** In 2002, Florida legislators enacted a state law that barred pupils from advancing if they failed the Florida Comprehensive Assessment Test's reading exam. As a result, 6,622 third-graders in Miami-Dade-County public schools were held back in 2003. However, a loophole in the law allowed the school district to (a) promote 207 of those children on the basis of a portfolio of their class work and (b) advance an additional 321 for their satisfactory scores on the nationally standardized Stanford-9 reading test (Pinzur, 2003c).

After 10,521 third graders in New York City failed at least one state exam in mid-2004 and were in danger of not advancing to fourth grade, 1,480 were granted reprieves because their class work was judged significantly stronger than their test scores. The remaining 8,041 who had failed were urged to attend a new summer-school program and, at the close of the summer session, to retake the English and math exams (Gootman, 2004b).

**Remaining problems.** When alternative evaluation methods are used to compensate for low test scores, advocates of strong testing programs can accuse schools of using deceptive tactics to avoid responsibility for the quality of students' achievement. In addition, assessing the value of class work (recitation, homework, workbooks, written quizzes, projects) involves a large measure of subjective judgment. Hence, critics can complain that a common measure of quality is not being applied to all students as it is in standardized-test programs.

## Develop a Different Evaluation System

**Type of damage—Many students labeled failures.** Students who have advanced significantly in terms of their own ability and past record can be dubbed failures if their state test scores are below the standard for their age and grade level. Under *No-Child-Left-Behind* rules, judgments of a school's annual yearly progress have been founded solely on the test results of groups of students as compared against a set criterion, not on how much progress students have made in relation to their individual records.

**District administrators' copy strategy.** The criteria for assessing students' progress or a school's effectiveness can include more than how close students' test scores come to a single group standard.

**Illustrative case.** Prior to 2004, educational achievement in New York City public schools was judged on the basis of state reading and math tests, with results ranging from a low of Level 1 to a high of Level 4. In late 2003, the city schools' chancellor, Joel I. Klein, announced the development of a new evaluation system that measured a student's achievement against that student's own progress in previous years. The system would also compare students' progress with that of their class, their school, and other students across the district and state. In addition, the scheme could be used to suggest the effectiveness of teachers by showing which teachers' pupils consistently achieved at a faster or slower rate of progress (Herzenhorn, 2003).

**Remaining problems.** When multiple types of evidence are collected, disagreements among groups—employers, politicians, teachers, parents, students—could be expected over questions of which sorts of evidence should be used for making which kinds of decisions. For example, should evidence from daily class work rather than from state test scores be used for deciding whether a student is promoted to the next higher grade? Should high-school graduation depend solely on state test scores, or should a student's own progress in relation that individual's past performance be included in graduation decisions? Should the socioeconomic backgrounds of schools' student populations be considered when schools' test scores are compared?

## Try New Curriculum Designs

**Type of damage—Too many students fail state tests.** Schools face punitive sanctions as a result of the high number of students failing language and math tests.

**District administrators' coping strategy.** On the assumption that their schools' current language-arts and math curricula are at least partially at fault for low test scores, officials can adopt other teaching materials and methods that might lead to higher test scores.

**Illustrative case.** For the 2003-2004 school year, New York City officials mandated "progressive" methods of teaching reading and math in all but the highest-performing of the city's more than 1,000 schools. The term "progressive" distinguished the new approach from curricula typically found in other larger urban districts that use such systems as (a) Open Court Reading (published by McGraw-Hill) or other step-by-step phonics approaches and (b) commercial math programs in which skills are built through repetition and standard calculations.

Throughout the New York district, Month-by-Month Phonics and Everyday Mathematics became the core of the reading and math programs. The phonics program featured spelling and rhyming activities as well as analogy, rather than directly teaching the letters and sounds that make up words. Math lessons used methods advocated by the National Council of Teachers of Mathematics. As a result, in a typical elementary school, teachers were more often reading popular children's books and discussing literature and the writing process than perusing a teacher's guidebook or drilling on phonics. Math lessons usually focused on everyday applications rather than drilling on multiplication tables and algorithms (Manzo, 2003a).

**Remaining problems.** When a district adopts a curriculum that differs from one advocated by funding agencies, schools may be in danger of losing support money. In the New York City case, millions of dollars in federal funds could be lost if officials in Washington decided that the city's curriculum innovations failed to meet the federal government's requirement that teaching methods be ones founded on convincing research. Another potential problem is that of retraining teachers to implement the new curriculum.

## Furnish Cash Rewards for Test-Score Improvement

**Type of damage—Insufficient teacher dedication.** The damage in this case is more direct than collateral, in that students' low test scores are attributed—at least partially—to a lack of the extra effort needed from teachers to raise scores.

**District administrators' strategy.** Teachers are offered monetary bonuses for improvements in their students' test results.

**Illustrative cases.** In the assessment of a cash-incentive pilot-program introduced into the Denver public schools in 1999, investigators concluded that the tryout version of the plan showed that focusing on a teacher's role in improving students' achievement could be an important impetus for change. The plan also recognized district factors that affected the quality of a school (Blair, 2004).

Teachers participating in the Denver plan were required to establish achievement goals for their class, with the goals approved by the school principal. For instance, an algebra teacher might set the goal of having 70% of her class show 40% growth from a pretest to a post-test. For each goal reached, a teacher received an annual bonus of $750. The assessment team found that the scheme "positively affected student achievement in many cases" (Blair, 2004).

Cash rewards for students and for their teachers have been credited with motivating Dallas, Texas, high-school students to perform well on college-level advance-placement exams. Each student passing an exam received $100 for every test passed, while teachers were paid $150 for each of their students who passed (Texas students, 2003).

**Remaining problems.** Cash-bonus programs are expensive, so they typically need contributions from philanthropists outside the school system. The Denver project received $4-million in external funds. Over a five-year period, the Dallas program was supported by $6.1-million from the school district and $2.1 from an electronics manufacturing firm. Such critics as Bob Schaeffer of the FairTest group, which monitors testing programs, have complained that the Dallas money "would be better spent on improving the education for poorly performing schools" (Texas students, 2003).

## Hire More and Better Teachers

**Type of damage—Unwelcome sanctions.** A continuation of substandard test performance by pupils can lead to such punishments as schools suffering public disgrace and the potential replacement of personnel.

**District administrators' coping strategy.** Hiring more teachers permits a school system to reduce class size and thereby focus more attention on individual students' academic needs. Hiring better-qualified teachers increases the likelihood that students will profit from more effective instruction.

**Illustrative cases.** In Western New York's Pendleton school district, Superintendent C. Douglas Whelan announced a plan to hire more teachers to help raise state test scores (Kowalik, 2004). Minnesota's Governor Tim Pawlenty proposed a pilot project in which five public schools would pay performance-based bonuses to *super teachers*—ones whose students dramatically improved their test results. School principals would be empowered to recruit, hire, and dismiss teachers outside of union contracts and tenure rules. Teachers could receive bonuses ranging from $20,000 to $40,000, depending on their students' test performance. The program—at an annual cost of $2.5-million to $5-million— would focus on schools that enrolled large numbers of disadvantaged students who had performed poorly on state tests (Walsh, 2003b).

**Remaining problems.** When administrators seek to hire more teachers and to conserve funds in the process, they are prone to favor candidates who are novices rather than hiring more-expensive veterans. But doing so entails the risk of employing candidates whose instructional skills are less effective than those of experienced teachers. Three additional problems with bonus plans like the Minnesota proposal are that (a) they are expensive, (b) they cannot ensure improved test scores for disadvantaged students whose academic progress does not depend chiefly on teachers' skills, and (c) teachers who do not receive bonuses can resent their more fortunate colleagues' higher pay.

## Offer Incentive Pay for Difficult School Assignments

**Type of damage—Shortage of skilled teachers.** Schools in dangerous inner-city areas or remote rural settings often fail to attract or retain competent teachers. Thus, children attending such schools are apt to receive inferior instruction.

**District administrators' strategy.**   Monetary bonuses can be offered teachers who are willing to work in difficult schools.

**Illustrative case.**   Over the three-year 2002-2004 period, nearly 1,400 North Carolina math, science, and special-education teachers each received as much as $1,800 extra to serve in poverty-area schools or in ones whose students had earned low scores on state tests.

**Remaining problems.**   After North Carolina education officials reviewed the most recent test results from schools in which teachers received extra pay, they questioned whether the bonuses were worth the expense. Test-score improvement in economically distressed communities fell well short of expectations. Furthermore, nearly half the teachers had taught in some of the state's most affluent districts, ones that already paid high salary supplements. In a survey of teachers' opinions about what incentives could induce teachers to work in low-performing, high-poverty schools, bonuses ranked fifth among enticements. Conditions that teachers placed ahead of extra pay were smaller classes, strong administrative support, adequate planning time, and extra support positions (Silberman, 2004c).

## Offer Teachers Bonuses

**Type of damage—Students' test scores fail to improve.**   Poor test results from one year to the next can lead to disgruntled parents, discouraged students, increased criticism of teachers, and dismissal of school personnel.

**District administrators' coping strategy.**   Like state officials, district administrators can furnish teachers cash rewards when their students' test scores improve.

**Illustrative cases.**   The Mesa School District—Arizona's largest with 74,500 students—placed nine of its schools among the state's top 16 in math-test scores during 2003. Mesa officials attributed much of the district's success to a program of retraining teachers and principals and to a $3,000 bonus for each teacher who significantly improved "student learning and parent satisfaction" (Kossan, 2003a).

In the Aldine school district, north of Houston, Texas, awards of $500 to $1,000 were paid to teachers and other campus personnel for meeting "verifiable performance standards." Between 1997 and 2003, bonuses rose from $322,000 to $3.7-million. According to Aldine Superintendent Nadine Kujawa, "As the dollars went up, the performance went up tremendously" (Do financial incentives motivate teachers?, 2004).

**Remaining problems.** Disadvantages of paying teachers for student test-score gains have appeared across the nation. The most frequent problem is that bonus plans can become very expensive, often abandoned after first introduced, thereby resulting in teachers losing faith in lawmakers' promises. That happened in California where officials who set up an award system in 1999 delayed bonuses the first year, then failed to pay them altogether because of the state's fiscal crisis. Authors of a 2003 assessment of the California plan concluded that among teachers, the motivating power of financial awards was minimal (Do financial incentives motivate teachers?, 2004).

Under a "career-ladder" plan in Texas, teachers competed for raises based on a review of their performance; but legislators eventually abandoned the scheme at the request of teachers' organizations that claimed the practice created division and tension. Teachers' groups contended that the money would be better spent raising salaries and restoring health-insurance stipends that legislators had cut earlier.

According to a study of incentive programs in Kentucky, Maryland, and North Carolina, teachers were often critical of incentive-pay plans, which they felt caused more stress and longer hours of work than positive outcomes. However, the researchers concluded that offering incentives could be "a potentially useful tool for policy-makers and administrators interested in focusing teachers, principals and educational systems on improving student performance" (Do financial incentives motivate teachers?, 2004).

## Provide Special Teacher-Training Sessions

**Type of damage—Implied teacher incompetence.** From the viewpoint of parents and the general public, a report of widespread low test scores can cast doubt on teachers' fitness and on administrators' ways of selecting, assigning, and supervising teachers.

**District administrators' coping strategy.** Officials' attempts to raise test scores can include furnishing teachers additional training in those subject-matter fields on which state tests focus.

**Illustrative cases.** Evergreen school district in the state of Washington developed an inservice-education program to train teachers in evaluating writing samples by the same method used for evaluating the state's standardized writing exams. District officials explained that the program's purpose was to equip teachers with "a deep understanding of how the scoring is done and how it relates to content standards" so teachers could aim writing instruction at aspects of composition that yielded high marks on state tests (Begay, 2003).

**Remaining problems.** Efforts to match teaching methods as closely as possible to test contents has the danger of restricting students' learning experiences. For instance, consider the teaching of writing skills. Writing can take many forms—fiction/nonfiction, description/persuasion, realism/fantasy, prose/poetry, news-reporting/editorializing, and the like. If tests include only one or two of these types, and teachers limit their instruction to those types, then students lose the chance to try the other forms of writing. In addition, if tests treat only the mechanics of writing (spelling, punctuation, verb-noun agreement, the location of pronoun referents, and such), and if teachers then limit their attention to the mechanics, then students are cheated of the opportunity to learn about the many kinds of writing contents, purposes, and styles.

## Improve the Outreach System

**Type of damage—Too few needy students receive tutoring.** The *No-Child Act's* provision for tutoring low-scoring students cannot succeed unless parents realize that free-cost tutoring is available and know the conditions under which it is provided.

**District administrators' coping strategy.** The school district can mount an aggressive program of informing parents and students of the available tutoring, its value, and how to take advantage of it.

**Illustrative case.** In New York City only 12.5% (30,359 children) of the district's 243,249 students who qualified for tutoring during 2002 actually signed up for such help. Consequently, the city spent less than half of the $27.5-million that was the minimum expenditure under the law for tutoring services. Officials believed the low-participation rate was at least partly the result of inefficient methods of informing parents of the program. Thus, for 2003 the district improved its outreach to families, with earlier notification, clearer correspondence, and help from parent program-coordinators. As a result, participation in 2003 rose to 19% (40,369 children) of the city's eligible students (Gross, 2003b).

**Remaining problems.** Improving a district's system of communicating with families effects no more than a modest rise in the number of pupils being tutored. In New York, the increase was only 6.5%, which still left over 80% of eligible candidates without special coaching. To raise the participation rate further would require overcoming other barriers—transportation difficulties, parents' reluctance to have children away from home during after-school hours, and students' unwillingness to spend leisure time studying.

## Require Summer School

**Type of damage—High failure figures.** Whenever students must pass a year-end state test in order to be promoted to the next higher grade or to graduate from high school, large numbers are likely to fail. Unwanted consequences that can result from the failures include hosts of irate parents, many disheartened learners, classes heavy laden with grade-repeating students, and a poor public image of the schools' efficiency.

**District administators' coping strategy.** A popular solution to the problem of grade repeaters is to require students who failed the year-end test to enroll in summer school for intensive study of the testing areas in which they had performed poorly.

**Illustrative cases.** In Philadelphia during 2003, a new policy made summer school mandatory for students in grades 3, 8, and 12 who had failed the state tests at the close of the school year. At the end of the summer session, 15,363 students—or 87% of the 17,675 students who had attended summer school—succeeded in the retesting and were promoted to the next higher grade or, in the case of the high-school seniors, earned their diplomas (Dean, 2003).

In Chicago's fourth year of required summer school for failing eighth-graders, 4,171 of the city's 31,199 eighth-grade pupils had to give up six weeks of their vacation time to attend a summer session. Of those, two-thirds were subsequently promoted, while 1,377 had to repeat eighth grade. Among the 1,800 Waco, Texas, children in grades 1-8 who were forced to attend summer school, 1,009 earned promotion (Johnston, 1999a).

Third-graders in Florida who failed the reading portion of the state test in 2003 were to be held back. When test results were compiled, the public learned that 23% (43,000) of third-graders were in danger of being retained. Because of the outcry set off by such large numbers, the rules were changed, allowing children to prove their reading ability through other methods. School districts also sponsored summer reading camps to give students a second chance at advancing to fourth grade. In Hillsborough County, 1,121 of the county's third graders (8.7%) were retained in third grade—double the number in 2002. However, 563 pupils moved up because of portfolios that attested to their reading ability and 371 were advanced on the basis of how well they performed on an alternative reading test after they had attended a summer reading camp (Ave, 2003).

**Remaining problems.** Whereas summer school may solve the promotion problem for the majority of students, there always will be a minority who will not improve sufficiently and thus become either grade repeaters or dropouts. In the Philadelphia example, 2,312 of those who attended summer school failed the retesting at the end of summer.

## Tutor to Reduce Grade-Retention Numbers

**Type of damage—High incidence of nonpromotion.** As noted earlier, massive nonpromotion can lead to a variety of unwelcome outcomes.

**District administrators' coping strategy.** Pupils who failed state tests can be offered special tutoring to remedy their shortcomings before they take make-up tests prior to the opening of the new school year. If they pass the make-up tests, they advance to the next grade rather than repeating their former grade.

**Ilustrative case.** New York City schools' chancellor, Joel E. Klein, in 2004 budgeted an additional $25-million for special tutoring in small groups and in summer classes of no more than 15 students to equip third-graders to pass state tests and thus avoid their spending another year in third grade (Herszenhorn, 2004a).

**Remaining problems.** Providing individual or small-group tutoring is far more expensive than regular classroom instruction. Furthermore, pupils frequently turn down tutoring opportunities because they or their parents find it inconvenient, as it often requires special transportation and after-school or weekend sessions.

## Improve the Quality of Classroom Visits

**Type of damage—School principals lack knowledge of classroom practices.** Principals are in a poor position to promote effective classroom learning that leads to improved test scores if they rarely visit classrooms or if they lack efficient observation skills when they do visit.

**District administrators' strategy.** Inservice training programs encourage principals to visit their schools' classrooms and improve the principals' methods of classroom observation.

**Illustrative case.** A Cooperating-School-Districts coalition of 61 school systems around St. Louis, Missouri, introduced a program of "classroom walk-throughs" designed to sharpen principals' methods of analyzing the quality of classroom instruction. The program consisted of an expert observer guiding a team of principals during a five-minute walk-through visit at each of a school's in-session classes. According to the director of the program, "A walk-through is not about judging a teacher; it is about judging the work" by focusing on how students are spending their time, how they interact with the teacher, how they respond to the visitor's queries, and what work-products are displayed on the classroom walls (Bower, 2004).

**Remaining problems.** One serious limitation of classroom visits is that the presence of a visitor—and particularly a visitor in a position of authority—can significantly alter what goes on. As a result, the principal may not see typical behavior and therefore is apt to draw an inaccurate conclusion about the quality of learning taking place. A second limitation is that a brief observation of a class cannot reveal what is happening in students' heads. Far more sophisticated evaluation methods are necessary for accurately judging how students' thought processes operate during a class session.

## Rescue Dropouts

**Type of damage—School-leavers' job opportunities curtailed.** Students who drop out before graduating from high school have difficulty finding well-paying, self-satisfying employment.

**District administrators' coping strategy.** School personnel can identify potential dropouts and make a special effort to help such students solve the problems that contribute to their precarious academic condition. Schools can also contact students who have already dropped out and help them continue their formal education.

**Illustrative case.** Education officials in Houston, Texas,—stung by the 2003 revelation that they had falsified reports of low dropout rates—sought to redeem themselves by launching a program to save students who had already left school before graduating or were in danger of doing so. The program, in place during the closing months of 2004, consisted of two components—a door-to-door canvass of homes and a restructuring of special classes for potential dropouts. As the 2004-2005 school year began, nearly 500 community leaders, parents, and school-district personnel visited homes of dropouts to encourage them to reenroll. At the same time, Houston's 24 high schools were divided into smaller "learning communities" designed to foster closer relationships between students and teachers. The aim of the program was to raise the district's high-school graduation rate from 75% to 85% and thereby surpass the state average of 83% (Austin, 2004).

**Remaining problems.** Steve Amstutz, principal of Houston's Lee High School, said that most students dropped out because "nobody's given them the pat on the back, the kick in the pants, the encouragement, or the support" needed to stay in school (Austin, 2004). Therefore, if down-sizing the high-schools' "communities" was not accompanied by serious efforts of teachers and counselors to give personal attention to students who were having academic difficulty, the 211,000-student school system's dropout rates would likely remain high.

## Feed Test-Takers

**Type of damage—Many students fail tests.** The greater the number of students earning unsatisfactory test scores, the greater the number who are despondent, require extra help, and are not promoted to the next higher grade. Large numbers of failing students also mean large numbers of distressed parents and the likelihood that schools will suffer sanctions under the *No-Child-Act* rules.

**District administrators' coping strategy.** On days when tests are to be administered, schools can offer pupils a nourishing snack on the assumption that (a) children's nutritional state can influence their test performance and (b) pupils often eat little or no breakfast before going to school.

**Illustrative case.** In 1996, schools in Hillsborough County, Florida, began furnishing pupils free breakfast on testing days. The practice of providing breakfast ultimately expanded to every day by 2003, with 40% of the county's 182,000 pupils taking advantage of the offer. The percentage rose even higher on days that the Florida Comprehensive Assessment Test was given (Stein, 2004).

**Remaining problems.** During times of tight money, adding the cost of free breakfasts to school budgets can be burdensome, especially if breakfasts are provided not only on testing days but throughout the school year.

# Individual-School Coping Strategies

School principals are obliged to respond to demands from three primary sources—the district superintendent's office, the school's own personnel, and the outside community served by the school. Attempts to cope with collateral damage at the school level can include (a) improving the social climate, (b) offering teachers extra pay, (c) offering students participation incentives, (d) encouraging adept students to retake tests, (e) promoting failing students, (f) raising test standards, (g) publicly identifying flaws in the testing system, (h) demanding a public correction of testing errors, (i) encouraging parents to fake pupil disabilities, (j) publicizing class comparisons, (k) falsifying students' class assignments, and (l) dismissing troublesome staff members.

## Improve the School's Personal-Social Climate

**Type of damage—Multiple unwelcome effects accompany low test scores.** As demonstrated throughout this chapter, a variety of undesired consequences can result from students' unsatisfactory test performance—increased dropout and nonpromotion rates, higher schooling costs because of more grade-repeaters, more criticism of school personnel, and damage to a school's reputation.

**District administrators' coping strategy.** Efforts are made to improve the social interaction among a school's inhabitants—officials, teachers, students, staff—in order to raise their morale and motivation, with higher test scores becoming one of the hope-for outcomes.

**Illustrative case.** Surveys of 1,700 California high schools between 1998 and 2002 showed that the largest gains in standardized-test scores occurred in schools that "tended to have low rates of substance abuse and violence, high percentages of students who exercised regularly and ate right, and school climates described as caring" (Viadero, 2003).

**Remaining problems.** Because substance abuse, lack of exercise, and improper nutrition are so strongly affected by conditions beyond the school's control, it is often difficult for school personnel to exert significant influence over such causal factors. However, there is hope for success in fostering caring attitudes among staff members and students.

## Offer Teachers Extra Pay

**Type of damage—Continuing poor test performance.** Schools in economically depressed and dangerous neighborhoods often have difficulty attracting and retaining highly qualified teachers, so that the unsatisfactory test performance of pupils in such schools is attributed at least partly to teachers' inadequate preparation and experience.

**School administrators' coping strategy.** To improve the quality of the teaching staff in socially and economically disadvantaged schools, administrators can provide well-qualified teachers special bonuses or "hardship pay" for accepting positions and for remaining on the job. This is an individual-school version of the state-wide bonus-pay practice described earlier.

**Illustrative case.** In Louisiana's Jefferson Parish, pupils' low test scores at Bonella St. Ville school brought penalties in the form of consultants demanding administrative changes and parents transferring their children to other schools. The school principal said she expected the next year's test scores to rise because the school furnished extra pay for certified teachers who would agree to stay at the school for at least three years. As a result of the incentive pay, certified teachers replaced many others who lacked the college course work or high scores on the teacher-preparation tests needed for certification (Waller, 2003).

**Remaining problems.** Not only may bonus programs strain the financial resources of schools that operate on tight budgets, but highly qualified teachers—in spite of the extra pay—are often unwilling to move into difficult schools that are known for their dangerous neighborhoods, a high proportion of English-limited students, substandard facilities, and uninspired leadership.

## Offer Students Participation Incentives

**Type of damage—Too few students take state tests.** Negative sanctions suffered by many schools under the *No-Child* regulations have resulted from fewer than 95% of the students appearing on the days tests are administered.

**School administrators' coping strategy.** Special incentives can be offered students for coming to school on testing days.

**Illustrative cases.** Brookwood High School in Atlanta was one of 135 Georgia schools cited in 2003 as failing to make adequate annual progress because the schools had fallen short of 95% student participation in the testing program. Thus, as a special inducement to attend school on testing days in 2004, Principal Jane Stegall announced a raffle that gave each test-taker a chance to win one of five MP3 music players or one of 50 movie tickets (Robelen, 2004b).

In North Carolina's Wake school district, just for taking the state High School Comprehensive Test, students had an extra point added to their fourth-quarter grade averages for every class, including math, art, and physical education. Thus, "a student with a 92 classroom average in English would receive a 93, the difference between a B and an A." If students passed both the reading and math sections of the test, they received two extra points, which could make the difference between failing or passing a class (Silberman, 2004b).

**Remaining problems.** Some expense is usually involved in providing incentives. In addition, not all incentives are attractive to all of the students who are tempted to be absent on testing days.

## Encourage Adept Students to Retake Tests

**Type of damage—Students' skills not adequately represented.** In states that require learners to pass competency tests in order to earn high-school diplomas, students are often obliged—or permitted—to try the tests two or three years before their graduation date. In effect, the test requirement can be fulfilled in grades 10, 11, or 12. However, those who have passed the exams as sophomores or juniors can be expected to be even more competent by the time they are seniors, a fact not reflected in the test scores used for assessing their school's performance under the federal *No-Child Act* rules. This means that a school could have reported higher exam scores if all students had been tested in their senior year. Consequently, when large numbers of students have met the high-school exit-exam requirement in grade 10 or 11, the report of the average achievement level for the school is inaccurately low.

**School administrators' coping strategy.** Skillful students who passed the graduation test in their sophomore or junior year can be asked to take the exam again in the latter part of their senior year. In the school's records for the *No-Child* report to the state, the results of students' senior-year testing will replace the results from the tenth or eleventh grade.

**Ilustrative case.** Some Arizona high-school principals urged older students who had already passed the Arizona-Instrument-to-Measure-Standards to take the exam again in the hope of pushing their schools up into a "highly performing" or "excelling" category (Kossan & Meléndez, 2004).

**Remaining problems.** Certain students—perhaps many—will be reluctant to take tests a second time because of the time the exams require and the anxiety students may suffer under high-stakes-testing conditions.

## Promote Failing Students

**Type of damage—Many nonpromoted students.** Whenever a state implements legislation that requires students to pass standardized tests in order to be advanced to the next higher grade, large numbers of students can be held back. Widespread nonpromotion can lead to a variety of unwelcome outcomes—discouraged learners, more dropouts, angry parents, overcrowded classrooms, and higher educational costs.

**School administrators' coping strategy.** Exceptions to the nonpromotion policy can be granted by school officials, so that children who failed one or more tests can still advance to the next higher grade. This is a school version of the state-waiver policy described earlier.

**Illustrative case.** In 2000, North Carolina education officials—alarmed at so many low-scoring students being moved up from grade to grade—ruled that those who failed state tests should not be promoted. However, exceptions were allowed to the strict application of the rule, so that two-thirds of the 8,535 third-graders statewide who did not pass the state's end-of-grade tests in reading or math in 2003 still advanced to fourth grade. Of the 3,300 fifth-graders and 6,300 eighth-graders who had failed, 80% were allowed to move up. School principals, rather than being required to automatically retain children who failed both the reading and math exams, were authorized to inspect each case and consider factors other than test scores that might warrant a child's being promoted. Important factors included the pupil's age and the quality of daily class work. If a child failed the tests three times, a panel of educators from outside the school reviewed the evidence and proposed how the case should be resolved (Silberman, 2003c).

**Remaining problems.** The granting of exceptions is strongly influenced by the personal opinions of principals about which conditions in a pupil's case deserve consideration (the pupil's diligence, attitude toward school, family support, parents' social status, success in subjects other than reading and math) and on how heavily each condition should weigh in a promotion/retention verdict. Consequently, whether a pupil is advanced depends heavily on which particular principal makes the decision, so the outcome is partly "luck-of-the-draw."

## Raise Standards

**Type of damage—Criticism for holding low standards.** School principals can be accused of being "too soft" and irresponsible if critics consider the school's student-achievement standards too low.

**School administrators' coping strategy.** Principals can raise standards by any of several means—build tougher tests, require higher passing scores, increase the amount of information covered on tests, reduce the percentage of students to be awarded high marks, or redefine the traditional letter-grade system.

**Illustrative case.** Dan Johnson, principal of Utah's Mount Logan Middle School, announced that the letter-grade *D* would no longer be considered a minimal passing mark. Instead, students would need to earn a *C* or better in order to be promoted. Johnson defended the policy by insisting that standards need to be raised so that students command deep knowledge and enduring understanding. "I never had one conference with a parent who thought this was a bad idea." In other Utah schools that had adopted the same policy, officials termed a *D*-grade "a glorified F." To help struggling Logan students earn at least *C*'s, the district established the Mountaineer Academy, where teachers, university students, and community volunteers offered aid in every subject before, during, and after school (D grade won't cut it, 2004).

**Remaining problems.** Declaring *D* a flunking grade could encourage teachers to award a *C-minus* mark to students who, under the former grading system, deserved a *D*. In effect, eliminating *D* as the lowest passing mark might contribute to grade inflation if teachers chose to promote low-performing students rather than face them again throughout another school year.

## Publicly Identify Faults in the Testing System

**Type of damage—Stained reputation.** A school's image is damaged when the public learns that the students have failed to meet test standards.

**School administrators' coping strategy.** The schools' reputation may be saved if administrators can offer convincing evidence through the news media that defects in the testing system, and not low-quality teaching, accounted for the report of unsatisfactory test scores.

**Illustrative case.** When the list of unsatisfactory schools in Illinois was announced at the close of 2003, administrators of more than 200 schools on the list publicly complained that errors in the testing system were responsible for their poor ratings. Most of the mistakes were in the way officials accounted for student test-participation rates. For instance, officials at some of the highest-scoring schools in the state—New Trier High, Lake Forest, Whitney Young, Lane Tech, Northside College Prep—argued that that their schools were listed as failing because not enough Asian and Caucasian students had taken the state tests, when actually the required 95% had been tested. The schools appeared to fall short of 95% because some students had not correctly checked a box identifying their ethnic status, which is a problem that is particularly apt to occur with students of mixed ethnic heritage (Grossman, 2003c).

**Remaining problems.** Once a school is reported as failing, it is difficult to correct the public's perception of the school by later reporting that the initial announcement was in error. People who read the first report may not see the correction. Or, even if they do see a retraction, the suspicion that the school is inferior may still linger in mind.

## Demand Public Correction of Errors

**Type of damage—School's reputation tarnished by erroneous test reports.** When mistakes are made in scoring exams or in reporting test results, and the mistakes lead to schools being labeled failures, the schools suffer an undeserved loss of public respect.

**School administrators' coping strategy.** School officials insist that the people responsible for reporting test results should issue a public correction of their previous inaccurate announcement.

**Illustrative case.** A computer-programming error in compiling a list of poorly performing schools in Michigan cast Allen Park High School into the needs-improvement category. Allen Park officials called on the state to admit the mistake and issue a public retraction of their placing the school on the failing list. The high-school principal, Janet McBurney, called the erroneous announcement "devastating" because the school had always done well on state tests. "We're not afraid of being held accountable . . . but we do ask that it be represented in a fair way" (Nichols, 2004).

**Remaining problems.** As Principal McBurney explained, being placed on the failing list was frustrating because "the impact this [press] release would have on our district is very difficult to recover from [even after] the correction is made" (Nichols, 2004).

## Encourage Parents to Fake Pupil Disabilities

**Type of damage—Many students fail test for promotion.** When grade promotion depends wholly on children passing high-stakes tests, many children risk being held back at the end of the school year.

**School administrators' coping strategy.** Principals who fear that too many of their pupils will fail a state exam may arrange to have children designated as suffering from such special handicaps as an attention-deficit disorder or a broken arm from an accident. The special-handicaps category is in addition to the "disabled" classification that is used for children with more permanent serious disorders—mental retardation, cerebral palsy, blindness, and the like. In New York, children meeting the special-handicaps criteria are given 50% more time to complete tests than are their non-impaired classmates.

**Illustrative case.** On the threshold of the 2004 springtime testing session at New York City's Public School 290, parents of third-graders received notices asking them to designate their children as having special handicaps, thereby giving the pupils extra time to finish the high-stakes state reading exam (Campanile, 2004a).

**Remaining problems.** In the PS 290 incident, parents who had received the request were angry at being expected to apply a handicapped label to their children whom they regarded as quite normal. The episode also cast doubt on the veracity and wisdom of the school principal who, at first, denied that the notices came from her office, but later admitted she had erred in sending out last-minute notices to parents of "at least three students to consent to test accommodations" (Campanile, 2004a).

## Publicize Class Comparisons

**Type of damage—Teachers singled out to bear the blame.** When principals report test scores only by grade level, without identifying how different classes in a grade have succeeded, they can incur criticism from two sources: (a) parents who want to know whether some classes have scored higher than others and (b) teachers whose classes have fared well but whose superior performance is buried in the averages reported for their grade level or for the school in general.

**Principals' coping strategy.** An obvious way to respond to critics is to publicize scores by class rather than only by grade or school.

**Illustrative case.** Juanita Nix, the principal of the 850-student Maple Lawn Elementary School in Dallas, Texas, posted large bar charts in the school corridor showing the passing scores for each class that took the Texas Assessment of Knowledge and Skills—including third-grade reading, fourth-grade writing, fifth-grade science, and sixth-grade mathematics. Nix said she thought everyone had a right to know how different classes performed. She admitted that her posting the scores was "a little gutsy" (Galley, 2003). Mike Moses, superintendent of the 166,000-student Dallas school district, praised Nix for effective leadership and for "having the courage to put a focus on teacher effectiveness" (Galley, 2003).

**Remaining problems.** Publishing class scores often draws the wrath of teachers whose classes have not achieved high scores. They protest that, by implication, they are being blamed for student inadequacies caused by conditions other than a teacher's methods of instruction—such conditions as students' out-of-school responsibilities, poverty, low native ability, peer influences, poor command of English, recent immigration to the United States, lack of home support for schooling, and more.

Nix's posting test scores drew criticism from the heads of the local teachers' union, who considered it an unprofessional act that did not improve students' learning by publicly humiliating teachers. According to one commentator, students' privacy rights are potentially violated when class scores are posted, because if a posted chart showed that "14 of the 18 children in the room passed the test, it might be possible to determine who failed and who passed" (Galley, 2003).

# Falsify Students' Class Assignments

**Type of damage—Students taught by poorly prepared teachers.** The chance that students will perform well on state tests is reduced if their teachers have a meager command of subject-matter and instructional methods. The *No-Child Act* requires schools to report the extent to which students are being taught by officially certified teachers.

**Principals' coping strategy.** To give the impression that students are being served by competent teachers—when, in fact, they are not—a principal can provide class lists showing that all students are in classes taught by properly certified personnel.

**Illustrative case.** A high-school math teacher in Nevada filed a complaint with the state board of education, claiming that the principal of his high school had told him that the grades of eight students who were not in his class were, nevertheless, being credited to him. According to the complaint, the purpose of the ploy was to give the impression that the eight had earned passing marks under a highly qualified teacher, as is required for complying with the *No-Child* standards (Galley, 2004).

**Remaining problems.** If the teacher's accusations prove true, the school principal is liable for dismissal, or at least for a reprimand. The principal's reputation also suffers in the eyes of the public.

# Dismiss Troublesome Staff Members

**Type of damage—School officials' integrity questioned.** Staff members who assume the role of whistle blower can damage the reputations of school officials by accusing officials of dishonesty in administering tests and in reporting test results.

**School administrators' coping strategy.** Administrators can respond to such charges by dismissing or demoting their accusers.

**Illustrative case.** A teacher from a Philadelphia kindergarten-to-fifth-grade charter school filed suit against the school's administrators, claiming they fired her after she informed school-district headquarters about testing irregularities at the school. She contended that she had been dismissed from her $50,000-a-year job three days after she had informed Philadelphia district officials of the testing infractions. According to her suit, school personnel had furnished students test answers, were lax in security measures during test sessions, and gave at least one student a test with some multiple-choice answers already filled in. That the school's staff was under pressure to have pupils do well on the test was suggested by their state test scores in 2002-2003 when only 6% of fifth-graders were proficient in math and only 18% in reading (Woodall, 2003).

**Remaining problems.** The charter-school officials face several problems. First, the suit, if won by the plaintiff, can result in the accused administrators losing their jobs, losing permission to operate a charter school, and being professionally scarred with reports of mendacity. But no matter who wins the case, the newspaper publicity about the charges can by itself damage the defendants' reputations. As for the school, its academic status in the eyes of the public can suffer from the publicity about how poorly pupils performed on the state math and reading tests. It is also possible that the teacher who filed the charges could experience difficulties finding a new job if, as a result of the lawsuit, she is viewed by employers as a potential troublemaker.

# Conclusion

As demonstrated by the cases in this chapter, educational administrators have displayed a wide range of responses to high-stakes-testing programs. In an effort to explain such a diversity of coping strategies, I would estimate that administrators' behavior results to a great extent from a combination of (a) their personal values, (b) their job skills, and (3) the multiple sources of social/political pressure they must endure.

Personal values are people's convictions about how they should act in matters of social relationships, curriculum offerings, educational opportunity, sexual conduct, property rights, religion, politics, occupational prestige, ways to spend money, recreational activities, the environment, and more. For instance, administrators' decision-making can be affected by whether they value more highly:

- Male/female sexual relationships than homosexual relationships
- Math/science knowledge than art/music knowledge
- A college education than trade-school training
- Republican-Party policies than Democratic-Party policies
- Christianity than Islam
- Football than hockey
- Americans than foreigners
- Using natural resources for society's economic benefit rather than leaving environmental resources in their original condition

Job skills are the techniques administrators use in doing the tasks their work involves, such tasks as planning budgets, setting school policies, responding to public criticism, hiring and firing staff members, working with agencies above and below them in the educational hierarchy, and the like. Administrators differ in how adeptly they perform such tasks, and those differences influence how well they cope with the problems of high-stakes testing.

A third potential influence on administrators' actions is the force of multiple sources of social/political pressure. Those sources and their degree of influence vary from one level of the schooling hierarchy to another. At the national level, administrators in the U.S. Department of Education are especially subject to pressure from the White House, Congress, state education departments, and lobbyists. For example, the *No-Child-Left-Behind Act* was strongly influenced by lobbyists from the nation's business community. At the state level, administrators in state departments of education face demands and appeals from the federal government, state legislators, the governor and his staff, school districts, individual citizens (particularly ones willing to provide funds for legislators' election campaigns), and lobbyists representing business groups (employers), textbook publishers, political parties, and teachers unions. Within individual school districts, superintendents and their staffs must contend with pressure from federal and state authorities, the local school board, local politicians (mayors, county supervisors), the chamber of commerce, employee unions, political parties, churches, school principals, teachers, and students' parents. Finally, within individual schools, principals and their aides are faced with demands and requests from all of the agencies above them on the educational ladder (federal, state, district) as well as from the school's teachers, support staff, parents, and students.

In summary, the position of educational administrator in a high-stakes climate can be a difficult assignment indeed, one that tests the person's values, job skills, and ability to juggle the conflicting demands from multiple sources of social pressure.

# 8

# The Public and Parents

Throughout this book the expression *the public* refers to the nation's adults who are interested in information about schools and who care about the efficiency of the schooling process. *The public*, in such a sense, can therefore be more accurately described as the nation's *informed and concerned adults*. But limiting *the public* to people who are informed and concerned still leaves the definition of *the public* unduly vague, because not all subgroups within the general populace hold the same opinions about high-stakes testing. Therefore, in this chapter's illustrative cases, specific types of subgroups of *the public* are often identified.

## Types of Coping Strategies

The 14 strategies described in the following pages range from techniques adopted by people who accept high-stakes testing as desirable to tactics aimed at defeating high-stakes testing and its sponsors. The strategies involve (a) supporting high-stakes testing, (b) seeking educators' advice, (c) informing other parents of testing policies, (d) punishing children, (e) demanding higher standards, (f) demanding lower standards, (g) expressing disgust about the tests, (h) removing children from testing, (i) rejecting school-transfer offers, (j) signing dropout-consent forms, (k) demanding changes in the testing law, (l) conducting demonstrations, (m) threatening boycotts, and (n) suing for the opportunity to inspect test items.

### Support High-Stakes Testing

**Type of damage—Educational improvements doomed.** Members of the public who see testing as a good way to improve schooling can have their hopes dashed if opponents of testing are successful in eliminating tests as determinants of grade promotion, graduation, and punitive actions against schools.

**The public's coping strategy.**  Advocates of testing can counter criticisms of tests by publicizing public support of high-stakes programs.

**Illustrative case.**  In 2004, proponents of testing cited a nationwide telephone survey of 1,508 Latino adults in which 75% of the respondents said standardized testing should be used to determine whether students are promoted or graduate, while 67% agreed that the federal government should require states to set strict performance standards for public schools (Survey, 2004).

**Remaining problems.**  Opponents of testing can attempt to counter supporters' survey evidence by publicizing the results of other polls which suggest that the approval of high-stakes plans is diminishing.  For instance, a January 2004 poll of American voters reported that 28% of respondents opposed the *No-Child* law compared to only 8% in January 2003 (Robelen, 2004c).

## Seek Educators' Advice

**Type of damage—Parents distressed by students' low test scores.** Learners are more likely to perform poorly on tests if they receive no help at home in how to study efficiently.

**Parents' coping strategy.**  Students usually earn higher test scores if parents monitor and guide their study habits.  Parents' ability to offer such help can be increased with advice from school personnel.

**Illustrative cases.**  Suggestions about promoting students' progress can be issued by schools via newspapers and letters to parents.  For instance, an article in the *Arizona Republic* about difficulties pupils faced with the state's achievement tests offered tips for parents from teachers. Parents were advised to (a) ask the school what their children are expected to learn at the particular grade level, (b) read aloud with their children (stopping periodically to ask children to explain what they have just read or to predict what might happen next), (c) help pupils in entertaining ways (such as using songs and flash cards for memorizing multiplication tables), and (d) monitor pupils' homework to see that it was consistently completed (Kossan, 2003b).

In Louisiana's St. Bernard's Parish, nearly 100 parents of eighth-graders at Trist Middle School accepted the opportunity to attend a Saturday *LEAP Fest*, conducted by 35 teachers, administrators, and retired teachers.  Parents could choose to attend any of the four 25-minute sessions in which teachers demonstrated effective ways to guide pupils' preparation for the LEAP (Louisiana Educational Assessment Program) exams that determined whether eighth-graders would be promoted to ninth grade. The organizer of the fest, former teacher Kathy Wendling, explained that they used portions of the LEAP test that children typically had difficulty with. The hope was that the refresher courses would assist parents in aiding their children with homework and with preparing for the annual state test, because some parents were unaware of how best to help pupils (Blakely, 2004).

**Remaining problems.** Two difficulties with implementing parent-guidance suggestions are those of (a) getting parents to read the advice and, (b) once those suggestions are understood, getting parents to consistently supervise children's study activities.

## Inform Other Parents

**Type of damage—Unaware parents.** High-stakes programs—and particularly the *No-Child* plan—offer a host of information for parents about help and requirements for various subgroups of pupils. However, many parents either lack access to such information or find the descriptions confusing so they fail to take advantage of the opportunities.

**Parents' coping strategy.** Parents who have a clear understanding of a school program's regulations can organize outreach campaigns in which they explain the program to other parents in language that poorly informed parents can understand.

**Illustrative case.** According to Lisa Tait in Lilburn, Georgia, parents are often desperate for information about state testing programs. Therefore, she volunteered to serve in a statewide education network that was organized to explain the *No-Child-Left-Behind* provisions to parents at churches, social-service centers, and Boy Scout meetings. As part of the network's effort, many Georgia school districts distributed letters and advertisements, some of which were intended for Spanish-speaking adults (Feller, 2004).

**Remaining problems.** It is often difficult to find competent and willing individuals to staff outreach programs in communities that must depend on unpaid volunteers for their personnel.

## Punish Children

**Type of damage—Pupils chastised for low test scores.** Two kinds of pupils—ones with limited English skills and ones suffering physical or psychological disabilities—have a particularly difficult time with tests that require English-language reading or writing skills. To help compensate for such disabilities, federal laws relating to handicapped and limited-English students require that schools offer them special help with class assignments, including aid with test-taking, such as having test items read to them so they can answer orally. However, high-stakes testing programs often forbid any sort of aid for students with handicaps, so that even diligent, well-informed learners can get low scores on tests.

**Parents' coping strategy.** Parents of students who have a limited command of English, and parents of the physically/mentally handicapped, may misunderstand that their children's low test scores have been the consequence of an inflexible regulation that prevented such students from revealing all they had learned. This misunderstanding is especially common in families that have immigrated to the United States and speak a language other than English. Such parents typically hope their children will adapt to American culture and compete successfully for jobs and social status. To fulfill this ambition, they want their children to do well in American schools. A method they may adopt for motivating an ostensibly reluctant scholar is to punish the laggard.

**Illustrative case.** To avoid the likelihood that parents might punish children for getting low grades on a high-stakes test, the superintendent of schools in a Maryland district delayed mailing individual test scores to parents. He said he was concerned that some of the pupils with disabilities or limited English might be chastised by their parents for earning low grades on the test, when their low grades resulted from a few test items having been read to them by teachers and, as a consequence, the company that scored the tests assigned such pupils failing marks for the entire test (Mathews & Mui, 2003).

**Remaining problems.** Families' traditional child-rearing habits are usually difficult to change. In some homes, corporal punishment and verbal abuse are thought to be effective motivators of good behavior, including successful academic performance.

## Demand Higher Standards

**Type of damage—Students are ill-prepared for higher education.** If achievement standards in high schools are low, graduates need remedial courses when they enter college.

**Higher-education officials' coping strategy.** State legislators and departments of education are urged to toughen promotion and graduation standards so as to encourage students to work harder in high school.

**Illustrative case.** Freeman A. Hrabowski III, president of the Baltimore County branch of the University of Maryland, advised the Maryland State Board of Education to raise test standards. He said that in international comparisons, American students usually come up short and that, on his campus, foreign students were better prepared, worked harder, and were "much more focused" than U.S. students. As an African-American mathematician, Hrabowski rejected the argument that blacks and Hispanics are incapable of reaching high standards. Therefore, minorities need not be held to lower achievement levels than whites. He said, "I realize it takes time, but you mustn't give up or lower the bar for some students" (Bowler, 2004b).

**Remaining problems.** Observers of the Maryland case suggested that the passing score had been set too high if thousands of Maryland students—most of them ethnic minorities—were denied diplomas. On the other hand, if the standard was set so low that everyone passed, the testing program would "become a mockery" and perpetuate the impression that the schools had unacceptably low expectations (Bowler, 2004b).

## Demand Lower Standards

**Type of damage—Large numbers of students flunk tests.** High fail rates result in discouraged students, more dropouts, increased class sizes at grade levels in which state tests are administered, increased educational costs, and distressed parents.

**Parents' strategy.** Officials responsible for setting standards are urged to lower the number of test items that students must answer correctly to pass tests.

**Illustrative case.** A 5,800-member grass-roots organization titled Parents Across Virginia United to Reform SOLs issued a public statement applauding the Virginia Board of Education for adopting new state-history-test cutting scores that more accurately reflected the standard-setting committee's views of what "barely proficient" students should be able to achieve (Wermers, 2003b). The parent group also pressed the board to lower the cutting scores for additional tests that large numbers of students had failed.

**Remaining problems.** Opponents of low test standards warn that reducing cutting scores encourages students to exert minimum effort rather than striving to do their best. Furthermore, when the pass-level is set so low that nearly all students exceed it, employers cannot be confident that high-school graduates are adequately literate and numerate.

## Express Disgust

**Type of damage—Students miss a well-rounded education.** When standardized tests play such a crucial role in determining children's academic progress and the fate of schools, teachers are prone to spend large blocks of time preparing students to take tests. In addition, the testing process itself reduces the time available for instruction. As a result, the breadth of students' education is narrowed.

**Parents' coping strategy.** Parents vent their frustration by complaining in the public press, on Internet chat groups, at PTA meetings, and at schools during conferences with administrators and teachers.

**Illustrative case.** In a letter to the *Frontline* television series, a mother said she had five children in grades 1, 3, 4, 6, and 7—all good students, and all engaged in test preparation "instead of real learning." She complained that the focus at their school was on getting ready for tests. Her seventh-grader finished his pre-Algebra course early and was then assigned to study exclusively in a test-preparation workbook. "High stakes testing is an experiment on my children, and the effects will be felt in the years to come" (VanDerwerker, 2002).

**Remaining problems.** Simply expressing disgust is unlikely to solve the problem of over-concentration on test preparation unless such complaints are followed by proposed alternatives and by the social/political pressure on school personnel necessary to ensure the adoption of the alternatives.

## Remove Children from Test Sessions

**Type of damage—Equating test-passing with education.** Parents see the emphasis on passing tests as a distortion of what they believe education should be.

**Parents' coping strategy.** In protest to high-stakes testing, parents keep their children home from school on testing days.

**Illustrative case.** A mother wrote to the public-broadcasting system's *Frontline* program to explain that she was keeping her third-grade son home when the Massachusetts state reading test was administered because she saw no way the test would diagnose her son's strengths and weaknesses in reading skills, particularly when the test results were not returned to the school until the boy was in fourth grade. She wondered what the schools were teaching about the value of real learning when the emphasis was on "winning the test game" (Guisbond, 2002).

**Remaining problems.** No change in instructional practices is apt to occur if only one or two parents keep their children home on testing days and if those parents only vent their distress through letters to the news media. Effecting constructive change in the content and methods of teaching typically requires tactics that gain the serious attention of school administrators, such tactics as having many parents keeping their children home, conducting widely publicized demonstrations, and voicing suggestions at well-attended PTA and faculty meetings.

Parents who boycott tests may cause their children to miss grade promotion. For example, New York City's Mayor Bloomberg warned that "The [third-grade] kids are going to have to take the test if they want to graduate" to fourth grade (Campanile, Seifman, & Mongelli, 2004).

## Reject Transfer Offers

**Type of damage—School transfer option unappealing.** As explained in Chapter 1, the *No-Child-Left-Behind* law gives students in a "failing" school the opportunity to transfer to another public school whose students have compiled a satisfactory test-performance record. Parents who accept the transfer offer are obligating their children to adjust to a distant and unfamiliar neighborhood, potentially hostile classmates, unfamiliar teachers and administrators, and unfamiliar buildings. Parents may view such conditions as harmful for their children, so the transfer offer becomes unattractive.

**Parents' coping strategy.** Parents decline the transfer offer and leave their children in the "failing" school

**Illustrative cases.** Throughout the nation, a large proportion of parents of pupils in schools labeled "needs improvement" have not accepted the opportunity to transfer their children. As mentioned in Chapter 5, fewer than 2% of students eligible to transfer actually moved to another school in 2003. In Virginia, parents of only 432 (2.2%) of the 19,030 students eligible to demand transfers took advantage of the opportunity (Wermers, 2003a). In Ohio, of 16,830 eligibles in Cleveland, 35 (2%) transferred; in Akron 76 (1.8%) of 4,088 moved; in Euclid five out of 750 (.6%); in Lorain 33 out of 1,133 (2.9%) (Okoben, Ott, Reed, & Matzelle, 2003).

**Remaining problems.** Some parents have not understood the transfer option, so more children might have moved if the opportunity had been clear to parents. Although the expectation behind the transfer plan was that pupils would perform better in a "nonfailing" school than in their "failing" school, in practice students often have not improved. Furthermore, as more poorly-performing students from "failing" schools enroll in "nonfailing" schools, the percentage of students not passing tests in "nonfailing" schools may increase.

## Sign Dropout-Consent Forms

**Type of damage—Increased dropout rates.** The introduction of high-stakes plans—and especially the advent of non-promotion and non-graduation policies—have been accompanied by more students abandoning formal education before the end of high school. In an effort to reduce dropout rates, school systems may require that parents formally consent to their children dropping out.

**Parents' coping strategies.** By signing consent forms, parents enable their offspring to end their formal education.

**Illustrative case.** In 2004, the Chicago school district—third largest in the nation after New York and Los Angeles—no longer allowed parents to telephone their consent to allow a high-school student to prematurely abandon schooling. In place of the phone option, the district drafted a letter that parents were obligated to sign before their teenagesrs dropped out. According to the district's chief executive, Arne Duncan, the letter was the district's method of being "brutally honest" about the consequences of a youth's abandoning school. Thus, students ages 16 to 18 and their parents were required to sign a letter acknowledging, among other things, that:

—I will be less likely to find good jobs that pay well, bad jobs that don't pay well, or maybe any jobs.
—I will not be able to afford many things that I will see others acquiring.
—I will be more likely to spend time in jail or prison.
—I will be more likely to rely on the state welfare system for my livelihood.
—I will be considerably less able to properly care for and educate my children. (Chicago schools, 2004)

**Remaining problems.** If permission letters are sent home for parents to sign, it is possible that (a) parents will not clearly understand the implications of dropping out (particularly if the parents are not fluent readers of English) or (b) a student will intercept the letter at home and forge the parent's signature. Thus, such a system works most effectively if a parent is required to sign the letter at school during a discussion of the dropout option with an administrator or teacher.

## Demand Changes in the Law

**Types of damage—High rate of failing schools.** Members of the public are distressed at the federal government's threatening to punish schools whose students fall short of unreasonable achievement standards.

**The public's coping strategy.** Apply political pressure on federal officials to correct objectionable features of the *No-Child Act.*

**Illustrative cases.** In late 2003, a group of educators and civic leaders formed the Citizens for Effective Schools organization that published a full-page advertisement in the periodical *Roll Call,* urging Congress to rewrite the *No-Child-Left-Behind Act.* The appeal was in the form of an open letter to President Bush, Education Secretary Paige, and members of Congress suggesting that the act should focus less on punishing schools that fell short of the *No-Child* standards and more on specifying ways to help schools improve. The letter's signers included leading members of the New York Urban League and the Education Law Center of New Jersey, as well as teachers and administrators around the nation (Schemo, 2003).

Similar objections to the *No-Child Act* came from school and community leaders in Wake County, North Carolina, who charged that the federal act had been politically motivated and designed "to undermine confidence in public schools." Whereas only 43% of Wake's schools had met federal standards, 98% had achieved North Carolina's own standards (Hui, 2003).

**Remaining problems.** The U.S. president and his staff who initiated the *No-Child* law, along with the members of Congress who voted in favor of the law, have been reluctant to admit flaws in the legislation, because doing so would suggest that they had exercised poor judgment in having sponsored such a program.

## Conduct Demonstrations

**Type of damage—High incidence of failing students.** Unexpected large numbers of students have failed to move up the academic ladder on schedule in school systems that require students to pass state achievement tests. The students' parents and friends have condemned the harmful effect of high-stakes testing on those youths' academic and occupational futures and their self-confidence.

**The public's coping strategy.** To attract politicians' attention to the high incidence of student failure in state testing programs, community members have conducted mass demonstrations that are reported in the press—newspapers, radio, television—and publicized over the Internet. The rallies are intended to frighten officials into (a) granting amnesty to students who failed the tests during the current year, (b) lowering test-passing standards in the future, (c) basing evaluations of student pro-gress on more evidence than just achievement-test results, and/or (d) furnishing more funds in support of the reform programs.

**Illustrative cases.** As noted in Chapter 1, an estimated 2,500 protesters rallied against Florida's high-stakes test in May 2003. The group in-cluded community and political leaders who condemned the policy that denied high-school diplomas to students who did not pass the Florida Comprehensive Assessment Test. The dissidents called for Governor Jeb Bush to grant amnesty to 12,500 Florida high-school seniors who would not receive diplomas and to more than 40,000 third-graders who would be held back because of their low FCAT reading scores (Pinzur, 2003a).

On a cold March day in Washington, D.C., several hundred parents, teachers, and children hiked to the Capitol and Department of Education to protest the *No-Child-Left-Behind Act.* The event had been organized by the Association of Community Organizations for Reform Now (ACORN) as a reaction against what protesters called the act's poor implementa-tion and underfunding (Drebes, 2004).

**Remaining problems.** Protest rallies most effectively influence public opinion when the rallies are well publicized via mass-communication media—newspapers, radio programs, and television broadcasts. But protestors fail to convey their concerns to the public if their gatherings are ignored by the news media. Demonstrations can harm rather than help the protesters' cause if they set off riots, result in injury or property damage, and seriously inconvenience the public.

## Threaten Boycotts

**Type of damage—High incidence of students failing tests.** As more school districts have used state test scores to determine whether students are promoted or held back, children from ethnic minorities and low-income families have been particularly in danger of being retained or of leaving high school without a diploma.

**The public's coping strategy.** Boycotts are intended to pressure offi-cials into changing evaluation methods and achievement standards that result in many minority students being denied promotion.

**Illustrative cases.** Opponents of testing policies in Florida planned several types of boycott in their efforts to force state officials to revise the policies. During the May 2003 mass rally, community activists threat-ened to boycott the state's lucrative tourist, citrus, and sugar industries if all high-school seniors who had failed the Florida Comprehensive As-sessment Test (FCAT) were denied diplomas. Subsequently, Florida lawmakers waived the testing requirement for students with disabilities whose individual education plans indicated that the FCAT did not accurately measure their abilities (Pinzur, 2003a).

A group of parents at Fort Lauderdale's Virginia Shuman Young Elementary School proposed to keep their children home when the FCAT was administered. If fewer than 95% of the pupils took the test, the school would be ineligible for the state's "A" rating and thereby would lose a bonus of $70,000 in state funds ($100 per pupil). In effect, as few as 25 students could sabotage the school, which had earned an "A" the past four years and had a strong chance of succeeding again if all students participated in the testing (Harrison, 2003).

**Remaining problems.** Mounting a successful boycott of industries requires widespread public cooperation that may be difficult to obtain, particularly when the boycott costs workers their livelihood and causes inconvenience for the industries' customers.

Parents who keep their children home on testing days may incur the ire of the school's staff and of other parents for causing the loss of state funds during times of tight budgets.

## Sue to Inspect Test Items

**Type of damage—Parents unable to help students prepare for tests.** Parents are better equipped to aid their children if they know the specific items of information on tests and the form of the test questions. If parents are prevented from analyzing tests, they may be ill-equipped to provide such help.

**Parents' coping strategy.** In an effort to force testing authorities to release past tests for analysis, parents can file lawsuits.

**Illustrative case.** In support of a lawsuit allowing parents to review the contents of past state tests, Gloria Pipkin (founder of the Florida Coalition for Assessment Reform) stated in a letter to Governor Jeb Bush, that coalition members felt strongly that "any test used to make life-altering decisions about children should be subject to scrutiny." The governor replied that the state could not afford to release the tests because creating new test questions each year rather than rotating questions—as currently practiced—would cost millions of dollars (Anti-FCAT group, 2003).

In mid-2004, the Florida state senate voted 40-0 to let parents review their child's state exam and its answers as a way of enabling them to "fully understand the problems a child faces in school and find the best resources to help." The legislation would limit test access to parents whose children failed the third-grade or tenth-grade tests. No one other than the parents, the student, and a school administrator would see the test, and it could not be taken from the room or copied (Kleindienst, 2004).

**Remaining problems.**   Lawsuits can be expensive, and appeals of court decisions may delay a final decision for months or years. In the Florida case, a state court found in favor of the parents, but government officials carried the case to the district court of appeal where the state court's decision was reversed until the state senate passed the parent-access measure in 2004 (Anti-FCAT group, 2003).

# Conclusion

Because the general public's knowledge of high-stakes testing depends so heavily on news sources, public opinion is apt to reflect the dominant beliefs about testing printed in newspapers and magazines and broad-cast over radio and television. Consequently, both the advocates and critics of high-stakes testing attempt to get their viewpoints widely dis-tributed through news releases to the press, news conferences, mass demonstrations, the results of opinion surveys, and quotations from "authorities" and well-known public figures. Consequently, the greater the success that testing advocates and their opponents have in dissemi-nating their views through the press, the more they influence public opinion. During the first year of the *No-Child* plan—2002—sponsors of the plan were more successful in winning public approval than they were in 2003-2004 when a mass of reports appeared about problems in testing programs' implementation. President Bush's approval rating on handling education dropped from a high of 71% in 2002 to under 50% by April 2004 (Leonard-Ramshaw, 2004).

In contrast to the general public, parents are prone to base their ideas of high-stakes plans on the experiences of their own children and on what they hear from other parents, from teachers, and from their school's administrators.

# 9

# Test-Makers and Test-Givers

The massive achievement testing required by state plans and by the *No-Child-Left-Behind Act* is a very expensive undertaking. The federal government's General Accounting Office in 2002 estimated that the cost of creating, administering, and scoring the act's required reading and math tests nationwide would be $3.9-billion over the seven-year period 2002-2008. That estimate was founded on the assumption that state tests would consist of multiple-choice items that could be scored by machine. However, if all states shifted to a combination of multiple-choice and open-ended essay questions, the cost would rise to $5.3-billion. And in states that also tested in subject fields other than reading and math —such as history, science, and foreign languages—the price would be a good deal higher (GAO reports, 2003)

States vary in the amount spent on testing, depending on such factors as the number of students involved, the costs of test-construction and test-revision, the types of test items, and the manner of scoring tests and reporting results. In the early twenty-first century, Massachusetts paid $190,870 for the development and administration of each assessment at an average cost (scoring multiple-choice and essay items) of $12.45 per test taken. In contrast, Virginia spent $78,489 for the development of each assessment with an average administration cost of $1.80 per multiple-choice test (GAO reports, 2003). The annual expense for the Stanford Achievement Test in California was $11-million (Garcia, 2002). Minnesota's tests in 2004 would cost the state an estimated $19-million to administer and millions more for implementing the demanding standards of the *No-Child-Left-Behind Act* (Draper, 2004).

State education departments rarely create and score the tests they use. Instead, they negotiate contracts with companies that develop exams, supervise test administration, score tests, and report the results. When measured by the number of state contracts, the most prominent test companies have been Harcourt Educational Measurement of San Antonio, Texas; CTB/McGraw-Hill of Monterey, California; and Riverside Publishing of Itasca, Illinois. A variety of smaller firms have also entered the lists in recent years. The competition among testing companies for contracts is intense because of the large profits involved. For instance, Pearson Education's test services accounted for $202.4-million of the firm's income in 2000 (The testing industry's big four, 2002). The Massachusetts contract with Harcourt for the period 2000-2004 was for $71-million (Rothstein, 2003d) until the state changed to Measured Progress beginning in 2005 at a price of $118-million (Rothstein, 2004a). In 2004 Arizona officials signed a five-year $45-million contract with CTB/McGraw-Hill (Kossan, 2004).

Test-preparation and administration does not always go smoothly, as shown in this chapter's description of collateral damage that can occur and of ways testers have attempted to deal with the damage.

## Testers' Coping Strategies

In the following pages, ways of coping with test-makers' problems include (a) rebuilding tests, (b) simplifying tests, (c) creating more difficult tests, (d) developing alternative exams, (e) devising tests for the disabled, (f) creating culture-neutral test items, (g) providing translation service, (h) revising faulty tests, (i) substituting other tests, (j) delaying test preparation, (k) paying for mistakes, (l) substituting alternative evaluation methods, (m) accepting alternative answers, (n) eliminating test items, and (o) discouraging cheating.

### Build Easier Tests

**Type of damage—High failure rate.** Whenever large numbers of students fail a test—including students considered by their teachers to be diligent and well-prepared—pupils are discouraged, their parents angry, and their teachers distraught.

**Test-makers' coping strategies.** Test creators, often at the insistence of politicians and their staffs, substitute less demanding items for an exam's most difficult questions.

**Illustrative cases.** The California State Board of Education voted to remove a variety of difficult questions from the English-language and math questions on the state's high-school exit exam and to replace those items with questions that measured more basic skills. The objectionable math items included ones requiring students to (a) calculate the lower quartile, median, and maximum of a data set and (b) use "stem-and-leaf" and "box-and-whiskers" plots for data displays (Board votes, 2003).

The New York State Education Department was widely criticized by educators for so many students failing the 2003 Math-A Regents examination. Critics complained that the exam was confusing and too difficult. As a result, the state education commissioner, Richard P. Mills, appointed a panel to examine the test, and he accepted the panel's recommendation that a new version be created with more multiple-choice items and fewer open-ended questions. In addition, the department in 2004 lowered the passing score to 28 out of 84 points on the test. To set that new standard, three groups of teachers had been appointed to review the revised test and a fourth group made recommendations for the scoring system. The department then applied its scoring chart to a sampling of 20,000 exam scores from across the state before releasing the system to schools. As a result, a higher proportion of students passed the graduation test in 2004 (Gootman, 2004a).

**Remaining problems.** Persistent issues regarding test-item difficulty include such questions as:

- What criterion should be used for judging the difficulty of test items? Should it be the percent of students getting the item wrong, or the kinds of students who get the item wrong, or subject-matter experts' opinions, or teachers' opinions?

- What range of item difficulty—from easy items to very demanding ones—should a test include, and on what rationale should that range be founded?

In the New York case, a number of math teachers and school administrators complained that the revised 2004 standard was overly forgiving so that passing scores were being awarded to students who had not mastered the material. Alfred S. Posamentier, dean of the City College of New York's school of education, believed the passing score was set too low when pupils who correctly answered only one-third of the questions were allowed to advance to the next higher math class. The chairman of the panel in charge of the Math-A revision, said, "You're going to get disagreement from passionate people about where those standards should be set. That's a normal dialogue" (Gootman, 2004a).

## Make Retake-Tests Easier

**Type of damage—High rate of students failing retake-tests.** When students retake tests that they had failed, they often fail again.

**Test-makers' coping strategy.** This is a special version of the build-easier-tests approach. The original tests are intended to be quite demanding. But to help more students pass a test after their first failure, test-makers prepare less difficult retake exams. Such a strategy enables officials to boast of high standards while, at the same time, helping ensure that enough students eventually pass so as to fend off criticism that too few students are making the grade.

**Illustrative case.** In October 2003 the chance to take a make-up exam was offered to 21,000 eleventh and twelfth graders who had failed the Florida Comprehensive Assessment Test earlier in the year. An additional 12,000 former students, denied diplomas because they had not passed the graduation test the previous spring, were also eligible to participate. Whereas the original FCAT consisted of both multiple-choice and open-ended questions that required written answers, the make-up version contained only multiple-choice items, thereby rendering the test easier to pass than the original. Nevertheless, a spokesperson for the state department of education assured the public that officials were confident that the test would accurately measure how well students commanded the skills they needed to move ahead. Versions of the FCAT that would be used in the future would still include both multiple-choice and short-answer questions (Pinzur, 2003b).

**Remaining problems.** Despite the claims of test-makers that an altered form of a test is as demanding as the original, critics are still likely to insist that substituting multiple-choice items for questions that require written answers reduces a test's rigor.

## Build More Difficult Tests

**Type of damage—School systems suffer sanctions.** Schools and their graduates can be punished if tests are deemed too lenient as measures of student competence. Sanctions can include (a) fines or the withdrawal of support funds from schools by government agencies, (b) the withholding of approval by academic accrediting associations, (c) the rejection of student applicants by universities, and (d) an unwillingness of employers to recognize students' diplomas.

**Test-makers' coping strategy**—More difficult items are added to tests.

**Illustrative cases.** Federal supervisors monitor state exams in an effort to ensure that the tests meet the *No-Child Act's* standards of reading and math skills. In 2003 the state of Georgia was fined by the federal government for giving a graduation test that federal officials considered too lenient. In response to the fine, Georgia's test-makers added seven tougher questions to the 2004 math and reading sections of the state's graduation exam (Tofig, 2004).

The 2004 version of the Texas Assessment of Knowledge and Skills (TAKS) confronted students with a more demanding high-school-graduation exam than those used in the past. The 2004 test—covering language arts, math, science, and social studies—was the result of complaints that previous versions had been unreasonably soft. Business leaders and educational organizations that advocated high-stakes graduation tests played an important role in setting the new TAKS standards. For example, a report from the American Diploma Project described the typical high-school-graduation certificate as a "broken promise" in preparing youths for a productive adult life. "Most high-school exit exams don't measure what matters to colleges and employers," according to the report, which was a collaborative effort of three think tanks—Achieve Inc., the Education Trust, and the Fordham Foundation—and endorsed by the Texas Business and Education Coalition (Zuñiga, 2004).

**Remaining problems.** The same problems faced in deciding whether a test is too difficult are faced in deciding whether a test is too easy.

- What criterion should be used for judging the difficulty of test items? Should it be the percent of students getting the item wrong, or the kinds of students who get the item wrong, or subject-matter experts' opinions, or teachers' opinions?
- What range of item difficulty—from easy items to very demanding ones—should a test include, and on what rationale should that range be founded?

Some reviewers of the more demanding TAKS standards claimed that raising the bar with harder test items imposed an unreasonable burden on ethnic minorities. The director of Harvard University's Civil Rights Project, Gary Orfield, called the new TAKS exam a "big mistake. It's not very predictive of success. It ignores all other aspects of the students" (Zuñiga, 2004).

## Develop Alternative Tests for Limited-English Students

**Type of damage—Learners with limited-English skills fail tests.** Students who have mastered the content of math, science, or social-studies tests can still fail tests if such students are recent immigrants or their home language is not English.

**Test-makers' coping strategies.** Two approaches to solving this problem have been those of (a) creating tests that are easier for limited-English students to understand and (b) adopting portfolio assessment techniques.

Two kinds of alternative tests that states have tried are ones in a student's native language and ones in "plain English." Native-language versions measure the same skills and knowledge as do the standard English forms but they are cast in a language commonly spoken in a student's home—Spanish, Chinese, Indonesian, or the like. Plain-English tests use simplified English vocabulary and sentence structures, thereby eliminating technical terms except those necessary in the subject being tested, such as the words *mean* and *graph* in a math exam.

Portfolio assessments depend on various forms of evidence of a student's skills and knowledge—written homework assignments, drawings, diagrams, and teachers' notes about the student's participation in discussions and group work.

**Illustrative cases.** The native-language option has been adopted by only a few states—such as Colorado, New York, and Texas—and in only a few subject fields, with Spanish the most common language into which tests have been translated. Many states have avoided the alternative-language approach because of the time and cost involved. A period of between one year and 18 months is usually needed for preparing and trying-out a translated version of a test. And the number of different languages can be very large. A Maryland official reported that it was obviously not feasible to attempt creating a separate test for each of the 192 languages spoken in the state (Zehr, 2003). A bill approved by the Florida legislature in 2004 would allow students to take the state math graduation exam in their native language. But observers of the Florida scene were waiting to see how the plan would work out in practice, since there were an estimated 200 languages that might need to be accommodated. The projected cost ranged from $21,000 for translating a test into one language to $4.2-million for 200 languages (Kallestad, 2004).

The plain-English option has been the more popular method for judging the achievement of limited-English students. In 1996, Illinois pioneered in preparing a language-arts test for English-language learners and subsequently developed a simplified-English version of the state math test. In 2002, Oregon introduced plain-English tests for math and reading. Wisconsin has permitted some students to present their work in their native language (Zehr, 2003).

In April 2004, the U.S. Department of Education issued a publication titled *Standards and Assessments: Peer Review Guidance* that gave detailed instructions about the sorts of alternative-assessment methods that could be used for evaluating the progress of severely disabled and limited-English students. The publication directed states to show that the alternative appraisal methods were valid measures of students' academic skills and produced scores that can be "'meaningfully combined with scores based on tests given under normal conditions" (Olson, 2004d).

**Remaining problems.** The most daunting difficulty with the task of creating alternative tests is the time and expense such work requires. Furthermore, a risk faced by states is that federal officials may not agree that either plain-English or foreign-language versions of tests qualify as suitable instruments under the *No-Child Act.* And using portfolio appraisals is even more problematic.

## Devise Tests for Developmentally-Disabled Students

**Type of damage—Disabled students cannot manage regular tests.** Learners with cognitive disorders are often classified into three categories of disability—mild, moderate, and severe. The ability of students to take the normal achievement tests varies from one of these groups to another.

**Test-makers' coping strategy.** Different assessment approaches are devised for the three levels of developmental disability. Mildly disadvantaged pupils can take modified paper-pencil tests, but the competence of moderately and severely handicapped pupils must be evaluated by other means, such as teachers' observations of pupils' class work or of tasks performed in a testing setting.

**Illustrative case.** Test-makers in Michigan created MI-Access tests for use with learners who suffered mild cognitive impairment. The tests were similar in form to the regular Michigan Educational Assessment Program, consisting of multiple-choice and open-ended questions that could be read by the students or by a test administrator. However, pupils who suffered moderate or severe cognitive impairment were rated by teachers who observed their performance on daily class activities. No overall score was assigned. Instead, the evaluation reflected what students with disabilities should know and be able to do at a particular grade level. In 2004, between 76% and 86% of fourth-, seventh-, and eleventh-grade students who took the MI-Access reading test exceeded the standard for their grade level. Between 54% and 68% reached or exceeded the standard for mathematics (Bailey, 2004).

**Remaining problems.** Some critics claim that assessments based on teachers' observations of impaired students' class activities are too subjective to be considered accurate reports of learners' knowledge and skills.

## Create Culture-Neutral Test Items

**Type of damage—Subgroups of society may be offended.** Some kinds of test questions may distress children or their parents who are members of a religious, ethnic, political, philosophical, or regional subgroup. If such items are included on tests, the subgroups may accuse testers of practicing harmful discrimination.

**Test-makers' coping strategy.** Eliminate any test items that might be regarded as insulting or provocative by members of any subgroup.

**Illustrative cases.** An informal survey of companies that supply tests to states revealed a variety of taboos that test-makers typically respect (Schouten, 2004). Unacceptable topics include

- Drugs, alcohol, sex, death, violence, family conflict
- Unattractive physical or psychological attributes (obesity, acne, lameness, mental deficiency)
- Names assigned to pets in test questions (Shep, Bitsy, Meg) that might be names of children's own pets or those of children's acquaintances
- Kinds of animals that might offend religious groups (pigs and dogs for Muslims, dinosaurs for anti-evolution-theory Christians)
- Objects and events unusual for a locality (snow in Louisiana, seashores in Kansas, farm machinery in Chicago, hurricanes in Montana)

**Remaining problems.** Education historian Diane Ravitch has criticized the sanitizing of test items not only for "making tests boring" but for distorting reality by ignoring the fact that the United States is a country of a great many cultures. "If we accommodate everyone's taboos" we are denying that "this is reality, and it's OK to learn about it" (Schouten, 2004).

## Provide Translation Service

**Type of damage—A high percentage of limited-English students flunk tests.** The proportion of learners from foreign-language backgrounds who fail state exams can reach as high as 80% or more. That many failures results in large numbers of English-limited students being retained in their present grade, being denied graduation diplomas, and dropping out of school.

**Test-givers' coping strategy.** On the belief that the way test contents are phrased in English is the principal cause of limited-English students failing state exams, officials provide translators to explain the test directions and questions in the students' home language.

**Illustrative case.** During 2003, Pennsylvania's public schools enrolled 38,288 students with limited English proficiency. On the reading portion of the Pennsylvania System of School Assessment (PSSA) test, only 18.3% percent of them earned passing scores compared with 60.3% of all students. In math, just 25.8% of English-limited pupils scored proficient or above, compared with 52.3% of all students. Reacting to these depressing figures, state education officials ruled in 2004 that students who were still learning English would be allowed to use bilingual dictionaries and have translators explain test instructions and questions in each learner's native tongue (Hardy, 2004).

**Remaining problems.** Skeptics were concerned that not all students would have access to translators, and even if they did, pupils' lack of familiarity with American culture could still hinder their performance. Other critics wondered whether pupils should be allowed to give answers in their native languages. In the opinion of Louis DeVlieger, an assistant superintendent in Pennsylvania's Upper Darby School District, "The intent [of the new regulations] is lovely; the practicality is a little more sticky," in view of the fact that Upper Darby had students from an estimated 70 countries who spoke more than 50 languages or dialects (Hardy, 2004).

## Revise Faulty Tests

**Type of damage—Confusion and low test scores.** Mistakes in test directions, in answer systems, and in the form of items confuse students, waste their testing time, and lead to erroneous test scores.

**Test-makers' coping strategies.** Correct flawed test items, methods of scoring, and reports of results.

**Illustrative cases.** In Minnesota, math scoring errors by a test-service company resulted in 7,930 students in grades 8-12 being listed as failing when they actually had passed. During the spring 2004 testing session in Hawaii's public schools, teachers discovered a variety of test errors—missing pages, mistakes in instructions, sample questions with incorrect answers—that could confuse children as they tried to finish the test within the set time period (Essoyan, 2004). The Hawaii Department of Education launched a test-quality investigation that would result in either throwing out incorrect test questions, giving students credit or partial credit for some questions, or having students retake portions of the tests (DePledge, 2004).

In Dallas, Texas, teachers complained about three dozen questions on the district's social-studies tests. Pertinent information was missing in some test items, other items were difficult to read, and maps lacked necessary details. For six of the questions, multiple correct answers were possible. One teacher complained that there was a mismatch between the content of the test and the course of study, "and then there's a possibility of two answers for some of the questions. I tell [students] just choose which one of the two you think it is. We don't know the answer" (Hobbs, 2004).

**Remaining problems.** Monty Niell, executive director of the watchdog FairTest organization, predicted that more mistakes are bound to occur in the future as test-makers struggle with the present-day trend toward "more testing, under higher stakes, with quicker turnaround, and more complicated tests" so that "all the major test companies have had problems" (Essoyan, 2004). A spokesman for one of the major test suppliers, Harcourt, pleaded that "We are human beings" and thus "sometimes make errors" (Essoyan, 2004).

## Substitute Other Tests

**Type of damage—Growing incidence of students failing graduation tests.** Large numbers of high-school seniors who are obliged to leave without diplomas have difficulty getting desirable jobs or gaining admission to colleges. As the failures mount, so also do parents' criticisms of legislators and school personnel.

**Test-givers' coping strategy.** Scores from tests other than the standard graduation exam can be used to qualify seniors for a diploma.

**Illustrative case.** In Florida, after 12,000 high-school seniors were denied diplomas in 2003 because they had failed the Florida Comprehensive Assessment Test (FCAT), the rules were changed so that a score from a nationally standardized college-aptitude test could be substituted for an unsatisfactory FCAT score. Thus, for a student who failed to get at least a 284 on the language portion of the FCAT, a 14 on the American College Test (ACT) or a 370 on the Scholastic Aptitude Test (SAT) would suffice. If the required 295 math score on the FCAT was not achieved, a 14 on the ACT or a 350 on the SAT would be accepted for graduation (Kallestad, 2004).

**Remaining problems.** Opponents of the alternative-test solution may argue that a substitute test does not measure exactly the same skills as the original test and therefore does not offer adequate evidence for awarding a diploma.

## Delay Test Preparation

**Type of damage—An accurate assessment of schools is not available.** Until students' learning is adequately evaluated, school personnel cannot identify which aspects of schooling need improvement and how to effect the improvement. Two factors that have hampered evaluation efforts in a high-stakes-testing climate are a shortage of funds for test construction and a lack of clarity about what high-stakes legislation means for test development.

**Test-makers' coping strategy.** Faced with tight state budgets and with confusion over what accountability legislation implies for evaluating student achievement, test-makers postpone the development and administration of tests.

**Illustrative cases.** A variety of states have reduced the number of subject fields and grade levels in which they give tests. The eliminated subjects are ones other than reading and mathematics (Hoff, 2002).

For the 2003-2004 school year, Oregon saved $4.5-million by doing away with writing tests for third-, fifth-, and eighth-graders. Testing in science at the fifth- and eighth-grade levels was also abolished, as well as the extended-response portions of fifth- and eighth-grade math exams.

Missouri would save $7.1-million in state funds by not paying for its science and social studies exams in 2003. As an alternative, school districts were given the option of paying $5.30 per student for administering the tests, and most districts accepted the option.

Massachusetts held off testing in social studies while the content of the social-studies curriculum was being revised.

**Remaining problems.** As noted earlier, delaying tests hinders schools' efforts to identify the strengths and weaknesses in students' achievement and to adopt methods for correcting weaknesses. This problem of a lack of evaluation information is most serious in the subject fields that are often bypassed in testing programs—subjects other than reading and math.

## Pay for Mistakes

**Type of damage—Test-makers' income diminished.** Companies that provide schools with testing services suffer financial loss if they fail to meet all provisions of their contracts with school systems.

**Test-maker's coping strategy.** As a means of encouraging test-makers to furnish schools efficient service, school authorities stipulate penalties —usually in the form of monetary fines—that test providers will incur if all contract conditions are not fulfilled promptly and accurately. Thus, if testing companies are to win lucrative contracts, they are obliged to agree with contracts' penalty clauses.

**Illustrative case.** In 2002, nearly 340,000 test scores for third-, fifth- and eighth-graders in Georgia had to be discarded because of errors by Harcourt Educational Measurement in comparing the 2002 scores with 2001 scores. Furthermore, the testing company had returned 2001 test results so late that schools could not meet deadlines in reporting student performance. Georgia officials renewed the Harcourt contract only after the company agreed to pay fines if there were errors again in the results or if the results were returned late (Jacobson, 2002).

Harcourt paid $425,000 to Nevada because of a mistake that lowered the scores of nearly 31,000 students who took the state's high-school math exit exam. The testing company also agreed to improve its quality-control procedures and to assume summer-school costs incurred by 736 tenth- and eleventh-graders who were mistakenly told they had failed the exam·(Hendrie & Hurst, 2002).

**Remaining problems.** When states and school districts include penalties in contracts, test-makers are motivated to perform their assignments efficiently, but penalties cannot guarantee that the testing process will be error-free. The people involved in testing can still make mistakes. In addition, when states include stiff-penalty provisions in their contracts, they can discourage test companies from bidding. For instance, after California penalized Harcourt for errors in administering the Stanford 9, not a single company submitted a bid when the state later sent out a call for creating a high-school exit exam (Boser, 2000).

According to Julia M. McMillan, a senior project associate with the Council of Chief State School Officers, large testing companies take on so many contracts that they make careless errors. However, they make so much money from state contracts that the cost of errors is easily written off. Hence, they find it more lucrative to have contracts with many states and risk making mistakes than to concentrate on furnishing a flawless product in only a few states (Boser, 2000).

## Substitute Other Evaluation Methods

**Type of damage—Students can suffer when errors are made in the testing process.** In a high-stakes-testing environment, students' fate—in terms of grade promotion, graduation, ability-grouping, and the like—depends on the accuracy of the entire testing process. Therefore, it is essential that, after students have taken tests, the exam results be reported accurately. This cannot happen if the completed tests are lost.

**Test-givers' coping strategy.** To compensate for the loss or damage of completed tests, officials can turn to other ways of judging achievement so that students will not be required to take the tests over.

**Illustrative case.** About 3,000 of the state tests taken by elementary-school children in eight Michigan school districts were lost during the 2003 testing period. The loss was blamed in part on Measurement Inc., a private company assigned to create and score the exams. School officials in the eight districts had to substitute other means of assessing pupils' progress. For instance, the Pinckney district already had in place a computer system for tracking learners' achievement, so information was available about how well children were succeeding in the subjects treated on the state tests—math, science, reading, writing, and social studies (Pardo, 2004).

**Remaining problems.** Federal authorities, whose *No-Child Act* stipulates that the appraisal of schools must be founded on state achievement tests, may not approve of alternative evaluation methods. Unlike Pinckney, some school districts may not have a student-progress system ready as an acceptable substitute for state test scores.

## Accept Alternative Answers

**Type of damage—Students not credited with correct answers.** Sometimes more than one available answer to a multiple-choice or fill-in test item is correct, although test-makers had not realized it. Consequently, students who select the alternate answer receive a lower score on the test than they deserve.

**Test-givers' coping strategy.** When alternative correct answers are brought to the attention of testing authorities, tests will be rescored to award students credit for such answers.

**Illustrative case.** The following item confronted eighth-graders who took the Massachusetts Comprehensive Assessment System science test in 2003.

In 1995, a private bus company in Washington, D.C., introduced a program to run all its tour buses with fuel obtained from soybeans. The buses are powered by:
    a. nuclear fuel
    b. biogas
    c. coal gas
    d. diesel fuel

According to the test-makers, the only correct answer would be "b—biogas." However, following the testing, a teacher in the Cambridge school system alerted the state department of education to the fact that "d—diesel fuel" was also correct, since soybeans can be a source of such fuel. After state officials verified the teacher's claim, they corrected hundreds of eighth-graders' scores, including those of 846 students who were elevated out of the "failing" category into "needs improvement" status. Two years earlier, a tenth-grader had found an alternative answer to a math question, so students who had chosen that answer were then awarded credit (Sataline, 2003).

**Remaining problems.** Rescoring exams in order to remedy testing errors can significantly increase the expense of a testing program. Furthermore, deciding on what constitutes a correct answer will sometimes involve a large measure of personal opinion, particularly in science, social studies, and English-language usage.

## Eliminate Test Items During Testing Sessions

**Type of damage—Defective items or answer systems.** While taking a test, students are confused and their time wasted as they try to decipher faulty test items, perplexing directions, and muddled answer systems.

**Test-givers' coping strategy.** Tell students to skip the items identified as defective, and explain in clear terms any baffling directions.

**Illustrative case.** High-school students taking the reading portion of the Utah Basic Skills Competency Exam were puzzled when they found 77 test questions but only space for 75 answers on the answer sheets. Test supervisors told them to leave the last two items out. Representatives from Measured Progress—the New Hampshire test company that had developed the exam—later directed school-district personnel to ignore questions 76 and 77 when scoring the tests (Lynn, 2004a).

**Remaining problems.** Taking time to correct exam directions or items during a testing session shortens the time students have to complete the exam, distracts them from their main task, and may invalidate the scoring of tests that are intended to be finished within a limited time period.

## Discourage Cheating

**Type of damage—Test scores are not accurate indicators of students' performance.** When low test scores in high-stakes programs result in serious consequences for schools, the likelihood is increased that school personnel will try illicit means to produce satisfactory exam results. When this happens, the purpose of testing is obviously defeated.

**Test-givers' coping strategy.** Supervisors of test administration can (a) monitor changes in test results from year to year to estimate results' validity and (b) punish school personnel who do not abide by test-administration rules.

**Illustrative cases.** The director of testing in Florida discovered several schools in Broward and Miami-Dade counties with improvements in scores on the 2003 state tests that were statistically unlikely. Those schools were ones with a higher incidence of questionable test results than schools throughout the rest of the state. Consequently, security measures were adopted for fostering error-free future testing in the two counties (FCAT answers, 2004).   In Brookesville Elementary School, a guidance counselor was suspended without pay for failing to follow the directions for administering the Florida Comprehensive Assessment Test.  The incident followed an earlier episode in which the same counselor had copied pages of the fourth-grade state exam in violation of the state's administrative code.  Other help not allowed by the code included giving test-takers access to test questions before the test, coaching test-takers during the test, making answer keys available, and failing to follow the written directions for administering the exam (Solochek, 2004).

**Remaining problems.**  If schools have honestly achieved unusual progress, their reputations can be damaged by publicity that they are being investigated for possible fraud.  And when evidence suggests that, indeed, cheating has occurred, it is difficult for test officials to decide if those schools' test scores should be used in assessing the schools' performance.  In the Brookesville case, district officials said the counselor's actions invalidated the testing session that she was involved with.  Whereas the students in that testing session would not be required to retake the test, their scores would not count toward the school's overall rating (Solochek, 2004).

## Conclusion

In the high-stakes test-making and test-giving business, the viewpoints of two groups of people are particularly important in explaining the coping strategies that are observed.  First are the testing companies.  Second are the state and district school officials most intimately involved in managing testing programs.

From the vantage point of testing companies, evaluating students' achievement is not a philanthropic endeavor conducted as a social service.  Instead, it is a highly competitive business whose chief purpose is to make money.  Therefore, a key factor influencing the ways company employees respond to collateral damage is how such strategies will likely affect company profits.  To protect themselves against serious financial loss through fines that they could incur if errors are committed in the testing process, companies include in their contract bids large enough costs to more than cover potential fines.  Furthermore, test-makers can be expected to blame other people—teachers, students, principals, state education department officials—for certain forms of damage.

From the vantage point of most education officials who are responsible for managing high-stakes programs, evaluating students' progress appears to serve two main purposes: (a) meet school achievement standards set by the government so that schools can receive government funds and (b) enhance the school system's public reputation. At an increasing rate, test results also determine students' grade promotion and high-school graduation. Unfortunately, managers of high-stakes testing programs appear to give far less attention to using tests for diagnosing individual students' strengths and weaknesses as a means of promoting each child's progress.

# 10

# Teachers

The term *teachers* in this chapter means individuals who directly offer instruction to individuals or groups. Therefore, persons who aid a single child in a one-on-one tutoring relationship and persons who instruct an entire classroom of learners qualify as teachers.

## Types of Coping Strategies

The following list of strategies moves from the most positive to the most negative. Positive strategies reflect teachers' acceptance and support of high-stakes testing. Negative strategies reflect teachers' dissatisfaction with high-stakes programs. The sequence includes teachers' (a) emphasizing tested subject-matter, (b) teaching to the test, (c) entering professional-development programs, (d) seeking certification, (e) adopting new instructional techniques, (f) showing parents how to help children, (g) depending on alternative evaluation methods, (h) adopting test-data-analysis software, (i) resenting intrusions into decision-making, (j) confronting politicians, (k) accusing the government of underfunding, (l) taking offense at *No-Child* demands, (m) refusing to test, (n) conducting public demonstrations, (o) proposing to sue the government, (p) avoiding difficult schools, (q) cheating to raise test scores, and (r) acquiring bogus academic degrees.

### Willingly Emphasize Tested Subject-Matter

**Type of damage—Schools (and particularly teachers) blamed for students' low test scores.** Not only are teachers embarrassed if their students perform poorly on state tests, but they risk censure and possible dismissal if test scores fail to improve at an ideal rate.

**Teachers' coping strategy.** Devote more time and effort to subjects that are the focus on high-stakes testing. Under the *No-Child Act*, those subjects have been reading and math, with science to be added later.

**Illustrative case.** Teaching reading to 23,000 third-graders in 64 Arizona schools confronted teachers with a special challenge, because 85% of the pupils came from homes in which English was a second language. A federal *Reading First* program provided the schools $105-million over a six-year period to pay for reading specialists, classroom materials, tutoring, and training that emphasized phonemic awareness, phonics, fluency, vocabulary, and comprehension. Under the plan, pupils would spend 90 minutes each day reading, three times the amount of time dedicated to any other subject. At the beginning of the school year, after assessment teams had identified pupils' reading weaknesses, teachers separated the pupils into learning groups to target the weak skills. Children who failed to make the expected gains were also given intensive tutoring before and after school (Melèndez, 2003).

**Remaining problems.** In the Arizona case, teachers said they lacked enough time to teach math, science, and social studies when 90 minutes a day was devoted to reading. Furthermore, the sorts of programs adopted in Arizona can be expensive and beyond the financial ability of many school districts unless they receive funding from outside the district.

## Teach to the Test

**Type of damage—Teachers faulted for students' poor preparation for tests.** Teachers are accused of incompetence when large numbers of students do poorly on tests.

**Teachers' coping strategy.** Analyze test content and diligently teach that content.

**Illustrative cases.** In Arizona's public schools, pupils have been required to take the AIMS test battery (Arizona Instrument to Measure Standards). To prepare children for the exam, teachers have been advised to ensure that children are learning the material tested on AIMS by following the AIMS guides furnished by the state department of education. Teachers are also advised to consult the sample test questions posted on the education department's Internet website (Woodall, 2003).

Such a teach-to-the-test approach was credited with pupils' success in a variety of Arizona school districts. For example, the proportion of fifth-graders at Jefferson Elementary who passed the AIMS math section rose from 26% to 44% over the three-year period 2001-2003. In 2003, third-graders at Mercury Mine Elementary scored among the highest for that grade level in Paradise Valley, with 98% passing in reading, 96% in math, and 93% in writing (Kossan, 2003a).

It is often difficult to determine whether teaching-to-the-test is a legitimate instructional tactic or, instead, is cheating. For instance, in mid-2004 a teacher at New York's City's Public School 123 reported to authorities that the school had retained copies of math tests from past years, and teachers used items from those tests in preparing children for upcoming exams. However, according to the school system's rules, all test papers—including unused or extra copies—were to be collected and sent to the testing headquarters after the exam was administered. On the bottom of each page of the saved booklets that teachers at PS-123 used for test preparation was the warning: "Secure material. Do not reproduce or discuss contents." The teacher who reported the incident at PS-123 said her school was not the only one violating testing regulations—"It's happening all over the city" (Campanile, 2004b). A few months earlier, nearly 4,000 New York City pupils in grades 3, 5, and 7, prior to test day had practiced 15 questions from the 2003 test. Because the test was thus compromised, those children were given the choice of having their tests re-scored without the 15 questions or taking a makeup exam (Campanile, 2004b).

**Remaining problems.** As mentioned in Chapter 2, teaching to the test may

(a) limit students' learning opportunities to only the information required to answer particular test items rather than equipping them with a wide range of skills and knowledge and

(b) encourage rote memorization of specific answers rather than promoting a comprehensive understanding of a field of knowledge and its underlying principles.

## Enter Professional-Development Programs

**Type of damage—Low student test scores resulting from inadequate instruction.** Inefficient teaching methods can contribute to students not succeeding well on tests.

**Teachers' coping strategy.** Teachers improve their instructional skills by engaging in professional-development activities through the use of inservice workshops, seminars, television programs, books, journals, study groups, and Internet courses and chat groups.

**Illustrative case.** Throughout the 2003-2004 school year, the Philadelphia public-school system scheduled bi-weekly Friday-afternoon sessions during which the district's 12,000 teachers studied ways to upgrade their skills in curriculum content, classroom management, and the district's standardized testing and evaluation tools (B. R. Brown, 2003).

**Remaining problems.** Inservice teacher-education programs are of questionable value if they (a) consist chiefly of one-hour speeches by imported "experts," (b) offer few if any specific classroom examples, (c) are not suited to the conditions that the participating teachers normally face in their classrooms (types of students, kinds of learning facilities), or (d) provide teachers no guided practice in applying the recommended techniques.

## Seek Certification

**Type of damage—Schools' unsatisfactory test results due to poorly trained teachers.** Clearly, a variety of factors can contribute to students' performing badly on state tests, with some factors—such as students' genetic endowment and home conditions—beyond the control of the school. But other causes are within the school's province—the most important being the quality of classroom teaching. That quality is chiefly influenced by the individual teacher's knowledge, skills, energy, and dedication. Teachers deficient in those characteristics are unlikely to prepare their students adequately for high-stakes tests.

A key requirement of the *No-Child-Left-Behind Act* is that all teachers, by the 2005-2006 school year, furnish evidence that they are "highly qualified" in the subject matter of their teaching assignment. According to the federal law, such evidence consists of a college bachelor's degree, a state teaching credential, and at least one of the following:

- A master's degree or equivalent undergraduate degree in the subject the candidate teaches.
- Complete national board certification in the subject taught.
- Demonstrated competence in subject matter, general knowledge, and instructional skills by using an assessment method that is evaluated by a local professional-development review team.
- Three years of teaching experience and 18 semester hours of study in a planned teacher-education program.

When judged by these criteria, thousands of the nation's teachers are not "highly qualified" and, therefore, are obligated to earn the stipulated qualification if they are to escape sanctions.

All states have established knowledge and skill standards that teachers are expected to fulfill and ways of certifying that teachers have met those standards. Regional and national teachers' associations also set standards and award certificates of attainment. The kind of evidence most often used for deciding that candidates for teaching are competent has been their satisfactory completion of teacher-education classes that develop the desired skills and knowledge. Sometimes candidates are also required to pass a written test focusing on educational theory and practice.

Whenever there is a shortage of certified teachers available for hire, school districts are left to appoint non-credentialed candidates—ones who lack certification. During the early years of the twenty-first century, there were many thousands of non-certified teachers in America's schools. An important goal of the *No-Child-Left-Behind Act* has been to ensure that every class is taught by a certified teacher. Under the act, schools are rewarded for complying with the certification provision and punished for failing to meet its standards.

**Teachers' coping strategy.** Non-credentialed teachers enter inservice programs that qualify them for credentials. Such programs are of various kinds—traditional preservice teacher-education classes, internships, mentored instruction, correspondence courses, television and radio programs, and study via the Internet.

At an accelerating pace over recent decades, teachers have opted for routes to certification that differ from the traditional full-time series of college courses. By 2003, 46 states and the District of Columbia had alternative ways of certifying elementary and secondary teachers. Between 1985 and 2003, an estimated 200,000 were licensed through alternative means, with most of the growth occurring since the mid-1990s. Over the 1999-2003 period, the rate was about 25,000 people per year. In 2002, states reported 144 different ways, other than traditional college teacher-education programs, for teachers to earn credentials (Alternative teacher certification, 2003)

**Illustrative cases.** Kentucky legislators in 2001 introduced a $2,000 annual supplement for teachers who earned National Board for Professional Teaching Standards certification, which has often been considered the nation's top licensure. Over the 2001-2004 period, the number of national board-certified teachers in Kentucky rose from 37 to 538 (Blackford, 2004).

Bryant Elementary School in Independence, Missouri, was reorganized as a professional-development school that hired expert teachers with the understanding that they would work with pupils and teacher-interns. The experts needed to be national-board certified and would serve as both classroom instructors and trainers of inexperienced interns who thus entered the profession "exposed to reflective practice and conversations about student learning that connect all faculty and staff" (Examples of education reform, 2004).

**Remaining problems.** A variety of conditions can contribute to a school district's inability to find enough fully credentialed teachers. Those conditions include low salaries, unappealing teaching conditions (dangerous neighborhoods, unruly students, remote rural locations), a rapid increase in the student population, and teachers remaining in the profession for only a short time. Thus, schools are often forced to hire people who lack some features of formal qualification.

## Adopt New Teaching Techniques

**Type of damage—Schools dubbed "failing" when pupils show up poorly on state tests.** Ineffective teaching methods can contribute to the low test scores that result in a school being placed in the "needs improvement" category and pupils being denied promotion or graduation.

**Teachers' coping strategy.** Invent or import more effective teaching methods and materials. Sometimes an improved teaching procedure applies to a single classroom, as when one teacher tries an innovative method. But other times a novel approach is introduced simultaneously throughout an entire school, district, or state. Such is the case when a district changes to a particular phonics program for teaching primary-grade reading skills. Or when a district requires that junior-high general-science classes follow a "demonstration-and-hands-on" instructional plan. Or when a state department of education recommends a specific high-school American-history textbook and its allied testing system.

**Illustrative cases.** California schools are rated by an Academic Performance Index (API) that ranges from 200 to 1,000 points, with 800 regarded as excellent. In the city of Oakland, the API for Acorn Woodland Elementary School rose 116 points (from 392 in 2002 to 508 in 2003). The improvement was attributed, at least partly, to teachers having children solve problems in a group (May, 2003). At McKinley Elementary, a San Francisco school enrolling a high proportion of children from disadvantaged homes, the API jumped 96 points (from 609 in 2002 to 705 in 2003). A combination of new teaching techniques was credited with the rise in test scores. For example, the teachers agreed on one skill to emphasize at a time in all their classrooms. In addition, pupils read to their teachers, to each other, and to older students. Each child also maintained an assessment file of charts and graphs on which to track reading progress (Knight, 2003).

The Beaverton School District in Oregon established a *Welcome Center* staffed by former classroom teachers and bilingual specialists fluent in ten languages. The staff improved the success of students from non-English-speaking homes by (a) welcoming immigrant families to the district and testing their children's proficiency in English, (b) training the district's teachers in methods of working with limited-English pupils, and (c) monitoring pupils' progress by collecting samples of their written work and of teacher' observations to identify children who needed extra help and ones who were skilled enough to move out of the special language program (Hammond, 2004b).

**Remaining problems.** A school district or state that mandates a particular teaching method or material may do more harm than good in some classrooms if the innovation (a) fails to fit the learning styles of the particular students, (b) is poorly suited to the instructional skills of the teacher, or (c) replaces an approach that has already been successful.

## Show Parents Ways to Help Their Children

**Type of damage—Low test scores cause students and their parents distress.** In a high-stakes climate, test scores increasingly determine whether students are promoted or graduate, no matter how the children perform in daily class assignments.

**Teachers' coping strategy.** Because family support of students' school progress can be such an important factor in their success, teachers can enhance that support by showing parents ways to prepare children for tests.

**Illustrative case.** Gulfport Elementary School in Pinellas County, Florida, landed in the state test's failing category in 2003. Subsequently, the school staff introduced ways to raise pupils' future scores. One third-grade teacher combined two innovations that promised better test performance. She launched an extended-day plan that kept children at school an extra one-and-one-half hours three days a week so she could coach them in reading and writing exercises and could demonstrate test-taking skills. She felt that the greatest improvement in reading-test scores resulted from increasing parents' participation by having them attend two weekend sessions on classroom activities and engage in a school-wide family reading night (Winchester, 2003).

**Remaining problems.** Parents are often unable or unwilling to attend meetings in which teachers demonstrate ways to promote children's test success. And those who do attend may lack the skill or patience to consistently guide their children's study at home.

## Depend on Alternative Evaluation Methods

**Type of damage—Students' knowledge and skills not adequately assessed by an annual state test.** As described in Chapter 3, multiple-choice tests are inappropriate devices for evaluating pupils' achievement of many of the school's traditional objectives. Therefore, depending solely on objective-type tests for judging students' school success produces a distorted picture of what children have learned.

**Teachers' coping strategy.** Use a variety of evaluation techniques for appraising students' achievement rather than depend solely on standardized multiple-choice and fill-in test items.

**Illustrative cases.** By mid-2004, Nebraska was the only state that had managed to negotiate a statewide portfolio-analysis system with the federal government. Rather than basing judgments of students' and schools' achievement solely on achievement-test scores, Nebraska's 517 school districts founded their evaluations on materials compiled for every student. A typical portfolio contained records of classroom assignments, district tests measuring pupils' progress toward local learning standards, a state writing test, and at least one nationally standardized test (Dell'Angela, 2004). To achieve equality of standards across the state, each district submitted its portfolios to state officials and a team of outside testing experts for review. Districts were then rated on both the proficiency of their students and on the quality and reliability of their portfolios.

In defending the plan, Nebraska Education Commissioner Douglas Christensen said that education was far too complex to be represented by a single test score, so the *No-Child* testing would be integrated into Nebraska's own more comprehensive evaluation system, "not the other way around. If it's bad for kids, we're not going to do it" (Dell'Angela, 2004). Christensen suggested that the portfolio approach rested on the "revolutionary concept" that teachers were more accurate judges of students' learning than were state tests.

Portfolios are not unique to Nebraska. They have been used in many of the nation's school districts, but usually not as substitutes for the *No-Child Act's* test requirement. Often portfolio evaluations are applied only to special groups of students. For example, in 2004 the school progress of about 7,700 severely disabled pupils in Illinois was judged by means of a portfolio plan called the Illinois Alternative Assessment (Olszewski, 2004).

**Remaining problems.** Three limitations of the portfolio system are that it is expensive, is time-consuming for teachers, and makes comparing districts difficult. In the Illinois case, teachers spent as much as 20 to 40 hours compiling portfolios of each child's work that was to be scored by a test contractor. Some observers have complained that portfolios tell more about a teacher's ability to compile and organize evaluation material than about a student's actual ability or progress (Olszewski, 2004).

## Adopt Test-Data-Analysis Software

**Type of damage—Test data not in a form useful to teachers.** The ultimate value of test information for improving schools' success lies in the use of test results by teachers for diagnosing and treating individual students' learning problems. This diagnostic function cannot be performed if the results of students' tests are not readily available to teachers in a form they can understand.

**Teachers' coping strategy.** Obtain computer software that recasts data into a form convenient for analyzing the test-performance patterns of individual students whose specific learning strengths and weaknesses can then be identified and remedied.

**Illustrative case.** Software for analyzing evaluation data can be purchased from a commercial supplier or created by a school district to suit the district's conditions. To help school personnel make wise decisions in selecting software, researchers at Johns Hopkins University reported their appraisal of a wide range of programs in a paper entitled *Software Enabling School Improvement Through Analysis of Student Data* (available from Johns Hopkins' Center for Research on the Education of Students Placed at Risk). The authors proposed that software well suited for student-data analysis should be easy to use, yield relatively rapid results, offer guidance for less sophisticated users, and enable users to study individual grades, classrooms, and students. In addition, teachers should be able to access the computer software from home as well as in school and have the information in a variety of forms, including "quick snapshots, query tools, and preformatted reports" (Olson, 2004b).

**Remaining problems.** One difficulty with commercial versions is that they often need to be altered to fit particular schools' needs. Although districts that create their own programs can fashion the software precisely to match their aims and conditions, doing so can be more expensive than importing a commercial product. In addition, local personnel do not bring to the software-creation task the extensive experience of commercial venders. The costs of adopting a data-analysis programs can range from $2 to $10 per student, depending on such factors as the features the software provides and the size of the school system.

## Resent Intrusions into Professional Decision-Making

**Type of damage—Teachers lack faith in a testing program's worth.** When teachers doubt the wisdom of high-stakes programs, they are offended by what they regard as a distorted view of what education should be. Thus, not only is teachers' enthusiasm for the *No-Child Act's* provisions dampened, but they may actively circumvent and weaken the implementation of the testing system.

**Teachers' coping strategy.** Publicly criticize what they regard as flaws in high-stakes programs.

**Illustrative cases.** The following are comments collected during surveys of teachers' opinions about the *No-Child-Left-Behind Act* (Wermers, 2004; Lynn, 2004b).

> It's interesting to note that almost everyone outside the classroom and education system can tell us how to do our job and what standards we must reach based only on the fact that they once sat in a desk in a classroom.

> The benefits are questionable, the promised money seems to be shrinking, and the accountability metrics are not what good teachers consider to be 'authentic assessment.'

> Sounds very good in theory but doesn't work very well in reality.

> The grades teachers give aren't enough anymore. Now, the state and the feds want to test and test and test before advancing or graduating students.

> If a few students lag behind their peers, an entire school is seen as failing under President Bush's sweeping education reforms.

> Business and higher education leaders complain about meaningless high-school diplomas. State lawmakers respond by passing more unfunded mandates.

**Remaining problems.** If teachers publicize their complaints, school officials may pay attention and attempt to make adjustments in high-stakes programs. But complaints may not be publicized, so that unsatisfactory features of testing may go uncorrected if school authorities (a) squelch and threaten "whistle blowers" or (b) accuse teachers of grumbling about tests in order to cover up their own incompetence.

## Confront Politicians Over High-Stakes Testing

**Type of damage—Disheartened educators.** Teachers are the people ultimately held responsible for improving students' test scores through better instruction. Teachers' zeal and their sense of doing the best for their students are diminished when they believe harm results from high-stakes testing.

**Teachers' coping strategies.** One way teachers hope to cause politicians to correct errors in testing programs is by presenting their opinions at legislative hearings or school board meetings.

**Illustrative case.** In testifying before a California legislative committee, Barbara Kerr (California Teachers Association president), reported the following results of a survey taken of teachers' attitudes about the state's high-stakes testing program.

- More than 80% of teachers (a) felt pressured to raise test scores and (b) believed the state testing program was not a successful motivator of students' achievement.
- More than 70% felt pressured to change their instructional methods in order to teach to the test. They believed that teaching-to-the-test (a) fails to encourage the most valuable kind of student learning, since it discourages the development of students' analytical skills, (b) reduces the range of material taught, and (c) diverts resources away from valued instructional materials and into test-preparation materials.
- More than 60% thought that (a) focusing instruction on the state test reduces the overall quality of students' education, (b) instruction for minority and lower-income students is limited by its attention solely to subjects that are likely to be on the test, and (b) high-school exit exams are inappropriate for students with limited English skills who have mastered the material in their own language.
- Over 50% agreed that the testing system widens the gap between the quality of education provided to poorer children and that furnished to more privileged children (Kerr, 2002).

**Remaining problems.** Representatives of large teachers unions usually have access to legislative bodies and individual politicians because of the number of voters the unions represent. Individual teachers who have grievances to vent or suggestions for educational reform enjoy far less access. And even when they can contact politicians or staff members, their opinions are often dismissed as petty and insignificant.

## Accusing the Federal Government of Underfunding

**Type of damage—Teachers faulted for not achieving high-stakes goals.** When insufficient money is provided to support the *No-Child Act's* provisions (testing, tutoring, instructional materials), students are more likely to perform poorly on tests and teachers can be blamed for the low test scores.

**Teachers' coping strategy.** With their unions as their representatives, teachers accuse politicians of failing to adequately fund the implementation of high-stakes programs.

**Illustrative case.** Sandra Feldman, president of the one-million-member American Federation of Teachers, reacted to President George W. Bush's 2004 budget proposal by telling news reporters that the union agreed with having clear standards and accountability, but that the federal program was not being funded adequately—"A [funding] increase that is billions short of what you need to carry out the mandates just doesn't do it." According to Joel Packer, a National Education Association staff member, the Bush administration actually proposed cuts in *No-Child-Left-Behind* funding in 2003 and 2004, but Congress restored the money (Bush defends education act, 2004).

**Remaining problems.** Whether more money would ensure that teachers would do a better job of equipping students to pass tests has been a much-debated issue. In the 2004 national election campaigns, Democrats charged that the Bush administration had failed to fund the *No-Child Act* adequately enough to prepare students for testing. In response, Republicans asserted that the federal funds had been quite sufficient for the task (Sanger, 2003; Sanger & Rutenberg, 2004).

## Taking Offense at No-Child-Left-Behind Demands

**Type of damage—Experienced teachers hate being labeled "unqualified."** As noted earlier, a key requirement of the *No-Child-Left-Behind Act* is that all teachers, by the 2005-2006 school year, furnish evidence that they are "highly qualified" in the subject matter of their teaching assignment.

**Teachers' coping strategy.** Privately and publicly, experienced teachers who do not fulfill all of the criteria of the *No-Child* "highly qualified" standard often express their distress at what they consider offensive allegations about their competence.

**Illustrative cases.** In Michigan an estimated 5,500 (5%) of the state's 110,000 teachers were "not highly qualified" under federal criteria. Typical of the teachers who were enraged over the new rules was Joanne Peurach, who had taught language arts for two decades in the Detroit area's Novi Middle School. She had both bachelor and master degrees, earned by majoring in education with a minor in English, but she did not meet the federal standard of having majored in English or language arts. Her reaction to her newly acquired "unqualified" status was: "It's totally an insult. If you were to do this to any other profession, they wouldn't stand for it" (Coates, 2004).

In support of Peurach's annoyance, Terri Moblo, head of the Novi Education Association vented her distress about teachers with very successful records being expected to confess that they were not highly qualified. And "even if teachers want to become 'highly qualified', there's no financial incentive" (Coates, 2004).

As a second example, the Montana 2003 teacher-of-the-year, Jon Runnals, traditionally taught several sciences—astronomy, geology, physics, and biology. "But since I don't have a degree in those subjects, I am not considered highly qualified," he explained, and was thus in danger of punitive actions. Although the *No-Child* law permits veteran teachers to demonstrate competency in each subject they teach by taking a test written by their state, Montana had no such test and lacked the money to create one (Dillon, 2004c).

Nevada lawmakers were warned in early 2004 that the federal "highly qualified" requirement could cause veteran teachers to resign rather than face more schooling, tests, and sanctions. Only two-thirds of the state's current teachers were "highly qualified." Thus, many others still needed to meet the federal standard. Officials reported that 83 teachers had retired in Washoe County during the past year—significantly more than in previous years (Educators: new law, 2004). Ken Lange, director of the Nevada State Education Association, said that veteran teachers made a particularly strong contribution to the quality of education by guiding new teachers. He said that kind of service was especially important because only about 30% of new teachers were still in the profession after five years (Educators: new law, 2004).

**Remaining problems.** Proponents of the "highly-qualified" requirements of the *No-Child* legislation dismiss veteran teachers' outrage as a sign of either laziness or the teachers' own lack of confidence in their fitness for the job.

# Refuse to Give Tests

**Type of damage—Too much time spent on testing.** When many days are required for administering tests, too little time is available for teaching.

**Teachers' coping strategy.** Avoid testing children.

**Illustrative case.** An Ohio law ordered teachers to administer a new state exam in reading, math, and writing to children in kindergarten, first grade, and second grade. In responding to the order, the president of the Cleveland Teachers Union, Richard DeColibus, said that giving the exams would consume at least five to eight days of class time because many of the tests had to be given to pupils individually. The assessment task included such things as listening to a child read, identify letters on a page, and place numbers in a sequence. School districts with a record of sufficient progress under *No-Child* regulations could choose to use their own home-grown assessments rather than the state's new tests. But districts that had failed to show enough progress were required to use the state exams.

DeColibus said, "We've told our people not to do it. To a teacher, instructional time is like gold. We simply refuse to give up that instructional time" (Stephens, 2003).

**Remaining problems.** When teachers decline to give tests, they open themselves to reprisals by district and state officials, such as publicized censure, delayed promotion, or dismissal. An additional problem in the Ohio case was that most teachers had received no training in how to administer the tests properly. The success of refusing to test is greater as the number of renegades increases, and particularly if they are represented by a union or association that wields political power.

## Conduct Public Demonstrations

**Type of damage—Schools' "failure" due to a shortage of funds.** Activities required for meeting achievement targets under the *No-Child Act* can be expensive (tutoring, bilingual specialists, inservice teacher training, new instructional materials). Schools' chances of meeting the *No-Child* standards are poor if the money to support the required activities is insufficient.

**Teachers' coping strategy.** Attract the attention of law-makers and the general public to the teachers' plight by organizing rallies that are given widespread television, radio, and newspaper coverage.

**Illustrative case.** As the central feature of Arizona's annual Education-Day celebration in 2004, hundreds of teachers rallied at the state capitol to voice their support for protecting public-school funding and for promoting early-childhood education. The event was designed to impress legislators with the importance of adequately financing educational reform (Juozapavicius, 2004).

**Remaining problems.** It is often difficult to recruit large numbers of teachers to participate in public demonstrations, because they fear being seen by government officials and the public as little more than grumpy malcontents and troublemakers. Vulnerable, hypersensitive legislators, school-board members, and administrators who are the targets of demonstrations may respond to the teachers' demands with reprisals—limit school funds, postpone or deny teachers' promotions, or find grounds for dismissing or demoting demonstration participants.

## Propose Suing the Federal Government

**Type of damage—Alarmingly high rate of failure among pupils and schools.** Critics of the federal *No-Child Act* cite a host of reasons that the law has caused so many children and schools to be called failures. A chief complaint has been that the federal government did not provide enough money to carry out the act's requirements.

**Teachers' coping strategy.** Urge state officials to file lawsuits that will force the elimination of the *No-Child Act*.

**Illustrative case.** Oregon's Governor Ted Kulongoski called the *No-Child* law "a hoax" in a speech to a gathering of Oregon school-board members. Subsequently, representatives of the nation's largest teachers union, the National Education Association, urged the governor to sue the Bush administration for not adequately funding the law's implementation (Hammond, 2003d).

**Remaining problems.** Three barriers to getting a governor to sue the national government are political risks, time, and money. If Governor Kulongoski had agreed to the suit, he could have invited retribution from Republicans in his own state and from the Bush administration. Furthermore, lawsuits are usually strung out over months or years and would distract the governor and his staff from other urgent affairs. Finally, lawyers charge high fees, so a suit against the national government could cost millions of dollars, a prospect not pleasing to taxpayers.

## Avoid Difficult School Situations

**Type of damage—A shortage of qualified teachers contributes to students' poor test performance.** School districts that offer low pay and unappealing living conditions fail to attract enough skilled teachers. As a result, their students are not well prepared for state tests and their schools are labeled failures because they are expected to meet the same federal standards held for schools in attractive, affluent communities.

**Teachers' coping strategies.** Shun schools that pay poorly and are located in discouraging settings.

**Illustrative case.** Dangerous inner-city schools and ones in isolated rural settings usually suffer extraordinary difficulty attracting and retaining competent teachers. Among those schools that face the most serious teacher-recruitment problems are ones that are located on sparsely populated, remote Indian reservations, such as the Standing Rock Reservation in North Dakota. With one of the lowest pay scales in the nation and little in the way of lifestyle incentives, many reservation schools have trouble attracting teachers, particularly in view of the newly imposed *No-Child* requirement that all teachers must have a major in the subjects they teach or go back to school to get requalified. Officials at Standing Rock Elementary reported that not even one candidate had applied for the science-teacher position that the school had advertised for months. Five teaching posts—including ones in reading and math—had been open for months at Belcourt, a school on the northern Turtle Mountain reservation, while there were 200 vacant teaching positions across the state (Harman, 2003).

**Remaining problems.** The prospects are dim for improving the recruitment of highly qualified teachers for schools in dangerous urban neighborhoods and inaccessible rural regions. In North Dakota, where two-thirds of college graduates move out of the state for better-paying jobs, Indian reservation schools are left with aging teachers who have little time or energy for retraining. Gloria Lokken, president of the state teachers' union, explained that the *No-Child* "highly quailfied" standard was unrealistic in rural schools where teachers offer instruction in three or four subjects. "We need some flexibility. This is not Philadelphia or Baltimore, where you have a teacher with a drama major who teaches five sections of drama and walks home" (Harman, 2003).

## Cheat to Raise Students' Test Scores

**Type of damage—Falsified reports of students' test performance.** Faced with the prospect of being blamed for students' poor test results, some teachers adopt illicit means for improving test scores. Such practices contribute to false reports of student progress that can invalidate the "school report cards" that are intended to help parents, taxpayers, and state officials evaluate the performance of schools and teachers. Cheating by teachers also sets a bad moral example for learners and violates the integrity of the entire testing process.

**Illustrative cases.** Over the 1999-2002 period, New York education officials found 21 proven cases of cheating. Teachers' deceitful acts included reading out answers during a test, sending students back to correct wrong answers, photocopying secure tests to use in test preparation sessions, inflating test scores, and illicitly reviewing tests in advance so as to tailor instruction to match specific questions.

Instances of teachers cheating in other states include the following (Gormley, 2003; Harrison, 2004)

- A Reston, Virginia, teacher was placed on paid leave in June 2000 and 18 eighth-graders were retested after they allegedly were prepped with questions that showed up on their state social-studies exam.
- Students at a Columbus, Ohio, school—praised for its test scores by President Clinton in 2000—said that adult tutors had guided their pencils to the correct answers or had calculated math problems while students took the mandatory state test.
- A grand jury in Austin, Texas, indicted 18 school officials in April 2000 for altering student tests.
- A Harvard study found cheating in Chicago that was motivated by teachers' need to improve standardized test scores. "We found cheating increased by 30% to 50% because of high-stakes testing," said Brian Jacobs of the John F. Kennedy School of Government at Harvard and co-author of the report "Rotten Apples."
- Students at Park Ridge Elementary in Pompano Beach, Florida, told investigators that, during the administration of the state tests in 2002, teachers had placed check marks next to correct answers.

In at least 75 out of 200 cases of alleged cheating in California schools, teachers were found guilty of such violations as whispering answers to students, photocopying test booklets so students could learn vocabulary words in advance, and erasing score sheets that had wrong answers and substituting correct ones. Whereas most violations led to reprimands, in some cases teachers resigned or were dismissed (Educators found, 2004).

Suspicion of test cheating can be generated various ways. In particular, a school's sudden dramatic rise in test scores can alert officials to the possibility of deceit, as in the case of a Massachusetts elementary school in which the number of fourth-graders failing the math section of the state test dropped from 60% to 2% over a two-year period (Vaishnav, 2003). In Florida, the state department of education refused to give Miami's West Little River Elementary School a grade, even though the school scored enough test points to rise from an F to an A. State officials told Miami-Dade schools to inform parents of children who had dramatic gains in test scores that those gains might be fake (Harrison, 2004).

**Remaining problems.** It is sometimes difficult to distinguish between legitimate and illegitimate aid for students. If a student has trouble figuring out the directions for taking a test, can a teacher properly rephrase the directions, or does that constitute unwarranted help? If the test is given in a noisy or disorderly setting, can a teacher properly allow more time to complete the test? If a student's eyesight is so poor that questions cast in small type are hard to decipher, should a teacher be allowed to read questions aloud to the student?

## Acquire Bogus Degrees

**Type of damage—False evidence of teachers' qualifications.** It is widely assumed that the more subject-matter knowledge and instructional skill a teacher brings to the job, the more adequately that teacher's students will be prepared for state tests. It is also assumed that teachers' college degrees and credentials reflect the level of their knowledge of what to teach and how to teach it. But if degrees and credentials are falsified, they represent an unwarranted claim of expertise. In other words, the skills and knowledge such teachers bring to their task is below the level that their "paper qualifications" suggest. Consequently, their students will not likely receive the quality of instruction expected from a properly certified educator.

**Teachers' coping strategy.** Under the pressure to meet the *No-Child Act's* "highly qualified" standards, some teachers acquire bogus diplomas—certificates that erroneously suggest the bearers have, through hard work, gained the high level of knowledge and skill that such credentials imply.

**Illustrative cases.** The expression *diploma mills* identifies enterprises that sell college degrees without requiring anything more than money from their applicants. Teaching is one of the few professions that directly connects college degrees and similar preparation to the salary scale. The more evidence of formal education (college preservice programs, inservice workshops, seminars, Internet courses) that a teacher compiles, the higher the salary paid. School districts, in operating such a system, face the problem of determining if the evidence of a teacher's education is trustworthy. One important indicator of trust is that the degree-granting institution has been endorsed by a respected state, regional, or national accrediting body.

An example of a diploma mill is the Liberia-based St. Regis University. In 2004, the Georgia Department of Education checked the records of the state's 130,000 teachers and discovered 11 who had presented advanced degrees from St. Regis. One was a middle-school math teacher who had received a $16,000 pay raise in 2003 upon submitting papers showing that she had earned a St. Regis doctorate (Chu, 2004).

Not all diploma mills are located overseas. Texas educational authorities have investigated a number of teachers who received salary increases on the basis of their presenting degrees from the now-defunct Crescent City Christian College that operated out of a house in Metairie, Louisiana (Morales, 2004).

**Remaining problems.** Because there are so many colleges and inservice-education programs in the world, it is often difficult for school districts to verify the status of a teacher's credentials. And not only have diploma mills been expanding their operations in recent years but, with the spread of the Internet, an increasing number of illegal entrepreneurs have been offering forged diplomas that supposedly were granted by legitimate universities.

# Conclusion

Teachers can differ markedly from each other in a variety of characteristics that influence their effectiveness, including such characteristics as their energy level, years of experience in the classroom, command of subject matter, and ability to control a classroom of students. In short, teachers—in their talents and personality traits—are a very diverse lot. Furthermore, the kinds of pupils and the kinds of environments in which teachers ply their trade can also be extremely varied. Managing 13 kindergarteners in an private elementary school in a wealthy suburb offers quite a different challenge than does teaching 40 public-high-school youths in a large city's dilapidated industrial district. Consequently, trying to identify what all teachers and their jobs share in common is a perplexing task.

However, in the area of high-stakes testing, it is possible to identify at least one characteristic in which teachers are much alike—they understand better than any of the other kinds of people described in this book (politicians, administrators, parents, the public, test-makers, students) the relationship between classroom practice and students' performance on high-stakes tests. That knowledge is vital to the planning of any system intended to account for how well schools are doing their job. But it is my strong impression that teachers are seldom assigned a significant role in planning high-stakes-testing programs. I am convinced that planners of such programs as the *No-Child* legislation could have avoided a goodly amount of collateral damage if they had seriously weighed the views of experienced teachers—teachers from different grade levels with varied kinds of students in diverse social settings.

# 11

# Students

Students, like teachers, are a motley assortment of individuals who differ from each other in many important ways—age, ability, health status, interests, ambition, personal appearance, social skills, home environment, cultural traditions, academic success, and more. Because students are such a diverse breed, they respond to high-stakes testing in diverse ways. Many of them study diligently and thus pass the tests without suffering ill effects. Others adopt special means for coping with high-stakes testing in their attempt to avoid unwanted consequences. This chapter focuses on such coping methods and on problems that may remain after those methods have been tried.

## Types of Coping Strategies

The 18 kinds of coping behaviors reviewed in the following pages involve students (a) retaking tests, (b) enrolling in special classes, (c) attending summer school, (d) adopting alternative ways to graduate, (e) earning a GED certificate, (f) trying alternative evaluation methods, (g) transferring to another school, (h) not taking tests seriously, (i) boycotting tests, (j) dropping out, (k) buying a diploma, (l) suffering distress, (m) publicly expressing disappointment, (n) not feeling challenged, (o) declining to take make-up exams, (p) rejecting transfer opportunities, (q) stealing test materials, and (r) threatening violence.

### Retake Tests

**Type of damage—High incidence of test failure.** Large numbers of students earn unsatisfactory scores the first time they take a state test. Consequently, many are in danger of missing promotion or graduation.

**Students' coping strategy.** Accept opportunities to retake tests.

**Illustrative cases.** To earn a high-school diploma in Florida, students have been required to (a) compile a specified number of course credits, (b) maintain an acceptable grade-point average, and (c) pass either the Florida Comprehensive Assessment Test (FCAT) or the General Educational Development test. Those who fail the FCAT can retake it as many times as they wish in grades 10, 11, and 12 (Grant, 2004).

**Remaining problems.** Students disheartened by failing a test once or twice may despair of ever passing. Therefore, not wishing to expose themselves to the likelihood of more failure, they avoid trying again. And a problem from the school system's perspective is that considerable expense is involved in retesting large numbers of students.

## Enroll in Special Classes

**Type of damage—Students fail to be promoted.** Children's chance of promotion to the next higher grade can depend entirely on how well they score on a high-stakes test, regardless of how adequately they performed on daily classroom assignments.

**Students' coping strategy.** Attend extra test-preparation classes or tutoring sessions.

**Illustrative cases.** As New York City third-graders in 2004 faced the prospect of not being promoted to fourth grade if they failed high-stakes tests, an increasing number of parents enrolled their children in extra classes. For example, one mother spent $380 for special Saturday courses at Queensborough Community College and $150 for extra test preparation at her daughter's school each morning before class. In Queensborough's program for third-graders, six sessions of reading preparation cost $185 and seven sessions of math preparation $195. Another parent paid $8,000 for private tutoring at a Sylvan Learning Center (Herszenhorn & Gootman, 2004).

In 2004, public schools in Connecticut had around 22,500 students who qualified for language-learner classes designed for students who were not fluent in English because they came from homes in which a foreign language was spoken. Among the 145 languages or dialects found among immigrant families, Spanish was the most common, used by 60% of the schools' language-learner students. Any school with 20 or more students speaking the same non-English language was obligated to offer a bilingual-education program. In schools without a bilingual program, instruction was primarily in English. Connecticut's language-learner students were required to take standardized math tests the first year they enrolled and to take tests in other subjects the following year (Thousands of immigrant students, 2004).

**Remaining problems.** Unless a school district has an efficient way to inform parents of special classes or tutoring for children who are in danger of failing tests, parents will not avail themselves of those opportunities. This communication problem is particularly serious for immigrants who have a weak command of English. Furthermore, unless the special help is free of cost, families living at the poverty level—whose children are most often at risk of failure—cannot take advantage of the aid.

## Attend Summer School

**Type of damage—Students fail to be promoted.** Not passing tests results in students being retained in the same grade for another year.

**Students' coping strategy.** For a chance to earn promotion after having failed tests in the spring, students enroll in summer-school classes and are then retested.

**Illlustrative cases.** An experimental group of 1,300 third-graders who failed Florida's Comprehensive Assessment Test in 2003 were required to attend 12 days of summer school during which teachers met with small groups of pupils for reading instruction. The success of the venture prompted officials in Hillsborough County to introduce a similar set of 18-day camps for poor readers from kindergarten through grade three. In the county's voluntary camps, 12 children spent four-and-one-half hours each day with a teacher, focusing entirely on reading skills (Ave, 2003).

Eighty-one percent of the students in Virginia's Prince William County who completed classes that were offered over the Internet in 2002 passed the state Standards of Learning test. As a result, in 2003 the online classes were expanded as a summertime offering to York County students (Samuels, 2003).

After the Philadelphia school district introduced a policy requiring summer school for learners who failed high-stakes exams, 17,675 students attended the 2003 summer sessions. Of that number,15,363 (87%) passed when retested after their summer study and thereby earned promotion to the next higher grade (M. M. Dean, 2003).

**Remaining problems.** Students often resent being required to attend school during a vacation period when their agemates are free to play or earn money working. Parents who wish to take their families on trips during the summer may resist sending their children to summer school.

## Take an Alternative Path to Graduation

**Type of damage—High-school seniors fail to graduate.** When high-school graduation depends on passing high-stakes tests, large numbers of students can be denied diplomas.

**Students' coping strategy.** Some school systems provide routes to graduation that do not include passing standardized achievement tests, so students who fail tests can choose to earn diplomas via such routes.

**Illustrative case.** To help certain students fulfill New Jersey's high-school graduation requirements, state officials established an alternative Special Review Assessment (SRA) program designed to aid a small percentage of youths who had unusual difficulty taking standardized tests. The program included a semester-long class for students who had failed at least one of the two sections of the regular High School Proficiency Test. During the class, students were taught material on which they had performed poorly on the test. At semester's end, they completed a set of state-developed questions and tasks to show they had learned the material. In 2004, 20% of the state's high-school seniors were on track to earn a diploma via the SRA system. Among the 30 neediest school districts, the proportion of seniors scheduled to graduate without passing the state's regular proficiency exam ranged from a low of 20% in Phillipsburg to a high of 70% in Newark and Trenton (McNichol, 2004).

**Remaining problems.** New Jersey's education commissioner, William Librera, told state legislators that about 20,000 seniors statewide were taking the SRA path to graduation, which he said was "well beyond where it should be. . . . I think SRA is part of the fundamental problem. It creates too easy an alternative that is applied too widely." In support of Librera's complaint was a letter from a Newark school-advisory-committee member reporting that at the city's West Side High School, 134 out of 150 graduates in 2003 had chosen the SRA route (McNichol, 2004).

## Select the GED Option

**Type of damage.** Seldom are students admitted to college or given the opportunity for desirable, well-paying employment if they lack a high-school diploma, and the chances of earning a diploma without passing high-stakes tests have become increasingly slight.

**Students' coping strategy.** The American Council on Education operates the General Educational Development (GED) testing service that prepares and distributes tests assessing students' skills and knowledge in English language reading and writing, math, social studies (including history), and science. The GED system was created after World War II to enable American war veterans to earn a high-school diploma without actually returning to school. By passing the tests, students earn a GED diploma, which is intended to be the academic equivalent of a regular high-school diploma. According to the Council, more than 860,000 adults worldwide annually take the GED exams, with one out of every seven high-school diplomas issued each year in the United States earned through the GED route. Individuals "who obtain scores high enough to earn a GED credential outperform at least 40% of today's high-school seniors" (Welcome to the Official Site, 2004).

The number of youths taking the GED path has grown rapidly in recent times. According to an economist at the Urban Institute in Washington, the proportion of youths earning GED's had doubled since 1989, whereas high-school graduation rates had slightly declined (Arenson, 2004). In 2001, when 2.8 million students received traditional high-school diplomas, about 266,000 teenagers earned GED certificates.

**Illustrative case.** In New York City more than 37,000 school-age students were in GED programs operated by the public school system in 2004, a figure up from 25,500 in 2002. Analysts suggested that trouble finding a decent job without a high-school diploma, combined with the difficulty in many states of earning a traditional diploma, was a strong factor in motivating dropouts to try the GED route. In New York State, much of the increase in the number of GED participants apparently resulted from the legislature requiring students to pass five Regents exams in order to graduate, so there was no longer a lesser diploma for weaker students. In addition, as the *No-Child-Left-Behind* law made high test scores the basis for rating schools' effectiveness, school personnel had greater incentive to discourage weak students from staying in school.

**Remaining problems.** The status of GED diplomas in the public's eye is a matter of continuing debate. Critics claim that the GED is generally viewed by educators and employers as a kind of "booby prize" for inept scholars. For example, Chester E. Finn, Jr., of the conservative Fordham Foundation, has deplored the increase of GED diplomas. "If the GED were a true 'equivalency' program, perhaps this would not be a foul deed, but it's widely understood that people presenting such a certificate in lieu of 'real' diplomas do not get as far in life" (Finn, 2004).

In response, the American Council on Education has claimed that "More than 95% of U.S. employers consider GED graduates the same as traditional high-school graduates in regard to hiring, salary, and opportunity for advancement" (Welcome to the Official Site, 2004).

246 Players' Coping Strategies

## Attempt an Alternative Evaluation Route

**Type of damage—Students with disabilities denied diplomas.** When students fail their high-school's graduation test and thereby do not graduate, their chances for well-paid and satisfying employment are significantly reduced, and their sense of self-worth can be diminished.

**Students' coping strategy.** Substitute evidence of competence other than test results to show they deserve a diploma.

**Illustrative case.** Education regulations in Massachusetts permit students with severe disabilities to offer a collection of their class work as an alternative to passing the state's graduation exam. Such portfolios typically include worksheets in math and English, essays, and drawings showing something about pupils' knowledge of science. Over the three-year period since the plan began in 2001, more than 2,000 high-school students submitted portfolios for evaluation. However, during that time only 47 candidates, or 2.4%, were awarded diplomas. The portfolio option has been available at other grade levels as well, with the state department of education receiving more then 15,000 submissions from around 6% of the public schools' special-education students (Schworm, 2004).

**Remaining problems.** Some observers have claimed that the standards for judging portfolios are too strict. Of the 700 high-school seniors who furnished collections of their work in 2003, none met the standards in math and English, although a few passed upon filing an appeal for a reevaluation. Lisa Guisbond of the Massachusetts Coalition for Authentic Reform in Education said she worried that officials simply expected such students to fail, but "The standards should be flexible and broad enough to be inclusive of kids of different talents and abilities" (Schworm, 2004).

## Seek Transfer to a Different School

**Type of damage—Students fear they will fail tests.** Students and their parents are convinced that the students' present school will not prepare them adequately for high-stakes tests.

**Students' coping strategy.** Try to move to a school with a reputation for having a high proportion of students performing well on standardized tests.

**Illustrative case.** The nation's largest school district, New York City, has offered learners from low-scoring high schools the opportunity to transfer to other public schools of their choice. By early 2004, students were allowed to apply to as many as 12 schools, compared to seven choices in 2003, with the options expanded to include dozens of additional small high schools that opened in 2004. A computer program designed to match learners' characteristics with schools' characteristics was introduced to upgrade the efficiency of the transfer process (Gootman & Herszenhorn, 2004).

**Remaining problems.** Despite the improvements in the transfer system, 12,000 to 14,000 students would not be admitted in 2004 to any of the New York schools listed on students' applications, although that figure was far better than the 35,000 who were denied transfer to any school of their choice in 2003. In early 2004, there were still openings in 91 schools; but among those were 12 that the state department of education had listed as "academically failing" and 14 that were identified as "dangerous" (Gootman & Herszenhorn, 2004).

Because of problems with New York's 2003-2004 transfer program, the city changed the plan for 2004-2005. School principals had complained that when over 7,000 students transferred to more successful schools in 2003-2004, the recipient schools had suffered overcrowding and a decline in teaching efficiency. In addition, the program had cost the city more than $20-million for transportation, labor, and other expenses in allowing children to transfer. For the autumn of 2004, fewer than 1,000 transfers would be granted, with priority going to poor children with low test scores. In defense of the new policy, the chairman of the city's education committee, Assemblyman Steven Sanders, said even though parental choice as an ideal might sound great, if in the policy's application "your child ends up in a school that is now grossly overcrowded, that's not so great for the child either" (Gootman, 2004c).

## Don't Take Tests Seriously

**Type of damage—Students aggravated by high-stakes tests.** Students can be annoyed by being forced to submit to so much testing, and they may see no good reason for taking tests.

**Students' coping strategy.** They rush through a test, marking items almost at random so the score they earn is not an accurate reflection of their actual knowledge.

**Illustrative cases.** Seven seniors at Lake Shore High School in St. Clair Shores, Michigan, carelessly raced through the 2004 Michigan Educational Assessment Program (MEAP) exam, thereby ending up with low scores. As punishment, they were assigned to three hours of detention and required to write a statement telling why the MEAP was important. The seven had already passed the MEAP in 2003 but, like their classmates, were offered a half-day off school on prom day if they took the exam again in 2004 in order to help boost the school's scores. They had accepted the offer but had failed to take the occasion seriously because they had already done well on the MEAP the previous year (Higgins, 2004).

When the California State Board of Education postponed the high-school graduation-exam requirement from 2004 to 2006, officials worried that students would interpret the postponement as a sign that the exam was not very important. Therefore, when students were assigned to take the test in 2004 and 2005 in its preliminary form, they might not try their best to perform well (Slonaker, 2003).

**Remaining problems.** In Michigan, the Lake Shore incident focused state legislators' attention on the usefulness of the MEAP. One senator complained that when students failed to see the relevance of the test, officials attempted all sorts of devices to try to make the test important, such as offering scholarships and free pizza for trying the test (Higgins, 2004).

Opponents of the MEAP suggested that the test should be dropped because it not only consumed much of students' time but colleges did not consider the MEAP results in their admission decisions so that many students viewed the test as unimportant (Higgins, 2004).

## Boycott Test Sessions

**Types of damage—Students' learning is not fairly assessed and test-taking uses too much time.** A well-balanced evaluation of students' learning and of schools' effectiveness cannot result from a single set of multiple-choice tests in a few subject-matter fields. Consequently, decisions about students' lives and the fate of schools, when based solely on high-stakes test results, are apt to be wrong. In addition, the value of state achievement tests for students may not be worth the time and bother that exam sessions require.

**Students' coping strategy.** Avoid going to school on testing days.

**Illustrative cases.** In Minneapolis and St. Paul, numbers of high-school students skipped school on the days that the Minnesota Comprehensive Assessments (MCA) tests were administered in 2003. The participation rate varied significantly from one school to another. Whereas in Minneapolis attendance ranged from 75% at North High to over 90% at Southwest, at St. Paul Central School nearly half of the tenth-graders who were scheduled to take the reading test failed to appear. Central's principal accounted for the students' absences by explaining that the students realized that the tests were not essential for graduation. "Last year, I told them they couldn't go to the prom, but that didn't intimidate them, [so this year] we're pulling them out of their classes. They either do it today or we're taking them out of their classes this week" (Walsh, 2003a).

In California, some of San Diego's brightest high-school seniors chose to opt out of state tests because they and their parents believed the amount of testing was unduly burdensome. Originally, 40 Bonita Vista High School students had rebelled because of the overwhelming number of difficult exams they faced—not only the state tests for the *No-Child* program but also advanced placement exams, international baccalaureate exams, and SATs important for applying to college. Eventually, after some pleading and implied sanctions from Bonita Vista's principal, 23 of the dissidents agreed to be tested but 17 remained unwilling to take part (Branscomb, 2004).

**Remaining problems.** For students, a boycott may result in punishment by school personnel, such as the loss of privileges, a reputation as a trouble-maker, low marks on report cards, and teachers being unwilling to write letters of recommendation. For school administrators, boycotts can be difficult to resolve if politically influential parents support their offsprings' actions.

## Drop Out of School

**Type of damage.** Students fail high-stakes tests, or at least they fear they will fail.

**Students' coping strategy.** Leave high school before receiving a diploma.

**Illustrative cases.** One study of high-school graduation rates in Massachusetts estimated that between 23% and 25% of eighth graders dropped out of school before earning a diploma, a figure higher than the 15% reported by the state's department of education. The graduation rate for blacks was 24 percentage points below that for whites, and for Hispanics was 37 percentage points below whites' (Ramer, 2004). Only 36% of Hispanic high-school students graduated, a figure far below the 53% national average for Hispanics. Around 50% of the Massachusetts' Afro-American students earned high-school diplomas, 15% higher than New York's rate of 35% (Rothstein, 2004b). In 2003—the first year that students were required to pass the Massachusetts Comprehensive Assessment System (MCAS) exam in order to graduate—the incidence of dropouts among seniors in Boston public schools rose from 7% to 7.7%, in Holyoke from 7.6% to 10.2%, and in Framingham from 1.2% to 3.7% (Vaishnav, 2004). However, a report from the politically conservative Manhattan Institute concluded that "Having a small number of students fail to graduate because of a test is offset by the improvements fostered in other students." In disagreeing with the conclusions from the Institute study, a Boston College researcher calculated that the state's graduation rate dropped from 76% in 2002 to 72% in 2003, with the rate among black students falling from 71% to 60% and among Hispanics from 54% to 45% (Rothstein, 2004d).

Gwinnet County, Georgia, reported that the 2003 high-school dropout rate of 6% was twice that of the previous year and most serious among Hispanics who left school at double the rate of their classmates (M. MacDonald, 2003).

In both 2002 and 2003, Texas had the lowest percentage of high-school graduates in the nation when 77% of Texans over age 25 had diplomas, the same percent as in 1993. Whereas other states' graduation rates improved over the years, so that 85% of Americans now had high-school degrees, Texas was still "treading water" (Spencer, 2004). Among ethnic groups in Texas, the lowest graduation rate was among Hispanics, the state's fastest-growing segment of the population, with only half of 4.3 million Hispanics age 25 and older having a high-school diploma.

**Remaining problems.** As noted earlier, high-school dropouts have far fewer chances for satisfying, well-paying employment than do students with regular diplomas or GED certificates. Rarely will dropouts be admitted to colleges.

## Purchase Private-School Diplomas

**Type of damage—Students fail to graduate from high school.** When graduation depends on students passing high-stakes tests, large numbers of youths can end their school career without a diploma.

**Students' coping strategy.** Buy a diploma from another school.

**Illustrative case.** Students who flunk high-school exit tests have been able to submit a record of their course work and supplementary educational experiences to North Atlantic Regional High School in Lewiston, Maine, and—for a $255 fee—receive a high-school diploma. North Atlantic Regional is a private school, designed to aid parents who home-school their children. More than 80% of North Atlantic's clients in 2004 lived outside of Maine, with the highest concentration of 400 in Florida where high-school graduation depended on passing the state's Comprehensive Assessment Test. Florida's education commissioner, Jim Horne, objected to the practice of purchasing out-of-state diplomas, but felt he could do nothing to prevent it. He was particularly concerned that the imported diplomas allowed youths to pursue higher education at such institutions as Miami Dade College, where North Atlantic Regional diplomas were treated the same as Florida diplomas.

When the administrators of North Atlantic Regional, Steve and Carol Moitozo, were asked about the school's operating methods, they reported that they analyzed applicants' course work, standardized test scores, internship activities, and other parts of an educational portfolio, then converted the evidence into measurable credits. "When a student has met Maine's graduation requirements—a set number of classes in subjects such as math and English—they receive a diploma." However, an official from the Maine Department of Education said the department did not recognize grades, credits, transcripts, or diplomas from North Atlantic Regional. Thus, potential students could be mislead by North Atlantic's claiming on its Internet website to "have the authority and privilege to grant high-school diplomas in the State of Maine" (Maine school giving diplomas, 2004).

**Remaining problems.** Colleges that expect applicants to have graduated from a program endorsed by a regional or state accrediting body may not accept students bearing diplomas from nonaccredited schools. Furthermore, students' reputations among their friends and relatives may suffer if they have failed to earn diplomas from the high schools they attended and, instead, have paid for a diploma from a mail-order or Internet source.

## Suffer Fright and Stress

**Type of damage—Heightened anguish.** Especially when grade promotion and graduation depend chiefly—or exclusively—on high-stakes-test scores, students can experience psychological pressure that diminishes their emotional well-being and their test performance.

**Students' coping strategy.** A potential threat to a person's welfare that raises the flow of adrenalin may produce greater alertness that improves the person's performance. But too intense a threat can immobilize the individual or result in counterproductive behavior—running away, weeping, destroying property, attacking others. Such coping is not a well-reasoned strategy but, rather, a desperate and confused automatic reaction.

**Illustrative cases.** As the New York City school system implemented the mayor's ruling that any third-grader who failed the 2004 tests would not be promoted, Schools Chancellor Joel I. Klein issued a statement recommending that children be well rested before the exam. However, teachers, parents, and third-graders across the city reported sleepless nights, butterflies in pupils' stomachs, and tears as the tests drew near. One mother complained that her daughter, a third-grader at Public School 203 in Queens, cried at night and turned into "a frazzle." She dropped off the softball team. Something had to give" (Herszenhorn & Gootman, 2004)

In Midland, Texas, four-year-olds in the Head Start program individually took their first standardized test, which consisted of a set of questions posed by a teacher about letter recognition, vocabulary, and math while she showed the child pictures of objects and events. The test was being applied to half-a-million Head Start children throughout the nation as part of the *No-Child-Left-Behind* effort. In Midland, Nate Kidder was typical of the four-year-olds being quizzed. At one point the teacher showed Nate a page with four black-and-white drawings and asked him to point to the one that matched the word *vase*. The boy chewed on his lip, obviously nervous, and pointed to the picture of a canister, not a vase. Another drawing showed a tree stump and grass sticking out of the water; children were expected to identify the picture as a *swamp*. After the session, the teacher explained that many children didn't have vases in their homes, and "We don't have swamps in Midland." She worried that standardized testing would damage the confidence of children like Nate, who, she said, was bright, but afraid of making mistakes. "If you ask him to do something [like the test questions], his smile freezes, and you see him worry, 'Am I going to get this right?'" (Rimer, 2003).

**Remaining problems.** Unless measures are taken to reduce severe stress, unfortunate educational outcomes can result, such as students dropping out of school, avoiding test situations, cheating, or vandalizing school property.

## Publicly Express Their Disappointment

**Type of damage—Their school denigrated.** A high school is cited in the news media by state authorities as needing improvement because the school fell short of having 95% of every subcategory of students taking the exit exams.

**Students' coping strategy.** By means of letters to newspapers, students air their anguish at the way their school has been branded.

**Illustrative case.** The following letter-to-the-editor, published in the *San Luis Obispo Country Tribune*, was signed by five students, a teacher, and an instructional assistant.

We feel that our school is unfairly labeled a "program improvement school." Arroyo Grande High School improved scores in all grades in English, math, science, and social studies. We worked hard to have a positive attitude about the tests (even though they take one-and-a-half months out of the school year). We worked hard to get everyone to take the tests. If two more students in one subgroup had shown up for the high school exit exam, we would have met all of the criteria. To add to the unfairness, the exit exam requirement was added after the fact. Perhaps the federal government is setting schools up for failure so the government has an excuse to cut Title I funding. (Dickinson, et al., 2003, by permission)

**Remaining problems.** Students who vent their concern in a public fashion may incur the ire of authorities who may then express their displeasure by censuring or punishing the youths.

## Don't Feel Challenged

**Type of damage—Gifted students' potential neglected.** When teachers spend so much time and attention on getting an entire class to earn at least a minimum passing score on tests, they can fail to help the brightest students make the most of their abilities.

**Students' coping strategy.** After they easily master the standardized test questions, bright students are bored rather than inspired to investigate more demanding and diverse skills and fields of knowledge.

**Illustrative case.** In the Massachusetts legislature, a pair of representatives submitted a bill to upgrade schools' attention to the educational needs of gifted pupils. The sponsors of the bill charged that the state's high-stakes tests in reading and math had focused attention solely on students who failed, so that now "We need to point out those who have succeeded" (Pappano, 2003).

Experts on educating the gifted claim that it's a myth to believe that highly capable students will achieve their potential on their own. Just as students with learning disabilities need properly trained instructors, so do very bright students. In addition, designers of curricula need to focus more attention on creating activities and materials that stretch the most capable students' abilities (Pappano, 2003).

**Remaining problems.** School districts may not be well equipped to identify children with academic potential, to develop or locate materials that sufficiently challenge the gifted, or to provide teachers adept at guiding highly talented learners. And in some communities, furnishing special opportunities for the most able students may be unpopular because it is thought to smack of elitism.

## Decline to Take Make-Up Exams

**Type of damage—Students never earn a diploma.** A growing number of states require that high-school students pass high-stakes tests in order to graduate. Students who fail those tests and thus lack diplomas find job opportunities and chances for higher education very restricted.

**Students' coping strategy.** For ones who fail a high-stakes test the first time, states offer opportunities to try the test again. However, many youths avoid retaking the tests. And the longer they have been out of school, the less likely they will attempt a make-up exam.

**Illustrative case.** Out of 4,178 students in the class of 2003 who failed the Massachusetts Comprehensive Assessment System exam, only 1,883 (45%) signed up for another chance to take the test, which they had to pass in order to graduate (Rothstein, 2003b). On the day the make-up test was given, only 468 of those who had registered actually showed up (Vaishnav, 2003a).

**Remaining problems.** Schools often lose track of students who have left school without graduating. Thus, it becomes impossible to inform dropouts of future opportunities to pass exit tests or to furnish them aid in preparing for a make-up exam.

## Reject Transfer Opportunities

**Type of damage.** Students may fail tests, partly because the school they attend provides inferior instruction. As a remedy, the school district offers students the chance to transfer to a school in which a higher proportion of students pass high-stakes tests.

**Students' coping strategy.** Refuse the option of transferring to a different school.

**Illustrative case.** In Michigan, 411 schools were required to offer transfer opportunities to pupils because the schools had failed to meet progress standards for two years in a row. However, many schools reported no transfer requests; and among ones that did receive requests, the number of students choosing to move was very low. In the city of Detroit, only 930 students from 130 schools asked to transfer. In Taylor, only 53 (5%) out of 1,033 students in three elementary schools chose to relocate (Moses & Osorio, 2004).

**Remaining problems.** When students decline the opportunity to enroll in a school with a record of better test scores, their own scores are not likely to increase if their own school's instructional conditions do not improve.

## Steal Test Materials

**Types of damage—Students and their schools are disgraced.** Pupils who fail high-stakes tests face the humiliation of nonpromotion, and their school suffers the shame of punitive action by the government.

**Students' coping strategy.** To enhance their test performance, students steal tests ahead of time.

**Illustrative cases.** At Leto High School in Tampa, Florida, a 14-year-old boy was arrested on a multiple felony charge of theft of intellectual property, burglary, and petty theft when he was caught with a copy of the math-test booklet for the Florida Comprehensive Assessment Test. A police lieutenant explained that "It's an unusual charge, but it's an official state-certified test of high importance." When the youth was questioned, he admitted that when he had left the testing room the previous day after finishing the reading portion of the FCAT, he had stolen a copy of the math exam from a test-administrator's desk and had worked out the answers at home prior to taking the math portion of the test the next day. As punishment, he was suspended from school for ten days (Grant, 2004).

**Remaining problems.** The expansion of sophisticated electronic technology in recent decades has enhanced students' ability to learn test answers ahead of time or to later improve their own test scores. Test items are frequently stored in computers. Hackers (students with high-level computer-programming skills) are sometimes able to break into a computer system containing tests and lift out test items and their answers, which are then distributed to the hackers' friends or clients. And because the results of a student's test performance are typically stored in computers, hackers are sometimes able to access those records in order to raise test scores. In addition, test-takers who carry cell phones, pagers, or hand-held computers into a test session may, during the session, receive answers to questions from companions outside the testing room. Consequently, it is becoming common practice for test-givers to confiscate such personal digital assistants before testing begins (Thomas, 2003).

## Sue the Government

**Type of damage.** Large numbers of youths—and particularly ones from ethnic-minority and low-income families—fail high-stakes tests and are thereby denied high-school diplomas.

**Students' coping strategy.** Hire attorneys to file lawsuits intended to force the state to rescind its requirement that students must pass standardized achievement tests in order to graduate.

**Illustrative cases.** Over the period 2002-2004, lawyers representing students filed a series of lawsuits directing state officials to abolish the Massachusetts Comprehensive Assessment System test. The cases gradually advanced through the court system until the Massachusetts

Supreme Court ruled that the state was within its rights to use the exam as a graduation requirement (Tench, 2004).

Attorneys for disabled students and their parents issued a class-action suit against the Alaska Board of Education, charging that the state's high-school exit exam discriminated against the disabled, who found it extremely difficult or impossible to earn a diploma. The lawyers' brief charged that the state had "created widespread confusion by repeatedly changing its regulations for disabled students and what testing modifications they can receive" (Lewin, 2004). According to federal law, handicapped students taking tests have a right to such accommodations as using a spell-checker or a calculator. Or a blind child may have the test questions read aloud. But the lawsuit contended that Alaska did not allow that same range of exceptions for students with disabilities who took the graduation tests; and many of those students, thoroughly discouraged, dropped out of school (Lewin, 2004).

**Remaining problems.** As noted in earlier chapters, lawsuits can be very expensive and can plod through the court system at a sluggish pace.

## Threaten Violence

**Type of damage—Fear of high-stakes tests.** Students can be intensely apprehensive about suffering serious consequences from failing tests.

**Students' coping strategy.** Disrupt testing with threats of violence.

**Illustrative case.** An 11-year-old sixth grader at Millennium Middle School in Tamarac, Florida, caused authorities to evacuate the school on the testing day when the boy anonymously called the emergency 911 operator to report that he had placed a bomb in the building. The threat was exposed as a hoax when a police bomb squad searched the school and found no explosives. Later the 11-year-old admitted the deed to his mother, who reported his confession to the police. He was arrested for making a false report about planting a bomb and was sent to a juvenile detention facility (Sampson, 2004).

**Remaining problems.** The sources of threats sent anonymously via letter, phone, or Internet are often impossible to trace, so that authorities are unable to locate and stop the perpetrators. Furthermore, it is difficult for school personnel or the police to estimate how likely such threats are real or merely pranks. Hence, it becomes necessary to act as if each threat was serious, and such action disrupts the orderly conduct of testing.

# Conclusion

As mentioned in Chapter 1, within the high-stakes-testing structure, students are at the bottom of the school's authority hierarchy. But even though they wield no official control, they are not without power. The methods they adopt to cope with tests exert a critical influence over the behavior of the other participants in the testing process—the politicians, administrators, public, parents, test-makers, test-givers, and teachers. When students respond to high-stakes policies by studying hard to do well on tests, life is pleasanter for the other people in the testing system. But when students respond by less acceptable means—earning low test scores (either purposely or unintentionally), avoiding tests, dropping out of school, cheating, refusing tutoring, falling ill, vandalizing—the lives of the other players in the testing game become difficult, and they turn to the sorts of remedies described in Chapters 6 through 10.

# 12

# Lessons to Learn

This final chapter is about "So what?" Or, more precisely, "So what lessons extracted from Chapters 1 through 11 might help lawmakers and educators hold students and schools accountable for the quality of learning without generating avoidable damage?"

Among many lessons that could be inferred from the contents of the previous chapters, the six selected for attention in the following pages concern (a) lawmakers' educational-planning competence, (b) the one-size-fits-all fallacy, (c) the international academic Olympics, (d) the constraint of finite space, (e) a static model versus a growth model, and (f) the value of pilot studies.

## Lawmakers' Fitness for Making Decisions About Educational Reform

Perhaps the most obvious lesson is that most lawmakers are not well equipped to decide how best to teach students of varied abilities who come from diverse cultural backgrounds. As observed in Chapter 6, too often lawmakers, as the result of their having been students themselves, appear to assume that they know what constitutes good teaching, without their recognizing that experiencing school as a student can differ dramatically from experiencing it as a teacher responsible for choosing what to teach at a particular hour, how to teach it to assorted learners, and how best to judge those learners' progress.

However, it is really unfair to expect legislators to understand the complexity of good teaching, because rarely do they bring to their job the kind of education and experience that informs them of the intricacies of effectively guiding various kinds of learners at different grade levels and in diverse cultural settings.  Most legislators are trained in law or business, so they can be expected to have little knowledge of how to deal effectively with a roomful of four-year-olds in a Head Start program, or with first-graders from Spanish-speaking homes, with restless junior-high pupils in an algebra class, with high school students who suffer learning deficiencies, or with members of an American-literature class for the gifted.  Yet legislators, with their restricted understanding, continue to issue laws that bear serious consequences for (a) the teachers and learners in such classes and (b) the schools the learners are obliged to attend.

In the current era of high-stakes testing, much education legislation has been urged on lawmakers by members of the business community who provide legislators financial support in elections and who are concerned with having high-quality candidates for employment in a high-tech economy.  Thus, laws bearing on schooling reflect such individuals' perceptions of what constitutes good teaching and of what should be done to reform schools that are deemed failures.  In effect, recent influential laws have been heavily affected by the perspectives of the business community and lawyers.  For example, Sandy Kress, a Texas attorney who helped construct the *No-Child-Left-Behind* law, was a former senior education adviser to President George W. Bush (Coates, 2004).

But legislators do not depend solely on their own experience and the wishes of their supporters from the business community.  They also solicit the opinions of "experts" from the field of professional education.  Such experts are usually educationists on the staff of the federal Department of Education or of a state education department, or else they are individuals summoned as short-term consultants.  Thus, a key influence over the quality of education legislation is the wisdom of those consultants.  In view of the type and amount of damage accompanying so many high-stakes-testing plans, it would appear that legislators have too often depended on poorly informed consultants, or else they have ignored the counsel of knowledgeable ones.  In the case of high-stakes programs, bad advice can easily result from a failure to include the opinions of various kinds of classroom teachers, school principals, and district superintendents.

So it is that laws about schools are shaped by politicians' own experiential backgrounds, the desires of their financial supporters, and the quality of the professional educationists whose advice they seek.  In addition, legislation is influenced by other features of the lawmaker's job, including (a) the public's expectations, (b) the appearance of action, (c) the locus of final responsibility, and (c) the passing of time.

The expression "public's expectations" refers to what people in general want the government to accomplish—with those wants typically voiced through such media as newspapers, magazines, radio, television, and the Internet. Hence, when the public is appalled by reports that America's schools are deplorably deficient, lawmakers become targets of a widespread demand that "the government should do something about it."

Legislators then feel compelled to respond by appearing to take corrective action. In the case of school reform, politicians can do little or nothing to ameliorate some of the most influential conditions behind the fact that American students have not outdone students in certain other countries on standardized tests. Those conditions include (a) a high rate of immigration from societies in which English is not the native language, (b) dysfunctional families, (c) cultural traditions that do not support formal schooling, and (d) the declining status of teaching as an occupation. Yet legislators appear to disregard such limitations as they issue regulations touted as adequate remedies for the ostensibly ailing education system. This appearance of taking action was illustrated in Congress's passing the *No-Child-Left-Behind Act* with strong support from both Republicans and Democrats. The act was heralded as the most dramatic, highest-funded federal educational initiative in the nation's history and as the savior of the American school.

However, publicizing such high hopes for school reform becomes politically dangerous if the hopes are not then demonstrated in practice. That danger is illustrated in the collateral damage from high-stakes testing programs chronicled in this book. But, fortunately for lawmakers, there are at least two escape routes they can take to absolve themselves of blame. Those routes concern (a) the locus of ultimate responsibility and (b) time.

The ultimate responsibility to improve schooling is located in the schools themselves. Each school's administrators and teachers must make the legislators' programs work. Hence, if students' test scores fail to meet high-stakes standards, lawmakers can blame teachers and principals for not doing their job. Such has been the case with the *No-Child* program. Thousands of schools throughout the nation have been dubbed failures, with the federal Department of Education placing the fault on school staffs, thereby leaving the *No-Child Act* virtually untouched. Hence, when legislators delegate the ultimate responsibility to teachers and principals, they can take credit for acting nobly by passing laws intended to elevate American students to the top of the world's testtakers, yet the lawmakers need not accept blame for flaws in their plan. As noted by Richard Elmore, a long-experienced authority on school reform, "Elected officials run on policy initiatives, not on their implementation" (Elmore, 2003).

Time can also help legislators escape responsibility for unwise decisions. Perhaps the most absurd assertion in the *No-Child Act* is the claim that all of America's public-school students will be at or above the *proficiency* level on reading, math, and science tests by 2014. But that claim—made in 2001—is fairly well insulated from serious political consequences by the intervening 13 years. By the time members of Congress come up for reelection in 2014 or 2016, their poor judgment in 2001 will likely have been forgotten.

> Policymakers generate credit for themselves, and for their bosses, by moving quickly from one issue to another within the dictates of two-, four-, and six-year electoral cycles, shipping their initiatives off to institutions that they understand only vaguely and episodically. (Elmore, 2003)

A question can now be asked about how legislators might act more constructively than by simply (a) ordering schools to achieve acceptable scores on standardized achievement tests and (b) punishing schools unless the great majority of their students do, indeed, achieve at—or above—a single national standard. One answer is suggested by the approach to learning improvement that Elmore developed after years of working intimately with individual school systems to raise the quality of the education they provide. Therefore, legislators could begin by recognizing how effective school reform actually works. For instance, the following are three of the principles that have come out of Elmore's experience with enhancing schools' effectiveness (Elmore, 2003).

- *Internal accountability precedes external accountability.* School improvement advances most successfully when administrators, teachers, and support personnel form a team whose members decide what they believe constitutes high-quality teaching and a suitable support system. By working together, staff members develop "consensus on norms of instructional practice, strong internal assessment of student learning [not limited to standardized tests], and sturdy processes for monitoring instructional practice and for providing feedback to students, teachers, and administrators," (Elmore, 2003, p. 9). Following that internal transformation, the school is ready to be evaluated by outside agencies.

- *Improvement is a developmental process that proceeds in stages; it is not a linear process.* In changing for the better, a school must divest itself of existing inefficient practices while its personnel learn and tryout new departures. This process can involve starts and stops, advances and plateaus. Only as improved ways of working are identified and mastered will the efficiency of such innovations be reflected in assessments of student performance. Thus, it is unrealistic to expect a regular pace of improvement in student learning from the outset of a reform effort.

- *Powerful leadership is distributed because the work of instructional improvement is distributed.* Expertise in a school is not the province of a single individual—a designated "leader." Instead, different sorts of talent that contribute to high student performance are held by different people—the principal, various teachers at different grade levels and in different subject fields, librarians, counselors, business-office personnel, and the like. Schools that are improving are ones that "pay attention to who knows what and how that knowledge can strengthen the organization" (Elmore, 2003, p. 10).

The foregoing principles are only three of those discovered by educators who have closely studied—and worked in—efforts to solve the problems of low-performing schools. Other tested principles can be found in the professional literature.

Implied in the above propositions is the understanding that schools can differ significantly from one another in factors that affect how they go about applying the principles. Such factors include (a) the characteristics of the students, (b) the characteristics of the staff members, (c) the economic and social-class composition of the community, and (d) the state's and school-district's political-power structure. Therefore, a specific plan for improving schools dictated by a central authority—such as the U.S. Department of Education or a state legislature—cannot be expected to succeed. What legislators can more profitably do than simply mandate high-stakes tests and threaten punishments is to (a) understand more about the process of school improvement, (b) fund activities which encourage and support that process, and (c) adopt a more balanced mode of assessing the progress of school reform. The nature of such a "more reasonable mode" is suggested under the topics that comprise the remainder of this chapter.

## The One-Size-Fits-All Fallacy

I noted in Chapter 1 that an essential characteristic of students which must be recognized if their educational needs are to be adequately served is this: Each student is, to some extent, different from all others in ways that affect how well they learn in school. In other words, Nature's rule is not "equality among individuals." Rather, the rule is "inequality." A school's clients vary from each other in their genetic inheritance (intellectual ability and style, physical attributes, energy resources), their background of experiences (family life, cultural traditions, health history, companions), their interests and desires, their emotional responses, their self-confidence, their manner of interacting with other people, and more. Consequently, the most demanding challenge the school faces is that of suiting instruction to every pupil's traits in a way that enables each to realize his or her greatest potential. That goal cannot be achieved if the school (a) sets the same academic-performance expectation for all students and (b) teaches all students in the same way. In short, one instructional "size" cannot possibly fit all learners

Unfortunately, the *No-Child-Left-Behind Act* and numerous state accountability programs violate this individual-differences principle in several ways. Under the *No-Child* plan—

- all students (no matter how they differ in ability, health, cultural tradition, socioeconomic status, community environment, and family composition)
- in every U.S. public school (regardless of the ethnic/socioeconomic composition of the student population, the school's financial support, the desirability of the community's living conditions, and the quality and stability of the teaching staff)
- are expected to reach the same achievement goal (*proficiency* level)
- at the same time (2014)
- in two subjects (reading, math—perhaps also science)
- as measured by a single method (an annual standardized achievement test, consisting entirely or primarily of multiple-choice items).

Therefore, it is hardly surprising that collateral damage would result from high-stakes-testing programs which failed to recognize significant differences among learners.

A question can then be asked about how the nation's public-education enterprise ever arrived in its present fix. At least part of the answer is found in the academic Olympics.

## The International Academic Olympics

As recounted in Chapter 1, the latter decades of the twentieth century witnessed increasing interest in applying the same academic-achievement tests in various nations. It was not the intent of the authors of those studies to set up a competition in which (a) pupils in one nation were pitted against those of other nations and (b) politicians and the public-communication media (newspapers, radio, television) would interpret the comparisons of countries' scores as indicators of each country's rank for intellectual quality on an international-prestige scale. Although such was not the testers' intention, that, nevertheless, was a prominent outcome of the testing efforts.

In the United States, whenever reports of cross-national testing showed American pupils being bested by pupils in other nations, the dismay expressed in the mass-communication media prompted politicians to declare that the students of the world's richest nation should be on the top rung of the international academic ladder. Just as in the athletic Olympics, where U.S. participants were expected to garner the most medals, the same was expected of students who represented America in what had now become—in fact, if not in name—an academic Olympics. Thus, the advent of cross-national testing in the language arts, mathematics, science, and civics served as a significant force behind the current high-stakes testing movement in the United States.

However, in their desire that American children and youths outscore those of all other countries, legislators and a sizable portion of the business community and general public failed to recognize vital factors which influence the ability of students and their schools to achieve the goal set for them—the goal of international academic superiority. Those factors are characteristics of the society within which a nation's schools operate—characteristics that schools can do little or nothing to change. The influence of such factors on academic performance can be illustrated in a comparison of two nations that have participated in international testing—Finland and the United States. Notice how the two countries match up in terms of (a) students' test scores and (b) features of the two societies that can affect test performance in such subjects as reading and mathematics.

## Test Results

In the early 1990s, 32 countries participated in the Second International Reading Literacy Study sponsored by the International Association for the Evaluation of Educational Achievement (IEA). Comparable tests in 21 languages were created to measure the mastery of several types of reading skill of 210,000 students from two age groups—9-year-olds and 14-year-olds. Among the 14-year-olds, Finland ranked number 1 (average score=560) in reading skills, and the United States ranked number 9 (average=535) out of the 32 countries (Elley, 1994, p. 57). Hence, teenagers in the United States did not do badly in comparison to the rest, but still they were outscored by 14-year-olds in Finland, France, Sweden, New Zealand, Hungary, Iceland, Switzerland, and Hong Kong. In effect, U.S. teenagers did not fulfill the hope of an ambitious American public and political leaders—the hope of whipping all rivals.

In 1999, 14-year-olds in 28 countries were tested for their mathematics and science knowledge. In math, the five top-ranking groups of students were in East Asia (Singapore, South Korea, Taiwan, Hong Kong, Japan). In science, four of the top five groups were in East Asia, with the fifth in Eastern Europe (Taiwan, Singapore, Hungary, Japan, South Korea). In mathematics, Finland was fourteenth and the United States nineteenth out of the 28 participating nations. In Science, Finland ranked tenth and the United States eighteenth (TIMSS 1999 Assessment Results, 2004).

## Influential Societal Conditions

Consider, now, five characteristics of the two societies—Finnish and U.S. American—that likely contributed to the superiority of the Finnish students over the Americans on reading, math, and science tests. The five are: population size, cultural homogeneity, rate of immigration, cultural traditions (particularly language patterns), and teachers' preparation.

By 2004, the population of Finland was around 5,220,000 and that of the United States 294,000,000. The United States not only had 56 times more people than Finland, but the Finnish population was more homogeneous than that of the U.S., particularly due to Finland's far smaller size and slower rate of immigration.

In 2002, only 3% (152,000) of the people in Finland had been born outside the country. Of those, nearly 104,000 were citizens of other nations—about 40% from the former Soviet Union, including 25,000 Ingrian Finns and 10,000 Estonians. Around 8,000 Swedish citizens also were living in Finland. Thus, the rather limited number of the country's foreign-born residents were mainly from countries close to Finland geographically and culturally (Peltonen, 2002). In the U.S. that same year, 11.5% of the population had been foreign born. Over 52.2% of those immigrants had come from Latin America, 25.5% from Asia, 14% from Europe, and 8.3% from elsewhere. Therefore, U.S. inhabitants were culturally far more diverse than Finland's residents.

As a partial gauge of the how the two countries' contrasting cultural patterns might affect schooling, consider the matter of students' language backgrounds. Finland has two official languages, Finnish and Swedish. In 2001, 91.3% of the population were Finnish speakers and 5.4% Swedish speakers. There were also about 1,700 people whose first language was Sami (a vernacular that shares many characteristics with Finnish) and 21,000 (0.4%) whose mother tongue was Russian (Peltonen, 2002). In dramatic contrast, according to the U.S. 2000 census, 18% of America's inhabitants (around 53 million by 2004) spoke a language other than English at home. Among the several hundred foreign tongues and dialects used, Spanish was by far the most common (about 28 million speakers). The next ten most prominent languages, in terms of numbers of speakers, were Chinese, French, German, Tagalog, Vietnamese, Italian, Korean, Russian, Polish, and Arabic (Language Use, 2003). Hence, nearly one out of every five American public-school children was obliged to take high-stakes reading and math tests in a language (English) not routinely spoken in the family. Furthermore, many of the most common home languages were linguistically far different from English.

Another advantage enjoyed by school children in Finland has been the highly phonetic nature of the Finnish language that enables learners to move rather easily from the spoken word to the written word. In comparison, the variegated linguistic origins of English vocabulary make phonics rules considerably less helpful to American learners as they seek to match a word's sound to the word's printed appearance.

Therefore, Finnish students, on the whole, could be expected to have less difficulty figuring out the language of achievement tests than would American students, and that difference could help account for the Finns' higher test scores.

A further aspect of culture that could well influence students' test performance is people's attitude toward schooling. Finns have a reputation for holding academic accomplishment in high regard. Parents urge their offspring to do well in school; and parents appear willing to sacrifice time, effort, and funds in support of that goal. In the United States, attitudes toward schooling—along with parents' ability and efforts to foster students' progress—seem to differ significantly across certain ethnic and socioeconomic groups. A likely indicator of attitude differences among ethnic groups is the set of cross-national comparisons in our earlier list of country scores from the 1999 IEA math and science tests. In that study, 14-year-olds in East Asia (Singapore, South Korea, Taiwan, Hong Kong, Japan) were on the top rungs of the achievement ladder. The suggestion that such success was due in large part to the emphasis on schooling in those societies is amply supported by opinion surveys and anecdotal evidence.

For high-stakes testing in the United States, one indicator of the impact of parental enthusiasm for schooling is the proportion of Asian-ancestry students who attend American universities that depend heavily on standardized tests for deciding which applicants they will accept. The University of California (Berkeley campus) serves as an illustrative case. Table 12-1 shows the percentage of students from different ethnic groups admitted to the university as freshmen for the fall of 2004 and the percentage of each of those ethnic groups in the state's general population in the 2000 census. The Berkeley branch of the University of California is a highly ranked institution that receives applications from far more well-prepared high-school graduates than it can enroll. The choice of which ones to admit is based chiefly on college-aptitude-test scores and high-school grades, along with evidence of broad-ranging interests and perseverance under difficult conditions. In Table 12-1, the figures relating to Hispanics and Asians admitted to the Berkeley freshman class are in striking contrast to the proportion of the two ethnic groups in California's general population. Whereas Hispanics represented nearly one-third of the state's residents, they comprised only 11% of the students admitted to the university. In contrast, Asians accounted for only 10.9% of the general population but for 40.6% of the Berkeley freshmen.

---

Table 12-1

**Ethnicity and U.C. Freshmen Admissions**
(in percentages)

| Ethnic Identity | U.C. Applicants Accepted 2004 (N=8,676) | California Census 2002 (N=35,116,033) |
|---|---|---|
| American Indian | 0.5% | 1.0% |
| Asian | 40.6 | 10.9 |
| Black | 2.4 | 6.7 |
| Hispanic | 11.0 | 32.4 |
| White | 35.5 | 46.7 |
| Other | 10.0 | 2.3 |

(Sources: (a) A Look at UC Berkeley, 2004, (b) *California Quick Facts*, 2002)

---

Table 12-1 data, when paired with the high scores of East Asia students in the IEA math and science study, support the proposition that cultural attitudes contribute substantially to how well students fare on high-stakes tests. Apparently the eagerness for academic success among immigrants from East Asia is greater in general than the enthusiasm of those from the Caribbean and from Central and South America. This discrepancy—and the resulting differences in academic performance across ethnic groups—obviously concerned the framers of the *No-Child Act* when they insisted that test results be reported for each group so as to highlight such inequalities. Hence, school personnel could then be urged to eliminate the differences between ethnic groups by raising the performance of Hispanics, blacks, and Native-Americans to a *proficiency* level. Schools that failed to do so would be subject to punitive action.

As a result of the *No-Child* rules, test-score reports have served to expose the effect of cultural attitudes toward formal education—attitudes that are likely a combination of social-class and ethnic perspectives. Consider these examples of the lag in Hispanic students' test performance.

- In North Carolina's Chapel Hill-Carrboro school district, the gap between Latino students' performance and that of white students increased from 2001 to 2003. Latinos' reading scores were 30 percentage points below those of whites and math scores were 25 percentage points below, thus representing greater discrepancies than the 16-percentage-point divide in reading and 17-percentage-point difference in math in 2001 (Ataiyero, 2003).

- At the close of 2003, Massachusetts school districts reported improvement in reading and math scores for students in general but, in a variety of districts, Hispanic students did not advance. Such was the case in Beverly, Amhurst-Pelham, and Waltham (Vaishnav, 2003b).

- Researchers studying school dropouts reported that an important factor related to dropout rates was the size of a state's Hispanic population, "because Hispanic youngsters drop out of school at a much higher rate than do other students" (Steinberg, 2003). The two states where the increase in dropouts was most apparent following the introduction of high-stakes tests—Nevada and New Mexico—were ones with high and rapidly growing Hispanic populations. Among eight states whose dropout rates rose most rapidly after high-stakes testing was introduced, five were ones with large Latino populations—Florida, Texas, New Mexico, New York, and Nevada (Steinberg, 2003).

Some observers have claimed that Hispanic students' academic difficulties stem, not from attitudes about schooling, but, rather, from a language barrier, because their home language of Spanish is at odds with tests written in English. However, the native languages of East Asians —Chinese, Japanese, Koreans, Vietnamese—differ far more from English in both their spoken and written forms than does Spanish. Nevertheless, East Asians as a group enjoy notably greater academic success in U.S. schools than do Latinos.

Therefore, in high-stakes testing programs, schools are being held responsible for raising the test scores of ethnic and socioeconomic groups that appear to hold deep-seated attitudes toward academic performance, attitudes that schools can do very little—perhaps nothing—to alter. Thus, in our comparison between Finns' and Americans' test scores, Finland's greater ethnic/cultural homogeneity—including attitudes toward schooling—is likely a significant influence behind the Finns' better performance. In multicultural America, ethnic and social-class viewpoints about academic performance appear to be quite diverse.

Another difference between Finnish and U.S. American societies is the preparation and status of teachers. All teachers in Finland hold at least a four-year university degree in the subjects they teach, and many have additional years of academic preparation. Partly because of this requirement, the profession of teaching is held in higher regard by the Finnish public than by the American public. A higher proportion of able college graduates—especially in math and science—enter teaching in Finland than in the United States. This problem of staffing all U.S. schools with high-quality instructors has been recognized in the *No-Child* legislation, which obligates schools to ensure that all teachers become fully credentialed if they are to escape unpleasant consequences. The expression "fully credentialed" in the *No-Child Act* means that properly prepared teachers must have at least a bachelor's degree in the subject fields of their teaching assignments, must complete an approved teacher-education program, and must be licensed by the state in which they teach. Consequently, a 20-year veteran teacher with an advanced degree in biology, but teaching one period of earth science would not be properly qualified. Likewise, a teacher licensed for grades 3 through 5 would not be considered properly qualified to teach grade 2. When judged by such standards, thousands of teachers in American public schools are unqualified, so they and their schools are subject to sanctions applied by the federal government and their state.

In summary, then, a number of differences between Finnish society and U.S. American society appear to serve as significant factors affecting students' success on high-stakes tests. So, how reasonable is it to hold U.S. public schools responsible for changing those factors or for ensuring that students earn high scores despite adverse societal/cultural conditions? However distasteful it may be to Americans, it seems inevitable that the students of certain other nations will, on the average, continue to outscore U.S. students in the academic Olympics. The American public and its political leaders, rather than expecting their youths—as a group—to defeat all comers, could more appropriately set their sights on improving the quality of education within the limits imposed by characteristics of U.S. society.

## The Constraint of Finite Space

It appears that many—perhaps all—planners of high-stakes-testing programs have neglected to pay enough serious attention to the following principle of physics: *A space that is completely full cannot accommodate anything new until something old has been removed.* So, if the time spent in teaching reading or math is doubled or trebled, the remaining time available for other subjects must be reduced. Or, as noted in Chapter 2, some of those other subjects may be eliminated rather than their instructional time being curtailed.

Therefore, an important problem educational planners face is that of choosing which parts of the curriculum must be sacrificed so as to provide additional time for test preparation. But some planners dismiss the finite-space problem by claiming that no extra time is required for reading and math if better teaching methods are adopted. They say that what is needed is greater teaching efficiency, not more time. In support of this conviction, the sponsors of the *No-Child* and state accountability programs have urged schools to upgrade their instructional practices by providing inservice courses for teachers and hiring new teachers who are well qualified. Indeed, improving teachers' skills is important. But upgrading instructional methods alone cannot be counted on to solve the problem of pupils not reaching high-stakes standards. Teachers find it necessary to spend more time preparing test-takers in the tested subjects, so, inevitably, less time is invested in other parts of the curriculum.

Some schools have sought to cope with the finite-space problem by enlarging the space—that is, they provide more instructional time (at least for the less-adept learners) by requiring students to attend tutoring sessions after school and on weekends, to enroll in summer sessions, to spend more hours on homework, and to follow lessons on the Internet. However, these ways of expanding instructional time can be expensive and are often unpopular with students and parents who find extra school hours a nuisance. Consequently, reducing time dedicated to non-tested subjects, rather than adding more instructional time, has become the common practice.

Under such conditions, it is particularly important for legislators, state-department officials, school-district administrators, and teachers to give serious thought to which educational goals, other than those in reading and math, are to be dropped when time devoted to the two tested subjects is increased. Legislators and state-department officials have attempted to solve this problem by (a) requiring testing in the subjects they believe should not be neglected (such as written composition, science, and social studies) or by (b) stipulating the amount of time each week to be spent on different subjects. However, efforts to "micromanage" instruction in such a fashion fail to accommodate differences from one classroom to another (in students' abilities and attitudes, kinds of instructional equipment, teachers' skills), thereby restricting teachers' freedom to match instruction to students' characteristics and to the teachers' own talents. If school time is to serve most economically for the benefit of all students, the judgment about how to use the time can most appropriately be made by skilled classroom teachers. Hence, if standards of achievement are set by others on the schooling ladder (state education departments, school districts, school faculty), teachers should be the ones to decide how to allocate the time students need to pursue those goals. Of course, such a plan will not work well with teachers who are short of skills and lack dedication to the job. But it seems unlikely that, in the cases of those inept teachers, instruction is going to be any more efficient if the time they are to spend on each subject is stipulated by some higher authority.

Another facet of the instructional-time-use problem is the issue of how test-makers decide on the level of reading and math skills that all students are to reach in order to be deemed *proficient* and worthy of a high-school diploma. For example, as noted in Chapter 2, critics have questioned the fairness of expecting all high-school graduates to pass math tests that include advanced algebra skills that will never be used in the great majority of graduates' post-school occupations.

In summary, matters of neglected subjects and of the standards required in tested subject-fields need greater informed attention on the part of decision-makers at all levels of the testing hierarchy, ranging from legislators to classroom teachers.

## Static Model and Individualized Growth Model

The expression *static model* in the present context refers to a single standard of test performance that all students and all schools are obliged to reach. This is the sort of model found in the *No-Child* plan and in most state testing programs. In contrast, the term *individualized growth model* refers to a system of student-performance standards that is adjusted to those characteristics of schools that influence how well students perform on academic-progress measures. Under a growth model, all students and their schools are not expected to reach the same goal at the same time but, instead, are to show reasonable progress from their present status toward a more desirable status. The various forms of a growth model that were recommended to the U.S. Department of Education over the 2002-2004 period—such as the one proposed by Jack O'Connell, director of California's State Education Department—were rejected by federal officials who chose to hold firmly to the static model of the *No-Child Act*.

To me, it's abundantly clear that a significant portion of the collateral damage depicted in previous chapters of this book could have been avoided if a growth model, rather than a static model, had been applied. If that is indeed the case, then why in the world did legislators and state education departments—often with the concurrence of local boards of education—embrace a static model? Two important reasons, I believe, are that (a) a static model is far easier to create and apply and (b) the sponsors of static models seem to know little about how effective educational reform is accomplished at the school level.

A key distinction between the static model of the *No-Child* variety and the sort of growth model I have in mind is found in the task that each poses for a school. The contrasting tasks are these:

- *Static model:* By a specified date, students in all schools will perform at or above the *proficient level* on standardized tests.

- *Growth model:* In each particular school—which in the near future will be compelled to operate under certain influential conditions—

students will advance a specified amount as judged by suitable assessment methods.

In order to implement the static model, federal or state officials need only identify the date at which the goal is to be reached, to define *proficient level* in terms of test scores, and to identify the tests to be used.

But implementing the growth model is far more complicated, because it requires several decisions about each school. For instance, "certain influential conditions" need to be estimated for the school. Such conditions include the composition of the student population, the skills of teachers and administrators, the home support to be expected from the students' families, the available funds for salaries and supplies, and the nature of the surrounding neighborhood (inner-city, wealthy-suburban, remote-rural). If performance goals set for the school are to be achievable, those goals need to be adjusted to the conditions. Furthermore, "suitable assessment methods" should be identified, and a reasonable amount of student progress in various areas of learning needs to be proposed.

The reason that growth-model planning demands so much time and energy is that it requires the serious participation of the school's personnel. A growth model is not the easy way out, but it does accommodate for the differences among schools in the conditions under which they must operate. Hence, individualized plans cannot be dictated by federal and state legislators or staff members in the U.S. Department of Education and state education departments.

Growth models can take various forms. One simple version that retains the reading- and math-testing features of the *No-Child* plan involves:

(a) testing students to determine their present reading and math skills,
(b) identifying conditions the school's staff members believe serve as constraints on students' test performance,
(c) estimating which of those conditions the school might reasonably be expected to improve, and
(d) proposing the amount of progress, in terms of test scores, that should be made within a specified length of time after the improvements have been introduced.

Critics of such an approach can quite rightly complain that not all school staffs are to be trusted to do such planning skillfully and honestly. Some staffs do not have the ability to analyze influential conditions and to propose improvements, and others are willing to "let things go on the way they are" because they lack the determination needed for effecting changes. Thus, a growth model needs participants from outside the school itself, participants who may improve the quality of the plan and can foster the open accountability that has become a public concern in recent years. There are several sources of outside participants, including a state department of education, another school in the same district, an educational-planning office in another district, or a university department of education. The resulting individualized growth plan—a product of the school staff's efforts and of help and monitoring from outside—is then published so the public will know the school's reform expectations.

It is apparent that growth models can be more elaborate than the one just described. For example, they can focus on a broader range of subjects than just reading and math, and they can extend their evaluation methods beyond the once-a-year standardized tests.

At this point, readers may contend that a growth model is nothing new. And indeed, most schools have been using such an approach for years, although often without external monitoring or advice. So the approach that I have described is already a familiar process in school-improvement efforts. But for many schools, that process could be much enhanced through (a) better staff training in the process and (b) the requirement that the resulting plan and its supporting rationale be open to public review.

Earlier in this section I suggested that a growth model would produce less collateral damage than the damage that results from static models. Therefore, a question can now be asked about what types of damage could be averted. Two of the most obvious types are (a) the very high number of schools that are labeled failures and (b) lack of attention to significant context conditions.

## Thousands of Schools Branded as Failures

Under the *No-Child* plan, all public schools within each state are expected to compete against a single standard that is expressed in terms of a particular number of test items that must be answered correctly. Schools that fall below the standard are said to "need improvement"—a euphemism interpreted by school personnel and the public to mean "failing." The higher the standard is set, the greater the number of failures. As illustrated throughout this book, the consequences of "need improvement" can be numerous and quite unpleasant—teachers and administrators are ridiculed and disheartened, parents are confused, a school's staff can be dismissed, and the school perhaps closed.

In contrast to the large number of schools called failures under a static model, a growth model can result in far fewer schools being punished and their reputations blighted, because each school does not have to contend with a single national or state standard. Instead, each is measured against its own improvement goals that are set in keeping with influential conditions under which the school is compelled to operate.

## Lack of Attention to Influential Conditions

The original version of the *No-Child* program held every student in every U.S. public school to the same standard of test performance, without regard for conditions that affect students' chances of passing tests. As problems arose in carrying out the *No-Child* plan, federal officials made slight adjustments in the expectations held for disabled pupils, for students from non-English-speaking homes, and for teachers who lacked full accreditation. But in the main, no recognition was given to societal conditions and students' personal characteristics that affect their ability to pass tests. Some results of such a *No-Child* policy can be illustrated with the following four examples of schools whose social and geographical contexts differ markedly.

---

**School A: An inner-city high school.** The school is located in an industrialized zone of a large city. A high proportion of the 3,500 students are from low-income families, many of which routinely speak a language other than English. The school draws most of its students from what are described as "dangerous neighborhoods" marked by a high incidence of drug traffic, robbery, assault, gang violence, and drive-by shootings. The locality has numerous one-parent families, usually consisting of a mother raising several children on her own. Most parents finished elementary school, but less than 35% ever completed high school in the United States. Many students are frequently absent from class as a result of illness or lack of interest in their studies. Dropout rates are high; graduation rates are low. Standardized-test scores for the school as a whole are well below the state average. Consequently, under the *No-Child* program, the school has been classified as "needs improvement." Because test scores have not risen sufficiently over the past two years, parents have been given the option of transferring their youths to other schools, and the school's administrators and teachers are now in danger of being replaced. The management of the school may even be turned over to a private company.

**School B: A suburban three-year middle school.** The neighborhood surrounding this school is described as "up-scale," inhabited by "upper-middle-class families of substantial financial means." English is the home language of nearly all students. More than 75% of the parents are college graduates. Most fathers and many mothers are in professional or business occupations. Students who do not already have a computer of their own at home have been loaned a computer by the school for use at home. In terms of standardized-test scores, the school ranks among the top five in the state. With rare exception, all of the middle school's graduates will earn a high-school diploma within a three-year period.

Financially, the school is in what observers describe as "very good shape" because of the district's host of expensive homes that provide a solid property-tax base and because the wealthy voters are willing to pass school-tax increases. Parents raise extra money to expand school facilities and furnish aid to disadvantaged learners—aid that would not be possible within the regular school budget.

The school pays high salaries, and it is located near an urban center that offers a host of cultural and entertainment options that appeal to teachers. The students are mostly from families that place high value on—and actively support—their children's academic achievement. Parents generally make sure that their offspring attend school regularly and "behave themselves." All of these conditions help attract skilled teachers and administrators. Thus, district officials have little difficulty hiring and retaining talented, dedicated staff members.

By *No-Child* standards, the school is a model of what an American school should be—a place where students consistently earn high scores on the state's once-a-year reading and math tests.

**School C: A four-year rural high school.** The great majority of the school's 329 students are from families living on an American-Indian reservation near the school. The reservation land and surrounding rural region are poorly suited for agriculture, are sparsely populated, and are distant from any city of substantial size. Most families speak a form of English that is mixed with expressions from their traditional tribal dialect. Financially, the school suffers from a low level of property-tax income, since the region lacks industries, major business establishments, and luxurious residences.

Although most students have a fairly good record of regular attendance, their performance on state reading and math tests continues to be unsatisfactory under high-stakes standards. Furthermore, less than 80% of the students were in school on the days the last round of tests was administered. As a result, the school has been listed as needing improvement. Parents have been informed that they can move their children to a different school, but no other high school is within reasonable traveling distance, so no one has accepted the offer.

The proportion of ninth-graders who ultimately earn a high-school diploma has been around 60%.

Because of the school's relatively low salaries, its remote location, and very few modern social amenities in the surrounding community, officials have great trouble finding and keeping competent staff members.

The problem is particularly acute for attracting fully accredited teachers of math, science, languages, and the arts.

**School D: A small-town elementary school.** This is one of three elementary schools in a town that has one junior high and one senior high. The pupils are from predominantly white working-class families whose home language is English. Many of the adults are employed either at the town's plastics-manufacturing plant or at a nearby state mental hospital.

Money to operate the school comes chiefly from local property taxes, state funds, and federal grants for disabled and socially disadvantaged pupils. The per-pupil level of funding is around the state average.

All members of the school's faculty—with the exception of one older kindergarten teacher—have full state credentials for teaching in an elementary school. The principal and several teachers have master degrees in education. Most faculty members have been at the school for at least five years.

On state reading, math, writing, and science tests over the past two years, scores for the pupils as a whole placed the school slightly above the state average. However, scores for 29 "disabled pupils" were low, resulting in the school being assigned the "needs-improvement" label.

---

As even these brief descriptions of our quartet of sample schools suggest, the four differ significantly in their chances of succeeding in present-day high-stakes-testing contests. Under *No-Child* rules, only one of the schools has made acceptable progress. The other three have fallen short.

Next, as an exercise in school-reform planning, let's speculate about how the status of the four might differ if each one's future were to be guided by an individualized growth model. The planners, in each case, are (a) a school's staff—typically in the form of a committee of able and willing members—and (b) one or more experienced planners from outside the school who help design the proposal and monitor its quality. This particular model is described in terms of the kinds of decisions the planners are expected to make.

First, consider the dual objective of the plan, which can be stated as both *an ultimate goal* and *an immediate goal*. The ultimate goal is that of *enabling all students to realize their highest learning potential.* Such a purpose is obviously an ideal that can never be perfectly achieved in practice, since the task is far too demanding, especially when students must be taught in groups rather than tutored individually. Nevertheless, the ultimate goal is useful because it identifies the direction in which schooling is aimed. Then, as a practical guide to how schooling might be improved over the next few months and years, we need an immediate goal, that of *altering the schooling process so students are learning more effectively in the near future than they have learned in the recent past.* Planners define that immediate goal by answering four questions:

- What conditions have limited students' ability to perform well on learning-assessment measures?
- Which of these conditions might we reasonably improve in the near future?
- What changes could we attempt for effecting such improvement?
- How much improvement could we expect within a specified length of time, such as five years?

The answer to the last of these questions forms the school's immediate goal. Thus, in contrast to a universally applied static model (whose achievement goal is set for all schools before any assessment is made of students' skills), the goal in a growth model is set only after students' achievement has been evaluated and estimates have been made of how much progress could plausibly be expected within a given time period.

In summary, the steps in planning the improvement of a school's instructional efficiency can consist of (a) evaluating students' present skills and knowledge in selected curriculum areas, (b) identifying conditions that appear to have constrained students' achievement, (c) estimating which of those conditions school personnel might be able to modify, (d) specifying steps for effecting the modifications, and (e) setting the student-performance goal (achievement standard) that will be pursued over a specified time.

Now let's imagine that such a planning process has been carried out in each of our four sample schools with the following results.

---

**School A: An inner-city high school.** In a five-year-growth plan, the top priority is to improve the English-language skills (reading, listening, speaking, writing) of the large population of limited-English students. The method of achieving this goal will consist of establishing two levels of special classes for English learners: (a) beginner level and (b) medium level. Enrollment in each class will be limited to ten students. As learners gain skill, they advance from the beginning to the medium class and then to a regular English class whose members are proficient in the language. Over the upcoming five years, the state language-test scores for the school as a whole should improve by at least 15 points.

As a way to assist students who need help with their class work and with test preparation, a peer-tutoring-and-counseling class will be established. The purpose of the class will be to train students in tutoring and counseling techniques that they will use while serving as aides in the school's counseling center. Class members will earn academic units toward graduation, gain the satisfaction of contributing to schoolmates' welfare, and enjoy the prestige of serving as professionally trained aides. The peer program should enable the school to expand its tutoring services significantly at little cost.

A parent-participation program will be introduced. The intent of the program is to use parents who are currently active in school affairs as the agents who encourage other parents to become constructively engaged with their teenagers' schooling. The program will operate through the school's parent-teacher association, with PTA parents visiting the homes of students whose parents might not know how to help their children succeed in school. The plan assumes that parents are often better at gaining access to—and winning the trust of—other parents than are school personnel, particularly when there are marked social-class, ethnic, educational, or religious differences between a teacher or principal and a particular parent.

A formal teacher-mentoring system will be established to help new members of the faculty solve problems they encounter on the job. The system involves pairing each new teacher with a veteran teacher who is responsible for meeting regularly with the newcomer to provide whatever aid seems needed. The purpose of the system is to ease the transition of new teachers into what is referred to as "an admittedly difficult school," thus (hopefully) improving the newcomers' efficiency and increasing the likelihood that they will become long-term members of the faculty.

The growth-model planning committee estimates that within five years, with the above innovations in place, test results should improve over recent scores by 15 points in English-language (reading, writing), 10 points in math, 10 points in science, and 10 points in social studies. In addition, the student dropout rate will lower from 16% to 10%, attendance rates will increase, and the number of discipline incidents will decline.

**School B: A suburban three-year middle school.** The growth plan features two main goals—improving overall test scores and expanding opportunities for the most advanced students.

Within a four-year period, state test scores will rise for the student body as a whole by 10 points above the most recent scores in English-language usage (reading and writing), math, science, and American history. The gain will result chiefly from improved performance by students who have scored the lowest in the past. Those students will be given small-group and individual tutoring in the subjects in which they have performed poorly on tests. Their parents will be encouraged to closely supervise their children's home assignments in those subjects.

Students, parents, and teachers have complained that the school offers too few opportunities for gifted students to (a) pursue more advanced learning tasks and (b) expand their learning opportunities in a broader range of subject fields, particularly in such areas as astronomy, geology, computer science, foreign languages, music, and art. Thus, the goal over the next four years will be to increase (a) the variety of study areas available to students and (b) the number of students in those areas. Steps toward that goal will include adding more special classes for the gifted, providing individual-project opportunities, and enrolling more students in courses available on the Internet.

In sum, the goal for test-score progress is a specific quantity—10-point gain within four years—whereas the goal for expanding learning opportunities is simply "greater-than-the-present-numbers" of fields of study and of participating students.

During the upcoming four-year period, progress toward the goals will be assessed annually and, if it seems desirable, the goals will be revised, that is, rendered either more lenient or more demanding in view of the progress made so far.

**School C: A four-year rural high school.** The four-year growth plan for the Indian-reservation school envisions (a) a 12% improvement in English-reading, English-writing, and math scores, (b) a graduation rate of 75%, and (c) enriched indigenous-culture instruction. To reach those goals, the plan calls for altering influential conditions in the following ways:

*Teacher recruitment and retention.* Three methods will be attempted for improving the recruitment of teachers.

First, in order to advertise attractive features of teaching at the school, a brochure that includes colored photographs will be mailed to the teacher-placement bureaus of the state's colleges and universities as well as to institutions in nearby states. The brochure will highlight the Native-American culture of the community and stress ways the school contributes to Indian youths fitting themselves for satisfying lives in modern America. The brochure is thus designed to appeal to graduates of teacher-education programs who are interested in cultural anthropology and wish to contribute to the future of the nation's original residents.

Second, an immediate means of upgrading the quality of instruction in such fields as science, math, and languages will consist of asking the closest state university to place teacher-education students from those subject fields at the reservation school for a one-semester or two-semester practice-teaching experience. Each student teacher will team-teach with a current member of the faculty. The idea is take advantage of the more up-to-date subject-matter and teaching methods that the university students might bring to the school while they are gaining practical classroom experience under the guidance of a veteran teacher.

Third, a philanthropic foundation will be asked to provide bonus pay to supplement the regular salary of teachers in the most-difficult-to-fill subject fields. The intention of the bonus pay is to increase the attractiveness of teaching at the school.

*Instructional efficiency.* From the nearest public university's department of education, help will be solicited for upgrading the current teachers' instructional skills in reading and writing. The program will consist of a series of Saturday study sessions conducted at the school by a university reading expert, supplemented with videotaped demonstrations of teaching reading and writing. The faculty members participating in the study sessions will receive extra pay. Funds to support the program will be sought from the state's Indian-affairs department.

*Parent outreach.* The planning committee believes that in the past the school has had too little contact with parents, particularly with parents on the reservation. As a consequence, there has been insufficient family support for students' academic progress. Therefore, in cooperation with the reservation's tribal council, meetings will be arranged with parents —in groups and individually—to explain (a) why family support of students' school efforts are important and (b) how families can help their youths succeed in school.

*Test attendance.* To encourage a higher rate of attendance on state-test days, the school plans to: (a) inform parents of test dates and of the importance of students' attendance by means of letters sent home, radio announcements, and parent-teacher meetings, (b) provide students free breakfasts on test days, and (c) conduct test-preparation sessions with students prior to test days so students are well acquainted with the form of the tests and with efficient ways of studying.

*Indigenous culture.* On the reservation, tribal leaders have voiced a growing discontent with what they view as the school's alienating young Native-Americans from their cultural heritage. According to the leaders, the school's curriculum is entirely foreign to—and frequently in conflict with—Indian traditions. Therefore, the growth model includes a tribal-culture component. A committee composed of tribal representatives, high-school faculty members, and a curriculum expert from the state university will propose ways to integrate indigenous-culture studies into the high-school curriculum. The goal is to have a reasonable plan ready for implementation by the end of the coming year.

**School D: A small-town elementary school.** The school principal and teachers are not distressed by their students' performance on the state tests, because the test scores are above the state average. Nor are staff members much disturbed by the school's being listed as needing improvement, because they believe it's ridiculous to expect disabled pupils to score as well on tests as do the nondisabled. Therefore, the growth model submitted by the planning committee for the upcoming six-year period focuses particularly on improvements specific to the local school district and this elementary school. The improvements concern (a) health-and-fitness education, (b) county, state, and regional history, and (c) the development of non-test assessment methods for the language arts, math, and science.

*Health-and-fitness education.* School-district officials, concerned about the nationwide obesity problem in children, seek to improve the health-study unit taught in the district at Grade 5. Two new tests will be created. One will be a paper-and-pencil exam measuring pupils' knowledge of health practices. The other will be a physical-fitness test requiring children to perform a series of exercises that reveal their physical condition. The paper-pencil test will be administered at the end of Grade 5. The physical-fitness test will be given at mid-year in all grades.

*Local history.* The county historical society has convinced school officials that more emphasis should be placed on county, state, and regional history in elementary schools. The society has also suggested that a history test be administered and that scores be publicly available so that progress in pupils' knowledge might be seen from one year to the next. The test will be given at the end of Grade 6, since local history is taught in Grade 6. The district's sixth-grade teachers, along with a test expert from the state education department, will create the exam.

*Non-test methods of evaluating reading, math, and science outcomes.* The school staff has been concerned about accurately judging the skills and knowledge of pupils who suffer either disabilities or a high degree of test anxiety. Therefore, a committee will be formed to devise a system of evaluating and summarizing pupils' daily class work in reading, math, and science. The system will be combined with state test results as the basis for grading pupils, providing remedial aid, and making grade-promotion decisions.

In summary, the school's growth model consists of (a) the expectation that state test scores will increase each two-year period over the coming six years, (b) pupils' knowledge of health practices and their physical fitness will improve over the six-year span, (c) pupils' knowledge of county, state, and regional history will increase, and (d) the evaluation of reading, math, and science skills will become more accurate as a result of an assessment system that combines class work with achievement-test scores. No specific amount of improvement (in terms of test scores or percentages of test items) is set for (a), (b), or (c) above. Instead, any degree of improvement will be regarded as evidence of progress.

# The Value of Pilot Studies

Imagine that an automobile manufacturer developed an innovative car —an Elevmobile—that could travel over any sort of terrain or body of water at great speed and at an extremely low operating cost because the vehicle used salt water as fuel. The car would be propelled forward by two engines that drove multi-blade propellers—one engine in front as a "puller" and the other in back as a "pusher." Furthermore, like a hover-craft, the car would rise several inches above the ground by dint of forced-air jets directed downward, thereby enabling the machine to move across land or water without touching the surface. As fuel, salt-water would be turned into energy by a hydrosodie converter. Now as-sume that the manufacturer—in great haste to get the Elevmobile to the market—produced 10,000 models and shipped them to dealers across the nation before trying out even one machine. Not a single Elevmobile en-gine was even turned on before all were sent off.

If such an event as this actually occurred, people would certainly be-lieve the manufacturer was daft for sending Elevmobiles to the market without testing them to discover and solve problems with the design. But sending off an untried innovation is what the federal government did with the *No-Child-Left-Behind* program. The plan was never tested in representative schools before it was applied nationwide. And this brings up the matter of *pilot studies*, which are small-scale tryouts of an innova-tion to find and correct flaws before the program is universally adopted. As in the example of the Elevmobile, planners of the *No-Child* initiative were able to draw on previous experience with certain elements of their creation. So, just as the manufacturer was acquainted with propeller and jet-driven craft, the *No-Child* planners were likely acquainted with in-formation about achievement tests, tutoring, standard-setting, and edu-cational finance. But they did not know how those elements might fit together with such new features as transferring students from "failing" schools, punishing schools with threats of closure, and requiring the same level of performance from students with disabilities as that ex-pected of the non-disabled.

I believe that much of the collateral damage that has plagued high-stakes-testing programs could have been avoided if the programs had been tried out before they became the law of the land. It's true that numbers of states and school districts have done small-scale testing of various educational reforms and thereby have profited by correcting un-expected errors before putting the reforms into general use. But in many instances, innovations have been mandated without their sponsors rec-ognizing ahead of time the defects that would produce troubles when the innovations were applied widespread.

In suggesting that high-stakes programs should first be tried out in representative schools, I use *representative* to mean a sampling of schools of different types in terms of key variables that influence the effect of high-stakes testing on students' success and on a school's fate. Those variables include:

- Grade levels (nursery school through high school)
- Student populations (ethnic mix, family backgrounds)
- Surrounding communities (remote rural, affluent suburban, impoverished inner-city)
- Characteristics of school staff members (educational backgrounds, age, experience, gender)

## Conclusion

As suggested in Chapter 1, the story of high-stakes testing is a tale of both victories and problems. The victories are in the form of improved student scores on standardized achievement tests, especially on reading and mathematics exams. The problems are in the form of collateral damage that can accompany the kinds of testing programs mandated by the U.S. government, by state governments, and by school districts.

It is obvious that this book has not offered an evenly balanced view of high-stakes testing, since there has been very little attention to victories and much attention to problems. However, presenting an even-handed view was not the book's intent. The purpose, instead, was to identify types of collateral damage and to describe ways that different players in the testing game have sought to cope with them. More precisely, in writing such a book I hoped to help readers understand

- How high-stakes testing can influence what the schools teach.
- How accurately standardized achievement tests assess students' progress toward different educational goals.
- How test-performance standards can be set, and how such standards can influence the fate of students and schools.
- Different ways test outcomes can be used.
- Types of collateral damage that can result from high-stakes testing.
- Conditions that affect which sorts of damage are likely to occur in which schools—such conditions as the composition of the student population, the type of neighborhood in which the school is located, the school's financial support, the talent and stability of the teaching staff, the skill of the school's administrators, the pattern of the curriculum, and more.

- The kinds of coping strategies adopted by different groups of participants in the testing movement—politicians and their staffs, administrators and their staffs, the public and parents, test-makers and test-givers, teachers, and students.
- Problems that may remain after different coping strategies have been attempted.

Writing the book has also prompted me to infer six lessons about how the kinds of damage described in Chapters 1 through 11 might be avoided—or at least diminished—in the future. Those lessons, which have formed the content of this closing chapter, can be summarized as follows:

- Rarely are politicians (the U.S. president, members of Congress, state governors, state legislators, school-board members) or most members of their staffs equipped to make well-informed decisions about classroom teaching—about students' aptitudes, instructional methods, learning materials, and methods of evaluating student achievement. Furthermore, the people whose advice politicians accept about such matters are too often poorly informed or else their advice is motivated by self interest, such as a desire to promote a political position, to spread a religion, or to sell textbooks, computers, or curriculum packets.

- When formulating proposals for improving students' achievement, planners should realize that it is folly to ignore influential differences among individual students, teachers, schools, families, and communities. One size—such as a single achievement standard for all students or all schools—cannot possibly fit all.

- Some of the important factors affecting students' success with achievement tests are characteristics of the surrounding society that schools can do little or nothing to alter. Among such factors are population size, the society's level of economic prosperity, cultural traditions, and the extent of ethnic/religious cultural diversity. People who ignore the influence of those factors are apt to hold unrealistic expectations for the ability of schools to raise students' test scores.

- Whenever the amount of instructional time in the school day is kept constant, adding new content to the curriculum or extending the time spent on a given subject means that some existing content must be removed or given less time. This fact of finite space is often ignored by people who suggest curriculum innovations. Thus, it is important for curriculum planners, when introducing a new practice, to decide which features of the existing curriculum could be sacrificed with the least harm to students' welfare.

- Many, if not most, high-stakes-testing programs assume the form of static models. The *No-Child-Left-Behind* plan is one such. A static model sets a single goal that all schools are to reach (an example of the one-size-fits-all assumption). When the goal is set high, many schools are unable to achieve it, so many of them become "failures." In contrast to a static model, an individualized-growth model sets each school's achievement target in relation to the school's estimated capacity to improve over a given period of time. The estimate is based on an analysis of factors affecting the likelihood that students' learning performance in their particular school will improve. Thus, given the reality of marked influential differences among learners and schools, growth models make better sense than static models.

- The collateral damage accompanying an educational innovation can be minimized if the innovation is first tried on a small scale, then refined on the basis of the tryout before being applied widespread.

# References

A look at Berkeley UC freshman admissions. (2004, June 1). *Associated Press.* Available online: www.gjsentinel.com/news/content/shared-gen/ap/National/Berkeley_Black_Admissions_Glance.html.

AAE teachers weigh in on NCLB. (2003, April). *Education Matters.* Available online: http://66.102.7.104/search?q=cache:swmof_41yeYJ:www.aaeteachers.org/newsletters/aprilnews03.pdf+NCLB+paper+work&hl=en&ie=UTF-8.

About SAT. (2004). *College board tests.* Available online: http://www.collegeboard.com/student/testing/sat/about.html.

Achievement test fails independent review. (1997, September 16). *ATA News, 32* (3). Available online: www.teachers.ab.ca/publications/news/_volume_32/ number_03/achievement.html.

Adequate yearly progress: A state snapshot. (2003, September 3). *Education Week.* Available online: http://www.edweek.org/ew/ewstory.cfm?slug=01ayp_sl.h23.

Aguilar, A. (2003, September 3). Illinois schools say federal school rules are roadblocks. *St. Louis Post-Dispatch.* Available online: http://www.stltoday.com/stltoday/news/stories.nsf./News/Education/D23A3E34D98AD90C86256D9600415B97?OpenDocument&Headline=Illinois+schools+say+federal+rules+are+roadblocks.

Allen, M. (2004, January 9). Bush's education plan gets mixed grades on anniversary. *Washington Post*, p. A09 Available online: http://www.washingtonpost.com/wp/dyn/articles//A1494-2004Jan8.html.

Alternative teacher certification. (2003). *National Center for Education Information.* Available online: http://www.ncei.com/2003/executive_summary.htm.

Anderson, D. R. (2004, January 6). High schools focusing on CIM see more seniors achieving certificate. *The Oregonian.* Available online: http://www.oregonlive.com/metrowest/oregonian/index.ssf?/base/metro_west_news/1073394363156660.xml.

Anti-FCAT group wants state to release tests. (2003, August 12). *St. Petersburg Times.* Available online: http://www.sptimes.com/2003/08/12/State/Anti_FCAT_group_wants.shtml.

Archer, J. (2003, September 24). Houston case offers lesson on dropouts. *Education Week.* Available online: http://www.edweek.org/ew/ewstory.cfm?slug=04Houston.h23.

Archibald, G. (2003, October 20). Education reform highlights scoring gap. *Washington Times.*Available online: http://www.washtimes.com/national/20031020-122546-5055r.htm.

Archibald, G. (2004a, January 13). Failing schools underreported. *Washington Times.* Available online: http://www.washingtontimes.Com/national/20040113-113134-1469r.htm.

Archibald, G. (2004b, March 28). Education act splits school chiefs. *Washington Times,* Available online: http://www.washtimes.com/national/20040328-115805-6114r.htm.

Archibald, G. (2004c, August 30). 12 million languish in failing public schools, report says. *Washington Times.* Available online: http://www.washtimes.com/national/20040829-114519-1566r.htm.

Are we there Yet? (2002). *Frontline, Public Broadcasting System.* Available online: http://www.pbs.org/wgbh/pages/frontlin/shows/schools/standards/bp.ntml.

Arenson, K. W. (2003a, October 14). Scaling back on regents standards. *New York Times.* Available online: http://www.nytimes.com/2003/10/14/education/14REGE.html.

Arenson, K. W. (2003b, October 23). Appeals system is urged for regents exams. *New York Times.* Available online: http://www.nytimes.com/2003/10/23/nyregion. 23REGE.html.

Arenson, K. W. (2004, May 15). More youths opt for G.E.D., skirting high-school hurdle. *New York Times.* Available online: http://www.nytimes.com/2004/05/15/education/15GED.html?ex=1085457600&en=babac3ee2bdba81fc9&ei=5070.

Armas, G. C. (2003, October 9). One in five don't speak English at home, data show. *San Luis Obispo County Tribune,* p. A3.

Ataiyero, K. T. (2003, November 21). School gap is good, bad. *News & Observer.* Available online: http://www.newsobserver.com/front/story/3039488p-2780777c.html.

Austin, L. (2004, September 7). Houston downsizes to tackle dropout rate. *Boston Globe.* Available online: http://www.boston.com/news/

education /k_12/articles/2004/09/07/houston_downsizes_to_tackle_dropout_rate/.

Ave, M. (2003, November 16). School year extends to let poor readers catch up. *St. Petersburg Times.* Available online: http://www.sptimes.com/2003/11/26/Hillsborough/School_year_extends_t.shtml

Azimov, N. (2003a, October 9). Few parents seize chance to transfer schools 'No child left behind' made offer mandatory. *San Francisco Chronicle.* Available online: http://www.sfgate.com/cgi- bin/article.cgi? f=/chronicle/archive/2003/10/09/MN198701.DTL.

Azimov, N. (2003b, November 13). High schools fear rate report—Graduation formula disputed, could lead to state takeovers. *San Francisco Chronicle.* http://www.sfgate.com/cgi-bin/article.cgi?f=/chronicle/archive/2003/11/13/BAG9H2MJ6933.DTL.

Azimov, N. (2004, March 10). More schools making the grade. *San Francisco Chronicle.* Available online: http://www.sfgate.com/cgi-bin/article.cgi?file =/c/a/2004/03/10/MNGCR5HRJD1.DTL.

Bacon, P. (2003, September 22). Struggle of the classes. *Time,* pp. 42-43.

Bailey, A. F. (2004, July 3). State students with cognitive disabilities meet or exceed test standards. *Detroit News.* Available online: http://www.detnews.com/2004/schools/0407/06/schools-202094.htm.

Barton, P. E. (2003, November 20). ETS report: Achievement gap will not close without understanding both school and societal factors. *Educational Testing Service.* Available online: http://www.ets.org/textonly/news/03111801.html.

Becker, J., & Hilderman, R. S. (2004, January 26). Va. seeks to leave Bush law behind. *Washington Post,* p A01. Available online: http://www.washingtonpost.com/wp-dyn/articles/A43173-2004Jan23.html.

Begay, J. (2003, August 29). Student test scores climb in county. *The Oregonian.* Available online: http://www.oregonlive.com/metronorth/oregonian/index.ssf?/base/metro_north_news/1062158388284260.x//ml.

Bennett, V. (2002). Testing the schools, discussion. *Frontline PBS Program.* Available online: http://www.pbs.org/wgbh/pages/frontline/shows/schools/ talk/.

Benton, J. (2004, April 14). TAKS standard is raised. *Dallas Morning News.* Available online: http://www.dallasnews.com/sharedcontent/dws/news/localnews/stories/041504dnmetmovingthebar.f5a5.html.

Bernstein, J. (2002, August 30. Test case. *The Texas Observer.* Available online: http://www.texasobserver.org/showArticle.asp? ArticleID =1004.

Bishop, T. (2003, November 25). School system sets new goals in achievement. *Baltimore Sun.* Available online: http://www.sunspot.

Net/news/education/bal-ho.schools25nov25,0,6166385.story?coll=bal-education-top.

Blackford, L. B. (2004, January 14). Teacher training incentive being cut. *Lexington Herald-Leader.* Available online: http://www.kentucky.com/mld/kentucky/news/local/7862892.htm.

Blair, J. (2004, January 14). Denver performance-pay plan yields student progress. *Education Week.* Available online: http://www.edweek.org/ew/ewstory.cfm?slug=18Denver.h23.

Blakely, A. (2004, January 9). School to hold LEAP Fest. *The Times-Picayune.* Available online: http://www.nola.com/education/t-p/index.ssf?/base/news-0/107363344019460.xml.

Blobaum, M. H., & Kowalczyk, N. (2004, April 19). New mandates force school-day changes. *Kansas City Star.* Available online: http://tinyurl.com/3a7od.

Board votes to alter high school exit exam. (2003, November 13). *San Louis Obispo County Tribune,* p. B5.

Boser, U. (2000, March 8). States face limited choices in assessment market. *Education Week.* Available online: http://www.edweek.org/register/register.cfm?mode=news (archive).

Bower, C. (2003a, September 3). Many area schools fail test. *St. Louis Post-Dispatch.* Available online: http://www.stltoday.com/stltoday/news/stories.nsf./News/Education/97ACE65FD9972E3186256D96003FFBF8?OpenDocument&Headline=Many+area+schools+fail+test.

Bower, C. (2003b, December 17). NEA chief says law sets goals too high for some disabled. *St. Louis Post-Dispatch.* Available online: http://www.stltoday.com/stltoday/news/stories.nsf./News/Education/ABAB944E25A348C5E086256DFF0012B6F7?OpenDocument&Headline=NEA+chief+says+law+sets+goals+too+high+for+some+disabled.

Bower, C. (2004, January 15). School administrators see how surprise visits to classrooms can improve teaching, learning. *St. Louis Post-Dispatch.* Available online. http://www.stltoday.com/stltoday/news/stories.nsf/News/Education/6102B7DE8D1E5E5F86256E1C00543041?OpenDocument&Headline=School+administrators+see+how+surprise+visits+to+classrooms.

Bowie, L. (2003, August 19). 131 stay on Md. list of failing schools. *Baltimore Sun.* Available online:http://.sunspot.net/news/education/bal-md.schools19aug19,0,732598.story?coll=bal-education-top.

Bowler, M. (2003a, May 6). Teachers fear social studies is becoming history. *Baltimore Sun.* Available online: http://www.sunspot.net/news/education/bal-md.history06may06,0,592349.story?coll=bal%2Deduca tion %2Dtop.

Bowler, M. (2003b, November 16). A tale of two test scores. *Baltimore Sun.* Available online: http://www.sunspot.net/news/education/bal

-md.edbeat16nov16,0,1500605.column?coll=bal-education-top.

Bowler, M. (2004a, March 10). Liberal arts may be left behind in Md. *Baltimore Sun.* Available online: http://www.baltimoresun.com/news/education/bal-md.edbeat10mar10,0,1963927.column?coll=bal-educati on-top.

Bowler, M. (2004b, March 31). A call to raise the standards. *Baltimore Sun.* http://www.baltimoresun.com/news/education/bal-md.edbeat31ma r 31,0,3602333.column?coll=bal-education-top.

Branscomb, L. W. (2004, May 5). Students skip state academic testing. *San Diego Union-Tribune.* Available online: http://www.signonsandie go.com/uniontrib/20040505/news_6m5tests.html.

Brown, B. R. (2003, October 23). Time out for teacher training: It gets an 'A' for excellence. *Philadelphia Inquirer.* Available online: http://www. philly.com/mld/dailynews/news/opinion/7080781.htm.

Brown, M. (2003a, November 21). School reform standards are getting tougher. *The Times-Picayune.* Available online: http://www.nola. com news/t-p/frontpage/index.ssf?/ base/news-0/1069401417119200.xml.

Brown, M. (2003b, December 7. Test scores fuel hope education reform is succeeding. *The Times-Picayune.* Available online: http://www.nola. com education/t-p/index.ssf?/base/news-0/1070780429191590.xml.

Brown, M. (2004, August 29). State reward money reduced for schools with good grades. *Tampa Tribune.* Available online: http:// www. tampatrib.com /FloridaMetro/MGBWYRMHGYD.html.

Bush administration eases testing restrictions. (2004, March 29). *USA Today.* Available online: http://www.usatoday.com/news/washing ton/2004-03-29-students-testing_x.htm.

Bush defends education act. (2004, January 6). *Richmond Times-Dispatch.* Available online: http://www.timesdispatch.com/servlet/Satellite? pagename=RTD%2FMGArticle%2FRTD_BasicArticle&c=MGArticle&c id=1031772939133&pat h=%21news&s=1045855934842.

Bushweller, K. (2003, October 1). Civic ignorance abounds, NCSL report concludes. *Education Week.* Available online: http://www.edweek. org/ew/ewstory.cfm?slug=05Report.h23.

*California quick facts.* (2002). U.S. Bureau of the Census. Available online: http://quickfacts.census.gov/qfd/states/06000.html.

Callahan, B. (2004, February 8). No child left behind ed tech grants. Available online: http://www.whro.org/education/nclb/.

Callas, T. (2003, September 18). N.J. high schools bristle at proficiency warnings. *Philadelphia Inquirer.* Available online: http://www.philly. Com/mld/inquirer/living/education/6799067.htm.

Campanile, C. (2004a, April 16). Shocking school 'cheating' plan. *New York Post.* Available online: http://www.nypost.com/news/regional news/18954.htm.

Campanile, C. (2004b, May 4). Math-test scandal. *New York Post.* Available online: http://www.nypost.com/news/regionalnews/23681.htm.
Campanile, C., Seifman, D., & Mongelli, L. (2004, April 20). Mayor: Boycott test & we'll fail your kid. *New York Post.* Available online: http://www.nypost.com/news/regionalnews/23049.htm.
Casas. M. (2003, October 12). The use of standardized tests in assessing authentic learning--A contradiction indeed. *Teachers College Record.* Available online: http://www.tcrecord.org/content.asp?ContentID= 11211.
Chestnut, C. R. (2003a, October 30). Federal law helps to create disparities in school class sizes. *The Oregonian.* Available online: http://www .oregonlive.com/news/oregonian/index.ssf?/base/news/1067518584 38070.xml.
Chestnut, C. R. (2003b, December 28). Algebra enters equation for graduation. *The Oregonian.* Available online: http://www.oregonlive.com /eduction/oregonian/index.ssf?/base/news/107253038711210.xml.
Chicago schools: Dropouts now must sign consent form. (2004, February 28). *USA Today.* Available online: http://www.usatoday.com/news/ education/2004-02-28-chicago-dropouts_x.htm.
Chu, L. (2004, May 5). Bogus degrees helping some teachers get raises. *Houston Chronicle.* Available online: http://www.chron.com/cs/CDA /ssistory.mpl/nation/2549518.
Coates, D. (2004, January 12). Demand to prove skills enrages veteran teachers. *Detroit News.* Available online: http://www,detnews.com/ 2004/schools/0401/12/a01-33058.htm.
Colorado must revisit school standards. (2003, December 12). *Rocky Mountain News.* Available online: http://www.rockymountainnews. com/drmn/opinion/article/0,1299,DRMN_38_2496585,00.html.
Colorado's awful history standards. (2003, September 28). *Rocky Mountain News.* Available online: http://www.rockymountainnews.com/ drmn/opinion/article/0.1299,DRMN-38-2299373,00.html.
Connors, L. L. (2004, January 27). A harder look at after-school help. *Christian Science Monitor.* Available online: http://www.csmonitor. com/2004/0127/p11s02-legn.html
Conti, K. (2004, January 8). Schools get head start in English immersion. *Boston Globe.* Available online: http://www.boston.com/news/educa tion/k_12/articles/2004/02/19/schools_get_head_start_in_english_ immersion/.
Curl, J. (2004, January 8). Bush to boost education funding. *Washington Times.* Available online: http://www.washtimes.com/national/2004 0108-111909-1981r.htm.

D won't cut it for students anymore. (2004, April 7). *Salt Lake Tribune.* Available online: http://www.sltrib.com/2004/Apr/04072004/utah/154885.asp.

Davis, M. (2003, May 28). Ed. Dept. invests $500,000 in team to tout its agenda. *Education Week.* Available online: http://www.edweek.org/ew/ewstory.cfm?slug=38warroom.h22&keywords=failing%20schools.

Dean, H. (2004, January 8). No-Child-Left-Behind should be more than a slogan. *Seattle Times.* Available online: http://seattletimes.nwsource.com/html/opinion/2001831790_dean08.html.

Dean, M. M. (2003, September 11). 2,312 students to redo their school year. *Philadelphia Inquirer.* Available online: http://www.philly.com/mld/dailynews/news/local/6742918.htm.

Deford, F. (2003, May 23). Physical activity is an illness plaguing children. *San Luis Obispo County Tribune*, p. B8.

Dell'Angela, T. (2004, April 12). Nebraska schools skip mandatory tests, *Seattle Times.* Available online: http://seattletimes.nwsource.com/html/nationworld/2001901192_nebraska12.html.

DePledge, D. (2004, May 6). Standardized tests checked for errors. *Honolulu Advertiser.* Available online: http://the.honoluluadvertiser.com/article/2004/May/06/ln/ln08a.html/?print=o.

*Description of the FTCE Tests.* (2004, February 2). Available online from the Florida Department of Education: http://www.firn.edu/doe/sas/ftce/ftcedesc.htm.

Dickinson, A., et al. (2003, September 8). Arroyo Grande High unfairly labeled. *San Luis Obispo County Tribune*, p. B8.

Dillon, S. (2003a, May 22). States cut test standards to avoid sanctions. *New York Times.* Available online: http://www.nytimes.com/2003/05/22/education/22EDUC.html.

Dillon, S. (2003b, November 5). School districts struggle with English fluency mandate. *New York Times.* Available online: http://www.nytimes.com/2003/11/05/national/05ENGL.html.

Dillon, S. (2004a, January 2). Some school districts challenge Bush's signature education law. *New York Times.* Available online: http://www.nytimes.com/2004/01/02/education/02RESI.html.

Dillon, S. (2004b, February 22). Bush education officials find new law a tough sell. *New York Times.* Available online: http://www.nytimes.com/2004/02/22/national/22CHIL.html.

Dillon, S. (2004c, March 2). Education chief again apologizes for 'terrorist' remark, *New York Times.* Available online: http://www.nytimes.com/2004/03/02/politics/02PAIG.html.

Dillon, S. (2004d, March 8). President's initiative to shake up education is facing protests. *New York Times.* Available online: http://www.com/2004/03/08/education/08CHIL.html.

Do financial incentives motivate teachers? (2004, February 3). *Arizona Republic.* Available online: http://www.azcentral.com/families/edu cation/ articles/0203incentives-ON.html.

Dobbs, M. (2003, November 8). Education miracle has a math problem. *Washington Post,* p. A01. Available online: http://washington post. com/wp-dyn/articles/A14117-2003Nov7.html.

Dobbs, M. (2004a, February 20). 'No Child' tests for schools relaxed. *Washington Post,* p. A01. Available online: http://www.washington post.com/wp-dyn/articles/A56123-2004Feb19.html.

Dobbs, M. (2004b, April 22). 'No Child' law leaves schools' old ways behind. *Washington Post,* p. A01. Available online: http://www.wash inngtonpost.com/ wp-dyn/articles/A32348-.

Draper, N. (2004, February 27). State's school testing costs add up. *Minneapolis Star Tribune.* Available online: http://www.startribune. com/stories/1592/4632557.html

Drebes, D. (2004, March 8). NEA chief criticizes Bush on education. *Washington Times.* Available online: http://www.washtimes.com/met ro/20040308-100631-5356r.htm.

Edley, C., & Wald, J. (2002, December 16). The grade retention fallacy. *The Boston Globe.* Available online: http://www.civilrightsproject. harvard. edu/research/articles/retention_edley.php

Educators found to be cheating system. (2004, May 21). *San Luis Obispo county Tribune,* p. B4.

Educators: New law may cause Nevada teachers to quit. (2004, February 25). *San Francisco Chronicle.* Available online: http://www.sfgate. com/cgi-bin/article.cgi?f=/news/archive/2004/02/25/state1300EST0 055. DTL.

Elley, W. B. (1992). *How in the world do students read?* The Hague: International Association for the Evaluation of Educational Achievement.

Elley, W. B. (1994). *The IEA study of reading literacy.* Oxford: Pergamon.

Elliott, J. (2003, September 12). Tougher standards for TAKS may wait. *Houston Chronicle.* Available online: http://www.chron.com/cs/CDA /ssistory.mpl/metropolitan/2094584.

Elmore. R. F. (2003, November). A plea for strong practice. *Educational Leadership, 61* (3), 6-10.

Essoyan, S. (2004, May 8). School tests widely flawed. *Honolulu Star-Bulletin.* Available online: http://starbulletin.com/2004/05/08/news/ story1.html.

Examples of education reform. (2004). *National Board for Professional Teaching Standards.* Available online: http://www.nbpts.org/edre-form/ index.cfm.

*Fair test.* (2003). Available online: www.FairTest.org.

FCAT answers to get cheater checks. (2004, February 25). *St. Petersburg Times.* Available online: http://www.sptimes.com/2004/02/25/State /FCAT_answers_to_get_c.shtml.

Feller, B. (2003, June 4). Teacher survey paints picture of dark side of education. *San Luis Obispo Country Tribune,* p. A6.

Feller, B. (2004, February 24). Secretary Paige stands by NEA claim. *Seattle Post-Intelligence.* Available online: http://seattlepi.nwsource.com/ national/apwashington_story.asp?category=1155&slug=Paige%20Tea chers%20Union.

Fessenden, F. (2003). How to measure student proficiency? *New York Times.* Available online: http://www.nytimes.com/2003/12/31/edu cation/31DIST.html.

Few students fleeing struggling schools. (2004, January 26). *CNN.com.* Available online: http://www.cnn.com/2004/EDUCATION/01/26/ education.review.ap/index.html.

Finn, C. E., Jr. (2004, May 20). Equivalent to what? *The Education Gadfly.* Available online: https://webmail.pas.earthlink.net/wam/msg822. jsp?msgid=420&id822=420-1&folder=INBOX&x=-348296781.

Fletcher, M. A. (2003, May 31). As high school exit exams cost diplomas, anger rises. *Washington Post,* p. A01.

Folts, James D. (1996). *History of the University of the State of New York and the State Education Department, 1784–1996.* Available online: http: www.nysl. nysed.gov/edocs/education/sedhist.htm.

Galehouse, M. (2004, February 10). Special-needs kids to take AIMS at their skill level. *Arizona Republic.* Available online: http://www.az central.com/arizonarepublic/local/articles/0210testhelp10.html.

Galley, M. (2003, September 17). Texas principal posts test scores of classes. *Education Week.* Available online: http://www.edweek.org/ ew/ewstory.cfm?slug=03Taks.h23.

Galley, M. (2004, May 26). Nev. teacher claims rosters altered to meet 'No Child' law. *Education Week.* Available online: http://www.ed week.org/ew/ewstory.cfm?slug=38Teach.h23.

GAO reports on state costs for NCLB testing. (2003, June). *National Association of State Boards of Education, Legislative Brief.* Available online: http://www.nasbe.org/Membership/Educational_Issues/Legislative _Brief/3_9.pdf.

Garcia, P. (2002, April 24). State Board of Education designates ETS as standardized testing contractor for 2003-2005. *California State Board of Education.* Available online: http://www.cde.ca.gov/board/notices/ star.pdf.

Gewertz, C. (2003, November 26). Educators endorse rules on accountability. *Education Week.* Available online: http://www.edweek.org/ ew/ewstory.cfm?slug=13Edtrust.h23.

Gilbert, H. (2003, August 29). Two dozen schools don't meet benchmark *The Oregonian.* Available online: http://www.oregonlive.com/metro north/oregonian/index.ssf?/base/metro_north_news/1062158274284 260.xml.

Goldstein, L. (2003, December 10). Final rules allow alternate assessments. *Education Week.* Available online: http://www.edweek.org/ ew/ewstory.cfm?slug=15web_nclb.h23.

Gootman, E. (2003a, September 11). 40%of city schools do not meet U.S. standards. *New York Times.* Available online: http://www.nytimes. com/2003/09/11/education/11SCHO.html.

Gootman, E. (2003b, September 30). New York City's schools fear a wave of transfers. *New York Times.* Available online: http://wwa.nytimes. Com/2003/09/30/education/30SCHO.html.

Gootman, E. (2003c, October 22). Math scores rise sharply across state. *New York Times.* Available online: http://wwwnytimes.come/2003/10 /22/nyregion/22MATH.html.

Gootman, E. (2004a, February 8). Now the regents math test is criticized as too easy. *New York Times.* Available online: http://www.nytimes. com/2004/02/08/education/08regents.html?pagewanted=all.

Gootman, E. (2004b, June 25). Promotions granted to 1,500 who failed 3rd grade tests. *New York Times.* Available online: http://nytimes. com/2004/06/25/education/25test.html.

Gootman, E. (2004c, July 17). New York City will limit chance to leave failing schools. *New York Times.* Available online: http://www.nytim es.com/2004/07/17/nyregion/17school.html.

Gootman, E., & Herszenhorn, D. M. (2004, May 16). Even with more choices, many don't get into preferred schools. *New York Times.* Available online: http://www.nytimes.com/2004/05/16/education/ 16school.html.

Gormley, M. (2003, October 28). Records show New York teachers cheating on tests to boost scores. *San Francisco Chronicle.* Available online: http://www.sfgate.com.cgibin/article.cgi?f=/news/archive/ 2003/10/28/nationalo329EST0449.DTL.

Grant, T. (2004, March 6). Tampa teen charged with FCAT felony. *St. Petersburg Times.* Available online: http://www.sptimes.com/2004/03 /03/06/Tampabay/Tampa_teen_charged_wi.shtml.

Gross, J. (2003a, August 29). Free tutoring reaches only fraction of students. *New York Times.* Available online: http://www.ny.times.com/ 2003/08/29/nyregion/29TUTO.html.

Gross, J. (2003b, November 6). Free tutoring is reaching more students in the system. *New York Times.* Available online: http://www.ny.time s.com/2003/11/06/education/06TUTO.html.

Grossman, K. N. (2003a, October 16). Top suburban schools listed among low scorers on state test . *Chicago Sun-Times.* Available online: http://www.suntimes.com/output/news/cst-nws-skul16.html.

Grossman, K. N. (2003b, November 7). Poor students buck trend at 27 schools. *Chicago Sun-Times.* Available online: http://www.suntimes.com/output/education/cst-nws-skul07.html.

Grossman, K. N. (2003c, December 10). Schools blast state test data that could lead to sanctions. *Chicago Sun-Times.* Available online: http://http://www.suntimes.com/output/news/cst-nws-skul10.html.

Grossman, K. N. (2003d, December 19). Conflicting city, federal school ratings due today. *Chicago Sun-Times.* Available online: http://www.suntimes.com/output/education/cst-nws-skul19.html.

Grossman, K. N. (2004). Schools pressured to dump bad students, critics say. *Chicago Sun-Times.* Available online: http://www.suntimes.com/output/education/cst-nws-drop09.html.

Guisbond, L. (2002). PBS Frontline discussion after the program. Available online. http://www.pbs.org/wgbh/pages/frontline/shows/schools/talk/.

Hammond, B. (2003a, October 30). Oregon spends more trying to close achievement gaps. *The Oregonian.* Available online: http://www.oregonlive.com/news/oregonian/index.ssf?/base/news/106751892338070.xml.

Hammond, B. (2003b, November 7). Schools chief hits reverse, slams parts of No Child Left Behind. *The Oregonian.* Available online: http://www.oregonlive.com/news/oregonian/index.ssf?/base/news/1068209836284091.xml.

Hammond, B. (2003c, November 24). Study: Test standards differ. *The Oregonian.* Available online: http://www.oregonlive.com/news/oregonian/index.ssf?/base/news/1069678810267471.xml.

Hammond, B. (2003d, November 26). Oregon considers challenging No Child Left Behind law. *The Oregonian.* Available online: http://www.oregonlive.com/news/oregonian/index.ssf?/base/front_page/106985153382400.xml.

Hammond, B. (2003e, December 5). Critics ask Wyden to fight education law. *The Oregonian.* Available online: http://www.oregonlive.com/education/oregonian/index.ssf?/base/news/1070629133241150.xml.

Hammond, B. (2004a, January 29). Schools record better marks. *The Oregonian.* Available online: http://www.oregonlive.com/news/oregonian/index.ssf?/base/news/1075381142263300.xml.

Hammond, B. (2004b, February 28). Teachers learn to close learning gap. *The Oregonian.* Available online: http://www.oregonlive.com/education/oregonian/index.ssf?/base/news/1077973686255140.xml.

Haney, W. (2002, July 10). Ensuring failure. *Education Week*. Available online: http://www.edweek.org/ew/ewstory.cfm?slug=haney.h21& keywords=achievement%20tests.

Hardy, D. (2004, January 29). State test translation plan raises concerns. *Philadelphia Inquirer*. Available online: http://www.philly.com/mld/inquirer/news/local/7820496.htm.

Harman, D. (2003, November 18). A crisis looms for some North Dakota schools. *Christian Science Monitor*. Available online: http://www.csmonitor/2003/1118/p12s01-legn.html.

Harrison, S. (2003, December 9). Boycott of FCAT threatened. *Miami Herald*. Available online: http://www.miami.com/mld/miamiherald living/education/7449436.htm.

Harrison, S. (2004, February 8). 'Unusual' FCAT scores raise questions. *Miami Herald*. Available online: http://www.miami.com/mld/miamiherald/living/education/7902627.htm.

Hegarty, S. (2003, November 7). Court rules father can't see son's FCAT. *St. Petersburg Times*. Available online: http://www.sptimes.com/2003 /11/07/State/Court_rules_father_ca.shtml.

Hendrie, C., & Hurst, M. (2002, September 4). Errors on tests in Nevada and Georgia cost publisher Harcourt. *Education Week*. Available online: http://www.edweek.org/register/register.cfm?mode=news (archive).

Herszenhorn, D. M. (2003, December 5). School system performance getting new measuring sticks. *New York Times*. Available online: http://www.nytimes.com/2003/12/05/nyregion/05SCHO.html.

Herszenhorn, D. M. (2004a, January 16). Special help for 3rd graders Is promised. *New York Times*. Available online: http://www.nytimes.com/2004/01/16/education/16school.html.

Herszenhorn, D. M. (2004b, March 16). Bloomberg wins on school tests after firing foes. *New York Times*. Available online: http://www.nytimes.com/2004/03/26/nyregion/16SCHO.ntml.

Herzenhorn, D. M. (2004c, May 13). Mishaps still plague citywide reading test. *New York Times*. Available online: http://www.nytimes.com/2004/05/13/education/13test.html?adxnnl=1&adxnnlx=1084640053-WoDRyR5pwXgJTLecJYEcXg.

Herszenhorn, D. M., & Gootman, E. (2004, April 19). City tests loom, and third graders feel the heat. *New York Times*. Available online: http://www.nytimes.com/2004/04/19/education/19school.html?ex=1083371942&.

Higgins, L. (2004, May 3). High schoolers' apathy could help kill MEAP. *Detroit Free Press*. Available online: http://www.freep.com/news/education/meap3_20040503.htm.

Hobbs, T. D. (2004, May 5). DISD teachers find fault with social studies tests. *Dallas Morning News.* Available online: http://www.dallasnews.com/sharedcontent/dws/dn/latestnews/stories/050504dnmetdisdtesting.27b0b.html.

Hoff, D. J. (2002, October 9). Budget woes force states to scale back testing programs. *Education Week.* Available online: http://www.edweek.org/ew/ewstory.cfm?slug=06tests-s1.h22.

Hoff, D. J. (2003a, July 9). N.Y. State seniors flunk exit exam, but get diplomas. *Education Week.* Available online: http://www.edweek.org/ew/ewstory.cfm?slug=42regents.h22.

Hoff, D. J. (2003b, October 1). Federal law bolsters case for aid suits. *Education Week.* Available online: http://www.edweek/org/ew/ewstory.cfm?slug=05Adequate.h23.

Hoff, D. J. (2003c, October 15). Forecasting failures, N.Y. delays raising exam threshold. *Education Week.* Available online: http://www.edweek.org/ew/ewstory.cfm?slug=07Regents.h23.

Hoff, D. J. (2003d, October 15). States facing staffing cuts, heavier load. *Education Week.* Available online: http://www.edweek.org/ew/ewstory.cfm?slug=07Capacity.h23.

Hoff, D. J. (2003e, November 5). Flaws could spell trouble for N.Y. regents exams. *Education Week.* Available online: http://www.edweek.org/ew/ewstory.cfm?slug=10Regents.h23.

Hoff, D. J. (2004, January 14). Pennsylvania district says ratings unfair in suit against state. *Education Week.* Available online: http://www.edweek.org/ew/ewstory.cfm?slug=18PAsuit.h23.

Hornbeck, M. (2004, March 3). Teachers told to train for test-giving. *Detroit News.* Available online: http://www.detnews.com/2004/schools/0403/03/e01-80945.htm.

Hotakainen, R. (2003, May 19). School tests stir backlash. *Minneapolis Star Tribune.* Available online: http://www.startribune.com/stories1592/3890057.html.

Hui, K. (2003, September 17). Teachers express frustration with No Child law. *News & Observer.* Available online: http://newsobserver.com/news/story/2876629p-2652561c.html.

Jacobson. L. (2002, July 10). Ga. Again faces scoring woes. *Education Week.* Available online: http://www.edweek.org/ew/ewstory.cfm?Slug=42caps.h21&keywords=achievement%20tests.

Johnston, R. C. (1999a). Firm but friendly pressure. *Education Week.* Available online. http://www.edweek.org/sreports/qc99/ac/mc/mc7-s1.htm.

Johnston, R. C. (1999b). Turning up the heat. *Education Week.* Available online: http://www.edweek.org/sreports/qc99/ac/mc/mc7.htm.

Juozapavicius, J. (2004, February 24). Teachers plan protest of law. *Arizona Republic*. Available online: http://www.azcentral.com/arizona republic/local/articles/0224Rally24.html.

Kallestad, B. (2004, March 23). FCAT failure may no longer be trouble. *Miami Herald*. Available online: http://www.miami.com/mld/miami herald/news/state/8252648.htm.

Kemper, V. (2003). Schools are skipping P.E. *Boston Globe*. Available online: http://www.boston.com/news/nation/articles/2003/09/30/ schools_are_skipping_pe/.

Kerr, B. (2002, January 18). Update on CTA's 1999 position bills: assessment and testing. *Politics and Legislation* (California Teachers Association), 12 (20). Available online: www.cta.org/Politics and legislation/ v12n20/bills_assessment.

Klein, S. P., Hamilton, L. S., McCaffrey, D. F., & Stecher, B. M. (2000). *What do test scores in Texas tell us?* Available online: http://www.rand. Org/publications/IP/IP202/.

Kleindienst, K. (2004, April 28). Senate backs parent review of FCAT, answers. *Ft. Lauderdale Sun-Sentinel*. Available online: http://www. sun-sentinel.com/news/local/florida/sfl-ffcat28apr28,0,5837555.story ?coll=sfla-news-florida.

Knight, H. (2003, November 6). McKinley school shines. *San Francisco Chronicle*. Available online: http://www.sfgate.com/cgi-bin/article.cg ?f=/chronicle/archive/2003/11/06/BAG0S2RA251.DTL.

Kohlberg, L. (1971). From is to ought. In T. Mischel (Ed.), *Cognitive Development and epistemology*. New York: Academic.

Kossan, P. (2003a, August 1). State schools boost scores. *Arizona Republic*. http://www.azcentral.com/arizonarepublic/news/articles/0801 testresults01.html.

Kossan, P. (2003b, September 3). Students stumble in AIMS math. *Arizona Republic*. Available online: http://www.azcentral.com/arizona republic/news/articles/o903aims03html.

Kossan, P. (2003c, September 29). 220 schools in Arizona on feds' underachieve list. *Arizona Republic*. Available online: http://www.az central.com/arizonarepublic/local/articles/o929fedlabels29.html.

Kossan, P. (2003d, November 17). Fix-it plan for poor schools plods along. *Arizona Republic*. Available online: http://www.azcentral.com/ arizonarepublic/news/articles/1117edsolutions17.html.

Kossan, P. (2004, March 30). McGraw-Hill gets contract to take over AIMS tests. *Arizona Republic*. Available online: http://www.azcentral. com/arizonarepublic/local/articles/0330AIMS30.html.

Kossan, P., & Konig, R. (2003, October 16). Fourth of schools in state fail to meet U.S. learning goals. *Arizona Republic*. Available online: http:// www.azcentral.com/news/articles/1016fedlabels16.html.

Kossan, P., & Melèndez, M. (2004, April 22). Students who passed pushed to retake AIMS: Schools hoping to boost rankings. *Arizona Republic.* Available online: http://www.azcentral.com/arizonarepublic/news/articles/0422AIMS22.html.

Kowalik, P. (2004, January 13). More teachers sought to improve test scores. *Buffalo News.* Available online: http://www.buffalonews.com/editorial/20040113/1057597.asp.

Kronholz, J. (2003, June 6). States' high-school exit exams are political bombs. *Wall Street Journal.* Available online: http://www.sfgate.com/cgi-bin/article.cgi?f=/news/archive/2003/06/06/financial 0907 EDT0036.DTL.

Langland, C. (2003a, October 9). Math, science education get a $12.5 million boost. *Philadelphia Inquirer.* Available online: http://www.philly.com/mld/inquirer/living/education/6966713.htm.

Langland, C. (2003b, November 23). Schools lagging in special education. *Philadelphia Inquirer.* Available online: http://www/philly.com/mld/inquirer/living/education/7330738.htm.

Langland, C. (2004, March 1). School chiefs to urge changes in 'No Child' law. *Philadelphia Inquirer.* Available online: http://www/philly.com/mld/inquirer/news/local/8074140.htm.

*Language use and English-speaking ability 2000.* (2003). Washington, DC: U.S. Bureau of the Census. Available online: http://www.census.gov prod/2003pubs/c2kbr-29.pdf.

Lawrence, C. (2003, September 28). Families get an education in No Child Left Behind. *Chicago Sun-Times.* Available online: http://www.suntimes.com/output/education/cst-nws-disney28.html.

Leo, J. (1993). 'A' for effort. Or for showing up. *U.S. News and World Report, 115* (15): 22.

Leonard-Ramshaw, M. (2004, April 18). Achievement test. *Boston Globe.* Available online: http://www.boston.com/news/politics/president/articles/2004/01/18/achievement_test/.

Lewin, T. (2004, March 17). Disabled Alaska students sue over exam. *New York Times.* Available online: http://www.nytimes.com/2004/03/17/education/17ALAS.html.

Lewin, T., & Medina, J. (2003, July 30). To cut failure rate, schools shed students. *New York Times.* Available online: http://www.nytimes.Com/2003/07/31/nyregion/31PUSH.html.

Liberman, B. (2004, February 12). Education chief defends No Child Left Behind. *The Times-Picayune.* Available online: http://www.nola.com/news/t-p/washington/index.ssf?/base/news-0/1076570718239670.xml.

Lynn, R. (2003a, September 3). Educators urge caution on reforms. *Salt Lake Tribune.* Available online: http://www.sltrib.com/2003/Sep/090

32003/utah/89299.asp.

Lynn, R. (2003b, September 9). Jordan does the math: $59M for 'competency'. *Salt Lake Tribune.* Available online: http://www.sltrib.com/2003/Sep/09112003/utah/utah.asp.

Lynn, R. (2003c, October 8). Minority students narrow gap. *Salt Lake Tribune.* Available online: http://www.sltrib.com/2003/Oct/1008200 3/utah/99859.asp.

Lynn, R. (2003d, October 14). Opt out of school reform? *Salt Lake Tribune.* Available online: http: www.sltrib.com/2003/Oct/10142003/utah/10 11810.asp.

Lynn, R. (2003e, November 21. Utah is behind on new ed rules. *Salt Lake Tribune.* Available online: http://www.sltrib.com/2003/Nov/112120 03/utah/223004.asp.

Lynn, R. (2004a, February 4). Tough test leaves some students testy. *Salt Lake Tribune.* Available online: http://www.sltrib.com/2004/Feb/02042004/utah/ 135536.asp.

Lynn, R. (2004b, April 4). Utah teachers say they are caught in the middle. *Salt Lake Tribune.* Available online: http://www.sltrib.com/2004/Apr /04042004/utah/153958.asp.

MacDonald, C. (2003, December 30). Poll slams Kilpatrick school plan. *Detroit News.* Available online: http://www.detnews.com/2003/schools/0312/30/c01-22270.htm.

MacDonald, C., & Feighan, M. (2004, February 3). Schools give selves A's, avert failure. *Detroit News*: Available online: http://www.det news.com/2004/schools/0402/03/a01e-54394.htm.

MacDonald, M. (2003a, October 9). County does well on state curriculum test. *The Atlanta Journal-Constitution.* Available online: http://www.ajc.com/metro/content/metro/gwinnett/1003/09crct.html.

MacDonald, M. (2003b, December 6). School dropout rate doubles in one year. *Atlanta Journal-Constitution.* Available online: http://www.ajc.com/saturday/content/epaper/editions/saturday/gwinnett_f31da36 0f3a331d51061.html.

Maine school giving diplomas to kids who flunk FCAT. (2004, February 29). *Boston Globe.* Available online: http://www.boston.com/news/education/k_12/articles/2004/02/29/maine_school_giving_diplomas _to_kids_who_flunk_fcat/.

Manzo, K. K. (2003a, October 15). N.Y.C. Hangs tough over maverick curriculum. *Education Week.* Available online: http://www.edweek.org/ew/ewstory.cfm?slug=07NYCCurric.h23.

Manzo, K. K. (2003b, November 5). Arts, foreign languages getting edged out. *Education Week.* Available online: http://www.edweek.org/ew/ ewstory.cfm?slug=10Lost.h23.

Marshall, K. (2003, October 1). Test prep—The junk food of education. *Education Week.* Available online: http://www.edweek.org/ew/ewstory.cfm?slug=marshall.h23.

Mathews, J. (2003, September 16). To educators, 'No Child' goals out of reach. *Washington Post,* p. A12. Available online: http://www.washingtonpost.com/wp-dyn/articles/A15836-2003Sep15.html.

Mathews, J., (2004, April 9). Federal education law squeezes out recess. *Washington Post,* p. B01. Available online: http://www.washingtonpost/wp-dyn/articles/A62558-2004Apr8.html.

Mathews, J., & Mui, Y. Q. (2003, October 10). Md. Faults U.S. law for poor scores. *Washington Post,* p. B01. Available online: http://www.washingtonpost.com/wp-dyn/articles/A5963-2003Oct9.html.

May, M. (2003, October 25). California school rankings improve. *San Francisco Chronicle.* Available online: http://www.sfgate.com/cgi-bin/article.cgi?file=/chronicle/archive/2003/10/25/BAG5R2JDF01.DTL.

McCleery, B. (2003, December 16). District sees results of its focus on ISTEP. *Indianapolis Star.* Available online: http://www.indystar.com/articles/4/102616-9034-016.html.

McElhenny, J. (2003, December 9). Turning MCAS test failure into success. *Boston Globe.* Available online: http://www.boston.com/news/education/k_12/mcas/articles/2003/12/09/turning_mcas_test_failure_into_success/.

McNichol, D. (2004, April 22). Fifth of high school graduates bypass test. *Star-Ledger.* Available online: http://www.nj.com/statehouse/ledger/index.ssf?/base/news-1/1082625985176343.xml.

Melèndez, M. (2003, October 13). Reading takes center stage. *Arizona Republic.* Available online: http://www.azcentral.com/news/ education/1013 ReadingFirst13.html.

Melton, R. H. (2003, September 10). Va. to put data on all schools on the web. *Washington Post,* p. B01. Available online: http://www.washingtonpost.com/wp-dyn/articles/A51737-2003Sep9.html.

Mendoza, M. (2003, September 30). Half of state's weak schools improve. *Arizona Republic.* Available online: http://www.azcentral. com/arizonarepublic/local/articles/0930schoollabels30.html.

Mezzacappa, D. (2003, October 26). Vallas critical of tutoring options. *Philadelphia Inquirer.* Available online: http://www.philly.com/mld/inquirer/living/education/7102892.htms.

Mezzacappa, D. (2004, June 19). Pa. moves to waive some teacher tests. *Philadelphia Inquirer.* Available online: http://www.philly.com/mld/inquirer/living/education/8960637.htm?1c.

Mollison, A., & Tofig-Cox, D. (2003, December 10). Rules on testing some disabled relaxed. *Atlanta Journal-Constitution.* Available online:

http://www.ajc.com/wednesday/content/epaper/editions/wednesd
ay/news_f36dec1b329ad18700e5.html.

Morales, K. (2004, May 21). 'Diploma mill' grads slip into schools. *Dallas Morning News.* Available online: http://www.dallasnews.com/shared content/dws/dn/latestnews/stories/052104dnmetdiplomamills.c32c. html.

Moses, A. R., & Osorio, C. (2004, April 2). Few use school transfer rule. *Detroit News.* Available online: http://www.detnews.com/2004/ schools/0402/04/e06e-54939.htm.

Mui, Y. Q. (2004, Feburary 25). Md. eases rules on tests tied to diplomas. *Washington Post.* Available online: http://www.washingtonpost.com/ wp-dyn/articles/A3309-2004Feb24.html.

National Commission of Excellence in Education. (1983). *A nation at risk: The imperative for educational reform.* Washington, DC: U.S. Government Printing Office.

Nichols, D. A. (2004, February 12). MEAP report card errors anger schools. *Detroit News.* Available online: http://www.detnews.com/ 2004/schools/0402/12/c03-62017.htm.

Oberthur, A. (2003, October 25). 90 percent score higher on key test. *San Luis Obispo Tribune,* p. B7.

Okoben, J. (2003, October 10). School law is unkind to Cleveland. *Plain Dealer.* Available online: http://www.cleveland.com/news/plaindeal er/index.ssf?/base/cuyahoga/1065778396207530.xml.

Okoben, J., Ott, T., Reed, E., & Matzelle, C. (2003, October 10). Students eligible for transfers decided most often not to go. *Plain Dealer.* Available online: http://www.cleveland.com/news/plaindealer/index.ssf? base/cuyahoga/1065778272207531.xml.

Olson, L. (2003a, March 12). 90 percent of Mass. seniors have passed graduation test. *Education Week.* Available online: http://www.edwe ek.org/ew/ewstory.cfm?slug=26caps.h22.

Olson, L. (2003b, March 12). State tests influence instruction, research says. *Education Week.* Available online: http://www.edweek.org/ ew/ewstory.cfm?slug=26caps.h22.

Olson, L. (2003c, April 16). Ga. Suspends testing plans in key grades. *Education Week.* Available online: http://www.edweek.org/ew/ewst ory.cfm?slug=31georgia.h22.

Olson, L. (2003d, August 6). 'Approved' is relative term for Ed. Dept. *Education Week.* Available online: http://www.edweek.org/ew/ew story.cfm?slug=43account.h22.

Olson. L. (2003e, December 10). In ESEA wake, school data flowing forth. *Education Week.* Available online: http://www.edweek.org/ew /ewstory.cfm?slug=15NCLB.h23.

Olson, L. (2004a, January 7). Data doubts plague states, federal law. *Education Week*. Available online: http://www.edweek.org/ew/ewstory.cfm?slug=16AYP.h23.

Olson, L. (2004b, January 14). Researchers sort out data-analysis software. *Education Week*. Available online: http://www.edweek.org/ew/ewstory.cfm?slug=18Software.h23.

Olson, L. (2004c, May 5). States seek federal ok for revisions. *Education Week*. Available online. http://www.edweek.org/ew/ewstory.cfm?slug=34Account.h23.

Olson, L. (2004d, May 26). Government offers guidance on standards and testing. *Education Week*. Available online: http://www.edweek.org/ew/ewstory.cfm?slug=38Assess.h23.

Olszewski, L. (2004, April 1). NCLB atrocities. *Chicago Tribune*. Available online: http://www.chicagotribune.com/news/printedition/chi-0404010291apr01,1,5608468.story?coll=chi-printnews-hed.

Paige: Houston schools criticized. (2003, December 15). *Dallas News*. Available online: http://www.dallasnews.com/sharedcontent/dallas/tsw/stories/121503dntexpaige.a511fa80.html.

Paige, R. (2003, March 14). *Remarks of the Honorable Rod Paige, U. S. Secretary of Education, to the National Association of State Boards of Education*. Available online: http://www.ed.gov/news/speeches/2003/03/0314 2003.html.

Pappano, L. (2003, October 19). In MCAS twist, some students may not feel challenged. *Boston Globe*. Available online: http://www.boston.com/news/education/k_12/mcas/articles/2003/10/19/in_mcas_twist_some_students_may_not_feel_challenged/.

Pardo, S. (2004, January 9). Michigan settles case of lost tests. *Detroit News*. Available online: http://www.detnews.com/2004/schools/040 1/09/b01-31269.htm.

Pasciak, M. (2004, February 6). Improved math-A test results debated. *Buffalo News*. Available online: http://www.buffalonews.com/editorial/20040206/1045106.asp.

Paulson, D. (2002, September 17). A plea to trust schools—not just tests. *Christian Science Monitor*. Available online: http://www.Csmonitor archive.com/csmonitor/display.jhtml?_requestid=167034.

Peltonen, A. (2002, November 21). *The population in Finland*. Available online: http://virtual.finland.fi/finfo/english/populat.html.

Pinzur, M. I. (2003a, May 23). Dump the test, thousands demand. *Miami Herald*. Available online: http://www.miami.com/mld/miamiherald/5925250.htm.

Pinzur, M. I. (2003b, October 9). 'Easier' FCAT given to those who'd failed. *Miami Herald*. Available online: http://www.miami.com/mld/miamiherald/living/education/6967059.htm.

Pinzur, M. I. (2003c, October 29). Hundreds of third-graders promoted. *Miami Herald*. Available online: http://www.miami.com/mld/miami herald/living/education/7130971.htm.

Postlethwaite, T. N. (1985). International Association for the Evaluation of Educational Achievement. In T. Husèn & T. N. Postlethwaite (Eds.), *The international encyclopedia of education* (Vol. 5, pp. 2645-2646). Oxford: Pergamon.

*Questions and answers on no child left behind: Testing.* (2002). Washington, DC: U.S. Department of Education. Available online: http://www. nclb. gov/next/faqs/testing.html.

Rabin, C. (2003, May 12). Leaders threaten boycott of FCAT. *Miami Herald*. Available online: http://www.Miami.com/mld/miamiherald/ news/state/5839954.htm.

Ramer, H. (2004, February 27). Study: Dropout rate remains around 25 percent. *Boston Globe*. Available online: http://www.boston.com/ news/local/new_hampshire/articles/2004/02/27/study_dropout_rat e_remains_around_25_percent/.

Rasheed, A. (2003, October 15). Orleans students snub free tutoring. *The Times-Picayune*. Available online: http://www.nola.com/news/t-p/ neworleans/index.ssf?/base/news-1/1066197485101260.xml.

Re: Here is what NCLB has to do with it. (2003, November 20). *Teachers Net*. Available online: http://teachers.net/mentors/discipline/topic 422 /11.20.03.12.17.47.html.

Richard, A., & Robelen, E. W. (2004, March 3). Federal law is questioned by governors. *Education Week*. Available online: http://www.edweek .org/ew/ewstory.cfm?slug=25NGA.h23.

Richmond, T. (2004, May 13). Wisc. attorney general says states can't be forced to comply with No Child Left Behind Act. *San Francisco Chronicle*. Available online: http://www.sfgate.com/cgi- bin/article.cgi?f=/ news/archive/2004/05/13/national2134EDT0867.DTL.

Rimer, S. (2003, October 29). Now, standardized achievement tests in Head Start. *New York Times*. Available online. http://www.nytimes. com/2003/10/29/education/292STAR.html?pagewanted=2.

Ritter, J. (2004, January 19). Gov pushes more P.E. in schools. *Chicago Sun-Times*. Available online: http://www.suntimes.com/output/news / cst-nws-gym19.html.

Robelen, E. W. (2003, September 3). State reports on progress vary widely. *Education Week*. Available online: http://www/edweek.org/ ew/ewstory.cfm?slug=01ayp.h23&keywords=failing%20schools.

Robelen, E. W. (2004a, March 31). Flexibility increased for federal testing mandate. *Education Week*. Available online: http://www.edweek. org/ew/ewstory.cfm?slug=29participation_web.h23.

Robelen, E. W. (2004b, March 31). Schools seek participation on test days. *Education Week.* Available online: http://www.edweek.org/ew/ewst ory.cfm?slug=29Participation.h23.

Robelen, E. W. (2004c, April 7). Opposition to school law growing, poll says. *Education Week.* http://www.edweek.org/ew/ewstory.cfm?slug =30Pen.h23.

Robertson, J. (2003, September 3). Missouri schools get failing grades. *Kansas City Star.* Available online: http:www.kansascity.com/mld/ kansascitystar/6677273.htm.

Rolly, P. (2003, November 11). Protesters rally to halt new 'omnibus education bill'. *The Salt Lake Tribune.* Available online: htttp://www. sltrib.com/2003/Nov/11022003/utah/utah.asp.

Rossi, R. (2003a, September 26). Few parents responded to offer of tutoring for children. *Chicago Sun-Times.* Available online: http:// www. suntimes.com/output/education/cst-nws-tutor26.html.

Rossi, R. (2003b, October 27). Feds: City falling short of school transfer goals. *Chicago Sun-Times.* Available online: http://www.suntimes. com/output/news/cst-nws-nclb27.html.

Rossi, R. (2004, April 7). Researchers blast policy of flunking kids. *Chicago Sun-Times.* Available online: http://www.suntimes.com/out put/education/cst-nws-repeat07.html.

Rossi, R., & Grossman, K. N. (2003a, September 3). Number of students eligible to transfer nearly doubles. *Chicago Sun-Times.* Available online: http:www.suntimes.com/output/education/cst-nws-left03. html.

Rossi, R., & Grossman, K. N. (2003b, November 5). 44% of state schools fail feds' test. *Chicago Sun-Times.* Available online: http://www. sun times.com/output/news/cst-nws-skul05.html.

Rothstein, K. (2003a, May 15). City would have graduated students who flunked MCAS. *Boston Herald.* Available online: http://www2.boston herald.com/news/local_regional/mcaso5152003.htm.

Rothstein, K. (2003b, July 22). Kids pass on MCAS: Many who failed choose not to retake test. *Boston Herald.* Available online: http://www 2.bostonherald.com/news/local_regional/mcas07222003.htm.

Rothstein, K. (2003c, September 30). Retests lift MCAS pass rate to 95 percent for class of '03. *Boston Herald.* Available online: http://www.2. bostonherald.com/news/local_regional/mcas09302003.htm.

Rothstein, K. (2003d, December 15). Three firms bid for pricey pact to administer MCAS. *Boston Herald.* Available online: http://news. bostonherald.com/localRegional/localRegional.bg?articleid=545.

Rothstein, K. (2004a, January 30). State hires new provider for MCAS test. *Boston Herald.* http://news.bostonherald.com/localRegional.bg? articleid=1589.

Rothstein, K. (2004b, February 26). Minority dropouts sky-high in Mass. *Boston Herald.* Available online: http://news.bostonherald.com/localRegional.bg?articleid=2232.

Rothstein, K. (2004c, March 30). MCAS grad waivers on upswing. *Boston Herald.* Available online: http://news.bostonherald.com/localRegional/view.bg?articleid=3072.

Rothstein, K. (2004d, April 29). Study: MCAS-like tests don't like dropouts. *Boston Herald.* Available online: http://news.bostonherald.com/localRegional/view.bg?articleid=13.

Roush, E. (2003, November 6). Dear homeroom. *Washington Post.* Available online: http://www.washingtonpost.com/wp-dyn/articles,/A3686-2003Nov5.html.

Russo, A. (2003, August 28). Flunking out. *Slate.* Available online: http://slate.msn.com/id/2087654/.

Samuels, C. A. (2003, June 7). Virtual high school will expand beyond Prince William. *Washington Post,* p.B07. Available online: http://www.washingtonpost.com/wp-dyn/articles/A26181-2003Jun6.html.

Sampson, H. (2004, March 5). Cops: FCAT behind scare. *Miami Herald.* Available online: http://www.miami.com/mld/miamiherald/news/local/states/florida/counties/broward_county/8109932.htm.

Sanger, D. E. (2003, September 9). Bush defends financing for schools. *New York Times.* Available online. http://www.nytimes.com/2003/09/09/politics/09BUSH.html.

Sanger, D. E., & Rutenberg, J. (2004, May 12). Education law will stand, Bush tells its detractors. *New York Times.* Available online: http://www.nytimes.com/2004/05/12/politics/12bush.html .

Sataline, S. (2003, December 9). Tweak to MCAS test boosts some scores. *Boston Globe.* Available online: http://www.boston.com/news/education/k_12/mcas/articles/2003/12/09/tweak_to_mcas_test_boosts_some_scores/.

Schaps, E. (2002, June 5). High stakes surveys. *Education Week.* Available online: http://www.edweek.org/ew/ewstory.cfm?slug=39schaps.h21&keywords=achievement%20tests.

Schemo, D. J. (2003, October 15). Education group calls for revised law. *New York Times.* Available online: http://www.nytimes.com/2003/10/16/education.html.

Schemo, D. J. (2004, March 30). New exceptions in testing law for some ill or injured students. *New York Times.* Available online: http://www.nytimes. com/2004/03/30/politics/30CHIL.html.

Schmitten, P. (2003, March 11). This paper work has got to stop. *Special Ed.net.* Available online: http://discussions.specialed.net/viewtopic.php?t=20.

Schools get waivers for algebra law. (2004, April 21). *Los Angeles Times.* Available online: http://www.latimes.com/services/site/premium/.

Schouten, F. (2004, June 28). Standardized tests take on shades of gray. *USA Today.* Available online: http://www.usatoday.com/news/education/2004-06-28-standardized-tests_x.htm.

Schworm, P. (2004, July 12). MCAS detour proves tough. *Boston Globe.* Available online: http://www.boston.com/news/local/articles/2004/07/12/mcas_detour_proves_tough/.

Sedam, S. R. (2003, December 10). Plans for different diplomas rankle officials, community. *The Gazette.* Available online: http://www.gazette.net/200350/montgomerycty/education/191611-1.html.

Senators take agency to task on tutoring. (2004, February 4). *St. Louis Post-Dispatch.* Available online: http://www.stltoday.com/news/stories.nsf/News/5647C74D5246CDF386256E31001C96F1?OpenDocument&Headline=Senators+take+agency+to+task+on+tutoring.

Shaw, L. (2003a, August 27). Hundreds of schools won't meet federal goals. *Seattle Times.* Available online: http://seattletimes.nwsource.com/html/localnews/2001631350_wasl27m.html.

Shaw, L. (2003b, August 29). Positives stressed in WASL results. *Seattle Times.* Available online: http://seattletimes.nwsource.com/html/education/2001659112_was129m.html.

Shaw, L. (2004, March 9). Lawmakers give students more chances to pass WASL. *Seattle Times.* Available online: http://seattletimes.nwsource.com/html/education/2001874861_wasl09m.html.

Silberman, T. (2003a, October 22). Debate rages over test goals. *Raleigh News & Observer.* Available online: http://www.newsobserver.com/front/story/2964606p-2718026c.html.

Silberman, T. (2003b, October 30). Tests put civics, science, behind. *Raleigh News & Observer.* Available online: http://www.newsobserver.com/news/nc/story/2986154p-2735923c.html.

Silberman, T. (2003c, December 3). Students fail state tests, still move up. *Raleigh News & Observer.* Available online: http://www.newsobserver.com/front/story/3100059p-2811937c.html.

Silberman, T. (2004a, February 23). Schools cut back on foreign language classes. *Raleigh News & Observer.* Available online: http://www.newsobserver.com/news/nc/story/3360671p-2992054c.html.

Silberman, T. (2004b, April 16). Schools raise stakes for test. *Raleigh News & Observer.* Available online: http://www.newsobserver.com/front/story/3516939p-3120327c.html.

Silberman, T. (2004c). Value of teacher incentives questioned. *Raleigh News & Observer.* Available online: http://www.newsobserver.com/news/story/1356053p-7479431c.html.

Simmons, T. (2003a, October 27). Efforts pay off to close achievement gap. *Raleigh News & Observer.* Available online: http://newsobserver. com/news/nc/story/2980957p-2731658c.html.

Simmons, T. (2003b, November 16). First, pass the tests. *Raleigh News & Observer.* Available online: http://newsobserver.com/news/nc/story /3029230p-2772863c.html.

Simon, S. (2003, September 8). St. Louis parents are fuming over school shift. *San Luis Obispo County Tribune,* p. A8.

Slonaker, L. (2003, May 7). Exist exam's new dilemma. *Mercury News.* Available online: http://www.bayarea.com/mld/mercurynews/news /local/5804056.htm.

Snyder, S., & Mezzacappa, D. (2003, August 21). 'Restructured' schools shine on tests. *Philadelphia Inquirer.* Available online: http://www.phi lly.com/mld/inquirer/living/education/6581701.htm.

Solochek, J. S. (2004, March 4). FCAT violation leaves job in jeopardy. *St. Petersburg Times.* Available online: http://www.sptimes.com/2004 /03/04/Hernando/FCAT_violation_leaves.shtml

Solomon, C. (2003, December 24). Revising rates for graduation stirs conflict. *Seattle Times.* Available online: http://seattleimes.newsource .com/html/education/2001822302_gradrates24e.html.

Spencer, J. (2004, June 30). Texas graduation rate worst in nation, again. *Houston Chronicle.* Available online: http://www.chron.com/cs/CDA /ssistory.mpl/metropolitan/2654323.

Standardizing unfairness. (2003, August 6). *Washington Times.* Available online: http://www.edweek.org/clips/.

States voice doubts about federal education law. (2003, December 10). *CNN.com.* Available online: http://www.cnn.com/2003/EDUCA TION/12/10/states.education.ap/index.html.

Stein, L. (2004, March 5). Eat your Wheaties! is new FCAT rallying cry. *St. Petersburg Times.* Available online: http://www.sptimes.com/2004 /03/05/Brandontimes/Eat_your_Wheaties_is_.shtml.

Steinberg, L. (2003, February 5). Does high-stakes testing hurt students? *Education Week.* Available online: http://www.edweek.org/ew/ewst ory.cfm?slug=21steinberg.h22&keywords=achievement%20tests.

Stephens, S. (2003, November 2). New exam for young pupils raises teachers' ire. *Plain Dealer.* Available online: http://www.cleveland. com/education/index.ssf?/base/isedu/1067772611211521.xml.

Stevenson, H. W. (1998). *A TIMSS primer.* Available online: http:// www.edexcellence.net/library/timss.html.

Superintendents: Replacing CATS will harm schools. (2003, December 15). *Lexington Herald-Journal.* Available online: http://www.kentucky .com/mld/kentucky/news/local/7494331.htm.

Survey: Hispanics more optimistic about schools. (2004, January 26). *CNN.com*. Available online: http://www.cnn.com/2004/EDUCAT ION/01/26/hispanics.education.ap/index.html.

Sweeney, E. (2003, December 11). Students face a feel-for-all. *Boston Globe*. Available online: http://www.boston.com/news/education/ k_12/articles/2003/12/11/students_face_a_fee_for_all/.

Tanner, R. (2004, February 23). Education Secretary Paige calls teachers union "terrorist organization." *Kansas City Star*. Available online: http://www.kansascity.com/mld/kansascity/news/consumer_news /8022280.htm.

Teacher of year snubs Bush aide over gaffe. (2004, March 5). *Boston Globe*. Available online: http://www.boston.com/news/education/ k_12/articles/2004/03/05/teacher_of_year_snubs_bush_aide_over_ga ffe_1078475875/.

Tench, M. (2003, November 18). Conflicting evaluations puzzle school. *Boston Globe*. Available online: http://www.boston.com/news/educa tion/k_12/msas/articles/2003/11/18/conflicting-evaluations-puzzle_ school/.

Tench, M. (2004, January 28). Students' legal bid vs. MCAS rebuffed. *Boston Globe*. Available online: http://www.boston.com/news/educa tion/k_12/mcas/articles/2004/01/28/students_legal_bid_vs_mcas_re buffed/.

Tessler, J. (2003, July 10). State board delays exist exam requirement. *San Luis Obispo County Tribune*, p. B5.

Texas students, teachers get cash for passing exam. (2003, December 15). *Houston Chronicle*. Available online: http://www.chron.com/cs/CDA /ssistory.mpl/metropolitan/2296274.

The testing industry's big four. (2002). *Frontline, Public Broadcasting System*. Available online: http://www.pbs.org/wgbh/pages/frontline/ shows/schools/testing/companies.html.

Thomas, R. M. (1960). *Judging student progress*. New York: Longmans, Green.

Thomas, R. M. (1965). A rationale for measurement in the visual arts. *Educational and Psychological Measurement, 25*, 163-189.

Thomas, R. M. (1986). Assessing moral development. *International Journal of Educational Research, 10* (4), 347-476.

Thomas, R. M. (1994). Approaches to setting and selecting achievement standards. In. A. C. Tuijnman & T. N. Postlethwaite, *Monitoring the standards of education*. Oxford: Pergamon.

Thomas, R. M. (2003). New frontiers in cheating. *Encyclopaedia Britiannica Year in Review—2002-2003*. Chicago, IL: Encyclpaedia Britannica, pp. 206-207.

Thomas, R. M., & Brubaker, D. L. (1971). *Decisions in teaching elementary social studies.* Belmont, CA: Wadsworth.

Thomas, R. M., & Brubaker, D. L. (1972). *Teaching elementary social studies: readings.* Belmont, CA: Wadsworth.

Thomas, R. M., & Murray, P. V. (1982). *Cases: A resource guide for teaching about the law.* Glenview, IL: Scott, Foresman.

Thomas, R. M., & Thomas, Shirley M. (1965). *Individual differences in the classroom.* New York: David McKay.

Thomas, R. M., & Titialii, T. (1973). *Measuring Samoan-language silent-reading skills.* Pago Pago: Government of American Samoa.

Thomas, R. M., Titialii, T., Harris, C. W., & Harris, M. L. (1973a). *Testing students' mental skills.* Pago Pago: Government of American Samoa.

Thomas, R. M., Titialii, T., Harris, C. W., & Harris, M. L. (1973b). *Testing students' physical skills.* Pago Pago: Government of American Samoa.

Thousands of immigrant students taking special English classes. (2004, April 26). *Boston Globe.* Available online: http://www.boston.com/news/local/connecticut/articles/2004/04/26/thousands_of_immigrant_ students_taking_special_english_classes/.

TIMSS 1999 assessment results. (2004). *Trends in international mathematics and science study.* Washington, DC: National Center for Education Statistics. Available online: http://nces.ed.gov/timss/results.asp#mathscience1999.

Tofig, D. (2003a, August 15). Some top schools earn low grades. *Atlanta Journal-Constitution.* Available online: http://www.ajc.com/friday/content/epaper/editions/Friday/metro_f3c397d8f0c1c07e00d9.html.

Tofig, D. (2003b, November 22). After review, 117 schools given better report cards. *Atlanta Journal-Constitution.* Available online: http://www. .ajc.com/saturday/content/epaper/ editions/saturday/metro_f3fb50b0b562201000c8.html.

Tofig, D., (2004, March 30). 7 questions added to test. *Atlanta Journal-Constitution.* Available online: http://www.ajc.com/tuesday/content/epaper/edi tions/tuesday/metro_0496a11db69890d100e6.html.

Union left behind on education lawsuit. (2004, June 28). *CNN.* Available online: http://www.cnn.com/2004/EDUCATION/06/28/teacher.politics.ap/index.html.

Vaishnav, A. (2003a, July 30). Low MCAS turnout prompts concern. *Boston Globe.* Available online: http://www.boston.com/dailyglobe2/211/metro/Low_MCAS_turnout_prompts_concern+.shtml.

Vaishnav, A. (2003b, December 5). School ratings raise concerns for Hispanics. *Boston Globe.* Available online: http://www.boston.com/news/local/massachusetts/articles/2003/12/05/school_ratings_raise_concerns_for_hispanics/.

Vaishnav, A. (2003c, December 10). MCAS cheating inquiry launched. *Boston Globe.* Available online: http://www.boston.com/news/education/k_12/mcas/articles/2003/12/10/mcas_cheating_inquiry_launched/.

Vaishnav, A. (2004, April 6). High school dropout rates are up sharply. *Boston Globe.* Available online: http://www.boston.com/news/education/k_12/mcas/articles/2004/04/06/high_school_dropout_rates_are_up_sharply/.

VandeHei, J. (2003, October 13). Education law may hurt Bush. *Washington Post.* Available online: http://www.washingtonpost.com/wp-dyn/articles/A17509-2003Oct12.html.

VanDewerker, M. (2002). PBS Frontline discussion after the program. Available online. http://www.pbs.org/wgbh/pages/frontline/shows/schools/talk/.

Viadero, D. (2001, January 11). How high the bar? *Education Week.* Available online: http:// www.edweek.org/ register//register.cfm? mode. = news?

Viadero, D. (2003, October 15). Academic achievement. *Education Week.* Available online: http://www.edweek.org/ew/ewstory.cfm?slug=07report.h23.

Waller, M. (2003, November 21). Most Jeff schools must undergo state reforms. *Times-Picayune.* Available online: http://www.nola.com/news/ t-p/capital/index.ssf?/base/news-1/1069401318119200.xml.

Walsh, J. (2003a, April 30). Big test? St. Paul Central students skip it in droves. *Minneapolis Star Tribune.* Available online: http://www. startribune. com/stories/1592/4052640.html.

Walsh, J. (2003b, October 2). Pawlenty pitches paying 'super teachers' up to $100,000. *Minneapolis Star Tribune.* Available online: http:// www. startribune.com/stories/1592/4129828.html.

Walsh, J. (2004, March 9). Minnesota's school testing results inflated. *Minneapolis Star Tribune.* Available online: http://www.startribune. com/stories/1592/4652640.html.

Wasserman, J. (2003, June 14). Schools chief urges delay in exit exam. *San Luis Obispo County Tribune,* p. B7.

Welcome to the official site of the GED testing service. (2004). *General Educational Development Testing Service.* Available online: http://www. acenet.edu/clll/ged/index.cfm.

Welsh, J. (2003, October 30). No Child Left Behind: A new option for struggling pupils. *Pioneer Press.* Available online: http://www.twincities. com/mld/pioneerpress/living/education/7135999.htm.

Welsh, J. (2004a, January 6). 'Seal of Honor' would promote test completion. *Pioneer Press.* Available online: http://www.twincities.com/mld/pioneerpress/living/education7640643.htm.

Welsh, J. (2004b, March 2). Split over No Child law leads to resignation. *Pioneer Press*. Available online: http://www.twincities.com/mld/pio neerpress/living/education/8081840.htm.

Werbitsky, E. (2004, January 8). Board lowers grade for Regents. *Buffalo News*. Available online. http://www.buffalonews.com/editorial/200 40108/1059166.asp.

Wermers, J. (2003a, October 23). More parents take advantage of federal law. *Richmond Times-Dispatch*. Available online: http://www.times dispatch.com/servlet/Satellite?pagename=RTD%2FMGArticle%2FRT D_BasicArticle&c=MGArticle&cid=1031771693473&path=%21news&s =1045855934842.

Wermers, J. (2003b, November 21). Group calls for lower standards. *Richmond Times-Dispatch*. Available online: http://www.timesdispatch .com/servlet/Satellite?pagename=RTD%2FMGArticle%2FRTD_Basic Article&c=MGArticle&cid=1031772226571&path=%21news&s=104585 5934842.

Wermers, J. (2004, January 19). Teachers give law mixed reviews. *Richmond Times-Dispatch*. Available online: http://www.timesdispatch. com/servlet/Satellite?pagename=RTD%2FMGArticle%2FRTD_BasicA rticle&c=MGArticle&cid=1031773174566&path=%21news&s=10458559 34842.

White, T. (2004, June 26). City school officials let students retake finals, get diploma. *Baltimore Sun*. Available online: http://www.baltimore sun.com/news/education/bal-te.md.promote26jun26,0,5936486.story? coll=bal-education-top.

Winchester, D. (2003, May 7). Schools hone strategies for FCAT. *St. Petersburg Times*. Available online: http://www.sptimes.com/2003/05/ 07/Southpinellas/Schools_hone_strategi.shtml.

Winerip, M. (2003, October 8). How a good school can fail on paper. *New York Times*. Available online: http://www.nytimes.com/2003/10/08/ education/08EDUC.html.

Winerip, M. (2004a, February 4). Principal sees mistake in plan to hold back 3rd graders. *New York Times*. Available online: http://www.ny times.com/2004/02/04/education/04education.html.

Winerip, M. (2004b, April 28). Making leaps, but still labeled as failing. *New York Times*. Available online: http://www.nytimes.com/2004/ 04/28/education/28education.html.

Wolfe, C. (2003, October 9). State board looks at scores. *Lexington Herald-Leader*. Available online: http://www.kentucky.com/mld/kentuc ky/news/local/6968312.htm.

Woodall, M. (2003, September 18). Suit alleges school gave answers to state tests. *Philadelphia Inquirer*. Available online: http://www.philly. Com/mld/inquirer/living/education/6787444.htm.

Zehr, M. A. (2003, November 26). States developing tests for English-learners. *Education Week.* Available online: http://www.edweek.org/ew/ewstory.cfm?slug=13Tests.h23.

Zuñiga, J. A. (2004, February 23). Making the grade. *Houston Chronicle.* Available online: http://www.chron.com/cs/CDA/ssistory.mpl/metropolitan/2415470.

# Name Index

# Subject Index

Atlanta, 67
Attendance, 64, 67, 73, 122
Australia, 15
Auditing methods, 160, 163-164
Authority, 107, 109
  defined, 109
AYP—adequate yearly progress,
  17, 19-20, 67, 74, 140

Behavior management, 31-32
Belgium, 15
Bilingual education, 242
Blacks. *See* African-Americans.
Bonus pay, 175-176, 182, 281
Boston, 5-6, 52, 70-71, 169, 249-250
Boycotts, 8, 193, 199, 202, 248-249
Bulgaria, 15

California, 8, 64-65, 70, 72, 75, 94,
  128, 159, 182, 205-206, 216, 237,
  248-249, 267-268
California Teachers Association,
  231
Canada, 5
CATS—Commonwealth Account-
  ability Testing System, 153-154
Caucasian students. *See* White
  students.
Center on Education Policy, 69
Certification. *See* Teacher certifi-
  cation.
Certificate of
  attainment, 133
  attendance, 6, 71, 133-134
  initial mastery, 134
Charter schools, 19-20, 56, 143,
  189-190
Cheating. *See* Test cheating.
Chicago, 38, 71, 74, 86-89, 91, 98,
  112, 178, 200, 212, 237
Chinese language, 266, 269
Citizen, 25, 28-30
Citizens for Effective Schools, 201

Citizenship education, 29-30
Civics, 13, 29, 36-37, 265
Civil Rights Project, 209
Class
  size, 98, 106, 125, 174-175
  work, 170-172
Classroom visits, 160, 179-180
Cleveland, 70, 87, 199, 233-234
Collateral damage, 5-9
  defined, 2
Colorado, 64, 173, 210
Completion items, 14
Computer,
  hackers, 255
  literacy, 28
  software, 229
Connecticut, 65, 149, 242-243
Consumer, 25, 32
Coping defined, 2
Corrective action, 19
Council of Chief State School Offi-
  cers, 126, 153, 216
CTB/McGraw-Hill, 206
Cultural heritage, 40-41, 212, 266,
  280-281
Curriculum, 77, 99-100, 106, 122,
  150, 160, 165, 168, 172-173, 190,
  215, 253, 270-271, 278, 281, 284
Cutting scores, 157-158
Cyprus, 14
Czech Republic, 15

Degrees, academic, 238-239
Delaware, 65
Democratic Governors Associa-
  tion, 126
Democratic National Committee,
  150
Democrats, 97, 119, 121, 124-127,
  144, 150, 190, 232, 261
Demonstrations, public, 8, 193,
  199, 201-202, 235
Denmark, 14

220, 227, 230, 241-242, 244-245,
248-249, 254
Group member, 25, 30-32
Growth model, 69, 153, 259, 272-
282, 286

Handicaps. *See* Disabilities.
Harcourt Educational Measure-
ment, 206, 214-216
Hawaii, 124, 213
Head Start, 252, 259
Health,
condition, 141, 160
education, 106, 282
High-stakes testing defined, 1-2
Hispanics, 4, 18, 53, 70, 113, 127,
152-153, 162, 167, 169-170, 194,
249-250, 267-269
History, 2, 17, 35-37, 52, 81, 129,
197, 205, 282
American, 29, 36, 81, 129, 279
Homework, 66, 132, 194-195, 271
Hong Kong, 15, 265, 267
Houston, 72, 94, 99, 114-115, 163-
164, 175, 180
HSPT—High School Proficiency
Test, 244
Hungary, 265

Iceland, 15, 265
IEA—International Association
for the Evaluation of Educational Achievement, 13-15, 263
Illinois, 38, 66-67, 71, 74, 83, 86-89,
91, 98, 112, 152, 186, 200, 210,
228, 237
Illinois Alternative Assessment,
228
Immigrants, 117, 120, 160, 166,
169-170, 188, 196, 226, 242-243,
261, 266
Incentive pay, 175-175
Indiana, 38-39, 168

Indians, American. *See* Native
Americans.
Individual differences, 11-12, 264
Individual growth model. *See*
Growth model.
Indonesia, 14
Inservice education, 103, 126, 160,
176-177, 223-225, 234, 238, 271
Instructional,
design, 80
materials, 118, 234
methods, 136, 152, 270
Internet, 127, 198, 201, 222-225,
238, 251, 256, 261, 271, 280
Internships, 225
Iowa, 15
Italian language, 266
Italy, 14

Japan, 15, 265, 267
Japanese language, 269

Kansas, 65, 75, 212
Kentucky, 63-64, 94, 153, 225
Korean language, 266, 269
Kumon North America, 91-92

Languages, foreign, 17
Latin America, 266
Latinos. *See* Hispanics.
Lawmakers, 259-263, 271-272
Laws, 161. *See also* No-Child-Left-
Behind Act.
Lawsuits, 55-56, 125-126, 160, 162,
189-190, 193, 203-204, 221, 235,
255-256
LEAP—Louisiana Educational
Assessment Program, 96, 195
Learning,
communities, 180
materials, 151
Legislators. *See* Lawmakers.

Tutoring, 77, 90-93, 118, 131, 149, 160, 162, 166, 168, 222, 242-243, 277, 279, 283

Unions, education, 139, 188, 232. *See also* NEA *and* AFT.
United States students, 14
University of California, 267-268
Urban Institute, 245
U.S. Congress, 37, 109-110, 119, 150-151, 155-156, 163, 190, 201, 232, 261, 285
U.S. Department of Education, 18, 110-112, 118-120, 147-150, 191, 210, 259, 261, 263, 272-273
U.S. President, 109-110, 285
Utah, 3, 39, 73, 125, 137-138, 148-149, 218
Utah Basic Skills Competency Exam, 218

Venezuela, 14
Vermont, 124
Vietnamese language, 266, 269

Virginia, 42, 79, 87, 124-125, 127-128, 167, 199, 205, 237, 243
Vocational education, 27
Vocational training, 27-28
Vouchers, school, 143

Waivers, 158-159
Washington, DC, 42-43, 66, 225
Washington State, 20, 53, 64, 73, 85, 131, 176
WASL—Washington Assessment of Student Learning, 3, 131
West Virginia, 65
Whistle blowers, 230
White students, 3-4, 18, 53, 131, 167, 186, 249-250, 268
Wisconsin, 125, 210
Work products, 45-46. *See also* Class work.
Worker, wage earner, 25, 38
Writing, 2, 17, 83, 168, 172, 176-177, 215, 217, 227, 233
Wyoming, 65